REFORMED HUMANISM

REFORMED HUMANISM

Essays on Christian Doctrine, Philosophy, and Church

David Fergusson

LONDON • NEW YORK • OXFORD • NEW DELHI • SYDNEY

T&T CLARK

Bloomsbury Publishing Plc, 50 Bedford Square, London, WC1B 3DP, UK
Bloomsbury Publishing Inc, 1359 Broadway, New York, NY 10018, USA
Bloomsbury Publishing Ireland, 29 Earlsfort Terrace, Dublin 2, D02 AY28, Ireland

BLOOMSBURY, T&T CLARK and the T&T Clark logo are trademarks of Bloomsbury Publishing Plc

First published in Great Britain 2024
Paperback edition published 2026

Copyright © David Fergusson, 2024

David Fergusson has asserted his right under the Copyright, Designs and Patents Act, 1988, to be identified as Author of this work.

For legal purposes the Acknowledgments on p. ix constitute an extension of this copyright page.

Cover image: Angel playing bagpipes, St. Giles Cathedral (© Ivan / Getty Images)

All rights reserved. No part of this publication may be: i) reproduced or transmitted in any form, electronic or mechanical, including photocopying, recording or by means of any information storage or retrieval system without prior permission in writing from the publishers; or ii) used or reproduced in any way for the training, development or operation of artificial intelligence (AI) technologies, including generative AI technologies. The rights holders expressly reserve this publication from the text and data mining exception as per Article 4(3) of the Digital Single Market Directive (EU) 2019/790.

Bloomsbury Publishing Plc does not have any control over, or responsibility for, any third-party websites referred to or in this book. All internet addresses given in this book were correct at the time of going to press. The author and publisher regret any inconvenience caused if addresses have changed or sites have ceased to exist, but can accept no responsibility for any such changes.

A catalogue record for this book is available from the British Library.

Library of Congress Cataloging-in-Publication Data

Names: Fergusson, David, author.
Title: Reformed humanism : essays on Christian doctrine, philosophy, and church / David Fergusson.
Description: London ; New York : T&T Clark, 2024. | Includes bibliographical references and index.
Identifiers: LCCN 2023049278 (print) | LCCN 2023049279 (ebook) | ISBN 9780567712745 (hb) | ISBN 9780567712783 (paperback) | ISBN 9780567712752 (epdf) | ISBN 9780567712776 (epub)
Subjects: LCSH: Religion and science. | Reformed Church. | Phenomenology. | Philosophy.
Classification: LCC BL240.3 .F46 2024 (print) | LCC BL240.3 (ebook) | DDC 230/.42–dc23/eng/20240126
LC record available at https://lccn.loc.gov/2023049278
LC ebook record available at https://lccn.loc.gov/2023049279

ISBN: HB: 978-0-5677-1274-5
PB: 978-0-5677-1278-3
ePDF: 978-0-5677-1275-2
ePUB: 978-0-5677-1277-6

Typeset by Deanta Global Publishing Services, Chennai, India

For product safety related questions contact productsafety@bloomsbury.com.

To find out more about our authors and books visit www.bloomsbury.com and sign up for our newsletters.

*To Holly Fergusson (b. 2021) and
Thomas Fergusson (b. 2023)*

CONTENTS

Acknowledgments	ix
INTRODUCTION: REFORMED HUMANISM	1

Part One
CHRISTIAN DOCTRINE

Chapter 1 THE DIVINE ATTRIBUTES: SOME METHODOLOGICAL CONSIDERATIONS	7
Chapter 2 THE POWER OF GOD: ITS USE AND ABUSE AS A THEOLOGICAL CONCEPT	24
Chapter 3 MAKER OF HEAVEN AND EARTH: THEOLOGY FOR CREATIONTIDE	40
Chapter 4 CHRISTOLOGICAL MAXIMALISM ASSESSED	55
Chapter 5 PROVIDENCE	70
Chapter 6 THE *IMAGO DEI*	81
Chapter 7 THE LAST JUDGMENT	95

Part Two
PHILOSOPHY

Chapter 8 HUME AS RELIGIOUS SKEPTIC	111
Chapter 9 ADAM SMITH ON ETHICS AND RELIGION	128
Chapter 10 NATURAL THEOLOGY AFTER DARWIN	140

Part Three
CHURCH

Chapter 11
THE THEOLOGY OF WORSHIP: A REFORMED PERSPECTIVE ... 159

Chapter 12
REFORMED THEOLOGY AND VISUAL CULTURE ... 171

Chapter 13
MAPPING THE CHURCH: CURRENT CHALLENGES OF HISTORY AND MISSION ... 180

Chapter 14
THE BIBLE IN MODERNITY ... 195

Chapter 15
REFORMED SOCIAL THEOLOGY: CONTEXTS AND CONSTANTS ... 212

Chapter 16
THEOLOGY AND THERAPY ... 228

Chapter 17
THE PLACE OF CHRISTIAN THEOLOGY IN THE UNIVERSITY ... 241

EPILOGUE

Chapter 18
THEOLOGY AND LAUGHTER ... 255

Bibliography ... 267
Index ... 287

ACKNOWLEDGMENTS

These essays offer reflections on a range of subjects. The work of a general practitioner, they combine a commitment to academic theology with engagement in church life. The most recent contributions, hitherto unpublished, have been written following my transition (during lockdown) in 2021 from Edinburgh to Cambridge. I am grateful for the friendship and intellectual stimulus of colleagues in both places. And, as ever, I am indebted to my wife for her constant support.

Many of the essays in this volume have appeared in other locations. I gladly acknowledge permission to reproduce them in lightly edited form. I am grateful to Matthew Fairhurst for his assistance with the preparation of the text and the index.

"Providence and Analytic Theology," in James Arcadi and James Turner (eds.), *T&T Clark Companion to Analytic Theology* (London: T&T Clark, 2021), 155–64.

"Humans Created According to the *Imago Dei*: An Alternative Proposal," *Zygon*, 48, no. 2 (2013): 439–53.

"The Last Judgement," in R. David Nelson, Darren Sarisky, and Justin Stratis (eds.), *Theological Theology: Essays in Honour of John Webster* (London: T&T Clark, 2015), 75–88.

"The Absence of God and Its Contextual Significance in Hume," *Journal of Scottish Philosophy*, 11, no. 1 (2013): 69–85.

"Adam Smith on Ethics and Religion," *Humanities and Culture*, 52 (2020): 53–72.

"Natural Theology after Darwin," in Andrew Robinson (ed.), *Darwinism and Natural Theology: Evolving Perspectives* (Newcastle: Cambridge Scholars Publishing, 2012), 78–95.

"Theology of Worship: A Reformed Perspective," in Duncan B. Forrester and Douglas C. Gay (eds.), *Worship and Liturgy in Context: Studies of Theology and Practice* (London: SCM, 2009), 23–35.

"Visual Images and Reformed Anxieties: Some Scottish Reflections," *Princeton Theological Review*, 21, no. 1 (2017): 25–34.

"Mapping the Church: Current Challenges of History and Mission," in A. B. McGowan (ed.), *Engaging Ecclesiology* (Eugene, OR: Wipf & Stock, 2023), 1–17.

"The Bible and Modernity," in Neil Messer and Angus Paddison (eds.), *The Bible: Culture, Community and Society* (London: Bloomsbury T&T Clark, 2013), 9–30.

"Reformed Social Thought," in Heleen Zorgdrager, Pieter Vos, and Eddy van der Borght (eds.), *Calling of the Church in Times of Polarization, Studies in Reformed Theology* (Leiden: Brill, forthcoming).

"Theology and Therapy: Maintaining the Connection," *Pacifica*, 26 (2013): 3–16.

"The Place of Christian Theology in the Academy Today," *International Journal for the Study of the Christian Church*, 21, no. 3–4 (2021): 212–21.

"Theology and Laughter," in Paul Middleton (ed.), *The God of Love and Human Dignity: Essays in Honour of George M. Newlands* (London: T&T Clark, 2007), 107–16.

INTRODUCTION

REFORMED HUMANISM

This collection gathers essays on selected themes, many of which have appeared in earlier forms and locations. The title is intended neither to designate a manifesto nor to articulate a single ideological position. "Reformed humanism" might better be characterized as an approach or a temperament. While not a term to which I am wedded, it may serve some purpose in characterizing a "theological mood" that seeks to navigate an (admittedly hazardous) course between the dismissal of modernity on one side and a capitulation on the other.

The term is ambiguous. "Humanism" is so capacious that some have judged it a useless slogan.[1] Since no one is likely to dispute the importance of human flourishing, we might all cheerfully subscribe to "humanism" in its generalized sense, thus evacuating it of any significance. Alternatively, humanism can be read as antithetical to every theological outlook. In affirming reason, science, and the pursuit of happiness, humanist associations typically define their position in explicit opposition to religion. Nowadays, the "non-religious" will frequently hire humanist officials to conduct wedding and funeral services. Even here, however, there is some ambiguity. The "scientific method" is an elusive procedure, to say the least, when metaphysical considerations of moral, aesthetic, and spiritual value are at stake. An appeal to a scientific approach seems as unlikely to resolve moral disagreements in our society, as an appeal to a theological standard. Meanwhile, the humanist stress upon values such as warmth, compassion, and generosity, however laudable, can hardly be considered a distinctive commitment since many religions are equally committed to the pursuit of human welfare, compassion, and generosity. In all of this, definitions are fraught with difficulty, and prone even to an implicit claim to moral superiority.

My use of the term "humanism" gestures toward a theological openness to the insights of other fields of knowledge and the subsequent need to accommodate these, even when this demands a rethinking of earlier positions. In some respects, this accords with the "humanism" of Renaissance thinkers who sought to

---

1. See John de Gruchy, *Being Human: Confessions of a Christian Humanist* (London: SCM, 2006), 25.

incorporate the best insights of classical culture within a Christian matrix.[2] Such an approach is governed by the recognition that Christian theology, even in its sacred scriptures, has borrowed and been shaped by whatever wisdom is available from outside the walls of the church.[3] Allied to this is a further conviction that the challenges of modernity cannot be bypassed by a wholesale retrieval of earlier theologies whether patristic, medieval, or post-Reformation. Robust claims for Christian distinctiveness have some merit, particularly in an age of church decline marked by loss of intellectual plausibility in our culture. A strong theology is likely to prove more attractive and endurable to those seeking to make sense of their lives at a time of cultural fragmentation. This may explain the reaction against the seemingly radical or liberal theologies of the postwar period. Yet the questions they sought to address remain with us, in particular those raised by the historical situatedness of Bible, doctrine, and church. Earlier assumptions, perspectives, and beliefs do not apply in their entirety. With its diverse witness and varied contexts, Scripture reflects the *Sitze im Leben* of its writers. The development of Christian doctrine is now harder to view as a linear unfolding of positions which, once established, become normative for successive generations.[4] The criticism of church practice by historians, gender theorists, and ethicists requires an assessment not only of what was done but also of what was believed. Positions that were once marginalized or anathematized such as universalism have now become more mainstream. If the term is allowed, the humanism that is advanced here is merely one that is alert to the criticism and insights that arise from without the domain of theology more narrowly conceived. The preposition "without" might suggest the image of a theological guild receiving input from disciplines that sit outside our field. Yet this may conceal the ways in which each of us absorbs an eclectic mix of intellectual influences and trends. The boundary between church and world does not so much lie outside of our domain; it runs through each of us as individuals with our different contexts, contacts, and influences.[5]

---

2. Some commentators have viewed the Renaissance humanism of the late thirteenth century onward, as well as its later Northern European manifestation in Erasmus and others, as a program of Christian reform. See Jens Zimmermann, *Humanism and Religion: A Call for the Renewal of Western Culture* (Oxford: Oxford University Press, 2012), 105–8.

3. This point has been made forcibly by William Schweiker in his remarks about "church" and "world" as "complex, interrelated, and ambiguous realities of forces, challenges, and possibilities" from which we cannot be hermetically sealed. See *Dust that Breathes: Christian Faith and the New Humanisms* (Oxford: Wiley-Blackwell, 2010), 6.

4. See David Bentley Hart, *Tradition and Apocalypse: An Essay on the Future of Christian Belief* (Grand Rapids: Eerdmans, 2022).

5. "The glory of God lies in a Love Supreme that speaks everywhere, sometimes confirming what we already believe but sometimes too challenging or even undermining what we suppose to be the case. Jesus learnt the value of pagan 'dogs'. So too can we." David Brown, *Divine Generosity and Human Creativity: Theology through Symbol, Painting and*

The decline of the church in the West has been matched and surpassed by its resurgence elsewhere in the world. This has contributed still further to the diversity of Christian theologies that populate the field; we should expect this trend to continue through the present century. The contribution of scholars from churches and groups that have been historically marginalized inside Western societies has also become increasingly significant. Their concerns and perspectives demand attention with further theological revision a likely outcome. Again, a humanism alert to the diversity of experience and context is to be preferred to a doctrinal rigidity that merely sidesteps the problems.

In all this, there remains a risk of a nomadic theology that becomes disconnected from the past. What makes a theology Christian, and how are we to understand the unity of the church? The celebration of diversity often comes at the expense of ignoring questions about the identity of the church as one, holy, catholic, and apostolic. Here the achievements of the ecumenical movement last century may be at risk. In qualifying "humanism" with the adjective "Reformed," I seek to represent a theological tradition that has viewed itself as both reformed and catholic; as catholic it represents a continuity with church tradition, and as reformed it is willing to reassess that in light of Scripture under the direction of the Spirit. The slogan *ecclesia reformata, semper reformanda* establishes a principle that reformation is never complete but is a task given to each generation. The church is reformed but always to be reformed. Yet there is much more to the Reformed tradition than this, and different ways of understanding its distinctiveness. Brian Gerrish characterizes it in terms of a series of intellectual habits—deference, criticism, openness, and practicality—rather than as a body of doctrinal positions, as in five-point Calvinism.[6] This looser description accords better with the more revisionist approach adopted here, particularly in relation to the openness to insights from other forms of inquiry.

> The original genius of the Reformed church, I believe, was that it borrowed gratefully from both the Lutherans and the Renaissance humanists, creating a "Christian philosophy" (as Calvin called it) that was at once faithful to the gospel and deeply committed to learning. I have no doubt that dependence on secular learning has sometimes led Reformed theology to make mistakes, but Zwingli and Calvin apparently considered it a worse mistake to isolate the gospel from secular thought.[7]

Architecture, ed. Christopher R. Brewer and Robert McSwain (London: Routledge, 2017), 74.

6. See also I. John Hesselink, *On Being Reformed: Distinctive Characteristics and Common Misunderstandings* (Ann Arbor: Servant Books, 1983).

7. Brian Gerrish, "Tradition in the Modern World: The Reformed Habit of Mind," in *Toward the Future of Reformed Theology: Tasks, Topics, Traditions*, ed. David Willis and Michael Welker (Grand Rapids: Eerdmans, 1999), 3–20 (16).

The title of John Calvin's best-known work, *Institutio Christianae Religionis*, is not wholly captured by its standard translation as *Institutes of the Christian Religion*. In the sixteenth century, the term *religio* did not carry its modern sense of one among several world religions. Closely related to *pietas*, the concept captures a combined commitment to devotion and service. This practical dimension is also heavily accentuated by Calvin. The purpose of his theological compendium is to inform the worship and service of God in the church and the world. "[W]e shall not say that, properly speaking, God is known where there is no religion or piety."[8] For this reason, he tends to eschew speculative questions and modes of inquiry. These are set aside in a concerted effort to concentrate on what is given to us to know and understand in this life. In this practical pursuit, he too has been characterized as a Christian humanist.[9]

In similar respects, the approach informing these essays commits to the practical and anti-speculative bent of the Reformed tradition. While aiming at coherence and plausibility, Christian theology serves a practical function in its being ordered to the life of the church for the world. I often return to the image, inspired by Wolterstorff's reading of Thomas Reid, of "living wisely in the darkness."[10] At best, we aspire to a theology that is faithful, credible, and useful, but there is much that will always remain provisional and open to revision.

---

8. *Institutes of the Christian Religion* 1.2.1, trans. Ford Lewis Battles (Grand Rapids: Eerdmans, 1960).

9. E.g. Nicholas Wolterstorff, "The Christian Humanism of John Calvin," in *Re-Envisioning Christian Humanism: Education and the Restoration of Humanity*, ed. Jens Zimmermann (Oxford: Oxford University Press, 2016), 77–94.

10. Nicholas Wolterstorff, "God and Darkness in Reid," in *Thomas Reid: Context, Influence, Significance*, ed. Joseph Houston (Edinburgh: Dunedin Academic Press, 2004), 77–102.

Part One

CHRISTIAN DOCTRINE

Chapter 1

THE DIVINE ATTRIBUTES

SOME METHODOLOGICAL CONSIDERATIONS

This chapter considers what is at stake in different approaches to the doctrine of the divine attributes. Before his untimely death in 2003, Colin Gunton's last book was on a topic that he judged to have been insufficiently related to Trinitarian doctrine.[1] Similarly, John Webster, one of his closest friends in the discipline, developed what he called a "theological theology."[2] Though seemingly tautologous, his title signaled a determined effort to focus on the doctrine of God as basal to all the doctrines. Others working in the field have pursued rather different approaches with alternative starting points, agenda, and emphases. But the preparation of this chapter has given me the opportunity to reflect on the work of two theologians who were my friends and whose absence from the contemporary field is much lamented. Despite fearing their disapproval of what follows, I gratefully acknowledge my debt to them.

Some of the challenges in framing an account of the divine attributes can quickly be noted. Should the attributes be unfolded at the outset or allowed to emerge in the course of one's theological system? Schleiermacher chose this second route to avoid abstracting what we say about God from our deepest religious affections. The most essential attributes—divine wisdom and love, along with their Trinitarian inflection—only emerged at the close of his *Glaubenslehre*. The majority of theologians, by contrast, have preferred to establish the attributes at the outset of their systematics, often with a bipartite distinction whether between the metaphysical and the moral, the transcendent and the immanent, or the incommunicable and the communicable. The term "attributes" is not itself entirely apt, since these suggest a set of predicates that combine contingently to make God who God is and not something else. But almost all accounts insist that the attributes belong together and characterize the one simple being of God from our creaturely perspectives. These might be regarded as formal rather than real

---

1. Colin E. Gunton, *Act and Being: Towards a Doctrine of the Divine Attributes* (London: SCM, 2002).

2. John Webster, *God Without Measure: Working Papers in Christian Theology, Vol. 1, God and the Works of God* (London: Bloomsbury T&T Clark 2016).

distinctions in the Godhead. In addition, a stress on divine ineffability is also apparent, whether as a function of human finitude or divine revelation, or both. We cannot imagine God, still less what it would be like to be God.

The consistency of the attributes is also questionable, and this too prompts a keen sense of the limitations of our knowledge. Core convictions about the power and the goodness of God quickly generate a problem of evil. But there are also challenges in thinking of divine omnipresence at times when God seems absent, hidden, or idle, and in nuancing the language of divine impassibility and immutability in relation to Scriptural language deploying anthropopathic images to describe God.[3]

In what follows, I consider different approaches to the doctrine of God which have substantive outcomes for the handling of the divine attributes. These are not exclusive of one another, though the differences of emphasis are important. In some ways, this must be a heuristic typology, rather than a nuanced characterization of approaches; indeed, one can plausibly argue that all three elements are present in the leading theologians of the church. But the extent to which one is given priority over the others will produce significant consequences. For that reason, a fundamental decision will have important repercussions for the rest of one's systematic theology. The three types that follow might be associated loosely with reason, Scripture, and experience. These labels provide an initial sense of the different sources that are at work here and the relative importance we attach to these.

Philosophical Approaches

One can begin with a philosophical justification of the existence of God as a single, necessary, all-powerful First Cause of everything else. It is sometime said that this dominates patristic approaches to the divine attributes, particularly in their borrowing from Platonist philosophy. Gunton argues this at some length in the opening chapters of *Act and Being*. On one reading of Aquinas, this is his preferred approach at the commencement of the *Summa Theologiae*, where the existence of God and some divine attributes follow from notions of God as First Cause qualified by a succession of necessary negations.

This also appears to be the preferred way of recent analytic philosophies of religion, for example, in Richard Swinburne's *Coherence of Theism* and *The Existence*

---

3. Different theological readings of "divine absence," "hiddenness," and "silence" have been attempted, particularly in post-Holocaust theology. In pointing to ways in which we are addressed by God, these expose forms of theological idolatry without recourse to a simple denial of divine presence. See Claudia Welz, "A Theological Phenomenology of Listening: God's 'Voice' and 'Silence' after Auschwitz," *Religions* 10 (2019): 139, doi:10.3390/rel10030139.

of God.⁴ He seeks to demonstrate (or show the probability of) God's existence as first cause, source, or origin of all matter and order in the physical universe. As first cause, God must work *ex nihilo* and cannot be identified with matter. Hence God is immaterial. And by a process of contrast and negation, we can figure out what God is not in order to be God. God is not an instance of a species. God does not belong to a genus. God is not limited or dependent upon sense data for knowledge. God is not compound, or finite or mortal or visible or subject to spatiotemporal limitation, and so on. Conclusions about divine eternity, omnipresence, and pure actuality can also be generated along these lines. A God with omni-properties provides a simpler hypothesis than one who is limited in some respect. In this way, we can construct something like an account of divine attributes that have a (more or less) classical form and are undergirded by philosophical arguments.

Gunton makes the point that this method tends to privilege the metaphysical rather than the moral attributes of God—he may be right in this regard. But, from this starting point, one might seek to connect the concept of God with further knowledge furnished by Scripture. This God is the God of Abraham, Isaac, and Jacob. This God is the Father of our Lord Jesus Christ, is one in three persons, and is made known to us in different ways. One outcome of this strategy is that the doctrine of the Trinity (*de Deo trino*) is treated after the doctrine of the oneness of God (*de Deo uno*) in the order of exposition.

What are the attractions of this framing of the doctrine of God? I can think of four that have featured in a variety of contexts.

There is the evidentialist strategy which seeks rational justification for general claims about God before entering upon an inquiry into more particular commitments. For a doctrine of God to get started, we need some proof of God's existence or at least a set of plausible reasons for such belief. It was prevalent from the early modern period, not only among deists but also among those who, like John Locke, adhered to more orthodox positions. This strategy reflects a preoccupation with epistemological questions. As has often been pointed out, people only seriously started to prove God's existence at a time when it was explicitly doubted.⁵ Philosophers did the same with proofs of the external world, largely under the impact of Hume's skepticism. Heidegger would later remark that the scandal was not the absence of a convincing proof but that it was ever expected and attempted time and again.⁶ Might philosophers of religion and theologians have worried unnecessarily about the priority of demonstrating God's existence to some imaginary skeptic? Were they drawn into a contest in which the rules were rigged from the outset?

---

4. Richard Swinburne, *The Coherence of Theism*, 2nd ed. (Oxford: Oxford University Press, 2016); *The Existence of God*, 2nd ed. (Oxford: Clarendon, 2014).

5. Michael J. Buckley, *At the Origins of Modern Atheism* (New Haven: Yale University Press, 1987).

6. Martin Heidegger, *Being and Time*, trans. John Macquarrie and Edward Robinson (Oxford: Blackwell, 1962), 249.

Yet perhaps we do need some proof or probabilistic case for God, if not the world. After all, it seems possible to doubt the divine existence. This is not as self-defeating as denying the extra-mental existence of material objects. To accomplish the task, a coherent concept of God is developed followed by a cumulative series of arguments for its probable instantiation. Even if this is not the route by which people come to faith, it offers rational justification. But, of course, it also sets the terms for a description of the divine attributes. In framing the hypothesis of a God whose existence is then to be demonstrated, it is necessary to give some content to the concept. Swinburne is explicit that this approach will rescue theology from fideism or positivism, and return it to the high intellectual standards set at earlier stages in the history of Christian thought. He seems unimpressed by much work in contemporary systematic theology.

> It is one of the intellectual tragedies of our age that when philosophy in English-speaking countries has developed high standards of argument and clear thinking, the style of theological writing has been largely influenced by the continental philosophy of Existentialism, which, despite its considerable other merits, has been distinguished by a very loose and sloppy style of argument. If argument has a place in theology, large-scale theology needs clear and rigorous argument. That point was very well grasped by Thomas Aquinas and Duns Scotus, by Berkeley, Butler, and Paley. It is high time for theology to return to their standards.[7]

Theologians have challenged Swinburne's work in different ways; some have even dismissed his approach as inclining toward idolatry with its hypothetical construction of a supreme personal being.[8] Yet, for anyone emerging from the skepticism of analytic philosophy in the 1960s and 1970s with its arid disputes around the meaningfulness of God-talk, his robust and positive approach was a breath of fresh air. With Plantinga and others, he demonstrated how a commitment to philosophical rigor could be allied to a strong religious faith. The revival of the philosophy of religion, in which he played a key role, ensured that the analytic tradition was not monotonously dismissive of all God-talk.

A second type of justification is that rather than affording a proof against skepticism, it is merely a way of introducing the idea of God. It positions the concept in such a way that a deeper exploration can then take place. If we start to think of God as cause, origin, source, or ground of everything else, then we start to get some purchase on the idea. We teach small children to think of God as the maker of everything, including ourselves. That gives them some orientation in what is involved in belief, prayer, and practice. Some cognitive psychologists,

---

7. Swinburne, *Coherence of Theism*, 7.
8. This criticism seems implicit in the hostile comment of D. Z. Phillips that such a God is at best "an averagely decent father." *Wittgenstein and Religion* (Basingstoke: Macmillan, 1993), 155.

for example, Justin Barrett, have even suggested on the basis of transcultural evidence that our brains may be inclined to codify God in this way.[9] And some leading Thomist scholars have claimed that this indeed is what Aquinas is doing at the start of the *Summa*.[10] His proofs are not developed in any detail. He is not engaged in arguing against atheists or skeptics. His strategy is the more modest one of positioning the concept of God in order to facilitate further exploration. From the outset indeed his project is deeply Scriptural and set within the context of faith seeking understanding. So the employment of a philosophical approach to the being of God in the Prima Pars can be construed as an exercise in Christian location rather than intending a fully developed doctrine of God.

A third reason for the approach might appeal again to Aquinas by pointing out that there is actually a bit more going on here than simply putting the ball in play. In his ruminations at the start of the *Summa*, there is a reflective purgation of false ideas of God. God is not one among many, or composite, or vulnerable to change, or conditioned by temporal limitation. Fergus Kerr claims that Aquinas's strategy at the outset of the *Summa* should be read not as an exercise in rationalist apologetics but better as an attempt through a negative theology to protect divine transcendence.[11] This process of refinement is also a dispossession of idolatrous intellectual habits. We cannot do theology without the kind of reflective acumen that is evident here. In the first volume of her systematics, Katherine Sonderegger appeals to Aquinas in her meditation on the oneness of God as revealed in Holy Scripture, particularly in Deuteronomy. This thought process, albeit speculative, take places within the context of faith, prayer, and adoration. The philosophical method now starts to be incorporated into a comprehensive theological programme. Divine Mystery is not a sign of our *failure* in knowledge but rather our *success*, she insists. It is because we know truly and properly—because we obey in faith the First Commandment—that God is mystery.[12] I associate this strategy with the second type which follows, but these remarks illustrate how one might use this more speculative approach as an ancillary device for purging religious elements of potentially idolatrous elements.

A final attraction, which may be underestimated, is its simplicity. It has a clarity and convenience in establishing a succession of omni-properties or perfections that can characterize God. One finds in many textbook treatments (e.g., Bavinck's *Reformed Dogmatics*) that they quickly follow this route in

---

9. Justin L. Barrett, *Cognitive Science, Religion, and Theology: From Human Minds to Divine Minds* (West Conshohocken: Templeton, 2011).

10. Brian Davies writes that the purpose of the five ways is "to set the ball rolling, not to bring the game to an end." *The Thought of Thomas Aquinas* (Oxford: Clarendon, 1992), 26.

11. Fergus Kerr, *After Aquinas: Versions of Thomism* (Oxford: Blackwell, 2002), 58. See also Janet Soskice, *Naming God: Addressing God in Philosophy, Theology and Scripture* (Cambridge: Cambridge University Press, 2023), 165–96.

12. Katherine Sonderegger, *Systematic Theology, Vol. 1, The Doctrine of God* (Minneapolis: Fortress, 2015), 24.

establishing the attributes, even while claiming Scripture as their norm.[13] Many of the post-Reformation confessions and catechisms also adopt this procedure. The theologian speaks here almost as a philosopher of religion before returning to more positive dogmatic claims. At the very least, an alliance is assumed between the philosophical approach and a Scripturally generated theology. This may be a recurring phenomenon in systematic theology—views that are simple, strong, precise, and easily communicated are often defended because the alternatives seem to lack these qualities in the same measure, for example, penal substitution, a deterministic providence, two-natures Christology.[14] If these are the attractions, what then are the problems?

One anxiety is that this concedes too much to philosophy, and particularly to the Platonic tradition, though one could say the same about later Kantian, Hegelian, and analytic trends in the discipline. If we deploy these resources and arguments at the outset, then a framework is established which will tend to distort or even control the witness of Scripture, for example, with reference to divine involvement in the world and our capacity to describe God in particular ways. This was Gunton's principal charge against classical theism with its dominant *via negativa*. The being of God was described by a cosmological argument that arrived at a description of God through a series of contrasts with the categorial features of created being. The procedure was thus built primarily upon what we cannot know about God rather than upon what is given to us to know. It was predicated upon failure rather than upon success. This can most readily be illustrated by his treatment of immutability and impassibility. For Gunton, these are generated not via a series of negative contrasts with creaturely change and suffering, but in positive terms of divine constancy (God is unchanging in the sense of remaining faithful to us) and peacefulness (the life of God is not disturbed by conflicting passions or emotions). By following this approach to the attribute, the God of the philosophers is set in an antithetical relationship with the God of the Bible. Others who have shared this skepticism around philosophical approaches include Luther, Pascal, Kierkegaard, Barth, and Jenson.

Within their critiques, there is concern around the detached and speculative air of accounts of the divine attributes. The fashioning and refining of the concept of the most perfect being is intellectually impressive, but does it resonate with lived faith, with the spiritual experience, prayer, rituals, and forms of life that characterize the church? Is this an exercise in metaphysical abstraction that suffers from a disconnect with the more messy and imprecise sensibilities of our faith? Does the framing of the divine attributes outstrip what we can believe and imagine, and what we are confident of saying as theologians to people of faith? Perhaps this

---

13. Herman Bavinck, *Reformed Dogmatics: God and Creation*, Vol. 2 (Grand Rapids: Baker, 2004), 118–37.

14. Whether this simplicity is merely apparent is at least an open question. Exercises in comparative theology with practitioners of other faiths might suggest otherwise.

pervasive sense of philosophical detachment has even discouraged theologians from tackling the subject at all, pushing us in other directions.

Yet, against this radical critique, we might ask whether the use of philosophical reasoning (if we can call it that) is unavoidable in a way that is not merely reactive but proactive. The tradition is constantly subject to critical inspection and the use of conceptual tools, in part derived from philosophy, is inevitable. One does not need to adopt an attitude of servility to a partner discipline to acknowledge this. Intellectual rigor may not deliver a fully coherent and credible concept of God on its own, but it might have a role in disciplining the lived faith of a community. At the very least, a deficient concept of God may have the effect of undermining some key tenets and habits of the faith. To that extent, the rationalist approach identified here must continue to have a necessary role to exercise.

I move now to a second type of approach.

Theology as Scripturally Driven

In approaching the divine attributes, we should acknowledge explicitly that concepts of God are contextually located within communities of faith that have their own forms of life, sacred texts, creeds, and patterns of devotion and worship. From these, we derive a positive theology that is embedded within the church. Christian theology is here conceived as a second-order form of Christian self-description. It takes place inside faith and attempts to describe the world from that perspective. In doing so, it is unashamedly confessional, though there may be scope for adjustments and absorption of insights and knowledge claims from elsewhere.[15] Luther, of course, charted this path in a striking manner in the Heidelberg Disputation.

For Katherine Sonderegger, we must begin with divine oneness as it is disclosed in Scripture and apprehended in the encounter that takes place only when, as she says, we are "on our knees." In the encounter with the God of Scripture, we are faced with the overwhelming sense of divine oneness and uniqueness which forbids all idolatry. "Attributes, and Perfections, all other disclosures of God as Word and Spirit are governed by and determined by Oneness, the surpassing Divine Uniqueness and Freedom. And just this is permanent mystery."[16]

---

15. This is acknowledged in the closing stages of George Lindbeck's *The Nature of Doctrine* (London: SPCK, 1984) where philosophical reasoning is accorded an important subsidiary role. "Confirmation or disconfirmation occurs through an accumulation of successes or failures in making practically and cognitively coherent sense of relevant data, and the process does not conclude, in the case of religions, until the disappearance of the last communities of believers or, if the faith survives, until the end of history." 131.

16. Sonderegger, *Systematic Theology*, Vol. 1, 25. Janet Soskice adopts a similar strategy in a book that appeared after this essay was written. See *Naming God: Addressing the Divine*

By contrast, Robert Jenson, though following the same approach, begins with the triunity of God's being and work, as this is narrated in Scripture. He deliberately sets this approach in contrast to a Hellenistic philosophical focus on the oneness of the eternal divine being on which everything temporal reposes. This is an "unbaptized God," to adopt the title of one of his books. Insufficiently Trinitarian in formulation, it fails to register the God whose being unfolds historically. The approach favored by Gunton in his discussion of the divine attributes largely follows that of Jenson.[17] It is unashamedly Trinitarian and critical of theologies that excessively stress the transcendence and unknowability of God, thus destabilizing the core claims of the Christian faith. In typically bold fashion, Gunton asserts:

> Aquinas having set up the ontological framework for his theology in the Five Ways by means of a general philosophical analysis of causation, everything else follows by a process of logical deduction. The attributes are those appropriate to a being who is the moving, efficient, material, formal and final cause of the cosmos. We have an analysis of the God-world relation in largely cosmological terms, untrammelled by reference to those particular divine acts in which God is revealed by Scripture actually to operate. That is to say, the basic concepts come from philosophical, or, should we say, Greek theology. We are in the presence of an entrenched tradition which owes more to Greece than Scripture and, despite modification, dominates the treatment of the attributes until this day.[18]

For Gunton, the divine attributes are more a function of Scriptural revelation appropriated in faith. These are ways of describing the God of the Bible rather than deductions of the ways in which the Creator must differ from the creation. This approach tends to contrast the God of the philosophers with the God of the Bible. In modern theology, its moving spirit is Karl Barth. Jenson, Gunton and Sonderegger are working in his slipstream, though not uncritically.

In discussing the divine attributes, Hendrikus Berkhof notes the enormous influence of *Church Dogmatics* II/1 even among those not regarded in other respects as followers of Barth. Indeed, it was this part volume of the *Church*

---

in *Philosophy, Theology and Scripture* (Cambridge: Cambridge University Press, 2023). The prioritizing of the divine names locates the doctrine of God within the sphere of faith as opposed to philosophical proof. In this way, Aquinas's work can be read as an exercise in *fides quaerens intellectum*.

17. Jenson himself seems less interested in developing an account of the divine attributes, stating merely that these are the terms predicated of God in our "speaking of the gospel." By narrating the story of God, we will make the divine attributes apparent. Robert W. Jenson, *Systematic Theology, Vol. 1, The Triune God* (New York: Oxford University Press, 1997), 223.

18. Gunton, *Act and Being*, 52.

Dogmatics that Hans Urs von Balthasar carried around with him, like a cat its kitten, as Barth remarked.[19] Berkhof's own treatment of the divine attributes reflects the same biblically oriented approach. Omnipresence rests on the belief that the transcendent God is always near to us; omniscience refers to a wise oversight; simplicity refers to the oneness and constancy of God; eternity describes God's surpassing yet surrounding of our own time.[20] These derive from the Scripturally focused confession of the faith community rather than proceeding from more abstract reflection.

A potential problem with this approach is its provincialism. Does it privilege one tradition and form of expression, thus ignoring the universal human experience of God and the validity of other traditions? A Barthian would respond that this is simply what the faith commits us to holding. It acts first and foremost as a judgment upon the church. Barth himself sought to nuance his position by claiming that the Word of God could be heard outside the church in secular parables (as he described them). And, in another image, he spoke of the little lights of creation which in their own way signify the one great light.[21] The charge of Christomonism irritated him intensely.

> As the Bible attests the one Word of God, and to the extent that the Church adopts and repeats this testimony, important human words are spoken, bright lights are set up in the human sphere and great and little revelations occur. Nor does it follow from our statement that every word spoken outside the circle of the Bible and the Church is a word of false prophecy and therefore valueless, empty and corrupt, that all the lights which rise and shine in this outer sphere are misleading and all the revelations are necessarily untrue. Our statement is simply to the effect that Jesus is the one and only Word of God, that He alone is the light of God and the revelation of God.[22]

The role of philosophy, moreover, is not excluded. It has to be critically appropriated and enlisted in the cause of articulating the Christian faith, but without assigning to it a controlling function whether intentionally or otherwise. Elsewhere, Barth spoke of "spoiling the Egyptians" to describe this eclectic and subordinate function of philosophy for the theological task.

Is the proof of the pudding in the eating? Barth arguably struggles more when it comes to a doctrine of creation or to articulating a theology of other religions,

---

19. See Eberhard Busch, *Karl Barth: His Life from Letters and Autobiographical Texts* (London: SCM, 1975), 302.

20. Hendrikus Berkhof, *Christian Faith: An Introduction to the Study of the Faith*, Revised ed. (Grand Rapids: Eerdmans, 1986), 113–54.

21. Karl Barth, *Church Dogmatics* IV/3 (Edinburgh: T&T Clark, 1961).

22. Barth, *Church Dogmatics* IV/3, 97.

though there are resources in his work that have been deployed in interesting ways for these tasks.[23]

A further difficulty may be that the approach adopted here fails to register the diversity of forms that Christian faith takes as it is enculturated in different contexts. Does it speak to our condition today in the face of pluralism, fragmentation, and the need for the building of coalitions? Part of its attraction was that it enabled a clear sociopolitical stance to be adopted, usually in the form of protest or rejection based upon a unique, distinctive, and authoritative revelation. This countercultural disposition worked well in the apartheid struggle in South Africa, which was a deeply Christian country at that time. But is this where we are today? Do we want to shout at people from a lofty height in an attempt to echo the heroic sounds of Barmen? Is the translation of distinctively Christian concerns into other vocabularies not part of the task of social concern and witness?

This acknowledgment of diversity is confirmed by Scripture itself. To reduce its content to a single pattern of promise and fulfillment in Christ may obscure the range of materials, some of which offer support for natural theology and a more detached philosophical reflection. One thinks here especially of the wisdom literature or passages from Acts 14 and 17. As James Barr has provocatively remarked, had a Barthian written Psalm 19, it would have taken a different form.[24] If we introduce other perspectives—in a self-consciously blended strategy—then we might more readily acknowledge mobility across space and time.

I doubt, however, whether this observation defeats the approach. One might argue for a Scripturally driven approach that can accommodate recognition of plurality as well as lights outside the church. The point of the approach is that the divine attributes are primarily descriptions of God that derive from a faith determined by Scripture, the practices of the church, and an intense focus on Jesus, rather than from a *via negativa* or arguments about causality from natural theology. Yet the different emphases in Scripture are both challenging and promising—challenging in that they resist assimilation to a single coherent set of divine attributes, promising in that the plurality of voices has a capacity to resonate with the different contexts in which faith is lived and expressed across both space and time.

A Scripturally driven method is capable of accommodating some blended elements of the more philosophical approach, and these may be useful in imposing a measure of coherence and unity upon the expressions of faith. We may rightly

---

23. This is evident for example in some recent summary essays. See Joshua Ralston, "Religion and the Religions," in Paul Dafydd Jones and Paul T. Nimmo (eds.), *The Oxford Handbook of Karl Barth* (Oxford: Oxford University Press, 2019), 637–53, and Sven Ensminger, "Barth and the Religions," in *Wiley-Blackwell Companion to Karl Barth*, Vol. 2, ed. George Hunsinger and Keith L. Johnson (Oxford: Wiley-Blackwell 2020), 869–80.

24. James Barr, *Biblical Faith and Natural Theology* (Oxford: Clarendon, 1993), 89.

begin from the primary deliverances of Christian faith in relation to its canonical scriptures, its liturgical habits, and its forms of life. But, as these are interrogated through a second-order reflective activity, more philosophical or speculative work will inevitably commence. This seems to be roughly what is happening in the recent theologies of Sonderegger and Webster, though I cannot do justice to them here.[25] Drawing on a different philosophical tradition, Jenson attempts something similar in his integration of divine being and action. Through a process of clarification and purgation, we can proceed to deeper understanding. This indeed might be represented as the kind of *a posteriori* work that some contemporary analytic philosophers of religion see themselves doing. Tim Mawson's recent treatment of the divine attributes in the *CUP Elements* series might be defended in this way. Within the community of faith, the concept of God involves ideas of divine personhood, presence, knowledge, power, action, and goodness. These require clearer articulation and, where possible, systematic clarity. Admittedly, there is a danger of seeking for a coherence that may elude us, of over-intellectualizing the faith, and in distorting the subject matter by the search for definition. Such intellectual longing should be tempered by reference to biblical themes regarding divine hiddenness. Though resisting any simple systematization, these provide both specification and publicly accessible norms.

> The angel, the pillar of cloud, and the face offer a variety of models of the presence of God, allusions and intimations rather than definition. Other more concrete models of that presence, the public institutions of the tent meeting, the ark, the covenant continually reaffirmed, and the tablets of the Decalogue, take up frail private and individual perception into the support of the wider fellowship of the community of the church.[26]

One could add that this public setting also includes philosophical reflection on the nature of the divine, neither to subvert nor to surpass, but to offer further clarity and the deepening that arises through insights borrowed from other traditions. Scripture itself, particularly its wisdom literature, offers some encouragement here.

This leads me to a further rejoinder to the aforementioned suspicion of the classical doctrine of the divine attributes in patristic theology. This is too beholden to something like the Hellenization thesis which ignores the variety of theological negotiations that took place in the second century as Christian scholars faced Gnostic, pagan, philosophical and Jewish criticism. The account of divine oneness, being, and action reflects these engagements with the surrounding culture by scholars deeply immersed in the practices of the church. As Robert Wilcken

---

25. Discussing the attribute of "aseity," Webster insists that this should not be treated as a cosmological derivation but as a revealed shining of divine splendor from which we understand both the divine being and its self-communication to the world. *God Without Measure*, 13–28.

26. William Johnstone, *Exodus 20–40* (Macon: Smyth & Helwys, 2014), 393.

argues, we might as well talk about the Christianization of Hellenism, though even this may reduce the creative ferment of the period.[27] A binary division between a classical theism derived from Greek philosophy and a Trinitarianism derived from Scripture is not sustainable, at least not as a broad-brush thesis that can adequately capture the diversity of Christian thought across several centuries. Even Augustine, so often the target of such criticism, was adamant that his Scriptural approach set him apart from the Platonists.

> None of this is in the Platonist books. Those pages do not contain the face of this devotion, tears of confession, your sacrifice, a troubled spirit, a contrite and humble spirit, the salvation of your people, the espoused city, the guarantee of your Holy Spirit, the cup of my redemption.[28]

Philosophical and Scriptural approaches inevitably move closer to one another, forming a combination. Again, this muddies the waters of my typology.

Starting with Religion

A third approach begins with the experience of God by way of phenomenological description. According to this strategy, an awareness of the divine can be discerned within the structures of human consciousness. The *sensus divinitatis* was already a familiar concept when deployed by Calvin at the outset of the *Institutes*. Following Romans 1 and Cicero, he regarded this as a feature of human life everywhere. Though he regarded it as confused, distorted, and prone to idolatry, he recognized its numinous and haunting qualities.[29] In modern theological projects, this has been evaluated more positively, often with respect to addressing epistemological questions. A phenomenology of universal religious consciousness can halt skepticism, while also having the advantage of identifying common ground across historical forms of religion. A further function for the Christian theologian has been its potential for problematizing human existence in religious terms, thus enabling revelation to be presented as its resolution. If the deliverances of a generic consciousness are lacking specificity, this creates the space for a more historically

---

27. "In many ways large and small the church fathers drew on the philosophical, moral, and literary traditions of the ancient world, but the Bible created a new milieu and unloosed their tongues by offering a fresh and versatile vocabulary to express the things they believed." Robert Wilckens, *The Spirit of Early Christian Thought* (New Haven: Yale University Press, 2003), 320.

28. Augustine, *Confessions* VII. xxi, trans. Henry Chadwick (Oxford: Oxford University Press, 1992), 131.

29. For analysis of Calvin on the *sensus divinitatis* see Edward A. Dowey, *The Knowledge of God in Calvin's Theology* (New York: Columbia University Press, 1952), 50–6.

particular definition. In this way, a phenomenology of religious experience can be doubly useful through its necessity and insufficiency.

Schleiermacher's description of a universal consciousness of being "absolutely dependent" has been highly influential, though recent readings of his work point to ways in which this is an intentional abstraction rather than a foundation of his system—there is no generic or natural religion, only particular faiths.[30] The sense of God as undergirding and informing the world is present in much of what Schleiermacher says, including the way he characterizes doctrines as religious affections put forth in speech and in his description of redemption as our sharing in Jesus' unbroken communion with God. The standard complaint is that this method tends to be subjective and indeterminate in outcome, with a resultant tendency toward doctrinal reductionism. Emil Brunner placed Schleiermacher on one side of a binary between a mystical and immanentist philosophy and a Word-focused theology of revelation.[31] When cast in these terms, a phenomenology of religious experience is vulnerable to the charge of human self-description apart from the domain of a genuine encounter with God.

On the other hand, a phenomenological approach might appeal to the spiritual experience of modern audiences with their inclination toward immanentism and search for common elements across all faiths. This may also represent a Christian constituency which is similarly conscious of the spiritual significance of nature, art and other forms of experience outside the church. The sense of God mediated through nature or art may be highly significant for people otherwise estranged from the language of Christian doctrine or the liturgical practices of the church. The messiness and imprecision of much of this makes theologians uneasy and may not be captured well by attempts at offering a single definition of religious experience. Yet this may be the ambivalent religious context in which we now find ourselves with its curious mixture of belief, half-belief, and unbelief.[32]

Familiar options are available, their variety suggesting that this approach is difficult to avoid while also inviting criticism about its plasticity. We are aware of a

---

30. Hans Frei claims that Schleiermacher provides a loose correlation between external and internal descriptions of Christian faith, rather than a method in which the particular merely represents one regional expression of the general. See *Types of Christian Theology* (New Haven: Yale University Press, 1992), 34–8.

31. Emil Brunner, *Die Mystik und Das Wort: der Gegensatz zwischen moderner Religionsaufassung und christlichem Glauben dargestellt an der Theologie Schleiermachers* (Tübingen: J. C. B. Mohr, 1928). For a critical assessment of Brunner's reception of Schleiermacher see Christine Helmer, *Theology and the End of Doctrine* (Louisville: Westminster John Knox Press, 2014), 47–58.

32. "Theology needs to take seriously the ten times as many people in Britain who express belief in God as attend church regularly, as well as conspicuous cases of religious experience formed outside of contact with those of faith." David Brown, *Divine Generosity and Human Creativity: Theology through Symbol, Painting and Architecture*, ed. Christopher R. Brewer and Robert McSwain (London: Routledge, 2017), 34.

presence at once mysterious and compelling. This comes not in isolation but "in, with and under" our awareness of some aspect of the world. One can cite Rudolf Otto's classical account of *Das Heilige*. Against Schleiermacher, he more firmly identifies the numinous as objective and outside of the self. We have a natural disposition for knowing the holy, though this is only manifested under particular historical conditions, the highest of which he discerns in Jesus.[33]

Karl Rahner's pre-thematic awareness of the Absolute describes the ways in which all human thought and action have a self-transcending aspect. Our existence presents itself to us as mysterious in terms of its origin and striving. The horizon of our consciousness is an ineffable mystery, always eluding our grasp. This transcendent orientation is inescapable for human beings, though we frequently find ways of suppressing and forgetting it.[34] As Schleiermacher before him, Rahner has been charged by his critics with anthropocentrism. Yet surveying his work fifty years on, one is struck by its constant orientation toward Christian life and faith, notwithstanding his openness to insights from elsewhere.[35] Rahner's approach might strike a chord with those who today occupy a position between belief and unbelief, perhaps in that inchoate space labeled "spiritual but not religious."[36] A haphazard and elusive sense of God haunts much literature today. Carol Ann Duffy's poem "Prayer" offers one well-known example. "Some nights though we are faithless, the truth/ enters our hearts, that small familiar pain."[37] Barbara Brown Taylor's story of her spiritual odyssey describes her moving away from the institutionalized forms of religion to retain a clearer sense of God. Instead of teaching people what they should believe about God, she says, the church might do better by taking an interest in their experience of God beyond its domain.[38]

Different phenomenologies are possible. One could attempt a more pantheist approach to spirit, or a sense of the divine invading and identifying with everything. Alternatively, some have adopted a stronger personalist framework to represent God in the language of disclosure, encounter, and demand. We find this in much post-Kantian theology. John Baillie provides an accessible example with his mid-twentieth-century notion of "mediated immediacy" set out in *Our*

---

33. Rudolf Otto, *The Idea of the Holy*, trans. John. W. Harvey (Oxford: Oxford University Press, 1958).

34. See for example Karl Rahner, *Foundations of Christian Faith* (London: Darton, Longman and Todd, 1978), 31–4.

35. Fergus Kerr has suggested that the key to Rahner's theology is "his experience and understanding of life in the Church—not his metaphysics of self-consciousness." *Twentieth-Century Catholic Theologians: From Neoscholasticism to Nuptial Mysticism* (Oxford: Blackwell, 2007), 94.

36. See Linda A. Mercadante, *Belief without Borders: Inside the Minds of the Spiritual but Not Religious* (Oxford: Oxford University Press, 2014).

37. Carol Ann Duffy, 'Prayer', in *Mean Time* (London: Anvil, 1998), 52.

38. Barbara Brown Taylor, *Leaving Church* (Norwich: Canterbury Press, 2011).

Knowledge of God.[39] According to Baillie, there are three paradigmatic ways in which our experience of God is mediated—through nature, through other people, and through the Christian story. God is known intuitively and not by way of inference, but always through some creaturely medium.

How does one develop an account of the divine attributes on this basis? Here Schleiermacher's approach remains instructive. What we can affirm of God is largely through a transcendental argument concerning the necessary conditions of the experience of being absolutely dependent. God is located outside the nexus of finite causes as infinite, eternal, immutable, and omniscient, these being interpreted in ways that are significantly redolent of the philosophical tradition noted at the outset. Descriptions of religious experience generally rely heavily on philosophical tools. In the closing sections of the *Glaubenslehre*, the two most specific and significant divine attributes are "wisdom" and "love," these representing the high point of the Christian doctrine of God.[40] The location of the attributes across the different sections of his work reveals the complex interplay of phenomenological, philosophical, and dogmatic themes. From start to finish, his must be viewed as a work of *Christian* theology.

A balanced and methodologically self-conscious approach is found in the opening volume of Pannenberg's *Systematic Theology*, where he begins with the phenomena of religion. Despite their manifest differences, these are represented as universal. Christian revelation, he claims, should be situated within the wider history of religion as offering one set of responses that makes positive sense of the total flux.

> Christian theology has to be interested in the question whether we have by nature a religious disposition. If not, if the development of the religious sense is the product of a subjectivity that exists apart from the religious aspect, as the expression of pathological aberrations in self-understanding, then the Christian assertion of divine reality has lost the basis of its plausibility.[41]

Yet, when he comes to the divine attributes, after dealing with the Trinity, Pannenberg notes, following a little-known study of Hermann Cremer[42], that causality will deliver only a minimal concept of God which needs to be expanded by reference to divine action, particularly to the love of God displayed in Christ. The so-called moral attributes cannot be established on any other basis.

---

39. John Baillie, *Our Knowledge of God* (Oxford: Oxford University Press, 1939).

40. Friedrich Schleiermacher, *The Christian Faith*, Vol. 2, ed. Catherine L. Kelsey and Terence N. Tice (Louisville: Westminster John Knox Press, 2016), 999–1017.

41. Wolfhart Pannenberg, *Systematic Theology*, Vol. 1 (Grand Rapids: Eerdmans, 1991), 157.

42. Hermann Cremer, *Die christliche Lehre von den Eigenschaften Gottes* (Gütersloh: C. Bertelsmann, 1897).

Unless governed by other norms, the limitations of this approach are readily discernible. Pannenberg acknowledges this danger. The phenomenological description may be given such priority that it becomes the controlling framework. The result is that the distinctive claims of Christian faith are captured and controlled by an alien frame of reference. Critics, as already noted in the case of Barth, charge the position with anthropological subjectivism. With its plasticity, it constitutes a retreat into the self and its projections, rather than an openness to an exterior divine revelation. We do not find God—God finds us.

From the other side, exponents of this approach have conversely been charged with a scarcely concealed Christian bias. The general description of religious experience or encounter with God is framed in such a way as to reflect an existing commitment to one faith tradition. Schleiermacher's Romantic critics who stood outside the church make this very allegation about the Fifth Speech in which natural religion is dismissed in favor of Jesus and the church.[43] Significantly, Pannenberg commends Schleiermacher for doing precisely this.[44] The general must in the end be normed by the particular, though the latter needs to be connected with some wider account of the *sensus divinitatis*. The correlation of the general and the particular is an ineluctable task of every systematic theology, even those more inclined to denigrate the former.

Conclusion

Methodological decisions about priority of approach will tend to generate different accounts of the doctrine of God. One lesson of this typological review is that a single approach pursued to the exclusion of others will result in some distortion of the subject matter. On the first, a classical account of divine metaphysical attributes will quickly appear with concentration on the concept of "the most perfect being." For the second positivist approach, the attributes are more descriptive of the God we encounter in Scripture and the life of faith, or we might more correctly say the God who encounters us. The third phenomenological route will tend toward a more elusive characterization of the divine by way of extrapolating from experience or encounter, though with some philosophical and Scriptural sifting inevitably involved.

Where does this leave us? In exploring each of these three approaches, their tendency to draw upon elements of the other two has been observed. Neither Aquinas, Barth, nor Schleiermacher quite fits the pigeonholes that have been neatly prepared for them by commentators and critics. An inspection of competing approaches points to the need to keep all three in play through a blended approach that refuses to allow one to dominate to the exclusion of the other two. Each of the

---

43. Friedrich Schleiermacher, *On Religion: Speeches to Its Cultured Despisers*, ed. and trans. Richard Crouter (Cambridge: Cambridge University Press, 1988), 95–124.

44. Pannenberg, *Systematic Theology*, Vol. 1, 165.

three becomes problematic if set in isolation. An integrated approach is required for a faithful, chastened, and religiously adequate description of God. Without philosophical rigor and criticism, theology will suffer incoherence while failing to offer intellectual satisfaction. Without attention to the lived faith of the church with its constant return to Scripture and tradition, theology will be threatened by abstraction and philosophical imprisonment. And without some sense of the encounter with God in multiple ways, the articulation of a Christian faith becomes only the self-definition of one religious community lacking recognition of a wider knowledge of God and the ways in which Christians nowadays inhabit different worlds and universes of discourse. All three perspectives need to find their place, though both the philosophical and the phenomenological approaches will eventually give way to the exposition of Christian doctrine within the contextual settings of the faith community. The first and third approaches might then be viewed as ancillary to the second while exercising important constraints upon it. The works of Anselm afford a historical example of a theologian who comprehended these different approaches in the *Monologion*, the *Proslogion*, and the *Cur Deus Homo*.[45]

Finally, why bother at all with divine attributes? Might we manage without them by speaking of God in relation to creation, Israel, Christ, and the church? The being of God will unfold through exposition of other doctrines, the attributes emerging only at the end or in passing. Several recent systematic theologies adopt this approach by briefly subsuming the attributes under forms of divine relatedness.[46] A response to this might offer two related considerations. The first is that we need to think of the being of God in relation to the actions of God, however imprecise and limited our capacity so to do. The subject of divine activity has to be characterized in some way if God's typical actions are understood as disclosures or intimations of who God is. God must be named, confessed, and approached in appropriate ways. And the attributes seem unavoidable here even if this points to a looser, less tight-fitting approach. In addition, the immense variety of names and images that are used of God in first-order Christian discourse require to be given some organization and unity as a necessary second-order activity, not least for the sake of regulating Christian worship and confession. Attempts to classify the attributes into two groups or to privilege a fundamental pairing gesture toward this need for an ordering of our thinking. Hence the subject requires continued articulation albeit in the different contexts in which we find ourselves.

---

45. I owe this observation to some comments of Clare Carlisle on an earlier draft of this chapter.

46. See for example B. A. Gerrish, *Christian Faith: Dogmatics in Outline* (Louisville: Westminster John Knox, 2015), 46–51.

Chapter 2

THE POWER OF GOD

ITS USE AND ABUSE AS A THEOLOGICAL CONCEPT

Introduction

The concept of the "power of God" has a long and complex history. Deeply embedded in Scripture and tradition, divine power is attested in the classical creeds whether as *omnipotens* (the Apostles' Creed) or παντοκράτορα (the Nicene Creed). Theology today faces a double bind. A maximal account of omnipotence might play it safe by extending the usual metaphysical compliments to God through drawing upon arguments that purport to demonstrate the absence of any limitation upon the divine essence. Yet the exegetical and theological difficulties with this account are compounded by anxieties around its ideological and ethical outcomes. By contrast, an account that seeks to deflate divine power, perhaps by subordinating it to the attribute of love, runs the risk of so diminishing the agency of God that much of what appears vital to the liturgical and confessional hope of the church is jeopardized. In what follows, I shall explore both of these options in an effort to outline a position that is at once tempered yet sufficiently robust to fulfill its necessary function in Christian faith.

Some self-examination might not go amiss at the outset. Stephen Sykes reflected on the subject of power over many years, wondering whether his preoccupation was borne of anxiety around his role as professor and later bishop. Did the abuses of power by those who held office in church and state generate belatedly some troubling questions about its nature and practice? Or has the rapid decline of the church in our time, at least in this part of the world, resulted in a questioning of power and status that have recently been lost? "Was a strong and influential Church, deeply entwined with the structure of government, inclined to look positively at the phenomenon of power, whereas a weak, marginalized Church has had all manner of anxieties and reservations about the same subject?"[1]

This chapter was first presented as a paper at the Society for the Study of Theology, April 2023. I am grateful for the comments offered in response.

1. Stephen Sykes, *Power and Christian Theology* (London: Continuum, 2006), x.

Political theologies today have generally preferred a register of protest to one of affirmation. No doubt, this has had something to do with the altered social location of the church. A different type of power can be exercised from the margins—this has its obvious attractions. Conversely, those of us who belong to national or established churches may be tempted to over-argue for the wider benefits of these arrangements. Meanwhile, many of us hold positions of restricted influence and relative affluence in the academy. Is it too easy to argue against traditional constructions of divine power while seeking to retain a degree of privilege in one's own domain? I've asked these questions of myself while composing this essay.

How should we define power? Stephen Lukes describes it as an "essentially contested term," its different characterizations reflecting the perspective and interests of the inquirer.[2] A concept that is amenable to multidisciplinary approaches, power might be taken to refer to the capacity of an individual to act or to achieve some goal. Whether exercised or not, this power represents the possibility for action belonging to an agent or group of agents. Hobbes and Weber are associated with this conception. An alternative account considers the influences exerted upon agents by institutions, authorities, and structures, often by a ruling group, class, or caste. Michel Foucault has exposed this more systemic conception of power, though it can be viewed as complementing, rather than replacing, the earlier model. An institution may restrain the power of one group of persons while protecting that of another. Hence power can be constructed both as a capacity for action and as the constraining effect of a system. In the case of divine power, we can blend these two notions, while also noting that their use must now be chastened by attention to some historical examples.

Divine Power in the Bible

Scriptural attestations of divine power are easily identified. These characterize the works of God in creation and redemption. As is often noted, the Hebrew verb *bara* is reserved for the actions of God, whether in terms of *creatio ex nihilo* or *creatio continua*. God creates in the beginning and then anew. "I am about to create new heavens and a new earth; the former things shall not be remembered or come to mind" (Isaiah 65:17). In Genesis 1, divine power is manifested in a serene sequence of divine speech acts in the six days of creation. This takes place gratuitously and not from any perceived need or lack in God. If the presence of the *tehom* is a residual hint of a more menacing reality, this appears to be subjugated to the power of Yahweh. Elsewhere, the Hebrew Scriptures attest divine power over natural and historical forces in manifold ways. This is dramatically manifested in the exodus from Egypt, and later in the return from Babylon represented as a second Exodus. Yahweh's power is displayed in these hinge events which are liturgically celebrated. Divine agency is extolled by comparison with the enfeebled

---

2. Stephen Lukes, *Power: A Radical View* (London: Macmillan, 1974), 9.

power of kings and horses (Psalm 33). Human trust and hope repose upon the rule of God who is above the nations. This image of transcendent height frequently accentuates the metaphysical difference between God and humans.

> It is he who sits above the circle of the earth,
>   and its inhabitants are like grasshoppers;
> who stretches out the heavens like a curtain,
>   and spreads them like a tent to live in. (Isaiah 40:22)

If the work of God is serene and effortless at the beginning, this hardly captures other actions of God which seem to require the use of more anthropopathic imagery. The extent to which divine agency is accommodated to the vicissitudes of creatures introduces themes of divine patience, struggle, interaction, and improvisation, particularly through the Deuteronomic history. The covenant has to be established, renewed, and reimagined in the history of Israel. A divine wrestling with resistant material is often recalled in the Psalms.

Furthermore, notwithstanding dramatic manifestations of power, such hinge events are comparatively rare in the Hebrew Bible, as Brueggemann notes.[3] Although they constitute a primary testimony, a secondary form of witness is elicited in which God remains present though frequently hidden in the quotidian world. With their more mundane attention to the rhythms of nature and the ordering of social life, this is apparent in the wisdom writers. Yet Scriptural testimony becomes complex in Qoheleth and Job where the inscrutability of God and the limitations of human knowledge become dominant themes. In this way, divine power is problematized by themes of hiddenness, silence, and complaint.

The God–world relationship is characterized by an ontological size gap that is both quantitative and qualitative. The power of God greatly surpasses all creaturely agencies. Exercised by right, divine dominion is displayed in judgment, chastisement, patience, mercy, and blessing. These actions of God are reiterated in the New Testament though with a Christological complexion, particularly in the Pauline discourse about the power (*dynamis*) and wisdom (*sophia*) of God being displayed in the scandal and folly of the cross (1 Corinthians 1:23-24). We might venture the claim that in Scripture the narration of God's works provides an account of divine power that destabilizes more generic and intuitive notions. As Karl Barth insists, the statement that "God is power" is irreversible; it should not be approached by enlarging and maximizing creaturely examples of power.[4] Instead, our idolatrous systems and practices of control are contested by the divine manifestation of power

---

3. Walter Brueggemann, *Theology of the Old Testament: Testimony, Dispute, Advocacy* (Minneapolis: Augsburg Press, 1997), 333.

4. "If we are . . . to understand God's omnipotence too in accordance with Scripture and therefore by the standard of God's self-revelation, we must in all circumstances understand it in this way, refusing to reverse subject and predicate." Karl Barth, *Church Dogmatics* II/1 (Edinburgh: T&T Clark, 1957), 524.

through constancy, forbearance, love, and seeming weakness. Power is not simply eschewed—it is refashioned according to the example of Christ.[5]

At the opening of the Letter to the Romans, Paul speaks of Christ as the Son of God in power (*en dynamei*) according to the Spirit (Romans 1:4). Whether this is an older formula is irrelevant here since the use of "power" is elsewhere apparent in Paul's description of the significance of Jesus, for example, as the "power of God to save" (Romans 1:16). Two features of this bear an important relation to creaturely expressions of power. The first is that the power of God, though displayed in weakness, withstands and overcomes earthly principalities and powers. Declared in Christ, this is the object of Christian hope in the lyrical section about the love of God at the end of Romans 8. Neither principalities nor powers (*dynameis*) will separate us from the love of God in Christ (Romans 8:31-39). The power of God thus negates and defeats other powers. This generates a second feature of divine power. God saves us from captivity to malign forces that entrap and hold us captive. The power of God in Christ is "unto salvation" (Romans 1:16). Its effects are both liberating and enabling—we are set free from all oppressive forces and empowered to live well. The connection between the kerygmatic indicative and the ethical imperative is close. Hence, the exhortation of Romans 12 is not a homiletic afterthought at the close of the epistle; it is central to the argument that the apostle sets out. The work of Christ is described in language of liberation, though this produces a subsequent tension between a redemptive condition and moral backsliding. Since we have been set free from the "elemental spirits," why persist as if we remained shackled to forces that have already been vanquished (Galatians 4:9; Colossians 1:20)?

The power of the cross, as described by Paul, is also freighted with eschatological significance. As a judgment of God upon the wisdom of the world, it cannot be separated from the final judgment of the world. The reversal of 1 Corinthians 1:18 is a sign and anticipation of what is to come. Commenting on this, Anthony Thiselton notes the parallel with the reversals in the Synoptic tradition where the exalted will be brought low and the humble exalted. Past, present, and future are brought together by the actions of God in Christ and the Spirit. In this way, the virtue of hope becomes an integral feature of the Christian life. The expected future, though mysterious and inchoate, informs experience, thought, and action.[6]

None of this is lacking in political significance. If power and authority reside primarily in God, then suspicion must surround attempts to claim any derived authority that is not disciplined by the law and the gospel. The witness of the prophets, the repeated critique of kingship, the encounter with Pilate in which his judgment is inverted, Paul's description of a new community in which imperial

---

5. In what follows, I am indebted to Beverly Roberts Gaventa, "Power and Kenosis in Paul's Letter to the Romans," in *Kenosis: The Self-Emptying of Christ in Scripture and Theology*, ed. Paul T. Nimmo and Keith L. Johnson (Grand Rapids: Eerdmans, 2021), 24–40.

6. Anthony C. Thiselton, *First Epistle to the Corinthians* (Grand Rapids: Eerdmans, 2000), 158–9.

practices are challenged—these have some bearing on the church's position within and its attitude to the *polis*. Oliver O'Donovan notes that the church's attitude to the state could take one of two modalities. Either the state could provide the conditions for the flourishing of the church, or it could provoke a hostile reaction from seeking to prevent this. "Either way the victory of Christ was the key to the relation."[7]

The Power of God in Christian Tradition

Pantokrator became a central term in framing early church discussions of divine power. As the Septuagintal translation of *sebaotha* and *shaddai*, it functioned as a divine name. *Pantokrator* captures a sense of holding power (*potentia*) over the world but also the authority (*potestas*) to exercise such power. As *pantokrator*, God exercises a legitimate power over all things. A deceptively simple account of this ascription is that God can do what God wills to do. Yet here a problem lurks for later developments of the doctrine of God. Granted that God can do what God wills to do—a view that has nevertheless been challenged by recent process theologies of which more anon—is there any sense in which God can do what God wills not to do? Two options present themselves here. On the one side, an affirmation of divine freedom requires that we must affirm multiple, if not infinite, possibilities which God could but does not actualize. Without this assumption, God is seemingly limited and bound by necessities over which God lacks control. A second option is to insist that there is no unrealized potential in God. The creation of the world is not the result of a process of selection, as if God were a decorator or planner with an array of options from which to choose. If everything God does has a sufficient reason, we should conclude that what God does not choose to do must have been excluded for some reason rather than capricious decision. Theologians as diverse as Anselm and Schleiermacher appear to have been attracted to this position. The gap between "will" and "can" must be closed when we reflect upon the uniqueness of God in relation to everything else.[8]

The tension between these two tendencies gave rise in the thirteenth century to the classical distinction between the absolute (*potentia absoluta*) and the ordained power (*potentia ordinata*) of God.[9] Though widely used, this distinction is generally not well understood. Its appearance as a formal distinction was seemingly a way of

---

7. Oliver O'Donovan, *The Desire of the Nations* (Cambridge: Cambridge University Press, 1996), 156-7. One might suspect that some elements of both could characterize a political system.

8. E.g. Anselm, *Proslogion* 7 in *Anselm of Canterbury*, Vol. 1, ed. Jasper Hopkins and Herbert Richardson (London: SCM, 1974), 97. Friedrich Schleiermacher, *The Christian Faith* (Edinburgh: T&T Clark, 1928), Section 54, 211-19.

9. The genealogy of the distinction is explored in an excellent critique by Gijsbert van den Brink, *Almighty God: A Study of Divine Omnipotence* (Kampen: Kok Pharos, 1993),

maintaining that there are real possibilities for God beyond those states of affairs that God has actually ordained. Stated thus, the distinction provided a safe way of preserving a classical account of divine freedom and power. There are not two sets of powers, either or both of which can be activated; instead, the distinction captures a conceptual gap between an abstract counterfactual set of possibilities and what God actually wills to do. Scotus insists that anything God does is brought about by his ordained power; absolute power refers more to unrealized, but logical, possibilities than to an executive capacity to override ordained powers.[10]

A more problematic account appears later in the Middle Ages where the absolute powers of God become "operationalized" (Oberman) in ways that disrupt and qualify the ordained powers.[11] While these remain aspects of a singular divine power and purpose, the distinction used in this way provokes a sense of God as always capable of acting beyond what we perceive as presently ordained.[12] It now assumes a function for which it had not originally been designed. (When applied to the legitimate powers of earthly rulers this could generate a sovereign right to override the legal order, rather than binding the sovereign irrevocably to protect it and abide by it.[13]) This use of absolute power as actual rather than merely conceptual opened up possibilities in late medieval discussions that were not previously contemplated, for example, whether God could utter a falsehood.

At the Reformation, such disputes were repudiated by Calvin as too abstract. We should focus only on what has been ordained for our knowledge of God's will and nature. At this point, his anti-speculative tendency serves him well. There is a practical benefit in focusing on what has been actualized rather than dwelling on counterfactual possibles or casting doubt on the reliability of what has seemingly been ordained. Admittedly, Calvin also holds that God can act outside the natural order by exercising the power of the miraculous. This construction of absolute power, if one can call it that, is a more benign use of the distinction as miracles are given to confirm and fulfill what is elsewhere revealed. More troubling, however, is the postulation of an inscrutable will of God in the divine decree. Although this is asserted as a corollary of divine grace, the foregrounding of predestination in Reformed theology is redolent of an absolute power that lurks behind an ordained moral and rational order. The decision to elect only some must be explained by the sheer will of God without reference to notions of desert, worthiness, or foreknowledge of choices. If this analysis is correct, then the fault here lies less

---

68-92. See also Francis Oakley, "The Absolute and Ordained Power of God in Sixteenth and Seventeenth-Century Theology," *Journal of the History of Ideas* 59, no. 3 (1998): 437-61.

10. See Richard Cross, *Duns Scotus* (Oxford: Oxford University Press, 1999), 59.

11. Heiko Oberman, "Via Antiqua and Via Moderna: Late Medieval Prolegomena to Reformation Thought," *Journal of the History of Ideas* 48, no. 1 (1987): 23-40 (39).

12. See the exposition in Henri Veldhuis, "Absolute and Ordained Power in Scotus' *Ordinatio* I:44," *Vivarium* 38, no. 2 (2000): 222-30.

13. For further discussion see Paul R. DeHart, "Leviathan Leashed: The Incoherence of Absolute Sovereign Power," *Critical Review* 25, no. 1 (2013): 1-37.

in the influence of late medieval nominalism—the Augustinian doctrine of predestination long predates these disputes—and more in a failure to determine the conception of divine power by reference to the gospel as announced for example at the outset of the Letter to the Romans.

Though often parodied, the construction of a divine decree with a double aspect lies deep in Augustinian theology. Attempts to separate Catholic notions of a single decree from Reformed accounts of a double whammy are largely unsuccessful, since it seems to follow that if only some are chosen then the remainder are not. But, leaving this aside, the flaw lies in an account of unlimited divine power not wholly constrained by the narrative patterns of Scripture. The story of Israel and the church has a universal scope. Divine love is unbounded. The commonwealth of God is capacious. Jesus' ministry is inclusive in intent. The cross is the power of God to salvation. If divine election is a way of expressing these convictions "upstream" in the primal decision of God, then we should view this either as a universal choosing of the whole world or alternatively as the particular vocation of some to bear witness to this. The calling of Abraham and Sarah does not entail a rejection of other peoples.

A chronic temptation for Christian theologians has been to succumb to implicit concepts of God defined by an absolute and basal power to which other supplementary attributes are added. To be sure, the idea of divine simplicity prevented this from ever being explicitly promulgated. The attributes are creaturely modes of expression that attempt to describe one simple and undivided divine essence that cannot be represented as an assortment of properties that could conceivably be divided. Hence, there can be no differentiation between necessary and accidental properties in God as there are in relation to created genera, species, and particulars. And yet descriptions of divine being and action have too often tended toward a prioritization of an absolute power that resulted in deleterious consequences. This is not restricted to arcane and neglected accounts of divine predestination. I offer several examples, not as exhaustive case studies but as material that might stimulate further discussion.

Human Dominion

It is now commonplace to lament the constructions of "dominion" that have arisen from readings of Genesis 1:26-27. As divine image bearers, human beings have been represented as exercising power over the created order. The Hebrew verb *rada* with its military connotations leans in this direction. This has resulted historically in attitudes and practices of proprietorial control, disposal, and despoliation. A pervasive assumption in earlier epochs, almost casual in its expression, was that plants and animals are ordered for our use and convenience. Thus Richard Bentley, the first Boyle Lecturer, wrote of how everything is made principally for our benefit and pleasure.[14]

---

14. Cited with other examples by Keith Thomas, *Man and the Natural World: Changing Attitudes in England 1500–1800* (London: Penguin, 1983), 17–20. See also David L. Clough, *On Animals: Systematic Theology Volume 1* (London: T&T Clark, 2011), 3–25.

In exploring the early modern literature on this subject through a series of startling examples, Keith Thomas notes that attempts to aggrandize human beings by virtue of some special set of capacities, for example speech, reason, or moral agency, provided ideological support for practices of hunting, meat-eating, vivisection, and extermination of vermin and predators. In addition, theological anthropology could also license gradations among classes of human being. Those that lacked or only partially instantiated distinctively human traits could be classed as semi-human or subhuman. More "primitive" peoples that lacked culture, technology, language, or Christianity could be regarded as brutish, thus legitimizing either their use or their forced development.[15] What is important in the present context is the manner in which a selective anthropocentrism draws ideological support from the notion of a dominion conferred by God in the creation story.[16]

There are, of course, ways in which the Genesis text can and ought to be reworked, particularly with respect to more benign notions of stewardship and shepherding. These are necessary correctives, though they also run the risk of over-determining the centrality and status of human beings in the economy of creation. The eucharistic liturgy often moves swiftly forward from a brief allusion to creation to the celebration of human beings as "the crown of creation." The account of human uniqueness that is embedded in this heightened anthropocentrism depends in part upon a linkage of divine power to human capacities. Dominion is primarily God's but is bestowed in some secondary privileged way upon our species alone with its status only a "little lower than God" (Psalm 8:5).[17] This strand in Scripture has arguably been over-determined in theological anthropology. The constant suspicion around the exercise of kingship in the Hebrew Bible might offer one way of constraining it in a more critical vein.

Providence

In accounts of providence, assumptions around divine power are also strikingly apparent in the literature. Two convictions are pervasive here. The first is that God would be diminished in some way if God did not control everything that happens. The divine writ must run everywhere if God is not to be reduced to a bystander or absentee landlord. Hence, it is fitting that God exercises dominion not only in an initial act of creation but in the superintendence of all nature and history. A second axiom that has governed reflection on God's providential activity is that every event must serve a divinely ordained purpose. This often resulted in the over-determining of battles, political forces, and individual fortunes as betokening a particular providential intention to be decoded by those with inside knowledge.

---

15. Thomas, *Man and the Natural World*, 41–50.
16. Thomas also draws attention to the support provided by ancient philosophy.
17. Although other translations of this text prefer "divine beings or angels," the connection between divine and human status remains.

Alexandra Walsham has written of how an emergent Protestant culture in early modern England sought to discern the hand of God in the everyday events and fluctuating fortunes of the faithful.[18] Often this resulted in a trivialization of divine intent and a spiritual over-determining of the physical realm. In a section of the *Westminster Directory of Publick Worship*, now largely ignored, pastors when visiting the sick are expected to inquire of them whether some bad habit or secret sin has been the occasion of their illness. They "shall exhort the sick person to examine himself, to search and try his former ways, and his estate towards God. And if the sick person shall declare any scruple, doubt, or temptation that are upon him, instructions and resolutions shall be given to satisfy and settle him."[19] The underlying assumption is that God has intended this particular physical effect for a spiritual reason.

In many theological texts of the nineteenth century, a similar theology of providence was repeatedly enlisted in support of slavery, free trade, and imperial expansion. Again, examples are not difficult to accumulate.[20] What is shocking about this literature, at least to a contemporary reader, is both the *extent* of providential discourse and the *confidence* of earlier generations that they had been singled out as God's decisive instrument. A useful benchmark is the fin-de-siècle series of Gifford Lectures of A. B. Bruce in 1896–8 on *The Providential Order of the World*.[21] Noting that divine providence seems to favor smaller nations for greater purposes—Israel, Greece, Rome, and the British Isles are cited—he argues for the benefits brought by established racial differences and the importance of avoiding inter-marriage, at least for a time. Bruce undoubtedly understands himself to be promoting a benign form of imperialism. He stresses that divine election is for the benefit of all, and that arrogance and belittling of other people are to be avoided. An emphasis upon human solidarity and universal benefit must always accompany forms of historical exceptionalism. Yet, in defending this position, he reveals the obvious dangers of a slanted providentialism which draws a straight line from the historical status quo to conclusions about the execution of a divine intention via human agencies.

There are at least two revisions required of this over-preening providentialism. The first is noetic. A much greater caution is required in drawing inferences about divine intentionality from observation of individual circumstances or political events, particularly when temptations of triumphalism are evident. If divine power is paradigmatically displayed on the underside of history, especially in the foolishness of the cross, then we should cease to measure its effects in terms of conquest, prosperity, or cultural progress. Second, this should be reinforced

---

18. Alexandra Walsham, *Providence in Early Modern England* (Oxford: Oxford University Press, 1998).
19. *Westminster Directory of Publick Worship*, Section on Visitation of the Sick.
20. See for example Stewart J. Brown, *Providence and Empire 1815–1914* (Harlow: Longman, 2008).
21. A. B. Bruce, *The Providential Order of the World* (New York: Scribner's, 1905).

by an ontic commitment to loosen the fit between what God wills and what happens in nature and history. A stronger differentiation of permission and will in God, as, for example, characterizes Orthodox theology, would serve us better in this regard. Though not without its own difficulties, such a distinction can enable us to accord a greater degree of autonomy to contingent forces. No longer burdened with the task of having to view everything as fulfilling a divine purpose, we can think of God working in and through these creaturely forces without exercising a meticulous control. God does not need to dominate in order to be God. The grace and freedom of creating a world out of nothing can provide the conceptual space in which God is immune from associations of pathological control.[22]

In this connection, it has become commonplace today to appeal to double agency as the solution to a range of theological problems. If we posit a non-competitive relationship between God and creatures, these belonging to different ontological planes, then a resolution of divine intentionality and creaturely contingency can be achieved. As these do not compete for the same conceptual space, we can allow each its full scope in different, but complementary, domains.[23] This position follows the classical distinction between primary and secondary causality in enabling an event to have two sets of causes, one creaturely and the other divine; though discrete, these are related by virtue of the primary guaranteeing the efficacy of the secondary. This move toward a complementarity of causal schemes has been employed inter alia to overcome the tension between divine determinism and human freedom, the efficacy of petitionary prayer, and the explication of the person of Christ in Chalcedonian terms.[24]

Nevertheless, while underscoring the need to avoid competitive accounts of double agency, this move faces the difficulty of either proving too much or too little. Although these levels of causal activity may be different and therefore not competing on the same playing field, some account of their correlation is required. If the primary causal activity of God is understood in terms of conservation and enablement, then it will tend to offer too little in respect of divine involvement in nature and history. On the other hand, if the primal cause guarantees the effective outcomes of secondary causation, then the freedom and contingency of the latter are called into question. These will become instrumentalized as the means by which the primal will of God is executed. This looks like proving too much with

---

22. This is argued, for example, by Rowan Williams, *On Christian Theology* (Oxford: Blackwell, 2000), 63–78. He quotes Jacques Pohier's remark that "God Does Not Want to Be Everything" (74).

23. For a seminal statement of this position see Kathryn Tanner, *God and Creation in Christian Theology: Tyranny or Empowerment?* (Oxford: Blackwell, 1988). The literature is reviewed by Simeon Zahl, "Non-Competitive Agency and Luther's Experiential Argument Against Virtue," *Modern Theology* 35, no. 2 (2019): 199–222.

24. A powerful recent example is Rowan Williams, *Christ the Heart of Creation* (London: Continuum, 2018).

its tilt toward earlier forms of determinism. And, in any case, does not the action of the Spirit in the world require us to adopt a more integrated model than the two levels suggest? Double agency is not to be abandoned—the price is too high here in terms of loss of divine involvement and oversight. Yet notwithstanding its importance as a rule of Christian discourse, it is unlikely to resolve intractable problems with the ease that is sometimes assumed.[25]

Christology

Within Christology, we find the most concerted effort in modern theology to inflect notions of divine power.[26] A key concept is *kenōsis*, following the Christ-hymn of Philippians 2:5-11. Different forms can be distinguished though these have sometimes converged.

In the standard approaches of nineteenth-century German kenotic Christology, kenosis was the means by which the divine person could become a human subject.[27] By divesting or suspending or transposing some divine attributes—the theories struggled to specify the most plausible process—the Son of God became incarnate. His full humanity was thus not compromised by the active possession of omnipotence, omniscience, or omnipresence. Emptied of these, the kenotic Christ was able to fulfill his earthly mission before resuming his full divine status upon ascension into heaven. Here a theory of kenosis was intended to safeguard a commitment to the full divinity and humanity of Christ without recourse to the conceptual problems of the Chalcedonian formula. If its "governing intention" (Macquarrie) could be maintained, then this was sufficient.[28]

The difficulty with these theories was twofold. The idea of a voluntary divestment of some divine properties seemed to compromise traditional notions of divine immutability and simplicity, while also generating conceptual puzzles that were at least as formidable as those of the Chalcedonian definition. Could the second person of the Trinity really set aside or transfer attributes and functions for a period of thirty-three years? A kenotic scenario had the seeming effect of delivering a temporary divine theophany rather than a genuine incarnation. If Christ is emptied of his divinity, in what sense is the Incarnation a revelation rather than a concealment of God? As a result of these perplexities, kenotic

---

25. For a sharp critique of the position, see van den Brink, *Almighty God*, 229–33.

26. In what follows, I have drawn upon material in "The Humility of God," in *Kenosis: The Self-Emptying of Christ in Scripture and Theology*, ed. Paul T. Nimmo and Keith L. Johnson (Grand Rapids: Eerdmans, 2021), 194–211.

27. For an overview see David R. Law, "Kenotic Christology," in *Blackwell Companion to Nineteenth Century Theology*, ed. David Fergusson (Oxford: Wiley Blackwell, 2010), 251–79.

28. John Macquarrie, *Jesus Christ in Modern Thought* (London; SCM, 1990), 383.

theories passed their high watermark sometime in the early twentieth century, though continuing to this day to attract their exponents.[29]

Despite these challenges, however, the concept of kenosis offered other possibilities. As the self-abasement of Christ, it could itself be revelatory of God. Instead of an instrument by which the divine Son was transmuted into the incarnate Christ, kenosis became the content rather than the form of divine revelation. Charles Gore was already moving in this direction in his reflections in *Lux Mundi*. A similar line was pursued by Sergius Bulgakov, Karl Barth, Hans Urs von Balthasar, and Donald MacKinnon. "Christ's self-submission to these conditions is to be seen not as an abdication of divine omnipotence but rather as its only authentic human manifestation."[30] This remark suggests a rooting of kenosis in the life of God itself, so that the Incarnation becomes its fullest historical expression. Instead of an instrumental act in which the divine is converted into a state appropriate to the conditions of human life, the kenosis of the Word of God in Christ corresponds to a love that eternally characterizes the divine life.

On this account, a Christological reframing of divine power can take place. The power of God is displayed in humility. The poor, the meek, the bereaved, and those who hunger for justice are declared blessed by Jesus. His victory is through the way of the cross. His resurrection appearances are displayed not in the trouncing of his enemies but in a return to his friends. The empowering Spirit is sent to people, not many of whom were wise by human standards, powerful, or of noble birth (1 Corinthians 1:26). Kenosis is no longer a divestment but a strange manifestation of divine power requiring a transposition of human standards.

Nevertheless, once again difficulties emerge along this path. These have been ventilated in recent critiques of atonement theories and valorizations of vulnerability. James Cone's *The Cross and the Lynching Tree* has become a recent *locus classicus*. Arguing against constructions of the cross in terms of vicarious suffering and penal substitution, Cone reclaims it as a historic sign of solidarity with the victims of suffering and injustice, and the promise of their vindication.

> The gospel of Jesus is not a rational concept to be explained in a theory of salvation, but a story about God's presence in Jesus' solidarity with the oppressed, which led to his death on the cross. What is redemptive is the faith that God snatches victory out of defeat, life out of death, and hope out of despair, as revealed in the biblical and black proclamation of Jesus' resurrection.[31]

Set against Cone's account are the anxieties of Delores Williams. The experience of multiple forms of surrogacy among African-American women problematizes

---

29. See David Brown, *Divine Humanity: Kenosis Explored and Defended* (London: SCM, 2011).

30. Donald M. MacKinnon, *Themes in Theology: The Threefold Cord* (Edinburgh: T&T Clark, 1987), 143.

31. James H. Cone, *The Cross and the Lynching Tree* (New York: Orbis, 2011), 150.

theologies of the cross which too often have been justified in terms of vicarious significance. Its ideological underpinning is too difficult for a reappropriation by those for whom surrogacy is the root problem. Instead, the ethical and spiritual focus of Jesus' life and ministry should be revitalized. Even alternative constructions of the cross, for example, Moltmann's, cannot overcome the deficit of the tradition.

> Even if one buys into the notion of the cross as the meeting place of the will of God to give up the Son (coerced surrogacy?) and the will of the Son to give up himself (voluntary surrogacy?) so that "the spirit of abandonment and self-giving love" proceeds from the cross "to raise up abandoned men," African-American women are still left with the question: Can there be salvific power for black women in Christian images of oppression (for example, Jesus on the cross) meant to teach something about redemption?[32]

In responding, Cone insists that the cross is an ineluctable and central element of Christian faith. He points to ways in which Shawn Copeland and other womanist theologians have sought to save it from its baleful legacy. To remove it as a potent symbol of Christian faith seems well-nigh impossible—one thinks here of Kähler's (somewhat misleading) description of the gospels as passion narratives with extended introductions. It is incumbent upon the theologian to produce an account of the crucifixion which describes its significance while heeding the salutary warnings of those who have been on the receiving end of earlier distortions. In this context, the criticism of Williams points to the importance of the *totus Christus* and of the need always to connect the event of the Crucifixion with what precedes and succeeds it in the gospel story. In isolation, the cross will suffer from implausible constructions of its meaning.

Related to this is a concern around stressing vulnerability and weakness as the way of redemption. Might this too readily slide into a cult of victimhood? Here feminist criticism has been rightly nervous around the inflated use of kenotic language.[33] As a corrective to patriarchal notions of control and domination, kenosis might be a useful category. But for those who seek and deserve greater autonomy and empowerment, the danger is that it merely reinforces a stereotypical subordination. There may even be a risk of rehearsing a disguised theodicy in which a recognition of vulnerability is commended, even celebrated, especially by theologians who have often occupied positions of privilege in their communities.

---

32. Delores S. Williams, *Sisters in the Wilderness: The Challenge of Womanist God-Talk* (New York: Orbis, 2013), 162.

33. For example, Daphne Hampson, *Theology and Feminism* (Oxford: Blackwell, 1990), 155. "*Kenōsis* is a counter-theme within male thought. It does not build what might be said to be specifically feminist values into our understanding of God."

The significant difference between the acceptance of limitation and its (deleterious) embrace as a positive good needs to be respected.[34]

Yet, following the Pauline line described earlier, we might construe an acknowledgment of weakness as a divine means of empowerment. Weakness and power are here not mutually exclusive. In the life of Christ, the active and the passive are complementary. A recognition of one's status before God is the way toward a fuller empowerment of the Spirit. Sarah Coakley's strictures for a strategy of self-dispossession through prayer make much sense in this context. "By choosing to 'make space' in this way, one 'practises' the 'presence of God'— the subtle but enabling presence of a God who neither shouts nor forces, let alone 'obliterates' . . . this special 'self-emptying' is not a negation of self, but the place of the self's transformation and expansion into God."[35] Yet the concept of kenosis should not do all the load-bearing here. If Christlike power is to be understood in relation to weakness, then its enabling of a range of actions requires stress—prophetic criticism, personal and communal empowerment, opposition to idolatry, and hope in the face of intractable problems. An overdetermining rather than a disciplined employment of kenosis may be the problem.

An important corollary will be a practical theology that enables us to think imaginatively about the ways in which grace and redemption are not so much superimposed upon the world but can work in, with, and under creaturely processes. Here an account of the Spirit's agency is a necessary counterpart to descriptions of the work of Christ. Poets and novelists may be better placed than systematic theologians to persuade us of this. Francis Spufford offers these hazardous thoughts after creating the counterfactual life histories of several children who perished in an air raid in 1944.

> Who knows it if it's true? But if the different bits and pieces of his life, rising, lofted as if by a bubble of force from below, are arranged in a messy spiral of hours and years, then mightn't it be the case, mightn't there be a place, mightn't there be an angle, from which you could see the whole accidental mass composing, just from that angle into some momentary order you could never have noticed at the time? Mightn't there be a line of sight, not ours, from which the seeming cloud of debris of our days, no more in order than (say) the shredded particles riding the wavefront of an explosion, prove to align? Into a clockface of transparencies. This whole mess a rose, a window. . . . Praise him in all the postcodes.[36]

---

34. This is argued by Karen Kilby in "The Seductions of Kenosis," in *Suffering and the Christian Life*, ed. Rachel Davies and Karen Kilby (London: T&T Clark, 2020), 163–74.
35. Sarah Coakley, *Powers and Submissions: Spirituality, Philosophy and Gender* (Oxford: Blackwell, 2002), 35–6.
36. Francis Spufford, *Light Perpetual* (London: Faber, 2022), 318.

A Radical Alternative

I have argued for an account of divine power that deconstructs creaturely distortions but in a way that reappropriates rather than renounces the notion altogether. Yet a more radical alternative is available in which divine power is significantly scaled down to exclude all other forms of action apart from that of persuasion. This is the route followed by process theology in the slipstream of A. N. Whitehead. Its attractions need to be acknowledged, particularly with respect to its dissolution of the problem of evil through an abandonment of divine omnipotence.

As an "omni-amorous" force, God is here described as working within creation through a process of allurement rather than coercion. A logic of control is abandoned in favor of one of persuasion. Following Whitehead, Catherine Keller argues for a divine presence which offers and receives love. This works by influence, though it is vulnerable to violence and resistance. Without creaturely cooperation, it cannot be effective. An immanent power within the created order, the divine seeks to realize values of truth, beauty, and goodness. "[T]he divine is within each of us, as an influence, an influx of desire—whether or not we share that desire as our own."[37]

Though often elusive, the imagery captures rather well one mode of divine action. Immanent and pneumatological, this has been neglected in many textbook treatments of divine power, especially where synergism has been viewed with suspicion. The work of the Spirit should include these characterizations of its force. Moreover, in perceiving the need for a middle way between the exercise of total control on one side, and a straightforward abandonment of creation to its own devices (as in many caricatures of deism) on the other, process theology has an intuitive appeal to those who might today identify as "spiritual but not religious."

In his study of "amipotence" Tom Oord argues for the relinquishing of all traditional claims for divine omnipotence and their replacement by the logic of an indwelling divine love. Although "omnipotence remains on life support due to high church liturgies and low church piety," he claims that it has had its day.[38] Oord regards the pastoral outcomes of such a shift as liberating—his postbag provides a good deal of evidence for this. While there are some doctrinal casualties along the way, including creation out of nothing and divine foreknowledge, these for Oord are disposable. The principal gain is the distancing of God from all that is evil—there is no sense in which this is willed, permitted, or justifiable. God must make do as best God can with the materials that lie at hand—these are not of God's making.

While this position deserves to be taken seriously in terms of its conceptual coherence and pastoral advantages, there are formidable difficulties in relation to

---

37. Catherine Keller, *On the Mystery: Discerning Divinity in Process* (Minneapolis: Fortress, 2008), 100.

38. Thomas Jay Oord, *The Death of Omnipotence and the Birth of Amipotence* (Grasmere: SacraSage Press, 2023), 118.

other elements constitutive of Christian faith. Restricted to one mode, the action of God within the world is described here in terms that make it impossible to conceive of God either as source or as final purpose. Hence an everlasting dualism of God and matter replaces a world that depends upon God for its existence and preservation. Similarly, a resolution of the world in which creatures are perfected—here eschatological and apocalyptic images seem indispensable— cannot be posited. Uncertain outcomes stretch into an indefinite future. One might respond that these are speculative matters which have little practical bearing. Yet the characterization of the Spirit's work though the language of sign and foretaste indicates the extent to which faith is inextricably bound up with hope. In the face of loss and death, we do not grieve as those without hope. Yet without the conceptual apparatus of creation, resurrection, and eschatology, it is hard to see what will ground such hope.

A further difficulty surrounds the account of divine action. Eschewing more interventionist approaches, a theology of attraction and persuasion seems simpler and more plausible. But is it? How does God persuade us except by some form of divine communication which presumably involves interaction with neurological processes or an opaque psychokinesis? The problem of divine action is, of course, not exclusive to any one position, but, despite its intuitive appeal, the process account may be no more immune to these challenges than any other.

Conclusion

A theology of divine power is beset by problems both theoretical and practical; these are readily illustrated by historical trends which run too deep to be easily dismissed. Yet the simple eschewal of power seems impossible if other theological commitments are to stand and hope to endure. Nor can power be abrogated in its human contexts. Government is necessary. Someone has to run the department. Churches will always require a polity and office bearers. The misuse of theologies of power should alert us to the practical risks involved in its unchecked exercise. Set against the backdrop of Christian claims about the power of God, there must arise downstream questions about the purpose of human power, its distribution, its checks and balances, and the accountability of its agents.

Chapter 3

MAKER OF HEAVEN AND EARTH

Theology for Creationtide

Introduction

My arrival in Cambridge represents a late career move after many years in Edinburgh. I was encouraged to consider its advantages by Professor Jim Aitken, our former Faculty chair, sadly no longer with us and now much missed. Had it not been for Jim's gentle exhortation and recommendation of Cambridge and this Faculty, I would not be here. Another person who helped facilitate the move is my wife—I was confident that she would veto the whole idea, thus sparing me any further reflection on the matter. But she told me that we needed a change and that this was not an opportunity to let pass.

So here we are, and I'm grateful for the stimulus of writing new lectures for new students, being enriched by a different set of conversation partners, the exposure to the pleasures of college life, a new ecumenical context, and the vigorous exercise afforded by attempting not always successfully to track down books in the University Library. I continue to find the study of theology exciting with its dual relationship to church and academy, the emergence of young, bright, and committed scholars, and the challenge of addressing new problems while drawing upon the rich resources of the past. Like the scribe trained for the kingdom of heaven, we are given treasures old and new.

My theme is one that I have pondered for some time both in church and university. An initial interest was stimulated by an invitation in Aberdeen in the mid-1990s to deliver a series of reflections on the theology of creation at the conjoint evening services of two parish churches. Two things immediately struck me. First, it was a subject that had been seriously neglected in my own education and indeed throughout much of the twentieth century with only a few notable exceptions. But it was also a doctrine that immediately aroused the interest of a wide audience. Why is this? The putative clash between science and religion, whether over cosmology or evolution, is largely around the plausibility of a divine Creator. The interpretation of Genesis 1, the best-known Scriptural passage apart

---

Inaugural lecture, delivered in the Faculty of Divinity, University of Cambridge, June 6, 2023.

from the Christmas stories, can always generate a lively conversation. And, most importantly, the ecological challenges that we face—climate change, pollution, and species extinction—have become increasingly urgent. These demand a revisiting of our theological traditions and their characterization of the natural world of which we are a part. Is Christian theology the problem or the solution, or might it be both? The interrogation and rethinking of earlier traditions have now elevated the theology of creation to the top of the agenda. While it's impossible to stay abreast of the articles and books now being published, I've learned that by setting essays on the subject students will often do the reading for me.

At the quotidian level, I have also wondered whether the disconnect between Saturday and Sunday in the lives of many Christian people has had something to do with the neglect of the doctrine of creation. Admittedly, this is speculative and probably parochial, even bourgeois. But people do spend much time on Saturdays around sports fields, or hill walking, fishing, gardening, cycling, and walking their dogs. Yet when they arrive in church the following day they hear little about the natural world and its diversity, our dependence on land, sea, air, and climate, and our connectedness with other creatures. We come almost immediately into an order of worship in which we confess our sins and seek forgiveness, as if requiring absolution from our Saturday pursuits. Here I exaggerate, and I don't underestimate the importance of the forgiveness of sins, but my claim is that this disconnect needs to be overcome not only theologically and liturgically but also in the wider life of the church in the world.

I shall seek to argue this first through a series of negations which together might be seen as a corrective program, and then offer three more positive remarks about how an ecological sensibility can be fostered in the life of the church.

One of my first teachers in theology was Elizabeth Templeton. An original thinker and skilled communicator, she once asked the class what *color* we considered theology to be. It seemed an absurd question based on an obvious category mistake. How could theology possibly have a color? Yet she generated a lively discussion. If there are liturgical colors then why not theological ones? One possible response is that theology used to be blue, but now it's become green. Our forebears were preoccupied with the blue beyond and how to get there. Today we're more concerned about the earth and the need to preserve it. The green image is one that is consciously cultivated. The recent book of Anglican liturgical resources that appeared in 2020 notes that a season of creation is now observed in many churches, usually in September and culminating in a harvest festival or with the feast of St Francis of Assisi on October 4. Unsurprisingly, its dust jacket is entirely green.[1]

Yet in prioritizing green we need to be careful to avoid a regional bias. I was alerted to this while examining an Australian doctoral thesis last year by Maina Talia, a student from Tuvalu, an archipelago of small islands in Oceania.[2] Tuvalu

---

1. *A Time for Creation: Liturgical Resources for Creation and the Environment* (London: Church of England Publishing, 2020).

2. Maina Vakafua Talia, *Am I Not Your TŪ/AKOI? A Tuvaluan Plea for Survival in a Time of Climate Emergency*, Charles Sturt University, PhD Thesis, 2022.

is faced with inundation as sea levels rise; it may well disappear in the coming generation, as the ocean erodes the coastline and rises from underneath the land. There is no high ground to which the population of *c.* 12,000 people can migrate. Shaped by the land, the sea, and ancestral graves, their entire way of life is under threat. As the fourth-smallest sovereign nation in the world they have very limited political power. Theologians in Oceania have complained about the color coding of contemporary theology. The sea is their livelihood, and an integral part of their habitat. Yet the green movement risks overlooking the marine crisis that threatens our planet. The "liquid continent" of Oceania that will suffer widespread destruction from global warming is in danger of being ignored. We should think about the sea as well as the land, both as a source and as a threat to life. A blue-green reading is needed for the whole household of creation.[3]

Traditional Deficits in Christian Theology

My first claim is that the creedal traditions of the church lack a capacious account of creation. It is, of course, a well-established axiom of Christian theology that the one God is the creator of everything, an axiom shared with Judaism, its parent religion, and Islam. Attempts to separate the God of Jesus from the Creator God of Genesis were resisted in the early centuries of the church. Dualism, in this form, was anathematized, there being a single economy of creation and salvation. The early creeds, as rules of faith for Christian instruction, included an opening reference to God as Creator. We see this in the two best-known and oft-repeated creeds—the Apostles' and the Nicene.

> *I believe in God, the Father Almighty, creator of heaven and earth.* (The Apostles' Creed, *c.* sixth century)

> *We believe in one God, the Father Almighty, maker of heaven and earth, and of all things, seen and unseen.* (The Nicene Creed, 381)[4]

These opening statements have a brevity which in its own way is majestic. The transcendence of God is affirmed, together with the dependence of everything upon our Maker. Here the power of God as almighty—*omnipotentem* or *pantokrátora*—is conjoined with the divine name of Father, thus offsetting any sense of sheer power or arbitrary force by the bold designation of God in parental language. Heaven and earth are also united. The sky above and the earth beneath seem to be the original

---

3. Nancy M. Victorin-Vangerud, "Thinking like an Archipelago: Beyond Tehomophobic Theology," *Pacifica* 16 (2003): 153–72. See also Meric Srikosz and Rebecca Watson, *Blue Planet, Blue God: The Bible and the Sea* (London: SCM, 2017).

4. For the Latin version of the Apostles' Creed with English translation see Jaroslav Pelikan and Valerie Hotchkiss (eds.), *Creeds and Confessions of Faith in the Christian Tradition* (New Haven: Yale University Press, 2003), 669. For the Greek of the Niceno-Constantinopolitan Creed with English translation see 162–3.

reference. There is nothing of which God is not the maker. The earth as well as the heavens testify to God's glory. J. N. D. Kelly suggests that the phrase "heaven and earth" slipped quite "casually and spontaneously" into the creed.[5] But perhaps we might also deploy this as a gesture toward possibilities of invisible realities that far exceed our imagination, a reminder of how little we know. One can work hard here from this opening statement to tease out some key ideas for creation theology; yet still this seems too brief, especially when one considers the much longer exposition of the second article about God the Son and to a lesser extent the third article concerning the Spirit. Doubtless, an important factor in this lapidary description of creation was that it was never the site of any major ecclesiastical controversy, unlike the relationship of the Word and the Spirit to the Father. From the late second century, the orthodox doctrine of creation out of nothing had become established and represented the consensus position of the church; it remained uncontested until quite recently. As a result of focus quickly shifting in the creeds from creation to Christ, no description was offered of the natural or social worlds, or of human beings, or the diversity of creaturely life. We are rapidly transported from the opening verses of Genesis to the drama of salvation narrated in the New Testament. This confirms David Kelsey's complaint that the story of sin and redemption has tended to occlude the story of creation in the life of the church; we have moved with unnecessary haste from Genesis 1 to Genesis 3 in our account of the faith.

This lecture is not an appeal for the theology of creation to exercise a totalizing place in Christian thought or worship. Admittedly, there's a risk of this converse danger in the recent turn to ecotheology with its relative disregard for other doctrinal elements. A properly articulated Trinitarianism of God as Source, Word, and Spirit will involve coverage of all three articles—the seasons of the Christian year with the addition of a period of time for creation should reflect this. A theology dominated by one idea, one theme, or one doctrine does not serve us well; distortions will soon emerge.

My second claim is that we have too long been preoccupied with the opening chapters of Genesis. These creation stories have become the site of significant disagreement between conservative and liberal tendencies. How we do interpret the six days of creation—as intervals of twenty-four hours, or eons of time, or as a religious parable that does not compete with the latest scientific findings? How is the relationship of Adam and Eve to be construed—as normative or mythical? And is the story of the original sin in Genesis 3 to be invested with the significance that it later attracted in Christianity, particularly in the work of Augustine following some comments of Paul in Romans 5? The opening three chapters of the Bible have continued to generate conflicting interpretations, some of their exponents believing that their claims for the text are constitutive for Christian doctrine and ethics. Yet

---

5. J. N. D. Kelly, *Early Christian Creeds*, 3rd ed. (London: Longman, 1972), 374. Kelly also notes the different Latin nouns—*conditorem*, *factorem*, and *creatorem*. He suggests that the use of "creavit" (Genesis 1:10) in the Vulgate (notwithstanding ἐποίησεν in the LXX) may have influenced the eventual preference for *creatorem* in the Apostles' Creed, though *factorem* became the preferred Latin translation of ποιητὴν in the Nicene Creed.

attention to the rest of Scripture underscores two points that seem incontestable. The first is that the writers and editors of Scripture itself were not as preoccupied as later commentators by these opening chapters of Genesis. There is almost no explicit reference to the Adam and Eve story until the intertestamental period when it commanded greater attention as a way of understanding the intrusion of evil upon the created order. And, second, other portions of the Hebrew Scriptures have much to say about creation. It is not merely the preamble to another story or the setting of a scene for a divine–human drama. In particular, the wisdom literature reflects in some depth, often with conflicting patterns of testimony, on the ways in which divine wisdom is expressed in the natural and social worlds. A capacious creation theology confronts us, but we risk neglecting it if we overdetermine the importance of Genesis 1 and the six days.

The lack of creedal development of creation theology has also been reflected in many of our liturgies. In the eucharistic prayer of thanksgiving, we travel swiftly again from the barest statement of creation to the story of sin and redemption. There is little by way of celebration of the natural world or recognition that we are not the only creatures loved by God. The recent Coronation liturgy drew upon Order One in *Common Worship* set to traditional language. The only reference to creation was in the Sanctus—"heaven and earth are full of your glory." Other prayers reference the act of creation but only as a transitional moment between the Sursum Corda and the Sanctus. Two examples, one Anglican and one from my own Scottish Presbyterian tradition, show the historical deficit to be ecumenical and trans-confessional.

> For he is your living Word;
> through him you have created all things from the beginning,
> and formed us in your own image.[6]

> We give thanks
> that in the creation of the world,
> When you laid the earth's foundation
> and set its corner-stone in place,
> The morning stars sang in chorus
> And the angels of God all shouted for joy.
> By the power of your Spirit,
> you made the universe;
> by the might of your Word
> you gave us life.[7] (*Book of Common Order*, First Order for Holy Communion)

There is some advance here on earlier liturgies by dwelling on the theme of creation, but still the tendency is to shift quickly to the making of human beings in the divine image. The language of the "crown of creation" is sometimes used

---

6. *Common Worship* (London: Church House Publishing, 2000), Order One, Prayer A, 184.

7. *Church of Scotland Book of Common Order* (Edinburgh: St Andrew Press, 1994), First Order for Holy Communion, 132.

before shifting to an acknowledgment of our defacing of the divine image. An obvious complaint is that this is too anthropocentric or humanocentric in its lack of attention to creaturely diversity, the material world becoming a stage on which we appear to heavenly acclaim.

One might respond that since the Eucharist is a memorial and representation of the Last Supper, we should not expect creation theology to feature prominently. Yet in most liturgies inspired by the ecumenical movement we seek to name God and to set the work of Christ within its fuller cosmic context. If there is to be a strong eschatological dimension, should not there also be a protological one that registers our place in a diverse, beautiful but fragile world? Attempts to remedy this have recently appeared, and further liturgical changes can be anticipated, not least through the ecumenical impact of Pope Francis's encyclical *Laudato Si'*.

> Lord of all life,
> you created the universe,
> where all living things reflect your glory.
> You give us this great and beautiful earth,
> to discover and to cherish.
>
> You give us the fish in the sea,
> the birds of the air,
> and every plant and tree;
> the life that sleeps in the winter earth,
> and awakens again in the spring.[8]
>
> Therefore with the whole realm of nature around us, with earth, sea, and sky, we sing to you. With the angels of light who envelop us, with all the saints before and beside us, with brothers and sisters, east and west, we sing to you. And with our loved ones, separate from us now, who yet in this mystery are close to us, we join in the song of your unending greatness.[9]

We find here a more expansive reference to the creation. These extended eucharistic prefaces reveal an intention to remedy early deficits. Yet they continue to suffer from a lack of boldness and inclination with their exclusive focus on the human within creation. Not everything exists for the sake of being given to us. Other liturgical resources might assist us, particularly the Psalms and the Benedicite, with their sense of the whole creation attesting the glory of God.

In her book *Church in Ordinary Time*, Amy Plantinga Pauw seeks to develop what she calls a "wisdom ecclesiology." Her project is to draw upon the resources of the wisdom literature to shape the life of the church outside the special seasons of the Christian year from Advent to Pentecost. With its focus on space rather than time, this involves a celebration of the everyday rhythms of life, a recognition of our earthly habitat shared with other creatures, and a heightened responsibility that we have for future generations. Plantinga Pauw is wary of a totalizing of

---

8. Prayer Two | The Church of England.
9. Communion Liturgy Iona 2020 (acny.uk).

Christology—"incarnation is not the sole bridge between God and creatures."[10] Attention should be directed to the texture of daily life in community, to our commonality with other creatures, and to the transformations that take place in the ordinary processes of the world. Water does not often pour forth from rocks and angels do not come for lunch. "Most days in church life are like that."[11]

As already noted, the neglect of creation is apparent in much modern theology, particularly in Protestant thought. This may be explained in part by the rejection of natural theology in German theology from Friedrich Schleiermacher to Karl Barth. Natural theology was viewed as the fruitless attempt to derive knowledge of God from the world without the aid of any special revelation. Condemned variously as idolatrous, vulnerable to philosophical skepticism, and lacking Scriptural support, natural theology was a distraction from the domains of ethics and history where God was to be found. To be sure, creation was acknowledged by virtue of the dependence of all things on God or as a distinctively Christian article in which Jesus is disclosed as the enfleshed Word of God through whom all things are created. But it fulfilled a largely secondary role in relation to salvation history. Karl Barth spoke of creation as the external basis of the covenant and the covenant as the internal basis of creation. While this has some potential, its tendency is to cast creation again as a stage for the divine–human drama, a necessary condition for the humanity of Jesus Christ. Some trends in twentieth-century biblical criticism confirmed this subordinationist role assigned to creation. In his *Old Testament Theology*, first published in German in 1957, Gerhard von Rad regarded the creation texts as a late addition to the core confession of Israel.[12] The focus was on salvation rather than creation with the result that "it took Israel a fairly long time to bring the older beliefs which she actually already possessed about it into proper theological relationship with the tradition . . . about the saving acts done by Jahweh in history."[13] Since then von Rad's claims have been significantly modified by the recognition that creation themes are more deeply embedded in the canon of the Old Testament. The presence of creation stories in every culture makes a more peripheral location problematic. The prophets, the Psalms, and the wisdom literature repeatedly attest the conviction that the God of Israel is the creator. "Our help is in the name of the Lord who made heaven and earth" (Psalm 124:8). An understanding of God as creator was not simply a presupposition or augmentation of Israel's faith—it was fundamental to its moral and religious identity.[14]

---

10. Amy Plantinga Pauw, *Church in Ordinary Time: A Wisdom Ecclesiology* (Grand Rapids: Eerdmans, 2017), 58.

11. Ibid., 3. The earlier remark is a citation from Ellen Davies.

12. This modifies a position already adopted in 1936. See Harm Goris, "No Creation Stories in the Holy Scripture: Von Rad's View on the Relation Between Covenant and Creation Revisited," in *Strangers and Pilgrims on Earth: Essays in Honour of Abraham van de Beek*, ed. E. van der Borght and P. van Geest (Leiden: Brill, 2012), 669–82.

13. Gerhard von Rad, *Old Testament Theology*, Vol. 1 (Edinburgh: Oliver and Boyd, 1962), 136.

14. See, for example, William P. Brown, *The Ethos of the Cosmos: The Genesis of Moral Imagination in the Bible* (Grand Rapids: Eerdmans, 1999).

Rolf Rendtorff later made the comment that the Bible begins with creation, whereas most of the Old Testament theologies of the last century began with history—this tells us more about the modern authors and their context than the Bible itself.[15]

Recent scholarship has uncovered a developed theology of creation in the Hebrew Scriptures. To take but one brief example, the book of Jonah conveys a powerful sense of the natural world over which God rules and in which human beings are placed in a position of trust. In disclosing his identity to the sailors, Jonah describes himself as a Hebrew who worships the God who made the sea and the dry land. Thrown into the tumultuous sea, he is saved by the large fish that swallows him. On dry land, he is shaded by the large bush that God appoints to grow over him. The short story ends with the sparing of the great city. "Should I not be concerned about Nineveh… in which there are more than a hundred and twenty thousand persons who do not know their right hand from their left, and also many animals?" (Jonah 4:11).

These materials provide a rich seam for Creationtide. The liturgical focus on the four gospels is not misplaced, but the relative neglect of the Hebrew Scriptures in much contemporary preaching is a missed opportunity. How many sermons have you heard on the Old Testament lesson in the past year? I might ask myself how many I've delivered. According to a 2019 Pew Research survey, only 61 percent of sermons in Catholic and mainline Protestant churches in the United States even mentioned a book of the Old Testament, compared to 90 percent for the New Testament.[16] As Plantinga Pauw suggests, not every address has to be about Jesus. He himself preached from the Hebrew Scriptures and recognized their importance. If we inflate his significance at the expense of the canon whose authority he acknowledged, then we do him a disservice. And some vital links with Judaism and Islam will be obscured.

A similar deflation of the doctrine of creation characterizes many of the textbooks prescribed last century. Although these do not feature prominently on reading lists today, they continue to repay study. Yet their handling of creation frequently disappoints and may explain its minimal coverage in the syllabus. J. S. Whale's manual of Christian doctrine was widely used in the second half of the twentieth century. Based on lectures delivered in this faculty in 1940, he offers a clear and historically informed account of the central doctrines. Yet his treatment of creation amounts to only a few pages. Whale takes it as almost a self-evident deliverance of Christian experience while noting its contrast with Deism which disconnects God from the world, Pantheism which confuses God and the world, and a Dualism which places them in opposition.[17] This may be valid as far as it goes, but it's too rapid and omits much that is important.

A notable exception to this trend is provided by another local example. Charles Raven held the Regius Chair from 1932 to 1950 and served also as Master of Christ's College and Vice-Chancellor. In his Edinburgh Gifford Lectures (1951–2),

---

15. Quoted by Terence Fretheim, *God and World in the Old Testament: A Relational Theology of Creation* (Nashville: Abingdon, 2005), xi.

16. An Analysis of Online Sermons in U.S. Churches | Pew Research Center.

17. J. S. Whale, *Christian Doctrine* (Cambridge: Cambridge University Press, 1941), 32–3.

he undertook the task, unfashionable at that time, of developing a theology of nature. He summarizes his case thus:

> Whereas Christendom down to and including our immediate predecessors like Bishop Gore had regarded the Universe as the theatre on the stage of which was played out the drama of Man's Fall and Redemption, our generation, taking evolution seriously, must see the theatre not as a mere setting, itself subsidiary and irrelevant, but as an integral and essential part of the play.[18]

Raven was also a naturalist and something of an ornithologist. In late career, he published *In Praise of Birds* (1950), in which he described them as having been a constant source of health and refreshment amid a busy life. "We have all met men and women who have given the best of themselves to the life of the open air, to help green things grow, to watching the ways of the beasts and birds. Such people, whatever their station, have a peculiar fragrance of character."[19] Raven describes his experience in France in 1917. His battalion of 800 men had been reduced to 150. Under further shelling, they sought shelter in a rat-infested trench. But, in the headquarters that had been constructed there, they discovered some swallows nesting. Amid the exhaustion and terror of the war, these birds became a sign of grace, a reminder of a better world. To observe them was to be lifted above the fear and misery of their war-torn condition.

The inherent goodness of the created order is celebrated across the Scriptures. This does not imply its perfection. The claim for the value of the world sits alongside a recognition of its disturbance, disorder, suffering, and death. It would take more than another lecture to explore this. But some comments are necessary. First, the fragility of the world and the repeated lapses that we both observe and commit generate a sense of falling away from the way things should be. An awareness of the tragic is shaped by counterfactual possibilities. This sharpens our longing for a world that is otherwise. A sense of loss and of what might have been accompanies much sorrow and regret. As Wallace Stevens once wrote, "death is the mother of beauty."[20] This is not to seek a justification or explanation for the flaws in creation, some of which seem inbuilt and others which we add through our own misdeeds. Along the border of creation theology there always runs the problem of evil. But we should beware of smuggling a theodicy, a justification for evil, into descriptions of the created order. Although this is God's good creation, its surd elements cannot be explained. It stands in need of redemption.[21] That may seem

---

18. Charles Raven, *Natural Religion and Christian Theology: The Gifford Lectures First Series, Science and Religion* (Cambridge: Cambridge University Press, 1953), 20.

19. Charles Raven, *In Praise of Birds* (London: Allen and Unwin, 1950).

20. Wallace Stevens, "Sunday Morning," in *Selected Poems* (London: Faber and Faber, 1953), 33.

21. David Bentley Hart notes the distinct and opposed meanings of the term *kosmos* in the New Testament. *The Doors of the Sea: Where Was God in the Tsunami?* (Grand Rapids: Baker, 2005).

unsatisfactory—in many ways it is—but this tension is generated by key claims at the center of Christian faith. However narrow and difficult, a path needs to be steered between an apocalyptic dualism and a bland optimism. Our love for the natural world cannot lapse into idolatry; yet gratitude for what has been created should remain a constant theme in Christian prayer.

Three Aspects of Creation Theology

In this second half of the lecture, I explore three themes, each of which can enhance a theology of creation today.

Creation as *Ex Nihilo*

A favorite essay topic today, the subject of creation out of nothing has recently come under greater scrutiny than at earlier periods. While Scripture does not explicitly teach a doctrine of creation out of nothing, it became firmly established in the late second century in opposition to two other options in the ancient world. These were the eternity of the world, the default position of classical philosophy, and the emanation of the world from the divine being itself—a view that was widely circulated in Gnostic myths. In rejecting each of these views, Christian theologians settled quite quickly on a doctrine of creation out of nothing. Creation was through the agency of the divine Word, but it was not from pre-existent matter. In defending creation out of nothing, Irenaeus and Tertullian tell us that creation is not out of something, whether that be chaotic materials or the divine being itself. The world is other than God but, in its entirety, it is of God's making. The *ex nihilo* is first and foremost a negation of other possibilities that distorted the relationship of God to the world. Unlike other doctrines that were disputed and expressed in contrasting ways, this one rapidly became the consensus position of the church.[22] After about 200 CE, it is uncontested and has never since become the source of any major confessional division. It received heavy reinforcement in the Middle Ages through a series of cosmological arguments in which the totality of all contingent existence was to be explained by the action of a transcendent and self-existent First Cause or Creator. Apologists today have sought to defend faith claims by invoking this line of defense. Only a God who creates everything that is not God can provide a sufficient explanation for the universe. This requires a creation that is out of nothing. As a speculative argument this has some force, though determining its precise probability is much trickier. But my question here is: what, if any, are the practical and pastoral outcomes of the doctrine of creation out of nothing?

The long-standing consensus in favor of an *ex nihilo* creation may explain the lack of critical attention to its practical outcomes. Only when a doctrine is called into

---

22. The standard historical work is Gerhard May, *Creatio Ex Nihilo: The Doctrine of "Creation out of Nothing" in Early Christian Thought*, trans. A. S. Worrall (London: T&T Clark, 2004).

question does it receive closer scrutiny and reconsideration. As is sometimes said, theologians only became serious about proving the existence of God when others began to doubt it.[23] So it has proved over the last thirty years or so as theologians have questioned whether the *ex nihilo* tradition pulls God and the world apart in ways that are problematic. Two sorts of difficulty have become apparent, these leading to experiments in alternative constructions of the God–world relationship. Does the classical position that God creates the world of out of nothing pull God and the world apart from one another in a way that renders God too remote and disengaged from cosmic processes? The other problem is whether it produces a schema in which God is depicted primarily in hierarchical and patriarchal terms of caprice, power, and control. The collective force of these anxieties has propelled some scholars toward a reconfiguration of the God–world relationship, more in terms of indwelling, intimacy, and persuasion. The world conceived as the body of God has some limitations as a metaphor or analogy, but it expresses, according to the critics of the *ex nihilo* tradition, a closer and more egalitarian model for understanding how God relates to the world. This is recommended as the antidote to the pathological symptoms of the older tradition.[24]

What seems clear from this critique is that it has stimulated renewed reflection on the *ex nihilo* account and on why it might be worth preserving upon suitable restatement. If we view it neither as a deduction from Scripture nor as an apologetic argument to demonstrate or raise the probability of God's existence, other features come into clearer focus. The making of the world is a free and unconstrained act of God but not in the sense that it is random. As a creation through the divine word or wisdom, the world displays a correspondence to God and remains dependent upon God for its continued existence. Since God does not need the world to satisfy some innate desire to control or dominate, God is free to love the world for its own sake, to accompany it, and to interact with it as a transcendent other who is neither a victim nor a hostage of creaturely forces. Far from distancing God from the world, the *ex nihilo* concept, for all its unimaginable mysteriousness, frames the relationship in a particular way. God and the world are to be neither separated nor confused, but bound together in relationship.[25] Thus stated, the doctrine can shape a vocabulary of love, grace, and mercy. As Susannah Ticciati has noted in this context, "true transcendence does not foreclose the possibilities of creation, but is their liberating context."[26] Considered in this way, the doctrine has a more limited grammatical function of framing the God–world relationship. This is achieved by excluding the alternatives. To say that creation is out of nothing is to say that it is

---

23. See Michael J. Buckley, *At the Origins of Modern Atheism* (New Haven: Yale University Press, 1987).

24. The most robust attack may be Catherine Keller's *The Face of the Deep: A Theology of Becoming* (New York: Routledge, 2007).

25. For a valuable exploration of this see Frank Kirkpatrick, *Together Bound: God, History and the Religious Community* (New York: Oxford University Press, 2004).

26. Susannah Ticciati, "Anachronism or Illumination? Genesis 1 and Creation *ex nihilo*," *Anglican Theological Review* 99, no. 4 (2017): 691–712 (704).

not out of something. We cannot imagine "nothingness," and it would be a mistake to describe it in terms of a metaphysical vacuum into which God posits all that is not God.[27] Its significance is more modest yet still profound. We can think of the world in its entirety in contrast to but never apart from God.

The World Is Our Home

A second feature of the doctrine of creation contributes further to an enhanced ecological sensibility. The world is our home. Given by God, it is intended as our natural habitat. Here much attention has been devoted to theological anthropology—the account of the human person created in the image of God. Much commentary has been produced on Genesis 1:26-27 in an effort to identify what properties or capacities might distinguish human beings from all the other creatures of the earth, thus conferring upon us a unique status in relation to God. One familiar mistake is to identify the divine element in the human person with consciousness or intelligence or the possession of a soul in contradistinction from the other animals. While there may be ways in which the degree of difference is quite striking, this does not capture what is intended by the image of God. Such strategies risk disconnecting the human person from the body and the natural world so that salvation is too easily construed in terms of a flight from this creaturely realm into a purer and more ethereal condition. Our heavenly home is somewhere beyond the blue—what is needed is a rescue strategy to lift us from a perishing world. Such scenarios can be deeply attractive under particular historical circumstances or at times of chronic pain and suffering. But the original text that speaks of the divine image in human beings seems to refer primarily to the role that we exercise in representing God within the created world. This can be overstated—most of the creation can flourish without us. To this extent, language of stewardship can be inflated in unhelpful ways. Yet there remains an important pastoral function in relation to the created world which emphasizes the extent to which the earth with its sea and land, and its different creatures, is our habitat and one in which we are assigned a vocation in relationship to the whole.[28] This is further reinforced by an anthropology that refuses to separate body and soul—we comprise a psychosomatic unity with the result that any extended hope must be envisaged as a renewal of our embodied and communal life, rather than an escape from it.

The expression, "There is no Planet B," has been popularized by the title of Mike Berners-Lee's book. At one level, this can be interpreted as a narrowly prudential insight. With global population set to rise above nine billion in the present century—a far cry from the Garden of Eden—our habits of consumption, modes of travel, food production, and use of technology need to be significantly adjusted if we are to survive and prosper as a species not just in one place but across the

---

27. Jürgen Moltmann is drawn to a similar strategy in *God in Creation* (London: SCM, 1985), 86–93.

28. See, for example, Michael Welker, *Creation and Reality* (Minneapolis: Fortress, 1999), 60–73.

globe.²⁹ Without a sustainable environment, we have no future. The colonizing of other planets remains for now within the world of science fiction. And scenarios of our minds being uploaded onto computer hardware also promise a future that most of us find deeply unattractive.

As we ponder this, the fragility of our planet becomes something more than a worry about our survival. Its intrinsic value as a habitat that evokes our wonder, admiration, and yearning speaks to us of something broader and deeper than a necessary resource for survival. Travelers to outer space have often spoken of the ways in which their perspective evokes a sense of love for their home on planet Earth. Some of the most striking photos are of Earth, and not just of hitherto unknown planets. John Calvin drew much consolation and inspiration from the contemplation of stars and planets. He considered astronomy to be "the alphabet of theology."³⁰ The grandeur of the world is evident in the vast order of the cosmos and the variety of life on earth. We are thus drawn with wonder to its Maker and to our lowly place under the stars. Perhaps this enlarged vision offered a serenity and sense of order that helped him forget the multiple health problems that afflicted him for much of his life. The Harvard and Smithsonian Center for Astrophysics seems to agree with him. Its website states that, "by asking big questions about the Universe and our place in it, we see ourselves as we are: together, voyaging through a singular moment in time on one very special but relatively minuscule planet among the vastness of space."³¹

Norman Wirzba has proposed a form of "iconic perception" which avoids the dangers of either instrumentalizing or idolizing the world. These are damaging in different ways and should be resisted. An iconic mode of perception is one in which we learn to love the world in relation to God as both its source and active presence.³² Here we repose upon the work of poets, artists, and mystics to capture this sense of belonging to a world that God creates and sustains in love. Mother Julian marveled at the sheer existence of a hazelnut. Hopkins, almost despairing over the way in which the world is sullied, wrote, "And for all this, nature is never spent; there lives the dearest freshness deep down things."³³ This evocative sense of belonging to something greater than ourselves is also captured in a striking passage from *Laudato Si'* that stresses our rootedness in place, land, and culture.

> The history of our friendship with God is always linked to particular places which take on an intensely personal meaning; we all remember places, and revisiting those memories does us much good. Anyone who has grown up in the hills or

---

29. Mike Berners-Lee, *There Is No Planet B: A Handbook for the Make or Break Years* (Cambridge: Cambridge University Press, 2021).

30. See his *Commentary on Jeremiah* 10:1-2 cited by Randall Zachmann, *Reconsidering John Calvin* (Cambridge: Cambridge University Press, 2012), 23.

31. How can astronomy improve life on earth? | Center for Astrophysics (harvard.edu).

32. Norman Wirzba, *From Nature to Creation: A Christian Vision for Understanding and Loving Our World* (Grand Rapids: Baker, 2015), 70–9.

33. Gerard Manley Hopkins, "God's Grandeur," in *The Poems of Gerard Manley Hopkins*, ed. H. Gardner and N. H. MacKenzie (Oxford: Oxford University Press, 1970), 66.

used to sit by the spring to drink, or played outdoors in the neighbourhood square; going back to these places is a chance to recover something of their true selves.[34]

Closely connected to this is the recognition that that this world will also be home for successive generations. Matter is constantly recycled—the atoms that constitute our bodies will survive us; there is continuity and succession built into the fabric of creation. So the divine commission in Genesis is one that carries a responsibility for the longer term. The Psalmist looks forward to children yet unborn who will sing God's praise. Though this recognition of the world as our home is not in itself a strategy for more responsible forms of action, it offers a spiritual and moral imaginary that can motivate and commit us to better practices for both the short and long term.

The Community of Creation

At this juncture, creation theology can be articulated with a Christology that is concerned with "all things" and not merely human beings. The significance of Christ is not with a portion of the human race, the elect, but with the whole creation. Rooted in a rural landscape and economy, Jesus draws upon the natural world in his parables. Animals are frequently mentioned in the gospels, even if their presence is often unobtrusive. As the incarnation of divine Wisdom, all things hold together in his life and work. The Letter to the Colossians uses this phrase—"all things"—five times in six verses (Colossians 1:15-20). Plantinga Pauw contrasts this with what she calls the "industrial strength Calvinism" that has reduced the scope of Christ's work to a limited portion of human beings.[35] The enfleshment of the Word of God underscores the ways in which this world is our dwelling place.[36]

A revitalizing of the theology of the Creed's first article will attend to the community of creation. We are not the only living things, nor a solitary animal. Thomas Aquinas reflected on why God did not just create human beings. If we see ourselves as the end point of creation, the crowning work, then we might wonder about this. Why did God bother to create so many species of bettle? Why ordain millions of years of dinosaurs roaming the earth? Aquinas hadn't been to Jurassic Park, but he had a decent answer. The wisdom and glory of God are more fittingly manifested in a world of creaturely diversity. "God's goodness could not be adequately represented by one creature alone. . . . For goodness which in God is simple and uniform, in creatures is manifold and divided and hence the whole

---

34. Pope Francis, *Laudato Si': On Care for our Common Home* (Vatican City: Libreria Editrice Vaticana, 2015), paragraph 84.
35. *Church in Ordinary Time*, 61.
36. Recent theologies of "deep incarnation" have stressed the connection between the nonhuman creation and the incarnate Word. See Niels Henrik Gregersen (ed.), *Incarnation: On the Scope and Depth of Christology* (Minneapolis: Fortress, 2015).

universe participates in the divine goodness more perfectly, and represents it better than any single creature whatever."[37]

The world of Eden is one that is populated by multiple species, and the subsequent covenant with Noah is one that spans the whole created order for future generations. Yet despite some hints and useful resources, theology has had too little to say about the theological status of animals and how it impacts upon their ethical status. This may have something to do with wider assumptions about nature as our property, placed by God at our disposal. Keith Thomas points out how in the early modern period many attitudes of proprietorial control, some resulting in cruelty, drew ideological support from assumptions about humans being set apart by God from other creatures. In this vein, Richard Bentley, the first Boyle Lecturer and Master of Trinity College, wrote of how everything is made principally for our benefit and pleasure—this was generally uncontroversial in his context.[38]

And yet we do have close bonds with domesticated animals and commit to species conservation in different ways. The RSPB can boast far more members than the aggregate number of all political parties. Other animals fascinate us in part by their distance and difference from our way of life—the speeches of God in Job reference the crocodile and hippopotamus as creatures. Amid all this, attitudes and practices to nonhuman species are deeply problematic, especially with respect to practices of rearing, feeding, housing, and slaughtering of animals for food production. Instead of dismissing or ignoring these problems, we can face these with the right motivation and sensibility and with readiness to listen to those with appropriate expertise.

A theology for Creationtide requires a more capacious treatment of the wider world—its goodness and purpose, our habitation of the earth, and our connectedness to other creatures. Neglected themes of conservation and preservation need to be foregrounded in prayer, praise, and proclamation. Wendell Berry expounds the ecological principle that we can't do one thing. Each action has some wider set of effects; everything in creation is related to something else and is dependent upon something else.[39] And in the cosmos human beings have a much smaller place than we like to imagine. In the paintings in the Lascaux Cave from c. 20,000 years ago, the hunter looks insignificant and vulnerable. Berry writes, "The Creation provides a place for humans, but it is greater than humanity and within it even great (people) are small."[40]

To deflate our significance is not to undermine the love of God which is sufficiently wide and intimate to embrace us all. This love is the ground of our hope both for ourselves and for the world as our home in all its rich diversity. The colors of theology must be many, not one.

---

37. *Summa Theologiae* 1a.47.1.

38. Cited with other examples by Keith Thomas, *Man and the Natural World: Changing Attitudes in England 1500–1800* (London: Penguin, 1983), 17–20. See also David L. Clough, *On Animals: Systematic Theology Volume 1* (London: T&T Clark, 2011), 3–25.

39. Wendell Berry, *The Unsettling of America: Culture & Agriculture* (San Francisco: Sierra Books, 1977), 46.

40. Ibid., 98.

Chapter 4

CHRISTOLOGICAL MAXIMALISM ASSESSED

Doctrines as Rules

In one of the most influential books to emerge in the 1980s, George Lindbeck advocated a rule theory of doctrine.[1] His proposal was that instead of viewing Christian doctrines as first-order propositions that either describe the being and action of God or symbolize religious experience—both options depend on competing models which he rejects—we should regard doctrines primarily as second-order rules for discourse. These provide a grammatical structure for Christian confession, governing its proper meaning and use in worship, prayer, and practice.

This rule theory of doctrine reposed upon a "cultural-linguistic" model of religion. A religion functions like a language. Drawing upon the work of Wittgenstein and Geertz, Lindbeck argues that one needs to become immersed in its forms of life, communal patterns of living, and rituals in order to understand a religion. The model was subject to intense discussion through the last decade of the twentieth century. Some lines of criticism emerged which might explain why the rule theory of doctrine has since been largely ignored. Although Lindbeck mentored an impressive group of pupils in Yale, many of whom would take up leading positions in the guild, they have tended to pursue other directions in their work. Yet there was much excitement surrounding the work of Lindbeck and his Yale colleagues, especially Hans Frei. Their work offered a way out of the seeming impasse of mid-twentieth-century liberalism and neo-orthodoxy. Sufficiently flexible to accommodate developments in other disciplines, they also promised a theology that was intellectually stronger and more self-confident in its assertion of a faith that could withstand the headwinds of secularization. Within the field of Christian ethics, Stanley Hauerwas emerged as a leading voice. And subsequent philosophical ballast became available in the writings of Alasdair MacIntyre.

Problems with the rule theory were raised from positions both to the left and to the right of Lindbeck. Could a doctrine not have a dual function which was *both*

---

1. George A. Lindbeck, *The Nature of Doctrine: Religion and Theology in a Postliberal Age* (London: SPCK, 1984).

regulative and confessional? Have Christians not always regarded their doctrines to be true in some stronger sense than the rule theory allows? That God is one in three persons and Christ both divine and human seem to be truth claims rather than grammatical rules. To some, there appeared to be a drift toward a non-cognitive position that merely viewed doctrine as a program for organizing the life of the community. The concept of culture that informed the account also seemed too static and monolithic. This problem was exposed in Kathyn Tanner's *Theories of Culture*, Tanner herself one of Lindbeck's most distinguished doctoral students. Cultures, she suggested, are more fluid and dynamic, and of course Christians inhabit not only the world of the church but other worlds which interact, collide, and fuse in interesting ways. It makes little sense to "fetishize" a set of rules that float above culture and remain immune to the vicissitudes of history. Further problems concern who are to be the appointed arbiters of rules and the extent to which divergence can be tolerated.[2] On the other side, there were fears that Lindbeck's proposal was covertly sectarian. In pulling up the drawbridge, he appeared to be demanding an ecclesiology that was hermetically sealed from the influences of the secular world. David Tracy famously remarked that the hands were those of Geertz and Wittgenstein but the voice that of Karl Barth.[3] Though a highly complex and contested field, one might also wonder whether Lindbeck's radical account of the dependence of experience upon language was quite right. Much of the way we encounter the world is theory laden, but not all experience can be encapsulated in that way. Recent studies from early infancy suggest that quite complex patterns of communication, interaction, and experience take place before the acquisition of language. And it is surely possible to discern some commonality of human experience across time and space.

These challenges to the rule theory of doctrine all came to the fore. To be fair, Lindbeck had already offered responses in his initial study, having anticipated some of the problems. But, in general, there appeared to be widespread unease with the position. One might also wonder whether the preoccupation with method could continue indefinitely. Theologians soon returned to substantive doctrinal and apologetic matters, leaving these second-order discussions to one side. Lindbeck himself would surely have approved of this turn to more traditional theological pursuits.

What was sometimes overlooked in this widespread discussion of *The Nature of Doctrine* was its *Sitz im Leben* in ecumenical dialogue. Hans Frei, Lindbeck's long-standing friend and colleague in Yale, pointed this out in a *Festschrift* essay.[4]

---

2. Kathryn Tanner, *Theories of Culture: A New Agenda for Theology* (Minneapolis: Augsburg Fortress, 1997), 138–43.

3. David Tracy, "Lindbeck's New Program for Theology: A Reflection," *The Thomist* 49 (1985): 460–72 (465).

4. Hans Frei, "Epilogue," in Bruce D. Marshall (ed.), *Theology in Dialogue: Essays in Conversation with George Lindbeck* (Notre Dame, IN: University of Notre Dame Press, 1990), 275–82.

Lindbeck had been a Lutheran observer at Vatican II, attending all its sessions in Rome. In his early work, he described the theological shifts that he detected there and in a later retrospective view he wrote movingly of how the council had inspired his work. The speech of Archbishop Elchinger in St Peter's in which he spoke of how Catholics had rediscovered the doctrine of justification by faith largely through the ecclesial communities of the Reformation suddenly reduced Lindbeck to tears. He remarked that this was the only time he had ever wept in public, apart from funerals.[5]

The rule theory of doctrine was originally intended to overcome ecumenical division. Despite its air of methodological abstraction, his work was firmly rooted in an ecclesial setting. If we can see particular confessional claims as contextual articulations of more fundamental rules, then it might be possible to reach agreement on these underlying rules despite their more specific outcomes having generated tensions under historical conditions which no longer obtain. *The Nature of Doctrine* devotes serious attention to papal infallibility, the immaculate conception, and the salvation of non-Christians. Given Lindbeck's immersion twenty years earlier in the conciliar debates, these elements of his work should not surprise us. One might speculate whether the loss of momentum in ecumenism, particular in the work of Faith and Order movement, provides a further explanation for the decline of interest in Lindbeck's work.

The search for ecumenical convergence drove Lindbeck to articulate the rules that Christians have tended to hold in common. One of these he describes as "Christological maximalism." This is the end point of three types of commitment that are constitutive of Christian faith—first, the monotheism that is inherited from Judaism with its claim that there is one God alone, the God of Abraham and Jesus; second, a constant focus on the historical specificity of Jesus of Nazareth; and, third, the maximalist view that the highest possible claims that can be made for a human being in space and time are to be made for Jesus. "Every possible importance is to be ascribed to Jesus that is not inconsistent with the first rules. This last rule, it may be noted, follows from the central Christian conviction that Jesus Christ is the highest possible clue (though an often dim and ambiguous one to creaturely and sinful eyes) within the space-time world of human experience to God."[6]

In assessing this description of Christological maximalism, one is taken into some deep territory within the doctrines of the person and work of Christ. What arguments might be advanced for the adoption of this rule?

An early high Christology can already be discerned in the New Testament. Martin Hengel once remarked that there was more rapid progress in the development of dogma in less than two decades of church history than in the next seven centuries.[7] Although one can reasonably claim that the Christology of

---

5. George A. Lindbeck, *The Church in a Postliberal Age* (London: SCM, 2002), 17–18.
6. Lindbeck, *The Nature of Doctrine*, 94.
7. Martin Hengel, *The Son of God: The Origin of Christology and the History of Jewish-Hellenistic Religion* (Minneapolis: Fortress, 1976), 2. He suggests that the formation of

Mark's Gospel is lower than the later Fourth Gospel, the earlier writings of the NT already make some of the strongest imaginable claims for Jesus. The Christ-hymn of Philippians 2:5-11, which is presumably pre-Pauline and already in circulation, refers to him as originally in the form of God. The category of divine Wisdom is closely identified with Jesus in 1 Corinthians 1:24. He is the one in whom, through whom and for whom all things are made (1 Corinthians 8:6). He is given the name that is above all names (Philippians 2:9). Terms such as Lord, which might be considered reserved for God, are ascribed to Jesus. God has previously spoken in many and diverse ways but now through a Son by whom the world was made (Hebrews 1:1-4). This theology of Sonship is further developed in the Fourth Gospel with its discourses reflecting the intimate relationship between the Father and the Son which even pre-exists the creation of the world (John 17:5). The cosmological Christology of the Epistles appears everywhere to imply a qualitative difference between Jesus and other revelations of God.

Much has been made in recent scholarship of the bracketing of Jesus with God in the devotional language of the New Testament. Larry Hurtado describes the liturgical features of early Christianity in terms of a dyadic structure. "The decisive step in treating Jesus as sharing in some way in divine glory and status was taken remarkably earlier, and was expressed both in Christological rhetoric and . . . this dyadic devotional pattern."[8] Richard Bauckham writes similarly of the emergence of a "Christological monotheism."[9]

Embedded within these Christological confessions are two base assumptions. The first is that Jesus is the fulfillment of what precedes him, particularly those scriptures that would become known as the Old Testament. The second is that Jesus is unsurpassable. His revelation is final not in the sense that God is no longer revealed to us, but rather that in every subsequent divine disclosure there remains an indispensable reference to the appearance of Jesus. To use Karl Barth's metaphor, each little light must be understood in its relation to the one great light. Given these assumptions, the concepts of Word and Spirit become necessary for future descriptions of the action of God in the church and the world. God continues to speak by the Spirit, but what we hear is ordered by the one Word. Hence the language of fulfillment and unsurpassability generated a high Christology which has consistently acted as the dominant constraint upon the liturgical and sacramental life of the church.

Related to this are further historical claims about the progress of dogma in the early church. Leaving aside the notable exceptions of the Oriental Orthodox and East Syriac traditions, an assumption of the ecumenical church is that the

---

doctrine in the early church was no more than a "consistent development and completion of what had already unfolded" in the twenty years following the death of Jesus.

8. Larry Hurtado, *Honoring the Son: Jesus in Earliest Christian Devotional Practice* (Bellingham: Lexham Press, 2018), 68.

9. Richard Bauckham, *Jesus and the God of Israel* (Milton Keynes: Paternoster, 2008), 18–31.

Chalcedonian formula represents a necessary development that resolved or at least constrained the inherent ambiguities in Christological dogma that had already emerged in the life of the church. By contrast with earlier scruples, much recent theological literature is surprisingly bullish in this respect. The 451 formula is often read as the inevitable metaphysical outcome of the early high Christology of the New Testament. Despite the political and intellectual wrangling that surrounded its definition, Chalcedon captured the essential ingredient of Christian faith that the Son of God, the second person of the Trinity, became fully human as Jesus of Nazareth without ceasing to be divine. A hypostatic union of the human with the divine was thus affirmed, this later being clarified by the introduction of the concepts of *anhypostasia* and *enhypostasia* that both avoided any incipient Nestorianism while reaffirming the full humanity of Jesus.

Yet criticisms of Chalcedon have persisted.[10] The Miaphysite churches of the East regarded the formula as compromising the Cyrilline commitment to a single divine–human person that emerged from the union. In teaching Chalcedon as the end of a process which resolved earlier disputes about the person of Christ, we have too often overlooked the subsequent controversies and later councils that registered the need for further clarification, for example in affirming the dyothelite view that Christ had two wills. Brian Daley notes that Chalcedon was neither a beginning nor an end. The variety of earlier Christologies should not be viewed as all pointing to Chalcedon; they have their own concerns and contexts. Nor did Chalcedon settle the issue as the controversies of Late Antiquity demonstrate. Its primary purpose is one of excluding unsatisfactory positions and establishing boundaries for subsequent reflection.[11] My own concern in this essay is with the modern critique of Chalcedon, though these early anxieties might be regarded as harbingers of later scruples.

Modern criticisms might be loosely described as logical, historical, and religious, though these tend to be everywhere interwoven. In the fifth century, concepts of *ousia*, *physis*, *prosopon*, and *hypostasis* served an important purpose in excluding positions that either divided the person of Christ or so stressed his divinity to the point of jeopardizing his humanity. Yet for many nineteenth-century theologians, it seemed impossible to conceive imaginatively of a divine subject assuming a human nature without detriment either to his divine identity or to his full humanity. In the *Glaubenslehre*, Schleiermacher illustrates this skepticism around the traditional dogma.[12] A nature is simply the aggregate of properties that make something what

---

10. These were generated by Christological concerns rather than any lingering disagreement around the Nicene doctrine of God. By contrast, modern concerns with Chalcedon have often, though not always, reflected underlying worries about the coherence of the classical doctrine of the Trinity.

11. Brian Daley, *God Visible: Patristic Christology Reconsidered* (Oxford: Oxford University Press, 2018), 1–27.

12. Friedrich Schleiermacher, *The Christian Faith*, Vol. 2, ed. Catherine L. Kelsey and Terence N. Tice (Louisville: Westminster John Knox Press, 2016), Sections 96–7, 581–608.

it is rather than another thing. For a single subject to have two natures therefore makes little sense. The Chalcedonian tradition lurches from affirming the unity of the person at the expense of either Christ's divinity or humanity, or else stressing the duality of the divine and the human in such a way as to imperil the unity of his person. The fruitlessness of this approach is illustrated by the controversy about whether Christ has one will or two. Schleiermacher's preferred approach is to see the significance of Jesus in terms of his God consciousness which is destined to redeem the human race.

These conceptual anxieties around Chalcedonianism have been reiterated in Bruce McCormack's recent study *The Humility of the Eternal Son*. Arguing against the notion of the hypostatic union, he claims that this results in the instrumentalizing of the humanity of Jesus by the divine Word, a tendency that he already detects in Cyril of Alexandria.[13] The human nature becomes a tool or mechanism by which the divine person accomplishes a redemptive purpose. But, in attempting to unite the human with the divine, the full personhood of Jesus of Nazareth is hollowed out. The individuating subject is not the human Jesus but the second person of the Trinity. To repair Chalcedon, McCormack instead advances the idea of a composite hypostasis, a divine, and a human person eternally uniting by virtue of their receptivity one to the other.[14]

This concern around the instrumentalizing of humanity by the divine Logos was already articulated by Karl Rahner in an essay to mark the anniversary of Chalcedon in 1951. While repeatedly stressing his allegiance to church tradition, he expresses the anxiety that the popular reception of Chalcedon has resulted in a Christology that fails to recognize the human person, Jesus of Nazareth, who is our Mediator. In its practical outworking, the metaphysics of the person of Christ tends to undercut some of our deepest existential concerns. "The formal schema nature-person is inadequate. We must conceive of the relation between the Logos-Person and his human nature in just this sense, that here both independence and radical proximity equally reach a unique and qualitatively incommensurable perfection."[15]

---

13. Bruce L. McCormack, *The Humility of the Eternal Son: Reformed Kenoticism and the Repair of Chalcedon* (Cambridge: Cambridge University Press, 2021), 39,

14. An alternative approach is followed in Ian A. McFarland's *The Word Made Flesh: A Theology of the Incarnation* (Louisville: Westminster John Knox, 2019). Arguing that the logic of classical Christology mandates a fuller account of the humanity of Jesus than the tradition has often provided, McFarland develops a "Chalcedonianism without reserve." This is a powerful exercise in both retrieval and correction.

15. Karl Rahner, "Current Problems in Christology," in *Theological Investigations*, Vol. 1 (London: Darton, Longman and Todd, 1962), 162. Unsurprisingly, Rahner's critics claim that he leans too far toward Nestorianism. See for example Thomas Joseph White, *The Incarnate Lord: A Thomistic Study in Christology* (Washington, DC: Catholic University of America Press, 2015), 73–125.

The second type of criticism reflects the historical turn of the modern period. Given repeated attempts to excavate the real Jesus within or behind the gospel narratives, the categories of Chalcedon seemed to conceal rather than expose a Jesus who was really like us in terms of bodily weakness, limited knowledge, and sociocultural determination. If the hypostasis that assumed a human nature was really divine, then the *persona* of Jesus as a human being seemed more apparent than real. One example of this is the various attempts to understand the miracle stories. Whether as exaggerated tales based upon genuine reminiscences, as myths with some deeper religious meaning, or as the authentic deeds of a charismatic teacher, the miracle stories had ceased to be operations of a divine nature that somehow undergirded or shone through the humanity of Jesus. The subsequent direction of gospel criticism suggests that a foregrounding of the Chalcedonian formula is either unhelpful or unnecessary for understanding Jesus in his historical context, even if some wish to retain it as a theological adjunct that remains consistent with their findings. The formula neither helps us to understand nor to follow the Jesus of the Synoptic tradition. Here intellectual skepticism is often allied to a religious concern. By investing Jesus with divine knowledge and power, the tradition, it is feared, renders him remote and unlike one who shares our human condition. In one sense, his stature and significance are inadvertently reduced.[16]

In this context, the emergence of kenotic Christologies can be viewed as an attempt to overcome the tensions in Chalcedon whether by reworking it or replacing it altogether. A commitment to the assumption of human nature by the Son of God can be maintained but only if some divestment or contraction of divine properties is held. On this basis, we can make better sense of Jesus as depicted in the gospels. He prays to God and talks of God in the third person; he hungers, thirsts, and grows tired; his noetic powers are limited to his historical condition. He speaks as someone of his time, rooted in the soil of Palestinian Judaism. These aspects of his life are not read as the accommodation of a divine person to the circumstances of his contemporaries; they render Jesus as he really was to those who knew him and followed him. Christology, at least in one of its phases, must begin from here.

Kenotic theories sought to capture the historical rootedness of Jesus, while also upholding the language of incarnation and the divine assumption of human flesh. The self-emptying of God in Christ, moreover, was the most striking instance of an immanent God immersed in the world of matter even to the point of suffering

---

16. See for example John Macquarrie, *Jesus Christ in Modern Thought* (London: SCM, 1990), 358. Admittedly, some exponents of Chalcedon argue that this does not commit us to the view that Jesus *qua* human was constantly aware of his divine identity. See Gerald O'Collins, *Christology: A Biblical, Historical and Systematic Study of Jesus*, 2nd ed. (Oxford: Oxford University Press, 2009), 252–3. How far this strays from the classical conciliar position is an open question.

on a cross. The attractions of the kenotic position were theological as well as Christological, particularly within Anglican theology after *Lux Mundi*.

Yet the demise of kenoticism can be traced to problems that had already surfaced in the criticisms of Isaak Dorner in the mid-nineteenth century. As a way of preserving the ascription of divinity to Jesus, kenotic theories generated even more conceptual puzzles than the formulations they sought to replace. Could God really cease to be fully divine in the Incarnation? If the divine being is concealed or abridged in some way, does this not compromise the character of the Incarnation as revelation? And what happens to the cosmic functions of the Word of God during Christ's thirty-three years on earth, if there is a temporary divestment of some divine functions on the part of the second hypostasis? An administrative reorganization among the persons of the Trinity seems absurd, not least on account of its tritheist leanings. And what of the eternal binding of the Word of God to our human condition, particularly in theologies of the Ascension which speak of the eternal humanity of the exalted Son? Kenotic theories must struggle with such notions. These sorts of difficulty came increasingly to the fore and led to the decline of kenotic Christologies, though the approach continues to have some advocates today, particularly within analytic theology.[17]

Contemporary Pressures on High Christology

There seems little doubt that these logical and historical problems come to the fore in modern criticisms of Chalcedon. But, in addition, a shift of emphasis in recent systematic theology also reflects a concern that the Christocentrism of earlier approaches has been to the detriment of other themes. While this leaves open the precise determination of the person of Christ, they address a need to focus to a greater extent on other doctrinal *loci* that are not explicitly about Jesus. Underlying this anxiety is a desire to avoid a narrowing of Christological concentration that prevents other doctrinal themes from receiving their proper due. There may also lurk a nagging concern that an extravagant use of a high Christology loses focus on the historical Jesus with a resultant failure to register his ethical significance and follow his example. Is this an unintended consequence of the classical tradition and perhaps a violation of Lindbeck's caveat about maintaining the historical specificity of Jesus?

David Kelsey, another Yale theologian, writes of the different plotlines that are woven together in Christian theology.[18] These comprise an account of creation and creaturehood, the story of sin and redemption, and the hope of eschatological

---

17. I discuss kenoticism more fully in "Kenosis and Divine Humility," in *Kenosis: The Self-Emptying of Christ in Scripture and Theology*, ed. Paul T. Nimmo and Keith L. Johnson (Grand Rapids: Eerdmans, 2022), 194–211.

18. David H. Kelsey, *Eccentric Existence: A Theological Anthropology*, Vol. 1 (Louisville: Westminster John Knox Press, 2009), 120–31.

consummation. Though discrete narratives, all three are drawn together into a single triple helix. But we distort them if we strive too hard to reduce them to one unitary narrative. According to Kelsey, this has tended to happen with overdetermined theologies of sin and redemption—these are not the whole story. In her recent work on ecclesiology, Amy Plantinga Pauw has registered a similar concern. Pleading for greater attention to be given to Hebrew notions of wisdom and to the theology of creation in the life of the church, she resists totalizing interpretations of the high Christology of the New Testament. This should not become a pattern into which all Creator–creature relations are absorbed.[19]

There might there be another set of religious anxieties that are harder to formulate but which suggest an undercurrent of reservations around the high Christology of church tradition. In his 1838 Divinity Address at Harvard, Ralph Waldo Emerson famously referred to the church's "noxious exaggeration" of the person of Christ. His charge was that this jeopardized human autonomy by overstressing our dependence upon the redemptive action of Jesus, while also overstating his significance to the detriment of other religious teachers and traditions. The stress on spiritual freedom was more likely to see Jesus as a guide or exemplar, alongside others, rather than the Saviour of traditional dogma.[20]

The attention devoted to other faith traditions has led to different Christological approaches. Jesus was not the only teacher or prophet. Within the historical study of religion, he has to be located relative to the founding figure of other religious and ethical traditions. In the late nineteenth century, Jesus was frequently regarded as representing the high point of religious evolution. By surpassing other traditions, the religion of the Incarnation stands in a relationship of fulfillment to these. The tendency here is to view incarnation as a difference in degree rather than one of kind. The presence of God in Jesus is more intense and saturated, but in a way that completes rather than annuls what precedes it.[21] Nineteenth-century writers also pondered the challenges that might be posed to traditional belief systems by the encountering of life forms on other planets. In many cases, such prospects were confidently united with traditional accounts of the person and work of Christ, but once that genie was out the bottle other possibilities such as multiple incarnations soon hoved into view.[22]

While robust defenses of Chalcedon seem less concerned with these problems, they continue to be registered in more recent literature. Writing in *The Myth of God*

---

19. Amy Platinga Pauw, *Church in Ordinary Time: A Wisdom Ecclesiology* (Grand Rapids: Eerdmans, 2017), 58. Here Pauw draws upon the work of Katherine Sonderegger, *Systematic Theology*, Vol. 1 (Minneapolis: Fortress, 2015), xix.

20. Emerson, *Political Writings*, ed. Kenneth S. Sacks (Cambridge: Cambridge University Press, 2008), 34.

21. See for example Edward Caird, *The Evolution of Religion* (Glasgow: Maclehose, 1893).

22. See Andrew Davison, *Astrobiology and Christian Doctrine* (Cambridge: Cambridge University Press, 2023).

Incarnate—a controversial collection of the late 1970s seldom cited nowadays—John Hick speculates that the future significance of Jesus will be more powerfully communicated outside the church. Describing Jesus as a "man of universal destiny," Hick suggests that his religious importance will be more authentically recognized and shared by different faith communities; his influence will become "the common property of the world."[23] This might also resonate with the more customized and eclectic approach to spirituality that is often taken as a feature of contemporary religiosity. The Emersonian affinities are not hard to detect here. Hick, like Emerson before him, continues to make some big claims for Jesus. In the case of extraterrestrial life, the jury is still out, though several rival proposals populate the field. The most conservative of these takes the view that the universal significance of Christ would require inter-galactic missionary activity, in the event that intelligent life were to show up elsewhere in the cosmos. Whether such a view would survive the cultural shock that such a discovery would engender is an open and speculative question. Other approaches support the hypothesis of multiple incarnations, though presumably this would require some empirical checking. But, even if sustainable, its corollary would be that the significance of Jesus is more provincial than earlier generations had taught. Rather than a single salvific event of maximal cosmic significance, its scope would be planetary, with other regions of the cosmos determined by their own local incarnations. This view has some *prima facie* plausibility and will continue to attract attention. But in this context, the salient point is that this may require some deflation of early claims in order to admit even the possibility of a multiplicity of incarnational events.[24]

Finally, the emergence of what is often called "world Christianity" has drawn attention to the multiplicity of Christologies that are evident today, many of these appearing uninterested or even dismissive of the abstractionism of earlier approaches.[25] The primary significance of Jesus is ethical, political, and spiritual. More theoretical discussions of the constitution of his person prescind from practical constraints which should be paramount in any contemporary Christology. C. S. Song's *Jesus the Crucified People* blends the story of Jesus with those of the suffering in a manner that either invites a low Christological construction or merely eliminates such concerns as symptomatic of our evasion of what matters most. Anthony Reddie's essay on Jesus as a black hero similarly points to ways in which a contextual reconstruction of Jesus' identity is not only permitted but also

---

23. John Hick, "Jesus and the World Religions," in *The Myth of God Incarnate*, ed. John Hick (London: SCM, 1977), 167–85 (184).

24. Although a further series of questions surrounds the Christian reading of Judaism, the problems of supersessionist attitudes cannot be laid at the door of Chalcedon. These are already apparent in the New Testament. As Rosemary Radford Ruether once remarked, "Anti-Judaism in Christian Theology Stands at the Left Hand of Christology. Anti-Semitism in Christian Theology," *Theology* 30, no. 4 (1974): 365–81.

25. The term "world Christianity" may itself be reaching its sell-by date, given its suggestion of a single brand.

demanded as a way of enabling Jesus to be with and for black people in the face of multiple forms of oppression. Though the work of Marilyn Adams may seem to offer a stark contrast in terms of its robust commitment to two-nature Christology, similar existential concerns come to the fore in her remark that in our frail animal condition, "we humans need not only emergency assistance to recover from the crisis of actual horror-participation, but a helper, a companion, and a teacher to enable, guide, and work with us all along."[26]

These are disparate themes—other faiths, eclectic forms of spirituality, the search for extraterrestrial intelligence, and the turn toward more political, pastoral, and ethically inclined Christologies—but they contribute to a *Zeitgeist* in which earlier assumptions have ceased to be intuitively plausible. While supporters of a classical Chalcedonian Christology have their responses to this, other approaches continue to be advanced and tested. Given their resonance for contemporary audiences, they are unlikely to be replaced by a consensus position determined by an agreed set of doctrinal rules. Notwithstanding this, there are some strong considerations against admitting an endless variety of Christological functions. What is politically or pastorally constructive in a given context is a valid pragmatic criterion, yet it is not the only critical standard. Attention to the claims of Scripture and tradition will be necessary if Jesus is to be regarded as more than the cipher of a loosely defined Christian consciousness. Questions about church unity also emerge, especially as the diverse forms of the church worldwide become apparent. Here Lindbeck's ecumenical commitments remain relevant. What holds the church together as a catholic and apostolic body united across space and time? And does this still matter to us? Furthermore, while functional approaches have significant traction for Christian witness, hermeneutical questions of a more theoretic type will eventually return. How are we to understand the person of Jesus Christ in relation to God? Why should we attach such significance to his life and teaching? In what ways do we understand him to be a living and present reality in the life of the church for the world?

An exponent of Chalcedon will also insist upon the importance of soteriological considerations. These were significant in shaping the Christological debates of the late fourth and early fifth centuries. If Jesus were neither fully human nor a single integrated subject, the healing of our human nature could not have been accomplished in the way intended. Later approaches, such as Anselm in the *Cur Deus Homo*, would view the Chalcedonian formula as axiomatic in the development of atonement theories. It is hardly surprising therefore that a similar ferment is currently taking place around contemporary discussions of the work of Jesus with concerns again expressed about the ethical outcomes or lack thereof in traditional views; any account of the person of Christ will thus be intertwined with convictions and consequences about his work.

---

26. Marilyn McCord Adams, *Christ and Horrors: The Coherence of Christology* (Cambridge: Cambridge University Press, 2006), 149.

Lindbeck Revisited

George Lindbeck's position may actually be more flexible than hitherto suggested. His rules are intentionally imprecise and subject to some negotiation. The analogy with language may assist here. The way it is spoken and written is never fixed. Fresh idioms, metaphors, and terms are constantly being coined. Novel ways of speaking with rhetorical force continue to be invented. One only needs to read Shakespeare or the King James Bible to appreciate the extent to which our language has evolved over several centuries. Nevertheless, we can recognize this as the same language in which many of the underlying rules persist. So it goes with Christian doctrine. Lindbeck advances the claim that different conceptual and symbolic formulations may articulate the same set of rules at different times and places. For example, the agreed formulae at the Councils of Constantinople and Chalcedon might have been the only possible outcomes under the conditions of Late Antiquity, but the rules that they instantiate can also be reflected in a different conceptual and symbolic idiom. Unlike the correlation of first- and second-order in Lonergan, the fit in Lindbeck between an implicit rule and its fullest metaphysical expression seems quite loose on closer inspection, thus admitting a degree of doctrinal mobility that was not initially apparent to critics on his theological left. "There may, on this reading, be complete faithfulness to classical Trinitarianism and Christology even when the imagery and language of Nicaea and Chalcedon have disappeared from the theology and ordinary worship, preaching, and devotion."[27] But he adds the intriguing observation that the classical creeds continue to be more useful than any modern substitute because their liturgical power is allied to a high degree of conceptual *unintelligibility*. The sheer unfamiliarity of key terms ensures that they function as open variables which can be supplied with whatever content is most effective in a given setting. Hence, what began in Lindbeck as a proposal that appeared to justify doctrinal immobility now emerges as something more fluid by virtue of the ways in which implicit rules of speech can deliver a significant diversity of content.

The advantage of this approach is that it can maintain a high degree of doctrinal continuity while accommodating some of the anxieties around Chalcedon noted earlier. Leaving aside the issue of "maximalism" for the moment, we can quickly register the extent to which the New Testament offers some very strong claims for Jesus. The terms *christos* and *kyrios* were rapidly established as terms of address, these indicating a belief in Messiahship and a lordship that placed Jesus alongside God in the devotional language of the early community. The belief in his resurrection from the dead as a harbinger of the general resurrection also placed Jesus in a different position from other teachers and prophets, for example, John the Baptist. Similarly, the deployment of Word and wisdom as Christological categories, even if not read in a proto-Nicene manner, expresses a belief in Jesus as the fullest disclosure of God, and one that provides a constant point of return, as, for example, in the opening

---

27. Lindbeck, *The Nature of Doctrine*, 95.

verses of the Letter to the Hebrews. This focus shapes the canon, the liturgy, and the sacramental life of the church, even to the extent, as we have seen, that other themes such as creation and pneumatology could be occluded. What holds this together is an underlying conviction that Jesus surpasses and is unsurpassed in his relationship to God and revelation of God. As a deep-seated assumption, this is "baked into" the very structure of Christian faith. Yet its Christological expression can be given in ways that do not require a strict and indefeasible commitment to the hypostatic union and two natures of Chalcedonianism. This leads me to some concluding thoughts about where Christology goes from here.

First, some of the proposals advanced by scholars in the postwar period last century continue to have traction, despite the tendency to reject these as either politically quietist or metaphysically insipid. Dismissed under the lazy rubric of "liberal Protestant," these have been among the most creative contributions to modern Christology. Donald Baillie wrote of the paradox of grace in the Christian life as being seen to the highest degree in the life of Jesus. We become most free as human persons when the grace of God is the animating principle of our lives. This blend of passivity and activity is fitfully achieved in us but appears most fully in Christ so that we can speak of his life as displaying both a divine and human character.[28] In similar vein, John Macquarrie describes the life of Christ as reflecting both the downward movement of the Word of God in a human life but also the upward response of Jesus of Nazareth. This is not the hypostatic union of classical Christology but an attempt to remain faithful to its "governing principle" through a different set of more historical and dynamic categories.[29] Karl Rahner's appeal for a more fully human Christ seems already to have followed a similar route, even while insisting upon its faithfulness to the conciliar formula. Registering the concern that classical Christology has too often led to an instrumentalizing of the humanity of Jesus in the popular consciousness of the church, he sets out a "Christology from below" which gives greater scope to Jesus as the one in whom our human potential is preeminently fulfilled. In his highly complex discussion, Chalcedon assumes the function of a formal marker that cautions against various Christological errors. But, rather than constituting an end of Christological definition, it remains in need of fresh elucidation in each age. Its historical consequence, Rahner suggests in the aforementioned essay, has been a regrettable monophysitism of the Christian imagination. In assuming humanity, Christ possesses this as an instrument. Yet he ceases to be a Mediator, except to himself.[30] The relationship of the human Jesus to God is occluded if we allow Chalcedon exhaustively to determine our thinking about his person. Yet it is the gospels' account of this Jesus as for God and before God which is important to mind and heart today. To the critic who alleges that is to concede too much to

---

28. Donald M. Baillie, *God Was in Christ: An Essay on Incarnation and Atonement* (London: Faber and Faber, 1948), 106–32.
29. Macquarrie, *Jesus Christ in Modern Thought*.
30. Rahner, "Current Problems in Christology," 157.

contemporary fashions, Rahner says simply that "it is quite meaningless to want to be modern on purpose."[31] His preferred solution is to combine approaches from above and below. We must think of the divine coming to the human in Christ, but also the human reaching to the divine. Though contrastive, these two movements are not in competition. The finite is created with this potential, and its fulfillment is given by grace. "The less we merely think of this humanity as something added on to God, and the more we understand it as God's very presence in the world and hence see it in a true, spontaneous vitality and freedom before God, the more intelligible does the abiding mystery of our faith become, and also an expression of our very own existence."[32]

These approaches will enable us to practice a Christology from below which makes sense of the intense historical work on the gospels of the last 200 years. The categories of "below" and "above" are undoubtedly vague terms that can mean different things to different writes. In an oft-quoted essay, Nicholas Lash once exposed their slipperiness.[33] There is no "pure" history of Jesus that is unadulterated with theological assumptions. The Christology of Mark's Gospel is often taken to be a low variety, yet it begins with a theological claim for Jesus which is reiterated in several places. He is presented as God's Messiah and God's Son. Historians may help us to explain what that might have meant in first-century Palestinian Judaism, but these claims are already theological with their thick references to religious and metaphysical concepts that have a previous history. Although Pannenberg's earlier work may have suggested a "proof" of the divinity of Jesus from historical work, his later comments on Christology from below make better sense. We need this approach in order to understand how faith in Jesus first arose among his earliest followers. Only in this way can we begin to comprehend its plausibility and significance for us too. This is a necessary procedure for the comprehension of faith. "To test and justify Christological statements about Jesus, Christology must get behind the confessional statements and titles of the primitive Christian tradition, reaching the foundation to which these point, which underlies faith in Jesus."[34] This historical work can illuminate the different dimensions of Jesus' appearance and provide a critical standard by which the proclamation of the church can be measured. We can also be alerted to the ways in which an understanding of Jesus' person is inextricably tied to his activity whether as teacher, healer, end-time prophet, crucified Messiah, and risen Lord.

Furthermore, this historical work may also make possible comparisons with other religious teachers and exemplars without fear of reducing these to instances of a single type. Each has their own particularity, doubtless with similarities and

---

31. Ibid., 153.

32. Ibid., 185.

33. Nicholas Lash, "Up and Down in Christology," in *New Studies in Theology*, ed. Stephen Sykes and Derek Holmes (London: Duckworth, 1980), 31–46.

34. Wolfhart Pannenberg, *Systematic Theology*, Vol. 2 (Edinburgh: T&T Clark, 199), 282.

differences emerging in the exercise of comparison. The Qur'anic view of Jesus is striking by virtue of its high estimate of his prophetic status and the quality of life that he exhibits. But on the subject of the Crucifixion and Resurrection, the Qur'an parts company with the New Testament, regarding it as mistaken in key aspects of its Easter story. These comparisons are fruitful in the process of promoting mutual understanding and a deeper appreciation of one another's scriptures. This applies *a fortiori* to our reading of the Hebrew Scriptures in the church with the benefit of insights from Jewish interpreters. But in the process of pursuing a Christology from below, we also find points of contact and similarity that are not to be dismissed.

These are programmatic points all in need of much elaboration. Where does this story leave us with respect to Christological maximalism as George Lindbeck's third rule? To a large extent, I have stuck with it, at least insofar as it permits of a good deal of flexibility with respect to its doctrinal expression. Yet maximalizing might not be best served by the inflation of the significance of Jesus at the expense of other important theological themes. The multiplicity of rules that govern Christian discourse, some of which can assume greater importance under new historical circumstances, entail that no one rule should be assigned a superordinate function. If that is correct, then there may be legitimate scope for a greater variety of Christologies across the world today, some high, some low, and others in between. These considerations might suggest that Christian theology should beware of any exclusivist maximalizing tendency that actually makes it harder for Christian people to understand and follow Jesus in the time and place in which they find themselves. Their faith cannot manage without a Christological *normativity*—Jesus remains the unsurpassed historical source and measure of faith—but proclamation does not always have to be about Jesus, nor does it have to speak of him in monotonous or inflated language over-determined by a metaphysics imposed upon us by the Chalcedonian formula, which has the unintended consequence of rendering him remote, thus obscuring much of what the gospel record seeks to make known.

Chapter 5

PROVIDENCE

Introduction

The term for "providence" seldom appears in Scripture. The Greek *pronoia* and the Latin *providentia* have a much richer provenance in classical philosophy, though these terms were soon used to express themes embedded in the stories of the Bible and the doctrinal tenets of Christian theology. In the early church, theologians assumed at least a partial alliance with the providential philosophies found in Stoic and Platonist philosophers.[1] Providence is about both divine foresight and provision. Nature and history are ruled by God, whether according to general principles or particular determinations. Like a wise ruler, God attends not only to the general terms of governing the cosmos, but also to the specificities of human affairs. The appearance of Christ came at the right time for the commencement of the gospel in the Gentile world; this was confirmed by the subsequent growth of the church which provided a further sign of divine foresight. Our actions have outcomes that are providentially ordered, particularly with respect to eschatological rewards and punishments. In these ways, philosophical notions of providence were adapted to distinctively Christian purposes. The main difference that emerged was one that tended to separate the churches of the Greek east from the Latin west. "Fate" was a Stoic notion that was held in the Christian east to compromise our divinely bestowed freedom—it was insisted by Orthodox theologians that some things are genuinely up to us—whereas in the west, "fate" tended to be affirmed as the servant of divine providence.[2]

---

1. For valuable explorations of the historical development of providentialism in early Christian theology see Silke-Petra Bergjan, *Der Fürsorgende Gott* (Berlin: De Gruyter, 2002), and Mark W. Elliott, *Providence Perceived: Divine Action from a Human Point of View* (Berlin: de Gruyter, 2015).

2. See Andrew Louth, "Pagans and Christians on Providence," in *Texts and Culture in Late Antiquity: Inheritance, Authority, and Change*, ed. J. H. D. Scourfield (Swansea: Classical Press of Wales, 2007), 279–98.

Although the theology of providence was largely an occasional theme in early Christian thought, perhaps an exercise in "irregular dogmatics," it was treated more systematically in the writings of the scholastics. For Aquinas, everything happens in accordance with the will of God. This is understood through a distinction between primary and second causality, which yielded a form of double agency. If the primal will of God is the first cause of every event, this is mediated by secondary causes. These are the created and intermediate forms by which the divine will is exercised. This distinction could conveniently preserve the integrity of human freedom and the order of natural causes, while ensuring that God could not be considered the author of sin and evil. Though with distinctive emphases upon Scripture, faith and divine sovereignty, a structurally similar account of providence re-appears in Calvin and the later Reformed tradition, again with recourse to the same philosophical tools, especially the distinction between primary and secondary causality, the latter appearing as subordinate to the former. The position is expressed succinctly by Bullinger in the Second Helvetic Confession (1566). "For God, who has appointed to everything its end, has ordained the beginning and the means by which it reaches its goal."[3]

The theology of providence was a dominant theme through much of modernity. Even in revisionist theologies not noted for their dogmatic convictions, providence often survived in an inflected form. Charles Taylor describes the ways in which the theologies of the Enlightenment could be cast as forms of "providential deism."[4] The confidence surrounding this providentialism is apparent in much of the literature until 1914, after which traditional approaches were increasingly questioned, revised, deflated, or articulated in a more defensive mode. In particular, more synergist approaches have been ventured which slacken the grip of a meticulous providence upon nature and history without abandoning Scriptural emphases upon a benevolent divine rule. Analytic philosophers of religion have been prominent in these experiments with the result that their work has moved on to more overtly theological terrain. This has enriched the exploration of newer models of providence while reinvigorating the assessment of classical approaches. In what follows, I shall examine recent discussion of the standard Thomist-Calvinist model and its Molinist revision, before exploring some alternative proposals.

The Classical Model

The classical model of providence, at least in the Latin west, is dominated by a commitment both to divine sovereignty and to the integrity of creaturely causes.

---

3. "Second Helvetic Confession," in *Reformed Confessions of the Sixteenth Century*, ed. Arthur C. Cochrane (London: SCM Press, 1966), 233.
4. Charles Taylor, *A Secular Age* (Cambridge, MA: Harvard University Press, 2007), 221–69.

Everything that happens is determined by the primal will of God but mediated through the secondary causes that we see at work in the material world. Divine sovereignty entails that nothing can occur that is not willed by God. Hence, the exercise of divine rule requires more than a foreknowledge of events—God must ordain, concur, and will that these take place, not simply "by a bare permission."[5] This position is sustained by a succession of arguments based on considerations around the divine being and the sufficiency of explanation, and buttressed by examples from Scripture. In articulating a maximalist doctrine of providence, theologians claimed that anything less would be unfitting for God and contrary to the teaching of Scripture. While this theology of providence was intensely debated and defended in the age of Reformed orthodoxy,[6] it would be a mistake to regard it as a Reformed invention. Its roots can be found in medieval scholasticism as the Reformed orthodox themselves had no difficulty in recognizing.

In expounding this theology of providence, Paul Helm has advanced several considerations in its favor.[7] These tend to focus on the coherence of the position and the Scriptural support that it commands. In addition, much attention is devoted to refuting contrary positions in such a way that the field is cleared of all but one possibility. It is argued that "risky" views of providence that accord too much scope to creaturely autonomy tend to compromise the sovereign rule of God as this is attested in Scripture. These views also lead to unwelcome assumptions about the loss of divine omniscience and eternity, and uncertainty around final outcomes. If God can be frustrated or compromised by human freedom or chance events, then this must weaken God's providence. A timeless, omniscient, and sovereign God becomes temporally bound, fallible in belief, and unable fully to secure an original intent.[8] Here we see how discussions of providence inevitably engage wider issues in the doctrine of God and, in particular, the coherence of classical theism. We should not be surprised therefore to find opponents of classical theism also advancing revisionist accounts of providence.[9]

The classical position continues to have an impressive list of defenders.[10] Strenuous efforts have been made to rebut objections concerning the theodicy

---

5. *The Confession of Faith*, Vol. 4 (Edinburgh: Blackwood, 1957), 11.

6. See Aza Goudriaan, *Reformed Orthodoxy and Philosophy, 1625–1750* (Leiden: Brill, 2006), 143–232.

7. Paul Helm, *The Providence of God* (Downer's Grove: InterVarsity Press, 1993).

8. Ibid., 54–5.

9. See for example John R. Lucas, *Freedom and Grace* (London: SPCK, 1976) and "Foreknowledge and the Vulnerability of God," in *Royal Institute of Philosophy Lecture Series*: 25, in Godfrey Vesey (ed.), *The Philosophy in Christianity* (Cambridge: Cambridge University Press, 1989), 119–28.

10. For example, Alexander S. Jensen, *Divine Providence and Human Agency: Trinity, Creation and Freedom* (Aldershot: Ashgate, 2014), and Vernon White, *Purpose and Providence: Taking Soundings in Western Thought, Literature and Theology* (London: T&T Clark, 2015).

problem and the charge of determinism. Although God cannot be presented as the author of sin and evil, God's rule extends over these in such a way that there is a permissive willing or concurring with creaturely causes. These are willed, but only in the sense that they are intended in the long run to serve both the glory and redemptive purposes of God. If we describe such causes as outside the will of God or unintended by-products of another process, then we merely generate some intractable problems. If God foresees what will happen, then God must in some way decree that this will take place unless we assume that there are events that God cannot control or rule. A bare permission is not coherent unless we view this as foreseen and willed. The world cannot surprise God or throw up unintended consequences without compromising divine sovereignty. It is for this reason that providence has sometimes been located within the doctrine of God—it is a necessary corollary of the divine attributes.

In this context, the classical distinction between primary and secondary causation continues to be expounded. Emerging in the Neo-Platonism of Proclus, this already had a long history in Islamic thought from the ninth century.[11] The differentiation of forms or levels of causality has at least five benefits for the theological metaphysician:

1. It protects the integrity of the system of natural causes—these can be described by the methods of the natural sciences and the social historian without reference to the supernatural as one among many forces at work.
2. Within this scheme, there remains scope for miraculous events which do not cohere with normal patterns of secondary causation—these can be attributed to the particular will of God in respect of their exceptional character.
3. The counterintuitive assumptions of occasionalism in which God is the hidden cause of every event to the extent that natural causes are apparent rather than real can be avoided. Secondary causes are genuine—they do not deceive us.
4. Primary causality enables the theologian to understand the total system of secondary causes as willed and ruled by God and therefore serving a providential purpose.
5. The distinction also allows a construction of human freedom as compatible with a form of divine determinism. The exercise of divine and human agency is neither a competition nor a zero-sum game. One form of agency does not recede in order that the other may flourish. These work together but at different levels; they are complementary rather than competitive.

In addition to its attractions, this scheme can draw upon Scriptural support from those passages which speak of God working through creaturely agencies but over-

---

11. See Richard C. Taylor, "Primary and Secondary Causality," in *The Routledge Companion to Islamic Philosophy*, ed. Richard C. Taylor and Luis Xavier López-Farjeat (London: Routledge, 2016), 225–35.

ruling them to fulfill a more primal intention. For example, the Joseph story could be interpreted along those lines. His brothers do evil in selling Joseph into slavery, but some deeper purpose ordained by God is thereby enacted. This does not abrogate the human agencies involved—the brothers act of their own volition and are held culpable—but with foresight God works in and through these to establish a higher purpose. Joseph's sojourn in Egypt eventually saves his people back in Canaan at a time of prolonged famine.

Given its explanatory power, seeming simplicity, and apparent fit, why have so many theologians demurred at this account, particularly in recent times?

Three fundamental problems can be identified with the classical view. The first is the free will objection. If God decrees and knows from all eternity what I shall do, then how is my decision to act free at the time immediately before that action? In what sense could I have done otherwise under the same conditions? Exponents of the classical view have often appealed to a compatibilist view of human freedom. If, for example, my free action is one that is determined by the condition of my mind and will prior to acting, then God can both know and determine this condition. On this view, there is no incompatibility between divine determinism and human freedom; indeed, the former is the guarantee of the latter. Critics of the classical view of providence, however, tend to favor a stronger libertarian account of freedom. If my action is genuinely undetermined at the time immediately prior to my decision to act in this way, so that I could have done otherwise, then my choice cannot be decreed from some timeless realm inhabited by God. In making this strong libertarianism an axiom for the theology of providence, the critic is then faced with some further adjustments to the traditional view. A second difficulty concerns the problem of evil. According to the classical view, God ordains everything that happens. This generates a meticulous providence that consolidates the connection between the divine will and manifold evils such as disease, natural catastrophe, malicious deeds, and tragic accidents. Theologians such as Calvin were willing to embrace this view on the basis that it was Scripturally warranted and ineluctable given the difficulties generated by its negation. But more recent work on the problem of evil has been reluctant to affirm this tight connection between the divine will and everything that happens. A stronger distinction between divine permission and willing is often introduced in this context, though as a historical note it is worth recalling that this has generally been maintained within Eastern Orthodoxy. A third difficulty with the classical view is its religious adequacy. The dynamic and interactive relationship between God and the world which is integral to prayer, worship, and service appears to be threatened by the view that the course of the future is fully determined by the primal will of God. The more cooperative and reactive elements of divine providence, which appear throughout Scripture, are not captured by the classical approach. Many people may have quietly defected from this mainstream view or privately harbored their doubts.[12] If we are to

---

12. Charles Wood, *The Question of Providence* (Louisville, Westminster John Knox Press 2008), 65.

embrace a stronger sense of God's wrestling with recalcitrant creaturely material and improvising to bring about God's ends, then an alternative account will be needed. For these reasons, recent scholarship has experimented with a variety of models that are preferred to the standard position of Thomists and Calvinists.

The Revival of Molinism

One way in which these criticisms can be accommodated without undue disturbance to the classical view is to revive the Molinist position with its appeal to middle knowledge.[13] On this account, we can distinguish three forms of divine knowledge. There is God's natural knowledge of necessary truths (e.g., 2+2 = 4) and there is God's knowledge of what God decrees shall happen (e.g., the fall of Adam and Eve). Additionally, there is God's middle knowledge of counterfactual possibilities which includes many conditional truths. For example, God knows what would happen in all the possible worlds in which free creatures exercised their libertarian freedom differently. The basic advantage of this position is that it enables full providential control to be maintained alongside creaturely freedom. In choosing this world from among all the possible options, God knows exactly what free creatures will do under all the circumstances that will arise. With this knowledge, God can then exercise providence to ensure all the desired outcomes. Yet what we do is genuinely up to us, rather than determined by God. The appeal to middle knowledge ensures that our free acts are protected and that God is no longer cast as the author of sin. Yet God's omniscience, sovereign will and providential control can all be maintained by the Molinist. More controversially, a Christological defense of middle knowledge has recently been articulated. The middle knowledge of God can guarantee that the human Jesus exercises true libertarian freedom but does so impeccably.[14]

Despite its initial appeal, there are formidable problems facing the exponent of middle knowledge. Does this really protect libertarian freedom? Critics have argued that if I am genuinely free at the moment of decision then God cannot know how I will act on the basis of all the antecedent conditions. In selecting this world for creating, therefore, God cannot know which of the many possible worlds has been actualized since its initial conditions cannot guarantee future outcomes. It seems that God must await our free decisions to learn which of many possible worlds this one will be, an outcome that will have consequences for the exercise of divine providence. According to this criticism, future conditionals are

---

13. For recent defenses of Molinism, see Thomas P. Flint, *Divine Providence: The Molinist Account* (Ithaca: Cornell University Press, 1998), and William Lane Craig, *The Only Wise God: The Compatibility of Divine Foreknowledge and Human Freedom* (Eugene: Wipf & Stock, 1999).

14. Thomas Flint, "The Possibilities of Incarnation: Some Radical Molinist Suggestions," *Religious Studies* 37 (2001): 125–39.

ungrounded and therefore indeterminate; for this reason, there is nothing that can be known until these are actualized.[15] A further problem is that God's sovereignty seems to be modified by the need for God to consult an array of possible worlds before selecting one of these. Like an interior decorator flicking through samples of paint color before making a selection, God is determined by a set of possibilities that are given and presented rather than willed. This loss of sovereignty in the appeal to middle knowledge was already noted in the seventeenth century—God was likened to Jupiter consulting the Fates before deciding what to do.[16]

Owing to these difficulties, a middle knowledge approach to providence tends to be squeezed by the classical view on one side and more revisionist approaches on the other. Either God determines this world more strongly than via divine middle knowledge or else God's accommodation of human freedom requires a more open approach to the exercise of providence. A variety of "openist" or "interactive" proposals can be discerned in the literature.

Interactive Approaches

Although the revisionist view has been closely associated with the movement known as "open theism," this was already evident in the work of analytic philosophers in the 1970s. Peter Geach once suggested that divine providence might be constructed on the model of God as a grand master of chess. No matter what moves the opponent makes, God can realize the divine intention by accommodating these in a strategy that will eventually result in check mate.[17] The parameters and the outcome are fixed, though the moves that will be made are in part conditional upon the decisions of the opponent. Hence God remains in control even while ceding some autonomy to creaturely agencies. J. R. Lucas advocates an improvised version of divine providence which is reactive but always successful by virtue of God's love, patience, and resourcefulness. God does not have one best plan, but an infinity of best plans capable of accommodating our mistakes. Lucas is ready to affirm divine temporality as well as an abridged account of omniscience in order to secure the coherence of his position. But these departures from classical theism are presented as gains in retrieving a more Scripturally adequate account of divine–human relations. Passages that refer to God's change of mind or conditionality in dealing with human beings are read, *pace* Calvin, not as metaphorical accommodations to our human mode of understanding but as genuine depictions of divine reactivity. Lucas offers the

---

15. William Hasker, *Providence, Evil and the Openness of God* (London: Routledge, 2004), 155.

16. Willem van Asselt, *The Federal Theology of Johannes Cocceius (1603–1669)* (Leiden: Brill, 2001), 167.

17. Peter Geach, *Providence and Evil* (Cambridge: Cambridge University Press, 1977), 58.

more personal analogy of the Persian carpet-maker who can accommodate the mistakes of his apprentice children in weaving a new design through a seemingly inexhaustible creativity.[18] A similar accommodation of libertarian freedom is also evident in Swinburne's adjustment of the traditional account of omniscience. God's foreknowledge cannot include an infallible awareness of the outcome of free decisions. To this extent, human freedom entails that divine foreknowledge is not incorrigible.[19] It seems that we add to the stock of God's true beliefs only as and when we make these decisions.

The more recent cluster of proposals described as "open theism" has developed this approach, mainly within Evangelical circles. Several strands of this more relational understanding of divine providence can readily be identified. The stress on human freedom is paramount to the extent that some outcomes are genuinely up to us. God may influence and cooperate with us in manifold ways, but the act of faith is one in which we freely assent to God. This is our decision, not God's. One consequence of this is that the construction of divine omniscience has to accommodate the openness of the future. Given creaturely freedom, the future is indeterminate. It is not so much that it is unknowable, but that there is nothing yet available to be known, even by God. So divine providence must find its way in a world (ordained by God) that is neither wholly knowable nor controllable.

Here open theism can make a virtue out of a necessity. A world characterized by creaturely autonomy and indeterminacy is part of the divine design. In the act of creation, God lets the world be. In this context, the concept of *kenosis* is sometimes employed. In conferring freedom and openness upon an evolving world, God resolves not to determine everything that happens by an act of primal will. There is a stepping back from a maximal providence that decrees each event. Yet, for the open theist, this does not signal a reversion to deism. God remains deeply involved in the life of the world but in modes of action that respect the conditions of creation. Hence instead of determinism, there is influence, interaction, improvisation, and other forms of divine activity that are intended to partner creatures rather than to control them. It is also argued that this makes better sense of the Bible, divine suffering, and the lives of the faithful. God is depicted in the stories of Scripture as engaging in multiple forms of interaction with God's people. Some biblical scholars have inclined to this approach, recognizing that it captures the more relational and anthropopathic imagery of Scripture than classical theism does.[20] And in the practice of petitionary prayer, we assume that we make requests of God, seek guidance and inspiration, and orient ourselves under God's direction toward the future.[21] To present this as the unfolding of what is already decreed

---

18. Lucas, *Freedom and Grace*, 39.

19. Richard Swinburne, *Providence and the Problem of Evil* (Oxford: Clarendon, 1998), 133.

20. Terence Fretheim, *God and World in the Old Testament: A Relational Theology of Creation* (Nashville: Abingdon, 2005).

21. Terrance Tiessen, *Providence & Prayer: How Does God Work in the World?* (Downer's Grove: InterVarsity Press, 2000).

and fixed in every detail seems to make a charade of our lives as we move into the future. As an accompaniment to the divine involvement in creation, the doctrine of God's timelessness is also abandoned in favor of a temporal God who can work in, with and through the creation. Finally, in its eschatological focus, open theism seeks to avoid the apparent unfairness of predestined outcomes by positing a salvation that is the result of our free assent to the work of God's grace in our lives. What is on offer here is not so much the revisioning of divine providence but a different theological scheme.

Though it reflects multiple historical and contemporary influences, much notable work in open theism has originated from with analytic philosophy of religion.[22] At the same time, its exponents have typically sought to distance themselves from process thought which is generally adjudged more heterodox in its doctrinal revisionism. Within open theism, there remains a strong account of divine action, of creation out of nothing, and a robust eschatology. In relation to theodicy, it offers some possible gains. Evil is the necessary by-product of a creation that possesses the stability and law-like structure necessary for creatures to exercise their freedom responsibly. We need a predictable and not wholly pliable world in which to grow and develop. The possibilities of sin and accident cannot be excluded from such a creation. How far this can be pressed into a theodicy is not always clear, but most open theists seem to assume that this is a better response to the problem of evil than anything that is available on the classical account.[23]

Open theism has produced an intense and frequently hostile debate that has sometimes resulted in excommunication from Evangelical circles, though patient dialogue has also proved possible.[24] Leaving aside its obvious departure from key elements of the classical tradition, we can identify the following problems. If God lacks complete foreknowledge of human choices, in what ways can providence be effectively exercised? Here the open theist can claim that God knows a great deal about the future by virtue of an awareness of antecedent conditions, of causal regularities and of human character. Although this does not amount to full omniscience in the traditional sense, God has sufficient knowledge of the world to influence it effectively. This seems about right, though when pressed it might slide in either of two directions. If God knows everything about us and is only rarely surprised by our free choices, then the overall position is not much different from the classical view with respect to the exercise of providence. In addition, it can be argued that divine permission and divine willing must be closely connected to the extent that what God permits are circumstances that God does not prevent. Here some form of divine concurrence and double agency begins to re-emerge

---

22. Hasker, *Providence, Evil and the Openness of God*; John Sanders, *The God Who Risks: A Theology of Providence* (Downer's Grove: InterVarsity Press, 1998).

23. Thomas J. Oord, *The Uncontrolling Love of God: An Open and Relational Account of Providence* (Downer's Grove: InterVarsity Press, 2016).

24. Christopher A. Hall and John Sanders, *Does God Have a Future? A Debate on Divine Providence* (Grand Rapids: Baker, 2003).

though there may be ways in which this can be distinguished from the classical view.[25] Yet, on this construction, the differences appear less stark. Alternatively, if God's foreknowledge is significantly curtailed by the openness of the future, then we might ask how much control can God really exercise, particularly if God is ontologically bound by kenotic constraints?[26] Might God in the end be powerless to realize God's primary intention? This is probably the most unnerving feature of open theism for its critics. Instead of affirming key aspects of faith and trust in God, it seems to undermine these by weakening God's capacities and generating human anxiety as to the eventual future. Can we really be sure that all will be well, if the conditions governing God's action are restricted in this way? Coupled with its sharp departure from a centuries-old tradition of providential theology, the claims of open theism appear too disconcerting for its critics. Some have argued in this context that a slide toward a more radical process theology is all but inevitable within this paradigm. And, from a more theological perspective, one might wonder whether its model of a divine–human partnership is too symmetrical, perhaps even anthropomorphic, thus threatening the core conviction that we are saved and transformed only by the mystery of an all-prevailing love. These debates will surely continue.

Conclusion

Several concluding observations are in order. First, the disputes between the classical, Molinist and openist positions may prevent a more nuanced theology of providence from emerging. The multiple forms of divine action in Scripture are not reducible to one single model, whether of control, of activating middle knowledge, or entering into a partnership with free creatures. In the interests of a more adequate account of the God–world relationship, the modes of God's action need to be narrated and clearly distinguished.[27] Accounts of divine action also suffer from an abstract quality or the search for the Grail of the "causal joint." Little attention is devoted to the actual uses of providentialism in the history of Christian theology and the practices of the church. W. J. Abraham has challenged this narrowing of focus by seeking a richer account more fully informed by doctrinal convictions that "reach for the full wealth of divine action showered upon us in the Son and in the Holy Spirit."[28]

Second, greater attention needs to be devoted to the question of how one can arrive at a lively belief in providence. In this context, Eleanore Stump has made a

---

25. David Fergusson, *The Providence of God: A Polyphonic Approach* (Cambridge: Cambridge University Press, 2018), 217–40.
26. See Oord, *The Uncontrolling Love of God*.
27. I seek to argue this in *The Providence of God*.
28. William J. Abraham, *Divine Agency and Divine Action: Systematic Theology*, Vol. III (Oxford: Oxford University Press, 2018), 155.

pertinent contribution in her identification of a personal knowledge that emerges only in encounter, relationship and a first-person narrative. This is set apart from the more standard and impersonal form of knowledge represented in analytic philosophy.[29] The personal knowledge that arises in relational contexts cannot be obtained except from its being lived and appropriated in a practical setting. This is of relevance to providentialism. Why would one believe in the efficacy of God's providence? It seems hard to deduce this on the basis of a more detached natural theology, though eighteenth-century versions of the design argument often attempted to do so. But as a practical orientation, informed by prayer and Scripture, it can make sense of one's life in relation to the world, to other people and to God. A conviction about providence can thus be represented as a way of responding to a narrative account of the world that sets our lives in a particular perspective and enables us to act accordingly. It must be inhabited and lived in order to be believed. John Cottingham writes of an "epistemology of involvement," while making it clear that this does not imply an uncritical submission that suspends rational objections.[30]

Finally, we should note that the role of analytic theology in these discussions is not easily delineated. This suggests that analytic techniques and approaches have been incorporated, often to good effect, in these debates, but that they cannot be isolated or pursued apart from other forms of inquiry. In particular, the need to engage with exegetical work and the history of dogma inevitably results in engagement with a range of different methodologies. This blending of skills and disciplinary strengths is to be welcomed.

---

29. Eleanore Stump, *Wandering in the Darkness: Narrative and the Problem of Suffering* (Oxford: Oxford University Press, 2010), 40–63.

30. John Cottingham, *Philosophy of Religion: Towards a More Humane Approach* (Cambridge: Cambridge University Press, 2014), 23.

Chapter 6

THE *IMAGO DEI*

The creation of human beings in the image of God is a theological platitude. A widespread and popular notion, its prevalence can be explained both by its early appearance in one of the best-known Scriptural texts and by its apparent ethical significance in explaining the sanctity of all human life. Reference to the *imago Dei* has become convenient shorthand in church reports and theological pronouncements concerning threats to personal dignity and the value placed on human life. But whereas its force is undoubtedly striking, its meaning is opaque. In what follows, I shall argue that the concept of the *imago Dei* is best interpreted as a signifier not of some ontological property or moral attribute that sets human animals apart from others, but as designating a complex identity that is established by a providential ordering of human life. As such, the *imago Dei* is not about any one thing, as if naming a mysterious anthropological ingredient which human beings possess but other creatures lack. To understand its meaning involves recourse to a more holistic description which includes functional, relational, and practical elements. In this way, a theological account of human existence requires to be narrated rather than defined by reference to a single property. This diffusive strategy, it will be further claimed, has the advantage of broadening the scope of theological anthropology to other sections of Scripture, and in ways that might prove fruitful for the dialogue with accounts of human evolution.

Imago Dei: *Rational Powers?*

For the most part, the Western theological tradition has identified the *imago Dei* with the possession of rational powers. These set human beings apart from other animals, placing us somewhere between angels and nonhuman animals in the chain of being. Augustine viewed the human mind as reflecting the divine Trinity in its self-conscious reflective activity. Anticipating the later *cogito* argument of Descartes, he writes, "We resemble the divine Trinity in that we exist; we know that we exist, and we are glad of this existence and this knowledge."[1] In knowing

---

1. Augustine, *City of God*, XI. 26, trans. Bettenson (Harmondsworth: Pelican, 1972). Philo appears to have been the first Jewish theologian to develop this identification of the

of our existence there is no possibility of deception, since this awareness of self does not depend on the truths of the bodily senses. Augustine acknowledges the very significant differences between God and creatures, and insists on our need of redemption. However, in the knowledge and gladness that we exist, there is nothing closer in all creation to God's own nature. This is made possible by a special act of creation in which God gives the human being a soul that is distinguished by its reason and intelligence. By virtue of this soul, human beings surpass all other creatures on the earth.[2]

Despite his Aristotelian leanings, Thomas Aquinas also attributes an intellectual potency to the human soul that enables it by divine grace to be raised to the beatific vision. Ordered in this way, the soul will naturally transform the conditions of its embodied existence. Human animals alone bear the image of God by virtue of possessing a rational soul.[3] This is true of all human beings, although they must be considered to bear the image of God less perfectly than the angels whose intellectual nature is superior. As elsewhere, his theology here closely follows Augustine. When dealing with Christology, Aquinas also speculates that, by virtue of the perfect ordering of his body by his soul, Jesus could have suffered no genetic disorder. Hence he would have been immune to leprosy or epilepsy, although he voluntarily submitted to such general deficiencies as hunger, thirst, and death.[4]

While generally eschewing speculative patterns of thought, John Calvin also locates the *imago Dei* in the distinctively spiritual and cognitive capacities of the soul.[5] Insisting that the *imago* is to be located in the soul rather than the body, Calvin states that it is immortal though created. His account of the image, however, is inflected with strong soteriological themes. After the Fall, nothing remains of the image of God except what is "confused, mutilated and disease-ridden."[6] A clearer understanding of the image is derived from Christ, our second Adam. In some measure, his image is evident in the lives of the sanctified, but its full luster will be displayed only in heaven. One consequence of this shift of perspective is that Calvin rejects Augustine's more speculative account of the human mind as an *imago trinitatis*, as also the attempt to see the divine image in human dominion of

---

imago with our spiritual capacities. For surveys of the history of interpretation see Claus Westermann, *Genesis 1–11*. (London: SPCK, 1984), 147–58, and Wentzel van Huyssteen, *Alone in the World? Human Uniqueness in Science and Theology* (Grand Rapids: Eerdmans, 2006), 111–62.

2. *City of God*, XII. 24.

3. Thomas Aquinas, *Summa Theologiae*, 1a.93.2, trans. Edmund Hill (Cambridge: Cambridge University Press, 2006).

4. Ibid., 3a.14.4

5. John Calvin, *Institutes*, trans. Ford Lewis Battles (Philadelphia: Westminster Press, 1960), I.15.3.

6. Ibid., I.15.4. For further discussion of Calvin's anthropology, see Charles Partee, *The Theology of John Calvin* (Louisville: Westminster John Knox Press, 2008), 80–105.

the world. The likeness of God lies within the internal good of the soul, largely lost in its post-lapsarian condition.

What is also apparent from a survey of the Western tradition is the way in which this anthropological tendency has been embedded in treatments of key doctrines such as sin, grace, the person and work of Christ, Mariology, and eschatology. A fuller treatment would require some exploration of these. Nevertheless, despite its scope and significance, this tradition of theological anthropology has been in difficulty since the nineteenth century. Attracting an array of criticisms, the traditional reading is now fractured for the following reasons.

The scientific account of human origins suggests a much greater continuity of human beings with other species. The earlier notion of a separate act of creation that individuates the human person by virtue of some distinct ontological property is harder to maintain, although revisionist theories have populated the literature. At any rate, belief in a first couple created *ab initio* in a state of moral, physical, and intellectual perfection is untenable given the findings of the natural sciences, at least since the time of Darwin. The conditions that govern suffering, disease, struggle, and death among species were prevalent long before the appearance of hominids. To attribute the causes of such hardship to the first human lapse is no longer credible, however attractive this may appear as an axiom of Christian theodicy. In much of the literature today, acceptance of this scientific claim is an unargued assumption. In other quarters, however, it is still fiercely resisted. This is less on account of its disturbance to the doctrine of creation and more through its wider ramifications for anthropology, ethics, and redemption.[7]

Recent exegesis of Genesis 1:26-27 has tended to reject the view that the *imago Dei* is to be identified with a distinctive noetic feature or single component of human existence. The holism of Hebrew anthropology renders this problematic, as is evident from the problem of translating any of the key nouns by the Greek or Latin equivalents of "soul" or "mind." Besides this, commentators have also pointed out that the notion of the image of God is largely absent from the Hebrew Bible outside the opening chapters of Genesis. Despite a cursory appearance in the first creation narrative, a disproportionate attention has been accorded this concept in Christian theology. Genesis 1:26-27 has been the focal point of discussion, rather than later references to the *imago* in Genesis or wider anthropological sections of the Hebrew Bible. Furthermore, we need to recognize that the dominant use of the *imago Dei* in the New Testament is in a Christological and soteriological context. As the true image of God, Christ is the one in whom we are to be recreated. In this respect, the *imago* is not so much protological as eschatological, thus constituting a divine promise rather than a description of our aboriginal existence.

This criticism of the tradition is also supported by trends in neuroscience that have increasingly revealed the ways in which the brain conditions the mental life

---

7. See for example Graeme Finlay, Stephen Lloyd, Stephen Pattemore, and David Swift, *Debating Darwin, Two Debates: Is Darwinism True and Does It Matter?* (Milton Keynes: Paternoster, 2009).

of the human person. While this does not refute the possibility of some form of mind–brain dualism, the significance of neurological events suggests that any top-down causal trajectory from mind to body requires to be qualified by recognition that the ways in which we think, speak, and act are significantly shaped by the assembly of the brain, itself the product of long processes of human evolution. Summarizing this recent consensus, Malcolm Jeeves has written, "One of the more consistent findings of research capitalizing on the convergence of experimental psychology, comparative neuropsychology, and brain imaging techniques has been how specific mental processes or even component parts of those processes appear to be tightly linked to particular regions or systems in the brain."[8]

A more philosophical line of criticism suggests that the Western stress on the soul or mind has produced a distorted account of how as human beings we understand ourselves. Fergus Kerr's work on *Theology after Wittgenstein* is an indispensable guide here with its compelling account of the distortion of personal existence as disembodied and deracinated in the writings of theologians from Augustine to Rahner. The ways in which meaning, language, and thought are embedded in physical and social settings have been occluded by accounts of the human person which privilege the possession of an immaterial soul or mind as the distinguishing characteristic of being human. The tradition has been haunted by the notion that the human being is really a "more or less deficient angel" (Cornelius Ernst) whose destiny is to transcend the physical limitation of other creatures.[9]

The anti-Cartesianism of thinkers such as Wittgenstein and Heidegger has been a powerful force in modern philosophy and has required a rethinking of many deeply held assumptions about human identity. A consequent stress on embodiedness and sociality is evident in much theological anthropology since the mid-twentieth century.[10] In some quarters, this has been conjoined with an attack on all forms of anthropocentrism in contemporary theology. The ontological privileging of the human person is viewed as ecologically problematic and neglectful of the moral status of other animals.

This criticism of the default setting of Western theology must also extend to its ethical outcomes. When the *imago Dei* and rationality are equated, there follows inevitably a tendency to view some human beings as more exemplary of the divine nature than others. Gender-biased assumptions about the relative distribution of rational powers are not hard to detect, these leading to the further erroneous claim that in some respects men rather than women more fully represent God. Against such reasoning of course stands the implicit equality of the sexes in Genesis 1:26-27.

---

8. Malcolm Jeeves, "Mind Reading and Soul Searching in the Twenty-first Century," in *What About the Soul? Neuroscience and Christian Anthropology*, ed. Joel Green (Nashville: Abingdon, 2004), 13–30 (17).

9. Cornelius Ernst, 'Introduction', *Theological Investigations*, Vol. 1, ed. Karl Rahner (London: Darton, Longman and Todd, 1961), xiii. Cited by Fergus Kerr, *Theology After Wittgenstein*, 2nd ed. (Oxford: Blackwell, 1997).

10. For example, John Macquarrie, *In Search of Humanity* (London: SCM, 1985).

But this tendentious outcome of the tradition reflects a strategy in which one element of our make-up is exclusively identified with the *imago*. If some are judged (implausibly) to possess it more than others, then an unacceptable hierarchy or even a binary distinction is established between those who are fully human and those who are not.[11] For this reason alone, we should avoid a simple equation of the *imago Dei* with our cognitive functions.

Alternative Interpretations of the imago Dei

More recent treatments of the *imago Dei* have reflected these concerns by offering alternative trajectories of interpretation. Relational accounts, to give one example, have sometimes appealed to the doctrine of the Trinity, the image of God being reflected in human interaction. Here the triune *perichoresis* of divine persons is mirrored by relations of freedom and love in society.[12] The shift in perspective has several undoubted advantages. In particular, it avoids the anthropological search for a single property or component of the human person by which he or she is distinguished from every creature, while at the same time breaking with the hierarchical connotations of the regnant tradition. Nevertheless, as an exercise in revisionism, this reading engenders two problems, neither of which is easily overcome. The first is its strained reading of the key Genesis texts. Even if later Christological texts might nudge us in this direction, there is little warrant in the Hebrew Bible for a Trinitarian or eschatological reading of Genesis 1:26-27. Its original setting in the creation theology of Genesis does not readily admit of such construction. For the Priestly writer of Genesis 1, the image is already a given that determines human existence; it is not something that is proleptically anticipated or realized only through eschatological fulfillment. We are already creatures made according to God's image.

Furthermore, this relational interpretation of the *imago* is beset with an abstractionism which makes it of limited anthropological significance. The function of Trinitarian categories in the early church was to maintain the unity and revelation of God in such a way that terms had to be reworked and pressed into service in hitherto unfamiliar ways. This was true *a fortiori* of the Greek concept of *hypostasis* which was used originally for the one divine being but later became the preferred term for the triune persons. In expressing a differentiated oneness, the

---

11. This theological tendency is criticized by Mary McClintock Fulkerson, "Contesting the Gendered Subject: A Feminist Account of the Imago Dei," in *Horizons in Feminist Theology: Identity, Tradition and Norms*, ed. Rebecca S. Chopp and Sheila Greeve Davaney (Minneapolis: Fortress, 1997), 99–115. See also Amos Yong, *Theology and Down Syndrome: Re-imagining Disability in Late Modernity* (Waco, TX: Baylor University Press, 2007), 155–92.

12. See for example Stanley Grenz, *The Social God and the Relational Self: A Trinitarian Theology of the Imago Dei* (Louisville: Westminster John Knox, 2001) and Alister McFadyen, "Imaging God: A Theological Answer to the Anthropological Question?" *Zygon* 47, no. 4 (2012): 918–33.

triunity of God had to be carefully distinguished from creaturely notions of both unity and plurality. The primary intention of the doctrine of the Trinity was never anthropological, as if the divine society were the archetype of a model human community. Hence the analogical move from the Trinity to creaturely relations *pace* Feuerbach could never be a simple one, especially as social models for God were generally combined with psychological ones in the classical accounts. Hence the term "person" could not be used univocally of divine and human persons.[13]

Relational accounts of the *imago Dei* have drawn upon the resources of personalist philosophy. Here the image is determined by the relationship of encounter and address established by God with human beings. In many ways, this makes sense of much of the subsequent narrative of Scripture with its account of a complex divine–human exchange. Human beings are determined by a relationship to God that is not restricted to an initial creative impulse or to the providential ordering of our anthropological condition. The divine–human relationship is one that continues throughout the stories of Scripture. This dramatic interaction is prefaced by the creation story, but its specification requires a history of address and response. In this way, relational accounts of the *imago Dei* are at least more adjacent to the Hebraic understanding of human beings under the rule of God than those that they succeeded. Personalist philosophy can capture elements of the divine–human relationship that ought to be preserved in any adequate account. Yet even this approach may be clouded by those earlier anthropologies that abstracted human beings from the earth and its other creatures. By isolating the divine–human encounter, such constructions tend to obscure the ways in which human beings belong to the natural order and are related to other creatures. Michael Welker points out that in more ecologically aware approaches personalist themes have been replaced or complemented by a stronger sense of the human being as belonging to the natural world. "The human being created in the image of God is to cultivate and preserve the community of creation and to exercise dominion in a certain form—namely, a form that bears responsibility for weaker creatures."[14]

This signifies a turn to more functional readings of the divine image in human persons, although even these now face the charge of an excessive anthropocentrism. The *imago Dei* is not so much identified with a defining component as that the whole person functions in distinctive ways under the rule of God. In some respects, this more modest reading of the *imago* is successful in making sense of its original context in the key Genesis passages while also being consistent with the psychosomatic unity of the self in both Hebrew and contemporary anthropology. Whether we read the verb *rada* in terms of dominion or stewardship, the proximity of this command to the *imago* verses confirms a functional reading. On the other

---

13. For criticism of social models of the Trinity see Karen Kilby, *God, Evil and the Limits of Theodicy* (London: T&T Clark, 2020), 5–16.

14. Michael Welker, "Creation and the Image of God: Their Understanding in Christian Tradition and the Biblical Grounds," *Journal of Ecumenical Studies* 34, no. 3 (1997): 436–48 (448).

hand, this simpler interpretation tends to shift the problems rather than resolve them. The issue of *which* functions are exclusively performed by human beings is not readily discerned in Genesis 1:26-27. And, if the *imago* texts no longer enable us to answer what the human being is or typically does, then we will have to find other ways of tackling this problem.

Toward a Diffused Interpretation

The divergent readings of the *imago Dei* in the reception history of Genesis 1:26-27 suggest that there is insufficient textual support fully to resolve these disputes. Moreover, the absence of any sustained reflection on the concept elsewhere in the Hebrew Bible may itself provide some scope for a more "diffused" reading of this text which in turn can generate other possibilities for theological anthropology. While maintaining elements of relational and functional readings, I shall attempt to sketch this rather different approach which seeks to make a virtue out of a necessity.

The Hebrew terms for image (*tselem*) and likeness (*demuth*) appear to draw upon notions from Egyptian and Mesopotamian culture in which a local ruler, viceroy, or physical statue can "image" the king.[15] Although this might imply the aforementioned functional reading of the *imago Dei* by which human beings exercise God's rule upon the earth, there are two reasons for hesitation. The first is that the image of God appears to be reflected by the whole human race rather than particular individuals deputed to exercise authority. Second, we know from elsewhere in Genesis that the divine presence is not mediated through human agents so much as displayed before human beings in a series of theophanies. The transcendence of God is signaled by an appearance *before* people rather than a presence mediated *through* them. In this respect, human beings do not have a sacramental significance in the Hebrew Bible, even though they fulfill a divine role in relation to others.

We should also consider the possibility that the inclusion of the key text in Genesis 1:26-27 may have been a later introduction in the P (Priestly) source to complement earlier appearances of the *imago Dei* in Genesis 5:1-3 with its bare reference to creation in the image of God, and Genesis 9:6 with its prohibition on the taking of human life on the ground that it is created in God's image.[16] These later instances are not so much explanatory of an initial citation in Genesis 1:26-27, but precursors to what became the more familiar adaptation of the concept. Genesis 5 might have been the earlier beginning of the P source later expanded by a further sequence of preceding events which set the concept in an originating context. According to this reading, Genesis 1 represents a new prologue that was

---

15. Here I am following Westermann, *Genesis 1-11*.
16. I am indebted here to A. Graeme Auld, "*Imago Dei* in Genesis: Speaking in the Image of God," *Expository Times* 116 (2005): 259-62.

placed at the front of a composite work and which offers a programmatic summary that anticipates later themes in P and non-P. The deliberate juxtaposition of image and likeness seems to confirm this more developed use of these related concepts. This, however, suggests that the *imago Dei* might be better understood as a marker or signifier of a history that will unfold, than a substantive notion that is central to Hebrew anthropology. What it signifies is that human beings have a central and distinctive place in the story that is about to be told. They are to become the object of divine address and encounter in a wide variety of ways, beginning in Genesis 2 but extending to the history of Abraham and his seed. The story to be narrated is of human beings and God, although other actors are also present—it is not only the God–human relationship that is constituted by the creation of heaven and earth. While the *imago Dei* here signifies our identity as God's covenant partners, what this entails will require subsequent narration in the stories of Noah, Abraham et al.

This reading of the text follows Westermann's analysis in important respects. It defuses the issue of what anthropological component the *imago* specifies while in turn diverting attention to other portions of the Hebrew Bible. One might see the text as indicating in a preliminary way *who* human beings are—they are situated within the created order in a particular way. As the addressees of God, a response is required of them. Beyond this, however, the text does not really resolve speculation as to *what* human beings are—the lack of interest in the *imago Dei* after the opening chapters of Genesis indicates that it is not the core concept of a developed anthropology, nor should it be.[17] We should abandon the search for that elusive ingredient that once located would explain how and in what ways human beings are distinguished from all other earthly creatures. To transpose Tyrrell's famous remark about the historical Jesus, the quest for the original *imago Dei* may offer little more than the reflection of those who gazed into the deep well of Scripture.

In pointing to a universal story of encounter between God and human beings, this account of the *imago* has an anticipatory significance. Instead of an ontology of the human, it heralds a plotline that will now unfold. Within this story, other creatures can also take their appointed place, hence avoiding any sense that a theological account of the human as created in the image and likeness of God must lead to the denigration of nonhuman creatures.[18] As a somewhat deflated reading of the Genesis text, which in the past has suffered from an over-determination of meaning, it can also facilitate the more eschatologically oriented use of the concept in the New Testament. At least three New Testament passages (Colossians 1:15; 1 Corinthians 15:49; 2 Corinthians 4:4; with Hebrews 1:3 as a functional equivalent)

---

17. Westermann also notes that this reading of the human being as addressee of God also avoids any collision with passages such as Isaiah 40:18ff., where God is incomparable and not to be depicted in images. *Genesis 1–11*, 158.

18. See Celia Deane-Drummond, "God Image and Likeness in Humans and Other Animals: Performative Soul-Making and Graced Nature," *Zygon* 47, no. 4 (2012): 934–48.

suggest that Christ is the true image (*eikon*) of God and that our destiny is to receive that image as we are raised to new life. This is a rather different employment of the *imago* concept in the context of our final fulfillment and needs to be recognized in this discrete and alternative sense, rather than attempting a Procrustean strategy of forcing different Scriptural usages into a single framework of meaning. In this latter sense, Jesus alone is truly the image of God; others become likewise by "imaging the image."[19] The gift is not bestowed originally but is given eschatologically. By connecting these somewhat equivocal uses of the *imago* to different settings in creation and Christology, we can also avoid the implication that redemption is the return of the human being to a perfect and aboriginal condition. Jesus does not restore what was lost in the Garden of Eden, so much as raise us to the estate that God intends, this being revealed proleptically in his resurrection from the dead. Recognition of these different usages of the concept might also spare us from rather sterile Protestant disputes about whether the image of God is lost at the Fall or merely defaced in some way before being restored. In addition, an uncoupling of the different senses of the *imago Dei* may have the added advantage of showing why the historical Jesus does not require the historical Adam. There is no exact parallelism between, on the one side what the image of God is and how it was lost and on the other, the way in which it will be regained.

Excursus—Kelsey on the imago Dei

David H. Kelsey's criticisms of the uses of the *imago Dei* as a systematic and organizing principle in Christian theology are instructive.[20] His contention is that the largely incommensurable uses of the concept in the Old and New Testaments prevent any single exegetical pattern emerging. An acute difficulty concerns the idea that the *imago* is in some sense given through Christ, either sacramentally (now) or eschatologically (in the future). This prevents the concept being deployed to describe human life more generally, which is precisely the direction in which Genesis 1 points. Theological attempts to unite these different exegetical uses generate further difficulties when the *imago* is held to be defaced or lost at the Fall, again a view for which there is no exegetical support in the Hebrew Bible. Human beings, whether pre-lapsarian or post-lapsarian, inside or outside the church, are made in the image and likeness of God. The universalism of *Genesis* seems unequivocal here.

By contrast, a schematizing of the different Scriptural uses of the *imago Dei* is attempted in Moltmann's *God in Creation*, where he stratifies the three notions

---

19. David Kelsey, *Eccentric Existence: A Theological Anthropology*, Vol. 2 (Louisville: Westminster John Knox Press, 2010), 1008ff.

20. Ibid., 895–1051.

of the created image, the messianic image and the eschatological image.²¹ This sequencing is attractive and Moltmann displays a sure-footed touch in arguing initially that the created image concerns not some element of our human constitution but the whole of human existence. Yet his attempt to integrate all three notions into a drama of sin, redemption, and eschatological fulfillment runs into trouble with the introduction of a distinction between our relating to God and God's relating to us. The former is lost through sin, but the latter remains so that our created existence continues to be determined by God's love. This then explains how and why the human agent can be considered *simul iustus et peccator*. But this move, while working within its own parameters, fails to connect with the ways in which Moltmann has already characterized human existence as representing God in all its facets. In addressing quite different questions—Kelsey describes these as *what* and *who* questions—Moltmann imposes upon the Scriptural material a single organizational pattern which it lacks. This may explain why Kelsey, by contrast, deliberately delays any sustained discussion of the *imago* until the final codas of his lengthy two-volume study of theological anthropology.

Kelsey's solution is largely to reserve the use of the *imago Dei* for its Christological and eschatological contexts. This enables us to answer the *who* and *how* questions of human existence but not the rather different question of *what* is a human being, a question that belongs more to the plotline of creation than to the stories of redemption and eschatological consummation. While these stories are integrated in important ways, they remain different narratives which are more clearly and unsystematically separate than in previous theological projects. As a result, the *imago Dei* does little work in the context of his theology of creation, Kelsey preferring to draw upon a wider range of Scriptural resources, particularly those from the Wisdom tradition. The attractions of this approach are that its separation of discourses alongside his careful exegesis of Scriptural passages produces a more supple and differentiated account of theological anthropology that avoids the Procrustean nature of earlier attempts to systematize theology around the *imago* concept. In this respect, it is a deflationary strategy that produces some real gains, not least in avoiding the over-determination of the Genesis 1–3 narratives in Christian theology.

But whether the concept of the *imago Dei* can be withdrawn altogether from creation theology is less clear. Its early appearance in the Hebrew Bible has ensured its place in important anthropological and ethical settings throughout the history of the church. The discarding of the notion in this context is hard to accomplish, given the ease with which it can be used to express key ideas in Jewish and Christian thought. My own proposal, therefore, seeks to retain it in the context of describing human existence everywhere and not only *en Christo*, but only as a theme which permits different and occasional variations, each of these requiring to be situated in wider narrative accounts of what it is to be human and of ways in which our

---

21. Jürgen Moltmann, *God in Creation: An Ecological Doctrine of Creation* (London: SCM, 1985), 215–43.

lives are multiply characterized as embodied, mortal, social, responsible, fragile, blessed, and many other things beside. What the *imago* concept does not enable is some shortcut to identifying a single property or function that differentiates us from other animals and which may be considered godlike in some privileged sense. Nor is it a moral concept which might suggest human virtue or justification in the presence of God. Here again it cannot be seen as denoting a single attribute or component which signals an ontological or ethical affinity with the divine nature. Within the theology of creation, our being made according to the divine image simply points to those forms and conditions of life that characterize human life in community. These become the locus of subsequent divine address and interaction in Scripture, the setting for a drama that enfolds, including the form that the Incarnation takes. But to overload the concept of the *imago Dei* is a mistake within the theology of creation, not only in relation to the exegetical adequacy of such a move but also as a result of the significant distortions that can arise from deploying it as an organizing concept. For this critical insight into a long theological tradition, we are indebted to Kelsey's groundbreaking study.

The imago Dei *and Human Evolution*

Despite Kelsey's strictures on the *imago Dei* in its setting in Genesis 1, the concept still serves a theological purpose. Its positioning of the concept at the front of the Bible enables us to develop some important aspects of biblical anthropology that may prove significant in a dialogue with theories of human evolution. For example, a salient feature of Genesis 1:26-27 is its universal scope. We cannot think of any human being as not bearing the image of God. To this extent, the use of the *imago Dei* can be ethically significant as it has been in Judaism with its less speculative tendencies.[22] Since the whole human race is created in the image of God, this determination is restricted neither to pre-lapsarian Adam nor to the covenant people. To this extent, we must assume that all human beings are addressed by God before and beyond the appearance of Abraham in the history of Israel. In some sense, human existence must always be understood as a religious existence, a theme taken up later in the Hebrew Bible where peoples other than Israel are positively related to God's providential action. Similarly, the pre-history of Genesis 1–11 points to ways in which all the peoples of the earth are theologically determined. Reminders of this are offered elsewhere in the canon, for example in the healing of Naaman the Syrian, and in Jonah's mission to Nineveh.

Other significant aspects of human existence seem to be assumed in the subsequent unfolding of the human relationship with God. The divine encounter is a social event. Peoples are collectively addressed by God and are the subject of divine promise, even when this is communicated to representative individuals,

---

22. See Alexander Altmann, "*Homo Imago Dei* in Jewish and Christian Theology," *Journal of Religion* 48, no. 3 (1968): 235–59.

such as the patriarchs, Moses, and the prophets. The encounter is also ethical in that the demands, judgments, and gifts of God require concepts of mercy, kindness, and justice. These are received by embodied agents who are rooted in the natural world. While they may be only a little lower than the angels in terms of their relationship to God and their appointed place in the cosmos (Psalm 8), in their transience and frailty they are also creatures of dust (Psalms 90 and 144).

Yet it is not only within social groups that human beings are addressed but also as persons. While there is a danger of reading into the text later assumptions, it seems that the address of God establishes a set of relations with embodied humans that are marked by freedom, interaction, responsiveness, dependence, and love. These determine the bonds between God and human beings, human beings and the creation, and human beings themselves.[23] This again militates against an essentialism in which only some are paradigmatically human. By being born of a woman, we are all set within a nexus of flesh and blood relations that characterize human existence under God.

Kelsey has also drawn attention to the proximate contexts in which human beings know and serve God, in particular the wisdom literature, which underscores the importance of the quotidian as ordained by God.[24] Often these proximate contexts have been ignored by theologies which move too swiftly to the story of redemption, as if Genesis 1-2 were merely the prelude to Genesis 3 and the story of a subsequent rescue. This has led to the constriction of anthropology in Christian theology whereby human existence is too exclusively characterized by its existential plight for which redemption in Christ and the ministrations of the church were offered as the remedy. By contrast, Kelsey wishes to establish distinct though interrelated plotlines for creation, salvation, and eschatological consummation in order that each displays its own integrity. This strategy enables him to say more about God's good creation and the place of human beings in it than is generally achieved in a preface to the doctrine of salvation. Our imaging of God in everyday existence is not confined to some religious province of life but is expressed in a multitude of human practices, institutions, and forms of life. As a teacher of wisdom, Jesus himself points to the presence of God in the ordering of everyday life. His commendation of the birds of the air and the lilies of the field recalls the providential order of the natural world celebrated in the wisdom literature. Here the warning of Bonhoeffer remains salutary:

> Only when one knows that the name of God may not be uttered may one sometimes speak the name of Jesus Christ. Only when one loves life and the earth so much that with it everything seems to be lost and at its end may one believe in the resurrection of the dead and a new world. Only when one accepts the law of God as binding for oneself may one perhaps sometimes speak of grace. And

---

23. This is developed by Terence Fretheim, *God and World in the Old Testament: A Relational Theology of Creation* (Nashville: Abingdon, 2005).

24. Kelsey, *Eccentric Existence*, 190ff.

only when the wrath and vengeance of God against God's enemies are allowed to stand can something of forgiveness and the love of enemies touch our hearts. Whoever wishes to be and perceive things too quickly in a New Testament way is to my mind no Christian.[25]

One of several gains here is a providential account of human existence not directly touched by the salvation history recorded in Scripture. This is important given our knowledge of how long human beings have inhabited the earth prior to the recorded history of the Bible. All people image God and can do so in mundane ways that relate to the typical features of embodied social existence. For the wisdom literature, everyday existence does not require to be characterized as fallen from an initial state of perfection and thus in need of recovery and restoration. As finite, it is fragile, vulnerable, and ambiguous but this is part and parcel of the created world that is declared good. Life is marked by typical practices, these including farming, manufacturing, managing households, child rearing, education, government, and science. Within this more capacious creation theology, there is scope for accommodating under divine providence long stretches of history and pre-history through which these practices developed. An account of creation that includes an anthropology of the everyday may be better placed to understand the evolutionary history of human beings as expressive of the wisdom and delight of God in creatures, especially human ones, than a theological anthropology which moves too rapidly from the definition of the *imago Dei* to the story of fall and redemption. When we then speak of redemption in Christ and eschatological hope, our approach can reflect the broad scope development of these wider themes in creation theology.

Conclusion

The concept of the *imago Dei* requires to be treated in this diffuse manner, rather than continuing the search for a single ingredient of which it is the referent. To this extent, the theology of creation just about manages without the idea of the *imago*, although its prominence in the tradition together with its place in the opening chapter of the Bible instead necessitates some repair work. A simple discarding of the concept under a "theology of the first article" would be prone to misunderstanding, as if tantamount to the affirmation that human beings were *not* created or sustained according to the image of God.

The *imago Dei* names us as God's creatures of flesh and blood, distinguished from, yet related to the other creatures of the earth in our ways of life. Yet it must do this as a signifier of the human condition before God rather than the specification of some elusive ontological or ethical ingredient. It is a mistake to assume that

---

25. Dietrich Bonhoeffer, *Letters and Papers from Prison*, ed. John W. de Gruchy, trans. Christian Gremmels et al. *Collected Works*, Vol. 8 (Minneapolis: Fortress Press, 2010), 213.

the failure of philosophers and theologians in the past to identify a key element corresponding to the *imago* could be remedied by modern science. To describe the ways in which God's wisdom is manifested in the divine image requires more patient and mundane description of human life drawn from other sections of the Hebrew Bible. This in turn can be complemented by the more eschatological sense in which Christ is the image of the people we shall become. In following this route deeper into the traditions of Scripture, we may discover resources that will enrich conversation with other fields of inquiry, while avoiding some of the pitfalls of the past.

Chapter 7

THE LAST JUDGMENT

Introduction

The essential task of Christian dogmatics, whether in postmodernity, modernity or premodernity, is one of patient, respectful attentiveness to the biblical testimony, allowing itself to be shaped by the hope which is there expressed, and quietly letting that hope disturb, shatter and re-make human thought and action.[1]

Throughout his writings, John Webster has reminded us of the need to articulate the teachings of the church in ways that are responsible in our present context, yet without enslavement to intellectual fashions. The last judgment seems a most unpromising locus for consideration today, a quaint item of mythology that evokes embarrassment or some nervous humor. In preparing a lecture on the topic, I was met by predictable responses of surprise and bewilderment on the part of colleagues. Their reaction reveals how the traditional four last things—resurrection, judgment, heaven, and hell—have fallen out of theological fashion. Christoph Schwöbel has noted that despite the twentieth-century insistence upon the eschatological character of theological speech, very little attention had been devoted to the specifics of the last things.[2] The focus has shifted from the *eschata* to the *eschaton* considered as the ultimate reality. Indeed the strange reticence in many modern theologians about the life to come, in particular the possibility of personal fulfillment, has attracted some criticism. Robert Jenson, for example, claims that the fundamental narrative shape of Jewish and Christian faith is disrupted if we cannot speak of a future ending, in both senses of "end"—the completion of a sequence and the fulfillment of a purpose. The

---

1. John Webster, "Eschatology, Anthropology and Postmodernity," *International Journal of Systematic Theology* 2, no. 1 (2000): 14.
2. Christoph Schwöbel, "Last Things First? The Century of Eschatology in Retrospect," in *The Future as God's Gift: Explorations in Christian Eschatology*, ed. David Fergusson and Marcel Sarot (Edinburgh: T&T Clark, 2000), 226.

Christian life seeks closure, Jenson insists, and only in God can closure be found.[3] Nevertheless, recent literature in both biblical studies and theology does reveal continued interest in the theme of the last judgment—perhaps more than we might suspect—and even some ecumenical convergence of approach. Occupying a significant place in the fabric of traditional Christian belief, this theme belongs to Scripture and the creeds.

In what follows, I shall argue toward the following points. First, the disparate and mythological Scriptural materials need to be organized around a central and controlling theme. Second, the excessive fear and gloom surrounding popular portrayals of the last judgment need to be overcome. The last judgment should be viewed as a bright rather than a dark mystery. Third, the focus of a theology of the last judgment should be on the person and work of the judge, namely Jesus Christ. This will ensure that the end is the completion of a work already determined in his cross and resurrection. Fourth, the last judgment is an element of the restoration of God's good creation. As such, it is an integral feature of Christian faith and hope for this world. Hope is not interrupted but fulfilled; hence, it must spill over from this world to the next, however mysterious that notion may be.

Scriptural Origins

The theology of the last judgment can draw upon significant, if disparate, Scriptural resources and, to a significant extent, the traditions of medieval art. The notion of a final and decisive judgment at the end of history has its roots in Hebrew traditions about the coming of God to execute justice for the righteous and the wicked. This governs both the life of individuals but also the corporate existence of Israel and the other nations (e.g., Psalm 1:5-6; Psalm 96:13). "The day of the Lord" is a recurrent expression among the prophets, usually referring to a time of punishment for Judah, Israel, and the other nations (e.g., Obadiah 15; Amos 5:18-20; Zephaniah 1:14-18). Other similar expressions ("on that day," "the days are coming when," "then") include the same reference to a single and definitive exercise of God's judgment. A few passages, perhaps of later origin, suggest an act of judgment and redemption beyond this world (Job 19:25-27; Isaiah 26:19; Ezekiel 37:1-14); in some cases, writers look to a final act of separation in which the righteous are rewarded and the wicked punished (e.g., Isaiah 66:24; Daniel 12:1-3). In the inter-testamental literature, an eschatological day of judgment becomes more pronounced (Wisdom of Solomon 3:18; 2 Esdras 14:34-35). This provided a set of resources that were adapted by the New Testament writers.

---

3. Robert Jenson, *Systematic Theology*, Vol. 2 (New York: Oxford University Press, 1999), 336.

In the Synoptic Gospels, Jesus speaks of the coming judgment, particularly in the apocalyptic sayings of Mark 13 and parallels. The term "day of judgment" is more characteristic of Matthew (10:15; 11:22; 12:36) and is given imaginative force by the Parable of the Sheep and Goats (25:31-46). While the notion of judgment is also present in the Fourth Gospel, there is a stronger emphasis upon Jesus himself as judge and the sense that judgment is already taking place with his appearance. "Now is the judgement of this world" (John 12:31). A future day of judgment is frequently cited elsewhere in the New Testament (e.g., 2 Peter 2:9; 1 John 4:17; Acts 17:31) while Paul refers to this as "the day of our Lord Jesus Christ" (1 Corinthians 1:8). The agents of judgment can include God, Christ, and even occasionally the saints (1 Corinthians 6:2). A condition of receiving a happy verdict appears to be conditional upon one's practice (Galatians 5:16-21), this leaving a subsequent challenge as to how it is to be squared with the strong Pauline account of grace. This is especially acute in Revelation 20:11-15, where the accent is on a final separation that is determined by one's own deeds. "And the dead were judged according to their works, as recorded in the books" (Revelation 20:12). One possible hint of a resolution of the tension between judgment and grace is at 1 Corinthians 3:10-15, where judgement has a purgative quality; God's judgment saves us from our sins, as if through burning these. One does not need to affirm a doctrine of purgatory to read the text in this way. While most passages appear to suggest a final comprehensive act of judgment that embraces all history—Augustine would later imagine how this is possible for the divine mind—other New Testament passages point instead towards a judgment on each individual immediately upon death (e.g., Luke 16:19-31; Hebrews 9:27). This timetable clash generates some theological puzzles. Can there be judgment for each of us at death, ahead of a final judgment at the end of time? Or are these continuous in some way? If my eternal destiny is already settled at death, does this make the last judgment redundant? And can there be justice or fulfillment for any one individual, apart from the nexus of relationships in which she or he is involved across space and time with other people and the wider created order? Further eschatological problems are not far away, including those that involve the notion of an intermediate state or soul sleep.

The Medieval Vision

However we resolve the problems set by the plurality of Scriptural references to the last judgment, it is clear that many of these passages exercised a strong hold upon the Christian imagination, particularly through the middle ages. A few examples must suffice here. The thirteenth-century poem the *Dies Irae* became a sequence during the liturgy of the dead and is still heard at the performance of many Requiem Masses (e.g., those of Mozart and Verdi). It has been described as the "most representative, the most culturally influential, and hence the most famous poem of the Latin middle ages."[4] The poem's stress is upon divine wrath, this being intended to awaken fear, trembling, and penitence among those who recite or hear it.

Dies iræ! Dies illa	Day of wrath, that day of burning
Solvet sæclum in favilla:	Seer and Sibyl speak concerning
Teste David cum Sibylla!	All the world to ashes turning![5]

Much of the imagery of the *Dies Irae* is drawn from Vulgate passages such as Zephaniah 1:15-16, Matthew's Parable of the Sheep and the Goats, and the "open book" of Revelation 20:11-15. This collation of Scriptural resources concentrates on individual judgment, the exposure of one's life in its totality and the threat of eternal perdition. It continues to haunt the Western mind, despite its being withdrawn from the post-Vatican II liturgy for the burial of the dead in favor of more positive and hopeful themes.

This graphic portrayal of the last judgment in the Middle Ages is also evident in the theology of Thomas Aquinas. Although his *Summa Theologiae* remained incomplete and without an eschatological conclusion, the later supplement, based on his earlier commentary on Lombard, together with material from the *Summa Contra Gentiles*, gives a clear impression of how he understood the matter. A great conflagration will occur with the cessation of solar and planetary movements. All will be consumed by the fire before being raised to judgment (cf. 2 Peter 3:10). The most likely location for a general judgment will be in the valley of Josaphat by Mount Olivet—the site of the Ascension. The risen dead will finally be separated into the blessed and the damned (apart from those who remain in limbo), their resurrected bodies accentuating the bliss or misery of their final condition. Much of this follows the interpretation of Scripture in Augustine's *City of God*, Book 20. For Augustine and Aquinas, the tension between an immediate judgment at death and a final judgment at the end of history is resolved with the notion of a double judgment. Our eternal destiny is fixed at death and remains unalterable. This is held in conjunction with the view that a time of purgation may be required between our death and postmortem bliss. But since the effects of our lives continue beyond the time of our dying, it is necessary for there to be a final judgment. This confirms the earlier judgment while also providing a fuller ordering of all that we have done. The first judgment determines our souls, while the final judgment determines us as resurrected bodies. But the verdicts are essentially the same; we are either saved or damned, and for identical reasons. Hence there are not so much two separate judgments but a double judgment continuous and consistent in every aspect.

---

4. Quote by Jürgen Moltmann, *The Coming of God* (London: SCM, 1996), 236.
5. Abraham Coles, *"Dies Irae" in Thirteen Original Versions* (New York: D. Appleton, 1864), 1 & 4.

Aquinas posits a real continuity between this world and the age of the resurrection. Our bodies that rise are the same in nature with all their essential parts. We are risen as if at the height of our youth, since this represents the fullest realization of our creaturely potential. He appears to identify this with the age of Christ when crucified.[6] In a glorified and embodied state, we enjoy the vision of God. By contrast, the resurrection of the damned merely intensifies their misery by inflicting sensible pains upon a body that cannot dissolve. Unlike Aquinas, Augustine dwells at some length upon the condition of the damned, comparing their state to captives who suffer intense bodily torture while yet continuing to survive. "But in the life hereafter the soul and the body will be connected in such a way that just as the bond that links them will not be unloosed by any passage of time, however long, so it will not be able to be broken by any pain."[7]

Although some variations on the theme of the last judgment are evident, this medieval vision is found in much of the artwork adorning churches. For largely illiterate populations, it was their primary access to the teaching of the church. Most famous is the later Renaissance work of Michelangelo in the Sistine Chapel, completed in 1541. The nudity and other graphic details reveal this to be a very human painting, characteristic of the Renaissance. Even the angels appear as purified humans, rather than otherworldly visitors. Its distinctive features are now widely celebrated by tourist guides. The pope's master of ceremonies, Biagio da Cesena, objected so much to the profanity of the images in the chapel that Michelangelo depicted him as an ugly Minos, judge of the underworld, with donkey ears and a snake biting his genitalia. On complaining to his employer, da Cesena was told that the pope's authority did not extend to hell.

While reflecting the medieval vision of the last judgment, Michelangelo's work is also classical in its portrayal of Greco-Roman conceptions of Hades and the ferryman, Charon, at the Styx. This may reflect the influence of Dante, whose work Michelangelo was believed to have studied extensively. Moreover, its overriding conception is circular rather than the more traditional layered depiction of heaven, earth, and hell, as in the orderly ranks of Giotto's *Last Judgment* (1306) in the Arena Chapel in Padua. At the center of the fresco in the Sistine Chapel is the figure of Christ, giving rise to discussions about whether this image reflects the new cosmology of Copernicus. What is most striking about Christ as judge is his apparent serenity. His raised hand could be interpreted as either offering a blessing or a rejection. There are not two faces of wrath and mercy, but a single, yet ambivalent, disposition. One line of interpretation suggests that this too derives from Dante. The final outcome of our lives is the result of choices that we have already made. So the role of Christ as judge is merely to confirm and expose what has been determined by our individual responses to the love of God. The horror

---

6. Thomas Aquinas, *Summa Contra Gentiles*, trans. Charles J. O'Neil (Notre Dame: University of Notre Dame Press, 1975), IV. 88, 329.

7. Augustine, *City of God*, Book 21, Chapter 3. Citation from David Knowles translation (Harmondsworth: Penguin, 1972), 966.

of the damned is in part the result of their being awakened to the truth about the lives they have led. Christ, as the embodiment of divine love and beauty, produces either attraction or repulsion among the living. But judgment is less the sudden intervention of God and more the inevitable outcome of what we have become.

> He is not the terrible judge, for there is no act of judgment. There is only the terrible drama of human choice. The Christ is the focus of the whole movement of the Chapel. He is the fundamental encounter with the reality of the sacred, the impossible paradox of the God-man, the desire and the terror, the beauty and the horror, the terrible contradictions that define humans in their response to it.[8]

The Reformation

With its focus on a Christ, now young, muscular, and beautiful, Michelangelo's fresco points beyond the medieval tradition even while participating in it. Attention is devoted less to the Scriptural record about the specific details of the last judgment, and more to the figure of the judge himself. In a very different way, the Reformation also provided this shift of focus with its concentration on the character of the one who will come again to judge the living and the dead. The last judgment is an important theme particularly for Luther, although this is sometimes noticed more by his biographers than his theological commentators.[9] According to Althaus, Luther's attention to the Last Day is accentuated by his tendency to think of an intermediate state of soul sleep from which we arise.[10] For each of us, this appears to happen immediately after death, just as if we had fallen asleep for only a moment. "A thousand years will seem as though you have slept a half an hour. As we do not know how long we are sleeping if we do not hear the clock striking during the night, so in death a thousand years will pass away still more rapidly. Before we shall be able to look around, we shall be beautiful angels."[11] But it happens for us all together, as we are awakened at the Last Day. So unlike the

---

8. John W. Dixon, *The Christ of Michelangelo: An Essay on Carnal Spirituality* (University of South Florida: Scholars Press, 1994), 75.

9. See Johann Heinz, "The 'Summer That Will Never End': Luther's Longing for the 'Dear Last Day' in His Sermon on Luke 21 (1531)," *Andrews University Studies* 23, no. 2 (1985): 181–6.

10. Paul Althaus, *Theology of Martin Luther* (Philadelphia: Fortress, 1966), 414ff. But against this interpretation, the consistency of Luther on this matter is questioned by Bernhard Lohse, *Martin Luther's Theology: Its Historical and Systematic Development* (Edinburgh: T&T Clark, 1999), 325ff. For further exploration of the divergence among the early Reformers on the intermediate state see Gergely Juhasz, "Resurrection or Immortality of the Soul?: A Dilemma of Reformation Exegesis," *Reformation* 14 (2009): 1–47.

11. From a sermon on Matthew 9, preached on November 10, 1532, the 24th Sunday after Trinity. See Martin Luther, *Werke: Kritische Gesamtausgabe* (Weimar: H. Böhlau, 1883),

double judgment of Augustine and Aquinas, there is a stronger accent on the final judgment in Luther.

In other respects, Luther's writings also represent a break with the medieval tradition. No longer an event for each individual, the last judgment heralds the renewal of God's creation. A corporate and cosmic event inaugurates the kingdom of God in all its fullness. For Luther, the resurrection of the dead is the final triumph of the gospel over the law of death; in this regard, his eschatology is not an appendix but a controlling theme of his theology. The hope of resurrection circumscribes our fear of death with a greater hope. He inverts Psalm 90—we say in the midst of life we are surrounded by death, but God says, no, in the midst of death we are surrounded by life.[12] For this reason, the Last Day is to be welcomed and longed for by Christians everywhere. It is the end of our tribulation and the commencement of God's new creation. So Luther could write to his wife of that "dear Last Day" (*lieber jüngster Tag*), a beloved day for which he longed, rather than the end he had feared in former times.[13]

Whether this eschatological orientation of Luther's theology was maintained in subsequent Reformation theology is doubtful. Calvin appears to have a more traditional approach which recalls much of the earlier medieval tradition. His insistence upon the immortality of the soul together with his early denial of soul sleep seems to place him closer to Aquinas than to Luther in key respects. While affirming the doctrine of the resurrection of the body in accordance with Scripture, Calvin also claims that the part of the self which bears the mark of the divine is immaterial and immortal, that is, the soul. Why else would Christ have said to the dying thief, "Today shalt thou be with me in paradise" (Luke 23:43)? For Calvin, the soul attains its final destiny at death, even though it awaits the resurrection of the body and the last judgment. Yet whether these add much to what has already been settled is less clear. The significance of the Last Day seems here diminished, a problem that is repeated by the *Westminster Confession* (1647) with its juxtaposition of the immortality of the soul and resurrection of the body, in a manner that conflates different anthropological and eschatological trajectories. Calvin himself appears content to sit with a kind of double judgment, with disembodied souls at rest awaiting a fuller glory that is promised them. But, unlike Luther, the day of resurrection seems to lack something of its momentous significance, despite Calvin's language of suspense. There remains an unresolved tension here.

---

349. The translation is borrowed from Althaus, *Theology of Martin Luther* (Philadelphia: Fortress, 1966), 416, note 52.

12. See Lohse, *Martin Luther's Theology*, 332.

13. Martin Luther, *Werke: Briefe*, 9: 175. See also Winfried Vogel, "The Eschatological Theology of Martin Luther: Part I Luther's Basic Concepts," *Andrews University Seminary Studies* 24, no. 3 (1986): 249–63. Vogel notes that the connotations of a fresh beginning in "jüngster Tag" are not readily captured in English (261).

Meanwhile, since Scripture everywhere bids us wait in expectation for Christ's coming, and defers until then the crown of glory, let us be content with the limits divinely set for us: namely, that the souls of the pious, having ended the toil of their warfare, enter into blessed rest, where in glad expectation they await the enjoyment of promised glory, and so all things are held in suspense until Christ the Redeemer appear.[14]

The Modern Era

When we move from the Reformation to the modern era, we encounter less discussion of the last judgment and some uncertainty on how this is to be handled. The causes of this are not difficult to identify, although each requires some qualification.

The shift of emphasis among Enlightenment thinkers to the providential action of God in this world led to a loss of focus on eschatological matters. Yet even among more theologically moderate writers of the eighteenth century, the hope of heaven and the fear of hell remain important for our ethical motivation. This is inflected in Kant's critical philosophy with his three postulates of practical reason, one of which is the hope of the *summum bonum*, a condition of life after death in which God ensures the coincidence of virtue with happiness. The morally regulative force of a final judgment is also stressed in his *Religion within the Limits of Reason Alone*. The prospect of having the details of one's life spread out before a judge is a useful image to maintain; its power to awaken conscience and to sustain our best efforts impressed Kant, as did the punitive force of hell. Similarly, Wittgenstein could cite the importance of the last judgment as providing a picture that organizes our lives. Believing in the last judgment, he argued, is not an empirical claim about what will happen when and where. "Here believing obviously plays much more this role: suppose we said that a certain picture might play the role of constantly admonishing me, or I always think of it. Here, an enormous difference would be between those people for whom the picture is constantly in the foreground, and the others who just didn't use it at all."[15]

A second difficulty is presented by the rise of biblical criticism which looks to the different *Sitze im Leben* and genres of the biblical texts, no longer seeking to harmonize these in a single narrative of the last judgment as Augustine and Aquinas had sought to do with their pre-critical hermeneutics. The resultant loss of confidence in a detailed eschatological story perhaps reflected some embarrassment with the naïve apocalyptic pictures of Scripture, prompting either their neglect or strategies of demythologization. Yet, as we noted earlier, this gave

---

14. John Calvin, *Institutes*, III.25.6. Citation from Ford Lewis Battles translation (Philadelphia: Westminster Press, 1960), 998.

15. Ludwig Wittenstein, *Lectures and Conversations on Aesthetics, Psychology and Religious Belief* (Oxford: Blackwell, 1966), 56.

rise to an eschatological reaction in twentieth-century theology with attempts to reappropriate the reserve and hope that characterized Christian faith from the outset.

A third concern surrounded the doctrine of hell which was so closely bound to standard treatments of the last judgment. From the seventeenth century, the idea of hell as everlasting torment became problematized, a steady decline in belief becoming evident. Alternative scenarios of purgatory, annihilation, universalism, and postmortem evangelism have all been proposed in recent times, each of these registering in different quarters a fundamental anxiety around the prospect of divinely sanctioned unending torture for the damned. How could God will or tolerate such an outcome for so many, or indeed even one single person? Yet, despite these anxieties around the prospect of damnation, some leading theologians continued to affirm and welcome its prospect. Jonathan Edwards could write of the beauty of hell in God's universe, while his famous sermon on "Sinners in the Hands of an Angry God" remains a compelling read in its exhortation to repentance. In the nineteenth century, the Oxford Movement, despite its insistence upon purgatory and prayers for the dead, continued to present a stark choice between heaven and hell. Edward Pusey's 1839 sermon on *The Day of Judgement* emphasizes the importance of contemplating our time of judgment to combat moral and spiritual laxity.

> Be this then ever before us; be our first thought, morning by morning to think of the resurrection, be our last night by night, the sleep of death, after which cometh the judgement . . . remember the parching flame, the never-dying worm, the everlasting fire, the gnashing of teeth, "the smoke of torment" which goeth up for ever and ever; and where they have no rest day nor night. Set heaven and hell before your eyes, so you may escape hell and by God's mercy attain heaven.[16]

John Henry Newman's *Dream of Gerontius*, a poem written in 1865 and set to music by Elgar, dramatizes the moment of death and the encounter with Christ. The soul asks, "Shall I see My dearest Master, when I reach His throne?" and the Angel replies, "Yes for one moment thou shalt see thy God. . . . One moment, but thou knowest not, my child, What thou dost ask: that sight of the Most Fair will gladden thee, but it will pierce thee too."[17] Commenting on this passage, Hebblethwaite notes how little room there is for a general judgment, a general resurrection, or even the resurrection of the body. The focus is almost entirely on the encounter of the individual soul with Christ, its judge.[18]

Nevertheless, despite the maintenance of traditional ideas of judgment and hell by figures in both Protestant and Catholic theology, the doctrine of eternal

---

16. *The Day of Judgement* (Oxford: John Henry Parker, 1839), 29.
17. John Henry Newman, *Dream of Gerontius* (Edinburgh: Constable, 1910), 46.
18. Brian Hebblethwaite, *The Christian Hope* (Basingstoke: Marshall, Morgan and Scott, 1984), 119.

punishment has undergone radical revision in many of the theologies of the nineteenth and twentieth centuries, in favor of views that are more patient of universalist interpretation. This may amount to the most significant paradigm change in theology since the time of the Reformation. As a shift that cuts across confessional boundaries, it has never been the subject of ecclesiastical division. There is support for universalism in the work of leading scholars including Barth, Moltmann, Rahner, and von Balthasar.[19] The earlier notion of an *apokatastasis*, once a marginal dogmatic tradition in Origen and Gregory of Nyssa, has now become more mainstream. Yet the absence of major ecclesiastical controversy may also have led to a failure to appreciate the shift in perspective that has taken place. Recent Catholic theology, in particular, stresses not so much a final separation, but the last judgment as a pedagogical process whereby the person is brought to an understanding of his or her life through an encounter with the love of God. The element of human freedom is stronger here than in Barth or Moltmann, but the emphasis falls upon divine love as pedagogical rather than retributive, so that there is a much more muted sense of the prospect of eternal damnation than we find in medieval traditions. "Christ inflicts pure perdition on no one. In himself he is sheer salvation. Anyone who is with him has entered the space of deliverance and salvation. Perdition is not imposed by him, but comes to be wherever a person distances himself from Christ."[20]

The affirmation of an *apokatastasis*, however, does not in itself negate the theme of judgment. In most theologies, it persists but is now transposed into a different key. A central insight is the identification of the crucified and risen Jesus with the judge of the world. He does not adopt a different *persona* from the Christ of the gospels, but continues to enact God's grace and mercy to sinners. His identity as judge is no different from his mission as savior of the world. This provides a Christological hermeneutic by which to interpret those passages in the New Testament which advert to a last judgment. Seen in this light, the last judgment cannot compromise in any way the justification of the ungodly, a judgment that has already been announced. The last judgment is the day of Christ; his judging of the living and the dead should not be viewed apart from the forgiveness of sins and our justification by grace.[21] So this final act is one of grace which includes but transcends the demands of justice. Its scope is inclusive and its mercy is unlimited. The justification of the sinner is rescued from a lazy acceptance by the display of God's faithfulness. This has already been accomplished so that the same Christ,

---

19. For a recent defense of universal salvation see David Bentley Hart, *That All Shall Be Saved: Heaven, Hell and Universal Salvation* (New Haven: Yale University Press, 2019).

20. Joseph Ratzinger, *Eschatology: Death and Eternal Life*, 2nd ed. (Washington, DC: Catholic University of America Press, 1988), 205. See also Zachary Hayes, *Visions of a Future: A Study of Christian Eschatology* (Wilmington: Glazier, 1989), 178–89 and Gerald O'Collins, *God's Other Peoples: Salvation for All* (Oxford: Oxford University Press, 2008).

21. See Eberhard Jüngel, "The Last Judgement as the Act of Grace," *Louvain Studies* 15 (1990): 389–405.

crucified and risen, will be our judge on the Last Day. For this reason, Karl Barth commends the Heidelberg Catechism's exposition of the Creed.

> Question 52. What comfort is it to thee that "Christ shall come again to judge the quick and the dead"?
>
> Answer: That in all my sorrows and persecutions, with uplifted head I look for the very same person, who before offered himself for my sake, to the tribunal of God, and has removed all curse from me, to come as judge from heaven.[22]

If we take our bearings from the verdict already announced in the crucifixion and resurrection of Christ, then his coming again can do no more or less than complete what has already been disclosed. There is not so much a double judgment as an outworking and fulfillment of a judgment already delivered which reaches out to our own death and towards the end of the world. What we say about death and the end of the world is set in the light of Christ. This requires both the revealing of the truth about ourselves and the world, but also our acceptance by a reconciling love. And it is difficult to see how or why this love would be withheld or withdrawn from anyone, given its intention and rootedness in the life of God.

Eberhard Jüngel has pointed to the therapeutic content of the hope of the last judgment. Our judge is Christ who has already been judged in our place. His return must therefore be viewed as the completion of what is already known and held in faith. As an accomplishment of what is anticipated, it represents a fulfillment of our deepest trust and commitment. The tension between the "already" of Christian existence and the "not yet" of eternal life is finally resolved in the resurrection of the dead. So our judgment cannot be seen apart from the glorious hope of resurrection. In the end, we do not face a frightening apocalyptic catastrophe; the dominant note of fear in so much of the Christian tradition should be replaced by that of hope in the resurrection. Instead, we are awakened to new life by the God of Jesus. To this extent, the parables of divine grace and generosity are our best index and analogue to the coming reign of God. This judgment must first give justice to the victims and establish a right order—in this respect, it includes elements of vindication and retribution—but these are directed to the prospect of a kingdom of peace. In the end, the work of God is restorationist rather than merely retributive.

Jüngel also points out that the judge is not blindfolded. The judge sees us clearly but comes to make peace with us and among us. This offers several corrective possibilities in relation to traditional notions of the last judgment. Each again has a

---

22. Barth comments, "A different note is struck here. Jesus Christ's return to judge the quick and the dead is tidings of joy. 'With head erect', the Christian, the Church may and ought to confront the future. For He that comes is the same who previously offered Himself to the judgement of God. It is His return we are looking for. Would it had been vouchsafed to Michael Angelo and the other artists to see and hear this." *Dogmatics in Outline* (London: SCM, 1949), 134.

therapeutic quality. First, we are released from judging ourselves. The judicial office is taken from us and transferred to Christ. We no longer have to judge ourselves or others. This is God's prerogative alone. Second, the passing of judgment to the savior of the world entails the healing of our wounds as our sins are simultaneously revealed and forgiven. We no longer require to suppress the past or to harbor bitter memories; all this can finally be resolved but only by a gracious God. Finally, the last judgment is not merely about the exposure of our misdeeds. It also includes a recognition of those actions that were the triumph of God's grace within us. Not everything that is disclosed is painful. Perhaps more than we imagine, we accomplish some good works that also require acknowledgement. "[T]he last judgement can praise what has really been done well as a good work with a clarity which is beyond our human judgement. The judge, before whom all our deeds will be revealed, acknowledges our good works."[23]

This notion has been strengthened by recent work stressing the essentially restorative rather than exclusively retributive nature of God's justice in Scripture. The accent falls not on "paying back" or "punishing" but on "putting right" what has gone wrong. Thiselton, for example, notes that while the Hebrew for judgment (*mishpat*) is generally rendered by the Greek *krima* or *krisis* in the Septuagint, the verb "to judge" (*shaphat*) is often associated with the Greek *dikaiosyne*.[24] It is a restoration of relationships that are disordered and broken rather than mere retribution. If this is how God justifies the ungodly in Christ, then we cannot think of the last judgment except in terms of a completion of this restorative action. Divine judgment and salvation are thus neither conjoined nor separated; these belong together within a single act of covenant faithfulness to God's one purpose. The Hebrew, as opposed to Greco-Roman concepts of justice, is corporate and restorative; it aims at the healing of broken relationships that are spiritual, ethical, and social in their different dimensions. Even while punitive and penitential elements are included in this notion of justice, its fundamental aim is toward restoration. Justice is not a private attribute that we might possess on our own; it is corporate and relational in its scope. Hence the establishment of such justice requires a general judgment and reordering of the world by God. Divine judgment is not only reactive but is proactive in its intention. There is a surplus of grace that does more than equalize the consequences of our actions.[25]

God's last judgment is already anticipated within the Christian life, particularly in the indelible sign of baptism. "To be baptized is to accept God's verdict of guilty, and so to be brought past the great assize and the final judgement of the last day

---

23. Jüngel, "The Last Judgement as the Act of Grace," 402.
24. A. C. Thiselton, *Life After Death: A New Approach to the Last Things* (Grand Rapids: Eerdmans, 2012), 167.
25. See Christopher Marshall, *Beyond Retribution: A New Testament Vision for Justice, Crime and Punishment* (Grand Rapids: Eerdmans, 2001), 47.

into the life of the Age to Come."²⁶ In this way, our divine acceptance already has an eschatological dimension by virtue of its binding and irrevocable status. Does this imply final acceptance only for people of faith? This seems unlikely since our faith is not the cause of God's loving us. If divine justice is restorative then we might expect people who have found faith difficult or impossible to be included in God's final act of restoration, alongside those whose lives have been oppressed by sickness, violence and poverty.²⁷

Why bother with a last judgment? Part of the answer must lie in the need for completion. The story of Israel and the Church has the character of promise. We still await its fulfillment, even if its outcome has already been determined. Faith is always closely accompanied by hope. Robert Jenson has remarked that "it is a chief disaster of the modern church, at least in its 'mainline,' that we think we can separate them, that we can believe in Christ without robust eschatological expectation."²⁸ Part of the embarrassment may be around apocalyptic expectation and naïve attempts to piece together a pre-eschatological sequence from the scattered texts of Daniel and Revelation. But if we see these as images of a single event in which everything finds its fulfillment in God, then we can maintain the vision of a last judgment and allow it to rest in its proper place within the Christian imagination.

What then are we to imagine? At least two features of the biblical accounts are fundamental. One is the sense of everything being put right and properly ordered. This requires judgment, but it is a judgment that takes place within the covenant faithfulness of God. Judgment has as its goal the reconciliation of all things in heaven and on earth (Colossians 1:20). A reconciliation that is final and complete will require our forgiving and being forgiven by others. But, as Miroslav Volf has argued, it will require even more than this. "Reconciliation will not have taken place until one has moved towards one's former enemies and embraced them as belonging to the same communion of love."²⁹ Without this reaching out to the other, we cannot participate in God's kingdom. If such reconciliation is not to be experienced as a further episode of oppression, this will require justice for the victim. So it is that the eschatological community brings us together not only with our own loved ones but with countless others from every tribe and language and nation. When Barth was asked whether we shall meet our loved ones again, he

---

26. Alan Richardson, *An Introduction to the Theology of the New Testament* (London: SCM, 1958), 341. See Thiselton, *Life After Death*, 175.

27. Thiselton makes the telling point that unbelief itself may be the result of forms of oppression or deprivation. Ibid., 182.

28. Robert Jenson, "The Great Transformation," in *The Last Things: Biblical and Theological Perspectives on Eschatology*, ed. Carl E. Braaten and Robert W. Jenson (Grand Rapids: Eerdmans, 2002), 35.

29. Miroslav Volf, "The Final Reconciliation: Reflections on a Social Dimension of the Eschatological Transition," in *Theology and Eschatology at the Turn of the Millennium*, ed. James Buckley and L. Gregory Jones (Oxford: Blackwell, 2001), 102.

replied, "Not only our loved ones."[30] Closely related to this is a second feature of the new creation—its sociality. We are furnished with images of a final gathering, whether this is a new *polis*, a feast, or the herding of a flock. The last judgment is not a private encounter, one on one with God. It is our being drawn together into a new community that is transformed in its relationship to God and thus in relation to each other. For this reason, it cannot determine me apart from others; this is something for all of us together.

Conclusion

What we mean by a last judgment is a divine work of completion that is anticipated in hope. As such, it belongs to the essence of faith in Christ. This is confirmed by much of the New Testament evidence. Nevertheless, we do not have the conceptual resources or knowledge to predict what this will be like, when it will take place, or what precise outcomes will follow. To this extent, it proceeds in many ways as a negative theology that excludes speculation about the ultimate future by providing symbolic pointers to a completion of our lives and that of the world. Death does *not* have the last word; we are *not* overcome by evil; injustices do *not* remain concealed; sin and guilt do *not* prevail.[31] The history of our theological traditions has been beset with images of fear surrounding the last judgment. These need to be replaced by more hopeful notes through a focus on Christ as our judge. Luther's theology of the "dear last day" already points in this direction. From this hermeneutical center, much of the Scriptural material needs to be reorganized and even demythologized. Such a theology will be more patient of a final *apokatastasis* than an irrevocable separation, though here again it can only gesture towards God's promised future rather than attempt a dogmatic definition of final outcomes.

---

30. Volf, "The Final Reconciliation," 89.

31. Christopher Morse approaches eschatology through a series of disbeliefs. The final eschatological disbelief—"That the One whose love has begun so good a work among us here and now will fail to bring it to fulfilment at the day of Jesus Christ" (Philippians 1:6)—requires a symbolic expression of the age to come, although this is best understood in terms of what it negates. *Not Every Spirit: A Dogmatics of Disbelief* (Valley Forge: Trinity Press International, 1994), 344.

Part Two

PHILOSOPHY

Chapter 8

HUME AS RELIGIOUS SKEPTIC

In narrating the final illness of Hume, Adam Smith records a conversation in which his friend reflected upon the reasons why he might wish to delay his journey across the Styx. He tells Charon, the ferryman, that perhaps he might correct his works for a new edition. This is dismissed as an excuse. Finally, he asks for time to see his work dismantle the prevailing systems of superstition. The boatman loses his temper. "You loitering rogue," he says, that will not happen these many hundred years. Do you fancy I grant you a lease for so long a term? Get into the boat this instant, you lazy loitering rogue."[1]

At a distance of three centuries, we can offer some assessment of the ways in which Hume challenged superstition and indeed what he might have intended by this late remark to his friend. Associated for much of his life with the city of Edinburgh, Hume became the doyen of the Scottish Enlightenment during the second half of the eighteenth century. Today he is regarded as the greatest philosopher to have written in English. Yet within his native context, he was also an exceptional figure by virtue of his views on religion. In Scotland, the Enlightenment was a movement that flourished on Presbyterian soil, many of its leading figures being clergy such as Robertson, Blair, Ferguson, and Reid, who distinguished themselves in fields other than theology. By contrast, Hume took a view on religion that was neither heterodox nor indifferent but explicitly hostile in important respects. He was attacked by the clergy on numerous occasions; some of it was vicious and vitriolic, including that of James Beattie, the Aberdeen philosopher, later memorialized in Joshua Reynolds's painting "The Triumph of Truth."[2] Never offered an academic position, Hume even endured an attempt to

---

1. David Hume, *Dialogues Concerning Natural Religion*, ed. Norman Kemp Smith (Oxford: Clarendon, 1935), 245.

2. James Beattie, *Essay on the Nature and Immutability of Truth* (Dublin: Thomas Ewing, 1773).

For discussion of the Beattie affair, see E. C. Mossner, *Life of David Hume* (London: Nelson, 1954), 577ff. Despite his cheap attack on Hume's skepticism, Beattie, a determined abolitionist, deserves credit for exposing the flaws in Hume's notorious comments on national characteristics. See the selection in E. C. Eze (ed.), *Race and the Enlightenment: A Reader* (Oxford: Blackwell, 1997).

have him excommunicated from the Kirk in 1755–6. Boswell famously described him as "the great infidel," an epithet that has since stuck.[3] In recent times, he has been valorized by the New Atheists as one of their own, a critic of religion who helped to turn the tide of reason against superstition.

In what follows, I shall present Hume as a skeptical naturalist, his views on both the practice and theory of religion being largely negative. Yet, while much of Hume scholarship today presents him as more explicitly atheist and dismissive of religion than he was able to appear in eighteenth-century Scotland, I make three further claims that modify this reading:

1. The question of God was never closed for Hume.
2. The existence of an intelligent creator was not a possibility that he judged capable of elimination.
3. There is a minimal form of theism and religious observance that he regarded as benign and even socially useful. In light of this, some comparisons will be drawn with today's New Atheists who regard Hume as their patron saint.

Hume wrote repeatedly on the subject of religion throughout much of his life. Although the material can readily be assembled into a single volume of writings, it covers a broad range of topics.[4] Almost everything he had to say on the subject remains of significance today whether in its philosophical, social scientific, or historical mode of study. Moreover, it seems clear that his writings on religion were of much importance to Hume himself. He was willing to suffer public hostility on account of his views, even if at times he took steps to conceal the real extent of his skepticism. Shortly before his death, he added further material to the manuscript of the *Dialogues*, while also making provision for their posthumous publication. Some have judged this work to be a philosophical masterpiece.

We teach our students that Philo is generally the mouthpiece for Hume, his skepticism throughout the conversation largely representing that of the author. Yet Philo's own position becomes curiously ambivalent in the penultimate paragraph of the *Dialogues* where he appears to leave open the possibility of a residual theism. Is this merely a dramatic device to conceal the author's convictions, or is Hume making a more serious philosophical move that prevents us from labeling him an outright atheist, in today's sense of that term? Commentators have divided over this issue of interpretation. There are certainly features of those closing remarks that must be seen as a smokescreen deliberately intended to

---

3. For example, Roderick Graham, *The Great Infidel: A Life of David Hume* (Edinburgh: Birlinn, 2006).

4. See Richard Wollheim, *Hume on Religion* (London: Collins, 1963), and Julian Baggini (ed.), *Hume on Religion* (London: Routledge, 2010).

conceal Hume's resting position. The claim that he has destroyed reason in order to make room for faith in revelation must be read in this way. This was simply a tactical move that enabled Hume to advance a thoroughgoing skepticism in his writings without causing the outright offence and censure that would have inevitably ensued in much of eighteenth-century Europe.

The use of skepticism to promote faith was a procedure that had been employed by different French writers, notably Montaigne and Pascal. It was a strategy that could be deployed to support the authority of the church over individual interpretations of Scripture, or more widely to set faith over reason. But the same device could also be used as a convenient means of disguising the real extent of one's skepticism, at a time when wholesale criticism of religion would have had deleterious consequences. Terence Penelhum notes that Bayle's *Historical and Critical Dictionary* of 1697 with its combination of "phenomenal learning, skeptical argument, and cynical cunning . . . provided a mine of anti-religious ammunition" for Hume and other Enlightenment figures.[5] As some of the most explosive material in Bayle is reserved for his footnotes, so in Hume's *Natural History of Religion* the attack on the religion of his own day is often more apparent in footnotes and citation. Bayle's rhetorical strategy is deployed by Hume—cast doubt on all popular forms of religion by subjecting these to tests of reason and evidence, but insist simultaneously that true faith must repose upon revelation. Hume had no intention of developing a theology of revelation, but this putative commitment provided him with a smokescreen behind which he could rehearse his arguments against natural theology.

A further tactical motive may have been Hume's resentment toward those such as Hutcheson and Leechman who represented the more liberal wing of the national Church of Scotland, but whose opposition to his appointment to the Edinburgh chair in 1745 proved decisive. Within Scottish Reformed theology, there had been a struggle since around 1700 between those who insisted upon an orthodox theology derived more or less exclusively from Scriptural revelation and "new light" thinkers who expressed much greater confidence in the powers of human reason leading to more heterodox emphases.[6] While heavily revisionist in their views on the Westminster Confession and more indebted to classical thinkers, especially the Stoics, this latter group within the Kirk had failed to support Hume's candidacy for the Edinburgh chair. James Harris has argued that Hume's preference for a "Calvinist rhetoric" in much of the First *Enquiry* can be

---

5. Terence Penelhum, "Hume's Views on Religion: Intellectual and Cultural Influences," in *Blackwell Companion to Hume*, ed. Elizabeth Radcliffe (Chichester: Wiley-Blackwell, 2008), 323–37 (330).

6. See W. I. P. Hazlett, "Ebbs and Flows of Theology in Glasgow 1451–1843," in *Traditions of Theology in Glasgow 1450–1990*, ed. W. I. P. Hazlett (Edinburgh: Scottish Academic Press, 1993), 1–26.

explained by his rejection of the providential Deism of this latitudinarian element. Hence Hume's veiled criticism of a rational approach to theology is not intended to provide support for the Evangelical party within the Kirk; his only point is the inadequacy of the moderate alternative.[7]

Yet, even allowing for such tactical maneuvers, Philo's remarks remain puzzling especially when one considers these to have been late additions, inserted shortly before Hume's death. "[T]he whole of natural theology . . . resolves itself into one simple, though somewhat ambiguous, at least undefined proposition, *that the cause or causes or order in the universe probably bear some remote analogy to human intelligence*."[8] Does this simply reduce religious belief to a point where it has to vanish altogether, thus requiring that we view Hume as a thoroughgoing agnostic? This was expressed by T. H. Huxley, "Darwin's bulldog," just over a century later.

> [I]f we turn from the *Natural History of Religion*, to the *Treatise*, the *Enquiry*, and the *Dialogues*, the story of what happened to the ass laden with salt, who took to the water, irresistibly suggests itself. Hume's theism, such as it is, dissolves away in the dialectic river, until nothing is left but the verbal sack in which it was contained.[9]

This seems nearly but not quite right.

The closing remarks of Part 12 of the *Dialogues* are neither a volte-face nor entirely a concealment of Hume's final position. For one thing, it accords with views that have already been developed in the *Dialogues* and elsewhere. The order of the universe, particularly its organic life forms, is mysterious and apparently in need of explanation. At least, it is not wrong to consider whether there might be an explanation. The Epicurean hypothesis, even though flagged as an alternative hypothesis in the *Dialogues*, is described by Philo as "the most absurd."[10] We know that in animals and human beings organization is accompanied by intelligence. That something akin to human intelligence is the source of order in the universe remains a possibility, and this we might call God. Is this consistent with characteristic Humean skepticism? Given the qualifications surrounding the claim, it seems that it is. While the theistic hypothesis is possible, it is difficult to attach a particular weight to its likelihood. Hume insists that we cannot get into a position to pronounce its probability, since we have had no experience of

---

7. James Harris, "Hume's Use of the Rhetoric of Calvinism," in *Impressions of Hume*, ed. M. Frasca-Spada and P. J. Kail (Oxford: Clarendon, 2005), 141–59. See also M. A. Stewart, "Two Species of Philosophy: The Historical Significance of the First Enquiry," in *Reading Hume on Human Understanding*, ed. Peter Millican (Oxford: Clarendon, 2002), 67–95.

8. Hume, *Dialogues*, 227.

9. T. H. Huxley, *Hume* (London: Macmillan, 1879), 146.

10. Hume, *Dialogues*, 182.

such an intelligence. The analogies, moreover, must be remote, given the inevitable differences between any distant cosmic mind and those of human beings whose intellects are determined by and directed toward the conditions of physical and social existence. Finally, while intellect appears to offer some possibility for an analogical inference, this cannot be said of other attributes attaching to human life, notably moral ones. The residual theism at the end of the *Dialogues* is amoral.[11] The analogy, Philo insists, cannot be transferred, with any appearance of probability, to the other qualities of the mind. So even if God exists in some inaccessible region, we cannot assume that God has any moral concern with the world. The evidence indeed suggests quite otherwise, rather than requiring our suspension of judgment. This also explains why Philo regards himself as moving to much stronger ground when the *Dialogues* turn from cosmic order to consider the problem of evil in Part 10. "It is your turn now to tug the labouring oar, and to support your philosophical subtilties against the dictates of plain reason and experience."[12] This is a tacit recognition that, with respect to the possibility of there being some cause of cosmic organization, Cleanthes has raised a significant question that cannot readily be dismissed. His position is not as hopeless as that of Demea.

Hume's final position on natural theology is therefore a nuanced one. True religion reduces to our giving a degree of intellectual assent to the proposition that "God exists," although it cannot ever be clear what this entails. This is the only form of "worship" that Hume will allow. Anything else is superstitious and debasing of our character. The consequence of this is that all practical manifestations of religion are called into question. The God whose probable existence is conjectured cannot be God as ordinarily understood. Therefore, a rational religious belief will have no possible bearing on human life. To this extent, all real (i.e., actual) religion is without intellectual foundation and, for other reasons, much of it is considered by Hume to be superstitious or fanatical.[13] While pleading for temperance and tolerance in matters of religious debate, some of his jibes display a mocking tone, hardly surprising perhaps given the treatment meted out to him by his opponents. His famous quip about the miracle by which the principles of understanding are subverted is one of several sarcastic sallies against the faithful.[14] This suggested the title of J. L. Mackie's *Miracle of Theism*, perhaps the most consistently Humean

---

11. Whether Hume goes all the way in arguing transcendentally that moral qualities cannot be ascribed to God, as Thomas Holden has claimed, seems less clear. See Thomas Holden, *Spectres of a False Divinity* (Oxford: Oxford University Press, 2010).

12. Hume, *Dialogues*, 202.

13. Here I am largely following the reading of Kemp Smith in his introduction to Hume, *Dialogues*, 24.

14. David Hume, *Enquiry Concerning Human Understanding*, ed. L. A. Selby-Bigge, 3rd ed. (Oxford: Oxford University Press, 1975), 131.

work in modern philosophy of religion.[15] Yet Hume's concluding remarks in the *Dialogues* suggest an *aporia* with regard to the origins of cosmic order. This yields a skepticism that confesses intellectual defeat. While the similar practical outcomes are apparent in the so-called "New Atheism" of the early twenty-first century, its tonality, as I shall later suggest, is less complacent and strident. The question of God is neither a pseudo-question nor one that is readily dismissed by Hume. The position he adopts is a counterculturaI contestation of key social tenets, yielding the possibility of a bare theism lacking any apparent practical value. But this is not the confident default setting of an established tradition, too readily dismissive of the claims of religion.

If this characterization of Hume's theological position is correct, then it might be viewed as belonging at the far end of the spectrum of deist positions that were advocated throughout the eighteenth century. "Deism" is a portmanteau terms that refers not so much to a single school of thought, owing allegiance to any one writer or body of literature; instead, the term denotes a range of Enlightenment views which tend to rest upon natural rather than revealed theology, and to maintain elements of Judeo-Christian beliefs about creation, providence, ethics, and the afterlife. At one end of the spectrum, it is an etiolated version of Christian orthodoxy, as in the case of some of the moderate clergy in Scotland. At the other end—shorn of providence, ethics, and the afterlife—it shades into skepticism and a practical atheism. This appears to be where Hume ends up in the *Dialogues*. Indeed, it may well be a settled position held over many years. In the essay on providence in Section 11 of the *Enquiry Concerning Human Understanding*, he had already written.

> All the philosophy, therefore, in the world, and all the religion, which is nothing but a species of philosophy, will never be able to carry us beyond the usual course of experience, or give us measures of conduct and behaviour different from those which are furnished by reflexions on common life. No new fact can ever be inferred from the religious hypothesis; no event foreseen or foretold; no reward or punishment expected or dreaded, beyond what is already known by practice and observation.[16]

Gaskin describes Hume's settled position as an "attenuated deism," although this might be further qualified by describing it as a *tentative* attenuated deism.[17] Against

---

15. J. L. Mackie, *The Miracle of Theism* (Oxford: Oxford University Press, 1982).
16. Hume, *Enquiry Concerning Human Understanding*, 146.
17. J. C. A. Gaskin, *Hume's Philosophy of Religion* (Basingstoke: Macmillan, 1978), 223. This largely accords with the readings of Kemp Smith in his edition of *Hume's Dialogues* and Alexander Broadie, *History of Scottish Philosophy* (Edinburgh: Edinburgh University Press, 2009). Much light is shed on how and why Hume held to such a position by Don Garrett, "What's True About Hume's 'True Religion,'" *Journal of Scottish Philosophy* 10, no. 2 (2012): 199–220. Garrett points out that the true religion espoused by Philo (and Hume)

this, Simon Blackburn has argued that the vague commitment at the close of the *Dialogues* constitutes an "inert proposition" or "bare claim" that is without content. "[I]t suggests no enquiry, and interacts with no desires or emotions, and guides no practices."[18] The affirmation of Philo is thus hollow, Hume having conceded nothing. In this poker game, one winner takes all. Blackburn claims that Kant and William James refused to pay up while Wittgenstein simply changed the rules of the game. But is Philo's proposition entirely inert? While lacking moral relevance for Hume, this claim does seem to place a question mark against the very existence of an organized cosmos. The universe might have an explanation or, to put it more cautiously, we could reasonably say that the absence of any explanation would be a puzzle. One outcome of this train of thought is that natural science cannot deliver all the answers. At the very least, there will be some residual questions that remain after science has done its explanatory work. To that extent, Hume's agnosticism is less self-confident and exclusive of possibilities than some species of today's New Atheism.

In his recent work, Daniel Dennett has suggested that Hume would have been bolder in his affirmation of outright atheism had he received the benefit of reading Darwin. Unable to explain the sources of order in the world, he had finally to revert to mystery and an appeal to the limits of human knowledge. But with later accounts of natural selection and genetic mutation, we can now explain far more in naturalistic ways than Hume realized. Describing the final position of Philo in the *Dialogues*, Dennett states that "[Hume] caved in because he just couldn't imagine any other explanation of the origin of the manifest design in nature. . . . The evolutionary revolution had to wait until Charles Darwin saw how to weave an evolutionary hypothesis into an explanatory fabric composed of literally thousands of hard-won and often surprising facts about nature."[19] In his more recent work, however, Dennett has suggested instead that the arguments of natural theology have reached a stalemate and that no breakthrough should be anticipated. What is more significant for him is not so much the *Dialogues* as the work begun in *The Natural History*. Perhaps even religion itself can be accounted for by neo-Darwinian cognitive psychology, thus placing on a more scientific basis the kind of explanation for religious belief and practice which Hume had already attempted.[20]

---

suffers from a lack of determinate probability in relation both to the degree of resemblance between divine and human intelligence and to the existence of the former. Thus Hume's epistemic claim at the close of the *Dialogues* is authentic but highly modest.

18. Simon Blackburn, "Playing Hume's Hand," in *Religion and Hume's Legacy*, ed. D. Z. Phillips and Timothy Tessin (Basingstoke: Macmillan 1999), 3–16.

19. Daniel C. Dennett, *Darwin's Dangerous Idea: Evolution and the Meanings of Life* (London: Penguin, 1995) 32–3.

20. Daniel C. Dennett, *Breaking the Spell: Religion as a Natural Phenomenon* (London: Penguin, 2007), 27.

To some extent, much of this is valid comment and follows in the tradition of Huxley's aforementioned commitment to Hume. Despite the publication of the *Dialogues*, the design argument continued to persuade a succession of later writers, including Paley and the authors of the *Bridgewater Treatises*. Its intuitive force together with the accumulation of scientific evidence seemed to make the design hypothesis unassailable to its defenders. By contrast, the criticisms of Hume were perceived as playful, ingenious, and slight. These could readily be overcome by counterargument. After the publication of *Origin of Species* (1859), however, all that changed. The design argument did not disappear, but it now had to be presented more cautiously, as the force was more fully felt of Hume's earlier criticisms.[21]

But whether Darwinism would have led Hume to a more forthright atheism is doubtful. One version of the eighteenth-century design argument is clearly made redundant by the principle of natural selection, namely that predicated upon observation of the matching of species to environment. That camels are equipped for desert conditions and polar bears for the North Pole is explained very well by Darwin without recourse to the hypothesis of divine providence. Similar comments might be made *mutatis mutandis* about the evolution of complex organs such as the camera eye—these have evolved incrementally as a result of mutations combined with the outcomes of natural selection. But whether this accounts for all types of cosmic organization is less clear. What about the motions of the planets and the origin of carbon-based life forms? Modern science can give us an account of their origins in terms of Big Bang cosmology but this too reposes upon there being a universe, or maybe a multiverse, that has the capacity to generate regions of space-time governed by scientific laws. The givenness of cosmic organization, including animal evolution, is not something that is readily explained, at any rate not to the point of exhausting all the possible "why" questions that can be posed. Hume's minimal deism thus remains a valid option, even for a post-Darwinian philosopher or scientist. To suggest that evolutionary theory must inevitably yield a full-blown and more self-confident atheism is to miss something of the subtlety of Philo's conclusions. Darwin himself did not commit to the full force of Huxley's skepticism. He may have lost much of his faith, but it did not lead him to espouse outright atheism or naturalism. He preferred to leave some questions open, it seems, even if traditional religious answers had long since ceased to satisfy. In turning away from orthodox dogma and practice, therefore, Darwin and Hume may have ended closer to one another, than to Huxley and Dennett.

Nevertheless, Blackburn and others are surely right that the practical outcome of the *Dialogues* is that God exercises no moral influence upon us, nor do we upon God. This entails for Hume that the claims of revealed theology are false; ceremonies, prayers, sacrifices, rituals, sacraments and fasting are either

---

21. See for example Robert Flint, *Theism* (Edinburgh: Blackwood, 1877). For further discussion, see John Hedley Brooke and Geoffrey Cantor, *Reconstructing Nature: The Engagement of Science and Religion* (Edinburgh: T&T Clark, 2000).

superstitious or fanatical. A binary opposition thus emerges between a thin philosophical theism and the actual practices and beliefs of the historical forms of religion. These depend upon particular beliefs about the divine nature and our capacity to influence it. Superstition appears in Hume's mind to be most closely associated with a religion of external ceremonies and rituals, no doubt with medieval Catholicism in mind, whereas enthusiasm is largely a Protestant phenomenon often marked by selectivity and intolerance.[22]

In *The Natural History of Religion*, there is a fuller discussion of the different forms of religion, this making it clear why, despite his comprehensive skepticism, Hume has a preference for the pagan religion of ancient Greece and Rome. With its plurality of gods, elaborate myths and anthropomorphism, this polytheism is more accommodating of diversity and tolerance. Its limited and quasi-human gods are more like fellow actors in a drama. Its focus on ritual and myth, rather than dogma, makes it less toxic. This ensures that pagan religion is more apt to produce virtues such as courage and generosity. By contrast, monotheism is altogether regarded as grim and demanding; it leans toward intolerance, violence, and the servile virtues. In our increasingly anxious and ingenious efforts to please the Almighty, we are drawn into all manner of irrational creeds and immoral actions. The long footnote, quoting Chevalier Ramsay, surely represents Hume's most bitter attack upon the religion of Reformed Scotland, including its cornerstone doctrine of double predestination.[23] With his moderate contemporaries, he recoils from the violence of the seventeenth-century Covenanting period, as is apparent in more satirical remarks from the *History of England*.

> Great were the rejoicings among the Scots, that they should be the happy instruments of extending their mode of religion, and dissipating that profound darkness, in which the neighbouring nations were involved. The general assembly applauded this glorious imitation of the piety displayed by their ancestors, who, they said, in three different applications, during the reign of Elizabeth, had endeavoured to engage the English, by persuasion, to lay aside the use of the surplice, tippet, and corner-cap. The convention too, in the height of their zeal, ordered every one to swear to this covenant, under the penalty of confiscation; beside what farther punishment it should please the ensuing parliament to inflict on the refusers, as enemies to God, to the king, and to the kingdom.[24]

Another notable feature of the *Natural History* is the way in which it undermines a central tenet of deism.[25] The assumption that there is a single natural religion

---

22. David Hume, *Selected Essays* (Oxford: Oxford University Press, 1996), 38–42.
23. Wollheim, *Hume on Religion*, 88.
24. David Hume, *The History of England from the Invasion of Julius Caesar to the Revolution in 1688*, 6 vols (Indianapolis: Liberty Fund 1983), Vol. 5. Chapter 56.
25. Martin Bell, "Introduction," in *Dialogues Concerning Natural Religion*, ed. David Hume (London: Penguin, 1999), 9.

common to all people is a premise of much deist writing in the eighteenth century. To this extent, deism is a project of recovery. By nature, we own a religion that is rational and ethical, and roughly commensurate with the findings of natural theology. This pure faith, however, has been overlaid with the superstitious claims and practices which have flourished for many centuries. By weeding these out, we can return to a common religion that is natural and self-evident. A *consensus gentium* will hence be established across confessional divisions. Yet the historical work undertaken by Hume is sufficient to cast serious doubt on the proposition that there is a single, natural, and monotheistic religion underlying all of the religious traditions of the world. The essentialist concept of a natural religion was no longer tenable. The historical contextualizing of all religious forms thus threatened a key motivational commitment of deism.

Hume does not appear to have favored a mitigated skepticism in matters of religion, as he did with respect to other types of belief. There is no natural tendency toward belief in this domain. Morality is independent of religion and is distorted by its intrusion. Gaskin argues that, despite some similarities, religious belief cannot be construed as a natural belief in Hume.[26] It is neither universal nor is its absence practically self-defeating, as for example, in the case of belief in the external world or other minds. Although it is a strong impulse, the religious is secondary rather than primary. This raises the further question as to whether Hume hoped for a society without religion. Does he explore the idea of a secularized society in which religion has altogether disappeared? Could a Humean perspective be embraced by every citizen?

When combined with his commitment to a naturalist ethics, Hume's views on superstition and enthusiasm appear to render a negative verdict upon most historical forms of religious belief and activity. Yet there are themes in his writing elsewhere which suggest a more nuanced position. Although not arguing for religion as a natural belief, he seems to assume that in practice all societies will be religious in complexion, even while this takes diverse forms. In the *History of England*, a model of establishment is advanced which shows a preference for an Anglican *via media* that resonates with Hume's views in other contexts.[27] The preferred form is a state religion. Released from the worst superstitions of the Middle Ages, this should retain many of its ceremonies, clerical orders and sensual forms of worship, while requiring a lower level of doctrinal commitment, after a cooling of the temperature raised by the divisive dogmas of the Reformation. Hume appears to believe that this is most likely to facilitate social harmony and civility when accompanied by state regulation, funding, and a high commitment to religious tolerance. At any rate, this is his declared preference in the *History of England*.

---

26. Gaskin, *Hume's Philosophy of Religion*, 120–6.

27. See Will R. Jordan, "Religion in the Public Square: A Reconsideration of David Hume and Religious Establishment," *Review of Politics* 64, no. 4 (2002): 687–713.

Was Hume seriously committed to this proposal? It is certainly a position that is argued, as opposed merely to being presented. The detail advanced in support of this model, the implied criticism of Scottish Reformed ideals, and the difference from the more disestablished type of church–state relation favored by Adam Smith suggest that it was his preferred position rather than another instance of diplomatic concealment. It was not simply a pragmatic or tactical response to appease a religious readership. Referring to the Elizabethan settlement, he writes:

> The ancient liturgy was preserved, so far as was thought consistent with the new principles: Many ceremonies, become venerable from age and preceding use, were retained: The splendour of the Romish worship, though removed, had at least given place to order and decency. . . . And the new religion, by mitigating the genius of the ancient superstition, and rendering it more compatible with the peace and interests of society, had preserved itself in that happy medium, which wise men have always sought, and which the people have so seldom been able to maintain.[28]

In other respects, this accords with his historical claim that religion appears to be a feature of all civic life, as well as his general preference for public ceremony and ritual over against highly particular dogmas that tend to be fiercely contested. Under a sacred canopy of a church regulated and sponsored by the state, religion is most likely to be rendered cohesive and benign in its effects. Doubtless, Hume as a skeptic sought only a national church that was moderate, latitudinarian, and undemanding of citizens. But this is rather different from Smith's more American-style model of a neutral state for a society populated by different confessional bodies, none of which is given political preference. This resonates with other remarks that Hume makes in the *Dialogues* and elsewhere. There is a "true" religion which is regulated by the calm passions. This is supportive of our natural moral impulses and can be evoked by a sense of wonder at the universe. Hume denotes this "true" religion not so much because he believed it with any conviction, but because it was plausible, worth tolerating and even promoting over other more toxic forms. With this mind, we might explain why the theological distance between Cleanthes and Philo appears to diminish somewhat in the closing stages of the *Dialogues*; this is the outcome partly of temperamental differences between friends.[29]

Genuine piety is described in the following manner in an unpublished draft introduction to Volume II of *The History of England*. Here Hume seems to be

---

28. Hume, *History of England*, Vol. 4, Chapter 40.

29. "Diverse judgements and expressions within this range may result from mere blameless differences in philosophical temperament—such as the notable differences between Cleanthes and Philo. These differences need not and should not breed animosity or hinder friendship, in Hume's view." Garrett, "What's True About Hume's 'True Religion,'" 218.

referring not so much to his own position as to a benign form of religion that is to be encouraged over against its alternative.

> The proper Office of Religion is to reform Men's Lives, to purify their Hearts, to inforce all moral Duties, & to secure Obedience to the Laws and civil Magistrate. While it pursues these useful Purposes, its Operation, tho' infinitely valuable, are secret & silent; and seldom come under the Cognizance of History.[30]

Hume's particular attacks on religion are unsettling and profound, precisely because the ground had already been prepared for this in his general philosophy. The *Treatise* says little about God, but precisely in doing so it offers an account of the natural and social world that has no need of theology. Alexander Broadie has pointed out that *The Natural History of Religion* could have been added almost seamlessly to the argument of the *Treatise*.[31] Hume's mitigated skepticism has no role for God either in its explanatory framework or its practical outworkings. The business of life can be conducted well, perhaps even better, without reference to the divine. For this reason, the most significant response to Hume was not George Campbell's reply to the essay on miracles or the later efforts to rehabilitate the design argument, however worthy these were. Thomas Reid's more widespread effort to set philosophy on a different basis was the most creative and constructive response to Humean skepticism in the Scottish Enlightenment. The attempt to offer an alternative account of our most deep-seated convictions about knowledge, the nature of the self, the external world, and the objectivity of moral and aesthetic values showed how much would be required for a satisfactory response. While Reid makes little effort in arguing specifically for divine existence through any single argument, he constructs a philosophy of the intellectual and active powers that lends itself more readily to theistic claims.

Two comments might be made about this approach. First, it shows that if one allows the role of God to be squeezed into a tightly demarcated religious province, then the design argument is unlikely to be persuasive or significant in its outcomes. Unless it is part of a much broader and more cumulative strategy of reasoning about the natural and social world then it will achieve relatively little. This is true *a fortiori* in late modernity when belief in God is no longer the default setting of Western society. As Charles Taylor argues in *A Secular Age*, this is the most profound difference between the contemporary world and the one that

---

30. Cited by E. C. Mosner, *The Life of David Hume* (Edinburgh: Nelson, 1954), 306. John Immerwahr notes that this passage is adapted in a speech of Cleanthes in *Dialogues*, Part XII. Philo appears to accept the proposition, adding that only the philosophical and rational kind of religion can function in this way. See "Hume's Aesthetic Theism," *Hume Studies* 22 (1996): 325–37 (333). For further exploration of what Hume intends by "true" religion, see Lorne Falkenstein, "Hume on 'Genuine', 'True', and 'Rational' Religion," *Eighteenth-Century Thought* 4 (2009): 171–201.

31. Broadie, *A History of Scottish Philosophy*, 187.

preceded the Enlightenment. For us, faith is an "embattled option" requiring not simple assent to one argument but the mustering of a broad set of intellectual and practical commitments.[32] Any response to Hume will have to widen the front of the argument. Second, even if faith can be maintained in the stronger realist setting provided by Reidian philosophy, the effects of skepticism may still prove significant. For Reid, the ineluctable principles by which our thinking and action are regulated are given for the negotiation of embodied life in the natural and social world. Our knowledge does not extend much further. At best, we can live "wisely in the darkness" with (just) sufficient awareness of God's ways.[33] The creeds and ceremonies of faith have a practical function in orienting us toward love of God, self, and neighbor. They may carry cognitive commitments, but these are limited in scope and imprecise in what they affirm. This may point to one of the abiding benefits of Hume's skepticism, even for the faithful. The limitations of theological reason can serve the cause of a moral religion, devotional practice, tolerance, and ecclesiastical self-criticism.[34]

The banishment of God in Hume's philosophy is an urbane achievement with neither dramatic nor tragic nor wistful consequences. This sets him apart from other European thinkers, in both theological and philosophical traditions. Luther's failure to locate God in worldly processes led to a sense of estrangement. The *deus absconditus*, the absent God, generated an existential tension that was only resolved by the figure of the suffering Christ. The ways of the crucified God eluded those of philosophy and religion. At least since Kant, the German theological tradition has generally been dismissive of the standard arguments of natural theology, claiming that its failure only points to the real location of God in human history and experience. Of course, there is nothing of this in Hume. Claims to revelation are equally suspect with little attention being given in his writings to the figure of Jesus. By contrast, other forms of agnosticism and atheism have a different tonality in later Western philosophy. Nietzsche dramatizes the death of God in modernity, seeing this as a difficult and heroic act with far-reaching consequences. In late Victorian England, while agnosticism may have been the default setting for many intellectuals, this is presented wistfully, with nostalgic and elegiac elements, in writers such as Matthew Arnold and Thomas Hardy. Even within the tradition of British empiricism, Bertrand Russell's atheism is of a more strident and dramatic form with its rhetoric of "unyielding despair." For Hume, by

---

32. Charles Taylor, *A Secular Age* (Cambridge, MA: Harvard University Press, 2007), 3.

33. Nicholas Wolterstorff, "God and Darkness in Reid," in *Thomas Reid: Context, Influence and Significance*, ed. Joseph Houston (Edinburgh: Dunedin Academic Press, 2004), 77–101.

34. This echoes earlier remarks of William Robertson to James Beattie defending the religious benefits of Hume's skepticism. "[A] little fluctuation, now and then, to the sceptical side, tends perhaps to humble the Pride of Understanding, and to check bigotry; and the consequences as to practice, I am inclined to think, are not very great." Cited by Mossner, *Life of David Hume*, 580.

contrast, the criticism of religion is a quietly therapeutic exercise for those willing to take the trouble. It need not induce existential *Angst*, cosmic despair, or moral nihilism. More redolent of the ancient world, his mitigated skepticism will prevent these from gaining purchase. The lesson of his philosophy, particularly his moral theory, is that one can live and act well without regard to God. On balance, it will be better for us if we are not obstructed or misled by the prejudices of faith.

In terms of the history of philosophy, Hume's position is a minority one. Kant and Hegel sought to reintroduce God, albeit in ways that were judged heterodox. Like Spinoza before him, Hegel was described as "God-intoxicated." Wittgenstein, whose views on religion were admittedly elusive, appears nevertheless to allow that religious discourse has an important role to play in expressing insights and commitments that cannot otherwise be stated. It is more akin to a box of tools that enable us to adopt and inhabit perspectives without which our lives would be impoverished, lacking a certain depth, discernment, and openness to the transcendent. But there is nothing in Hume which suggests that even a regulative account of religious language and practice might have some real advantages over other philosophies. The intention appears to be one of dispelling its irrational and baleful hold over human beings, as opposed to assimilating it within a naturalist framework.

We can speculate about the contextual factors that contributed to this. Unlike Boswell, Hume was someone who appeared able to live and die well, without any recourse to religious sentiments, rituals, or hopes. His criticism of religion is not that of someone who craves faith but cannot find it, or who feels keenly the absence of a rational creed. He suffers no religious crisis after the swift loss of faith in his adolescence. Another factor may also be the religion of his early-eighteenth-century upbringing in the Scottish lowlands, in the wake of the violence of the Covenanting era. The Reformed theology and worship of the period must have appeared "gey dreich" to someone entering upon the exciting intellectual world of the early Enlightenment. It would take another 150 years before Scottish church life embarked upon a systematic renewal of its worship, sacramental practice, preaching, music, and church architecture to bring it closer to the Anglicanism seemingly preferred by Hume.[35] Yet Hume does not adopt the emerging moderate position of Hutcheson and many of those clergy who became his friends and supporters. His indifference to religion and its institutions sets him at a distance from most of the other thinkers of the Scottish Enlightenment, with the possible exception of Adam Smith. That other great critic of eighteenth-century Presbyterian church life, Robert Burns, was a younger contemporary of Hume. He exposed the hypocrisy of the "unco guid" and generally set his face against the prevailing orthodoxy, but without abandoning religion altogether. There are many more positive religious notes in Burns than in Hume.

---

35. See A. C. Cheyne, *The Transforming of the Kirk: Religious Scotland's Victorian Revolution* (Edinburgh: St Andrew Press, 1983).

Others have read Hume as a man ahead of his time. In the writings of the so-called New Atheists today, he has come into his own. Richard Dawkins assumes that a cocktail of Hume and Darwin will prove lethal for all forms of religion. The multifaceted attack of Hume on religion is replicated, if intensified, in much of this literature. Dawkins follows many of Hume's standard criticisms of the proofs for God's existence. The citation of the problem of evil bears similarities to Parts 10 and 11 of the *Dialogues*. The attack on sacred texts as populated with miracle stories and unedifying tales is reminiscent of Hume's famous essay on the subject, while the claim of Christopher Hitchens that "religion poisons everything" in its individual and social effects recalls much in the *Natural History* and other works.[36]

Nevertheless, despite their obvious alliances, there are probably two related ways in which Hume would have been uneasy around the New Atheism. Its confident assertion of the non-existence of God might appear an overreaching of the power of reason. Much of Hume's criticism is that our experience is too limited to enable us to pronounce over questions surrounding the origin of the universe. Peter Atkins's inflated claim that we should expect science eventually to answer the question, "Why there is something rather than nothing?" would have been unlikely to secure the support of Hume.[37] There may be many questions that remain incapable of resolution, given our human condition. The capacity of science to produce a new metaphysics might have been greeted with a similarly skeptical response. And Hume would surely have been skeptical around credulity attached to the explanatory concept of memes.

The tonality of the New Atheism might also have disturbed Hume, particularly its tendency to scoff at religionists as either fools or knaves. Dawkins often writes as if exponents of faith should be creationists, fundamentalists, and biblical literalists for the sake of consistency. He is reluctant to enter into conversation with revisionist positions which offer alternative constructions in ways that seek the coexistence of religion and science. Hume's *Dialogues* by contrast are a model of interpretation *in optimam partem*. His opponents, especially Cleanthes, are given a fair and sympathetic hearing. The art of civilized conversation and friendly disagreement is exemplified, even when the differences run deep. For that reason, the rhetorical strategies of the New Atheists with their strident and condescending overtones would probably have elicited some rebuke from Hume himself.

He might have preferred to position himself alongside other humanist voices who have urged the need for collaboration between advocates of tolerance, civility and social justice, whatever their religious hue. At the risk of frivolous anachronism, we might ask what Hume would have made of buses in London and Edinburgh parading the message, "There's probably no God. Now stop worrying and enjoy

---

36. Richard Dawkins, *The God Delusion* (London: Bantam, 2006), and Christopher Hitchens, *God Is Not Great: The Case Against Religion* (London: Atlantic Books, 2007).

37. Peter Atkins, *On Being: A Scientist's Exploration of the Great Questions of Existence* (Oxford: Oxford University Press, 2011), 12ff.

your life." Is this the public triumph of skepticism or the nadir of a reflective secular humanism? It is hard to see Hume disagreeing much with the content of that slogan. Its light and urbane tone is more Humean than Nietzschean. Yet the medium might have offended him rather more. Is this just too vulgar, a descent into sloganizing rather than arguing? Is there an atheist fanaticism that also has its bad consequences? Is this likely to induce the calm and measured discussion on the subject which he urged upon his critics? Or is it indeed a strategy that might prove counterproductive by triggering a reflux of intemperate religious enthusiasm? With his skepticism about the inevitability of human progress, Hume might have entertained that prospect.

Finally, what of Hume's reception among later Scottish philosophers and theologians? My impression is that later generations, including scholars who identified broadly with the Kirk, have learned to value Hume and have sought to include him in a noble tradition of distinctively Scottish philosophers. Cairns Craig points out that the late-nineteenth-century reading of Hume located him within a Scottish tradition that was no longer fundamentally at odds with Hutcheson and Reid.[38] Henry Calderwood and James Orr, both products of the United Presbyterian Church, wrote sympathetic studies at the turn of the nineteenth century, even if Calderwood sought implausibly to identify the real Hume with Cleanthes.[39] Hume's skepticism contributed to the refining of faith, thus playing a positive role, albeit in ways that he himself did not directly intend. Kemp Smith, who remained a theist of sorts, wrote one of the finest studies of Hume's philosophy and sought to position him close to Reid in his espousal of a philosophical naturalism.[40] The Divinity Faculties in Scotland ensured for many years that the *Dialogues* remained a prescribed text. Scottish theologians, it seems, took some pride in the view that while Hume may have been a skeptic, he was at least their skeptic and better than any of the others.[41] For that reason among others, he deserves to be better known and valued in contemporary Scotland. His nuanced criticism of religion should enable us to think twice, to realize the danger of believing too much in the wrong things, to remain alert to the follies and prejudices of the faithful, aware of the mobility of religious forms across history, while listening patiently to those who see the world differently in the expectation that we will profit from them.

---

38. Cairns Craig, *Intending Scotland* (Edinburgh: Edinburgh University Press, 2009), 91–5.

39. Henry Calderwood, *David Hume* (Edinburgh: Oliphant, Anderson & Ferrier, 1989), James Orr, *David Hume and His Influence on Philosophy and Theology* (Edinburgh: T&T Clark, 1903).

40. Norman Kemp Smith, *The Philosophy of David Hume: A Study of its Origins and Central Doctrines* (London: Macmillan, 1941).

41. I explore this further in "Hume Amongst the Theologians" in David Fergusson and Mark W. Elliott (eds.), *History of Scottish Theology, Vol. II: The Early Enlightenment to the Late Victorian Era* (Oxford: Oxford University Press, 2019), 301–13.

As a critic of religion, Hume deserves to be eulogized in his native land at least as much as Robert Burns. Although the toast to the immortal memory of the mitigated skeptic is an intriguing prospect, it is unlikely that we shall ever have Hume Suppers. Yet at least he is worthy of greater public recognition than he currently receives. But as the ferryman at the Styx informed him, these things take a long time.

Chapter 9

ADAM SMITH ON ETHICS AND RELIGION

Religious Shifts in the Scottish Enlightenment

The eighteenth-century Scottish Enlightenment was a cultural and intellectual movement rooted in Presbyterian soil. Clergy of the Church of Scotland were at the forefront of many of its key developments. These included leading figures such as William Robertson (1721–93), Thomas Reid (1710–96), Adam Ferguson (1723–1816), Hugh Blair (1718–1800), and George Campbell (1719–96). All flourished in the second half of the eighteenth century within the ancient universities of Scotland. Their work would not have been possible, however, without the significant shifts that had taken place in Scottish culture and theology earlier in the century.

After 1700, Scottish theologians began to turn away from the disputes that had marked Reformed orthodoxy in the seventeenth century. The Covenanting era had been succeeded by the Glorious Revolution (1689) and Act of Settlement (1701). The civil strife and violence of the former period had given way to a time of relative Presbyterian stability. Greater economic prosperity now appeared to be a consequence of the Treaty of Union (1707). At the same time, newer philosophical trends were imported from the European continent and England. Increased latitude of thought, some of which is quite surprising in its context, became evident in the work of several professors. A culture of "moderatism" gradually found favor, despite some fierce resistance from the courts of the church. In the minds of its exponents, this was integral to a peaceful and prosperous society no longer marked by religious intolerance, arcane dogmatic disputes, and factionalism. Within this milieu, different intellectual preoccupations became widely established. Earlier debates about the extent of the atoning work of Christ, the depravity of the human condition, divine election, and the nature of assurance were displaced by discussion of the innate moral sense endowed by the Creator, the nature of virtue, the civilizing role of the Christian religion, and the sublimity of the teaching of Jesus. All of these signaled a confidence in the power of reason which contrasted with earlier emphases upon the clouded nature of human judgment and the need for divine revelation. Despite these shifts, however, the philosophy and religious thought of the period retained a strong Christian theistic cast.[1]

Francis Hutcheson (1694–1746), Professor of Moral Philosophy in Glasgow, was the leading figure of the early Scottish Enlightenment. Enjoying the patronage of the Earl of Islay, the most powerful Scottish politician of his day, Hutcheson set about transforming the culture of the university and the church. Lecturing in English rather than Latin, he reached a wider public through his accomplished literary style. His Sunday evening discourses on the truth of the Christian religion attracted popular audiences. While his moral philosophy stressed a natural moral sense, this was traced back to the wisdom of the Creator who had endowed us in this way. Owing to his intellectual brilliance, gentle disposition, rhetorical skills, and political acumen, Hutcheson was largely successful.

Hutcheson also wished to maintain the necessity of religious belief for moral motivation. Without belief in the ordering of the world and the vindication of our best efforts, we are likely to be undermined and demoralized in our projects. (There is a foreshadowing of Kant here.) Belief in God, in providence, and in a future state are vital supports for the moral agent. These can reassure us in the face of anxiety, sustain us when things go badly wrong, and secure our perseverance over the long haul. Hutcheson's religion belongs to what Charles Taylor has aptly called "providential deism."[2]

The so-called Moderate party dominated the Church of Scotland from the 1750s until the early nineteenth century. Committed to the principle of patronage, by which the landowning classes played a decisive role in the appointment of clergy, they represented political and social stability through the principles of Enlightenment philosophy and theology. The sermon was a key instrument in the promotion of this culture. Instead of long *ex tempore* discourses on the points of Reformed doctrine, preaching was characterized by a more polished style, a carefully crafted text, and apologetic arguments with a stress on moral principles. The theological emphasis of Moderate preaching rested upon the wisdom of the Creator, the teaching of Jesus, the providential ordering of nature and history, and the prospect of eschatological rewards and punishments.[3]

The influence of classical culture permeated this movement. The teaching of rhetorical style was mediated through classical figures such as Aristotle. Of particular philosophical significance were the works of the Stoics, especially Marcus Aurelius, Cicero, and Epictetus. The resonance of Stoicism with the "providential deism" of the Enlightenment ensured that some of its key tenets

---

1. For further background, see Thomas Ahnert, *The Moral Culture of the Scottish Enlightenment 1690–1805* (New Haven: Yale University Press, 2015).

2. Charles Taylor, *A Secular Age* (Cambridge, MA: Harvard University Press, 2007), 221.

3. See Stewart J. Brown, "Moderate Theology and Preaching c. 1750–1800," in *The History of Scottish Theology*, Vol. 2, ed. David Fergusson and Mark Elliott (Oxford: Oxford University Press, 2019), 69–83.

would be transposed into eighteenth-century terms.⁴ This suggested the possibility of a measure of natural goodness that counteracted an excessively negative (Calvinist) estimate of our fallen nature.

Somewhat ironically, therefore, the most distinguished figure of the Scottish Enlightenment was also its most avowedly skeptical. David Hume (1710–76) offered an account of ethics that was wholly independent of religious belief or practice. For Hume, our moral passions are rooted in our natural and social constitution, requiring no explanation beyond this. Religion, by contrast, can interfere with these by a surfeit of superstition and enthusiasm. These are the enemies of social stability and require to be tamed by appropriate political arrangements. Our intuitive sense of moral objectivity is to be explained by our propensity "to stain and gild the world" with the colors of the mind.⁵ The language of moral objectivity is a projection on to the world of virtues that are either natural to our constitution or contrivances to promote our social well-being. This is especially evident in his discussion of justice as an artificial virtue. Morality does not require religious explanation or underpinning. We can live well, often better, without the constraints of religious dogma.

Hutcheson and Smith

Hutcheson was Adam Smith's (1723–90) teacher and his predecessor in the Chair of Moral Philosophy in Glasgow. Some lines of comparison enable us to appreciate the similarities and differences. Hutcheson's ethical theory sets the context for much of Smith's *Theory of Moral Sentiments* (TMS), first published in 1759, with its stress on moral feelings. Drawing on the analogy of aesthetic judgments, Hutcheson argues that moral approbation reposes upon a sense of what is pleasing in human conduct. In particular, the feeling of benevolence plays a central role in ethical life. It "recommends the generous part by an immediate undefinable perception" without regard to our own interests.⁶ The tendency in Hutcheson is to regard moral sense as a particular faculty with which human beings have been endowed. Though this may be deficient in some persons, just as general perceptual capacities can be impaired, it is a universal capacity. A pervasive assumption in Hutcheson is that this has been implanted by the Creator. Hence, despite the concerns of his conservative ecclesiastical critics who feared that Hutcheson attributed too much to our natural capacities, there is a close link in his thought between ethics and

---

4. See James Harris, "The Place of the Ancients in the Moral Philosophy of the Scottish Enlightenment," *Journal of Scottish Philosophy* 8, no. 1 (2010): 1–11.

5. David Hume, *Enquiries Concerning Human Understanding and Concerning the Principles of Morals* (EHU and EPM), ed. L. A. Selby-Bigge, rev. P. H. Nidditch (Oxford: Oxford University Press, 1975), 294.

6. Francis Hutcheson, *A System of Moral Philosophy: In Three Books* (London: 1755), I.4.xii.

religion. Nature, including its human elements, has been providentially designed by God to further our well-being. The design argument rehearsed by Hutcheson stresses not only the harmonies of the solar system and the fruitfulness of the earth, but also the intellectual, moral, and spiritual constitution of human beings. And these reflections lead him to argue both for the metaphysical and moral attributes of God. His system might be described as a species of theological naturalism. Our moral capacities are rooted in our human nature with its inherent dispositions. But these provide powerful evidence of the wisdom and goodness of our Creator. This also leads Hutcheson to stress the importance of piety for the sake both of glorifying God and reinforcing our ethical commitments. We should reflect upon the attributes of God. These are worthy of contemplation and enhance the moral sense. And, through participating in public worship, we give outward expression to this and become bound with others in the pursuit of common moral and religious ends.

> A constant regard to God in all our actions and enjoyments, will give a new beauty to every virtue, by making it an act of gratitude and love to him; and increase our pleasure in every enjoyment, as it will appear an evidence of his goodness: it will give a diviner purity and simplicity of heart, to conceive all our virtuous dispositions as implanted by God in our hearts, and all our beneficent offices as our proper work, and the natural duties of that station we hold in his universe, and the services we owe to this nobler country.[7]

Hutcheson's theological commitments are everywhere apparent. Though he differs from his Reformed predecessors in attributing much more to nature, philosophical reason, and our innate goodness, he stands as a formative influence for a Moderate theology. In his philosophy, an ethical naturalism is allied to doctrines of creation, providence, and eschatological rewards.

When we come to Adam Smith, we find obvious similarities but also some significant differences of emphasis. In the opening chapter of TMS, he follows Hutcheson's rejection of ethical egoism, criticizing Mandeville for a restriction of human motives to self-interest. Our natural tendencies include a consideration of others without reference to any advantage accrued for ourselves. Our ethical judgments are rooted in our natural capacities. Smith makes much of the role of sympathy in which we are able to place ourselves in the position of other people and to judge accordingly what is proper, honorable, just, and so forth. The ideal perspective to which we should attain is that of the impartial spectator whose judgments provide an exact standard for moral evaluation. But greater attention is given by Smith to the ways in which the different virtues arise in a range of social contexts and are embedded in forms of human life. Much of TMS is devoted to moral psychology with the result that the need to invoke a distinct moral sense endowed by the Creator is largely circumvented.

---

7. Ibid., I.10.iii.

In discussing Hutcheson, Smith acknowledges his debt.[8] A rationalist approach to ethics cannot provide a full account of moral approbation and motivation. We can discriminate and calculate particular rules of morality by use of reason, but distinguishing what is right and agreeable from what is wrong and disagreeable cannot at the outset be generated by reason. This is the domain of sentiment as Hutcheson clearly saw. Only "immediate sense and feeling"[9] can render virtue desirable for its own sake. Yet Smith also expresses some skepticism around Hutcheson's invocation of a distinctive moral sense that accounts for our moral perception and motivation.[10] His account both proves too much and too little. In proposing a distinctive moral sense for the heavy lifting in his theory, Hutcheson (and other sentimentalists) have named a term which has hitherto been obscure in moral philosophy. Why has this only recently been identified, Smith asks, if it is so pervasive and deeply rooted in our constitution? Would not other cultures and civilizations have noticed this earlier? Here Smith echoes the anxiety that Hutchesonian ethics still has associations with an implausible innatism, whereby he invokes a special category in the absence of any other explanatory mechanism. At the same time, Smith reckons that Hutcheson's appeal to a moral sense cannot account for the diverse range of moral feelings that can variously be expressed in anger, elevation, admiration, gratitude etc. By describing the ways in which sympathy connects us with the perspective of other agents, we can broaden notions of self-interest, pleasure, and pain to accommodate wider social dynamics. In particular, the utility or beauty of a system that works well for us can be appreciated and promoted. In this way, Hutcheson's naturalism is deepened without recourse to a special moral sense endowed by the Creator. The different directions in which these forms of ethical naturalism move enable us to reflect further on why religion plays a much less prominent role in Smith's moral theory than in Hutcheson's.

Adam Smith on Religion

Given his reticence and some of the shifts in his writing, it is not surprising that a range of different views has been attributed to Smith. These include a Christian theology that is shared with other moderate thinkers, a theistic Stoicism that was increasingly accentuated in his philosophy, and a deep skepticism that was much more carefully concealed than that of his close friend Hume. Some recent writers

---

8. Adam Smith, *The Theory of Moral Sentiments*, ed. D. D. Raphael and A. L. Macfie (Indianapolis: Liberty Fund, 1982), VII.iii.2.7–9.

9. Ibid.

10. Daniel Carey, "Francis Hutcheson's Philosophy and the Scottish Enlightenment: Reception, Reputation and Legacy," in *Scottish Philosophy in the Eighteenth Century, Volume 1: Morals, Politics, Art, Religion*, ed. Aaron Garrett and James A. Harris (Oxford: Oxford University Press, 2015), 36–85.

including Phillipson,[11] Kennedy,[12] and Heydt[13] have argued that Smith is much more closely aligned with Humean skepticism than with any obviously theistic position. Others have argued for a more vigorous, if concealed, theological underpinning.[14] My own view is that Smith retained elements of Moderate theology but that these were not of obvious personal or intellectual significance, and that at the very least there is some drift from the tenets of Christian orthodoxy.[15] But, since Smith's views were well concealed, much of this debate is conjectural.

Smith's closest relationship throughout his life was with his mother who died in 1784 in her ninetieth year. A devout Presbyterian, she attended the Canongate Kirk; together with its manse, it is situated next door to the Smith home at Panmure House on Edinburgh's Royal Mile. Adam Smith probably accompanied her to church on many a Sunday. At the time of her death, he wrote to his publisher:

> Tho' the death of a person in her ninetieth year of her age was no doubt an event most agreeable to the course of nature; and, therefore, to be foreseen and prepared for; yet I must say to you, what I have to other people, that the final separation from a person who certainly loved me more than any other person ever did or ever will love me; and whom I certainly loved and respected more than I shall ever love or respect any other person, I cannot help feeling, even at this hour, as a very heavy stroke upon me.[16]

This moving passage tells us only of the mutual affection between a son and his mother. As far as indicating Smith's own theological beliefs it offers us very little. We have to assume that Smith would have respected his mother's piety and done little or nothing to disturb it. But the reference to a "final separation" does not betoken the absence of a belief in an afterlife. Christians can talk of a final parting

---

11. Nicholas Phillipson, *Adam Smith: An Enlightened Life* (London: Allen Lane, 2010).

12. Gavin Kennedy, "Adam Smith on Religion," in *The Oxford Handbook of Adam Smith*, ed. Christopher J. Berry, Maria Pia Paganelli, and Craig Smith (Oxford: Oxford University Press, 2013), 464–86.

13. Colin Heydt, "The Problem of Natural Religion in Smith's Moral Thought," *Journal of the History of Ideas* 78, no. 1 (2017): 73–94. For a rejoinder in defense of Smith's theological commitments, see Paul Oslington, "The 'New View' of Adam Smith in Context," *History of Economics Review* 71, no. 1 (2018): 118–31.

14. Jacob Viner, *The Role of Providence in the Social Order* (Princeton: Princeton University Press, 1972); Lisa Hill, "The Hidden Theology of Adam Smith," *European Journal of the History of Economic Thought* 8, no. 1 (2001): 1–29; Paul Oslington, "Divine Action, Providence and Adam Smith's Invisible Hand," in *Adam Smith as Theologian*, ed. Paul Oslington (London: Routledge, 2011), 61–76.

15. For this more mediating position, see Gordon Graham, "Adam Smith and Religion," in *Adam Smith: His Life, Thought and Legacy*, ed. Ryan Patrick Hanley (Princeton: Princeton University Press, 2016), 305–20.

16. Phillipson, *Adam Smith: An Enlightened Life*, 262.

at death, without implying the lack of hope beyond the grave. Smith's mother can be used neither to confirm nor deny his faith.

His relationship with the dying Hume is also of much interest, though again it raises as many questions as it answers. As Hume's closest friend at the close of his life, Smith became his literary executor. Despite being tasked with arranging the posthumous publication of the *Dialogues Concerning Natural Religion*, Smith was reluctant to be drawn into a public controversy. In the end, the manuscript was entrusted to Hume's nephew who quickly ensured its publication. The effect was not as divisive as Smith had feared. Perhaps as reparation for this refusal, Smith instead published a letter to his publisher describing the manner of Hume's death as befitting that of the most perfectly wise and virtuous man of his acquaintance. While no traces of faith or hope were evident, Hume remained amiable and cheerful to the end. Smith remarked to a friend. "Poor David Hume is dying very fast, but with great cheerfulness and good humor, and with more real resignation to the necessary course of things, than any Whining Christian every dyed with pretended resignation to the will of God."[17] These are strong words, but do they signify that Smith is in accord with Hume's agnosticism and merely avoided its advocacy on account of his aversion to public controversy? Again, the evidence is slender either way, though he seems to have shared Hume's disdain for the manifestations of religious enthusiasm, intolerance, and sectarian division.

More significant are the extensive adjustments to portions of the *Theory of Moral Sentiments* in the sixth and final edition of 1789. The best-known deletion is the passage on the atonement in which an extended reference to the standard Reformed understanding of the atoning work of Christ's death is replaced by reference to a universal religious conviction regarding future rewards and punishments. "In every religion, and in every superstition that the world has ever beheld, accordingly, there has been a Tartarus as well as an Elysium; a place provided for the punishment of the wicked, as well as one for the reward of the just."[18] Smith's emendation undoubtedly suggests a departure from a more orthodox theological position. But it remains consistent with much of the regnant moderate theology of the day which maintained a system of eschatological rewards and punishments while typically presenting Christ as a moral teacher and exemplar. Smith appears to distance himself from Christian theories of atonement, but not necessarily from all forms of "providential deism."

The critical remarks about religion in the *Wealth of Nations* (WN) are also taken to signify this more skeptical attitude to religion.[19] Like Hume, Smith is suspicious of religious groups that dominate society to the extent of repressing and persecuting opposition. Both Roman Catholics and Protestants are subject to this criticism at different historical moments. Smith's preferred option is for

---

17. Ibid., 244.
18. TMS 2.2.3.12.
19. Adam Smith, *An Inquiry into the Nature and Causes of the Wealth of Nations*, ed. R. H. Campbell, A. S. Skinner, and W. B. Todd (Indianapolis: Liberty Fund, 1981), 5.1.3.

a balancing of smaller sects, none of which can then dominate civic life. These will tend to respect other groups and coexist in the same social space—hence his advocacy of an American model of church–state relations by contrast with Hume's preference for a benign establishment. As Kennedy notes, competition is Smith's solution for religious as well as commercial monopolies.[20] And he appears to favor Presbyterianism over Episcopacy as a form of church government owing to its distribution of power and authority.[21] Yet Smith also notes some tendency toward narrow-mindedness and an over-bearing moral rigor among the sects. This can be counteracted, he judges, by the study of science and philosophy and in "the frequency and gaiety of publick diversions."[22] Yet there is little here from which moderate theology would dissent.

I doubt that we can find a window into Smith's soul at any point in his literary output. Some diminution of his Christian convictions seems apparent, though perhaps this is the older man becoming less constrained by public opinion and the need for approbation. Or maybe Smith, like so many of us, was a man of fluctuating and uncertain theological opinions. The direction of travel may incline toward skepticism on key Christian tenets, even while much of the framework of his ethical philosophy strongly suggests something like a providential deism. Though Heydt argues persuasively for a strong naturalism of conscience in Smith and a "psychological genealogy" of religious belief, there remain too many passages in his writings that invoke religious belief and practice as important for ethics. Are we to believe that Smith is really dissembling here for the sake of conformity and a temperamental reluctance to engage in public controversy, especially as many of these passages survive his late-life revisions? Admittedly, the absence of "piety" from his list of virtues is strikingly egregious in an eighteenth-century Scottish context, but again this may reflect a more minimalist natural religion animated by a growing skepticism about positive religion and its "whining" practitioners. There are many people who have given up on the church and the conventions of religious practice without abandoning their belief in God. Smith may be numbered among them.

The references to providence in TMS 3.5 are generally positive, strong and in accordance with Stoic philosophy. There is an order of nature, governing the world and human affairs. Our duty is to assent to this and to accept its conditions. The dictates of duty are presented to us as the will of God. Belief in God reinforces our moral motivation and performance. The tenor of Smith's writing is shaped in part by his reading of Seneca, Zeno, and Epictetus on the subject of divine providence. This represents a theory of general providence, rather than the special providence that is also a constitutive feature of Reformed theology. Smith's invocation of a standard of "exact propriety and perfection" to which our human norms can only approximate has some religious possibilities. The notion of an "archetype of

---

20. Kennedy, "Adam Smith on Religion," 471–2.
21. Ibid., 473; Graham, "Adam Smith and Religion," 316.
22. WN, 5.1.3.

perfection" produced by a "divine artist" enables us to make a distinction between what is generally approved in society with what ought to be approved, even if these can never be entirely separated.[23] One might argue that the providentialist categories that shape Smith's philosophy lean in a theistic direction—it seems possible to develop elements of TMS in this way. And yet Smith never makes the same moves that we find in Hutcheson. There is no explicit attempt to use ethics, economic order or the domain of nature as evidence for the divine existence. Although he notes the efficacy of religious images for our moral performance, everything he says is consistent with a theological non-cognitivism. To view belief in God as helpful for moral purposes does not constitute an argument for the veracity of such belief. Smith does not go there at any point in his philosophy. The possibility remains open for others to make the necessary argumentative moves as many of his successors did. Yet Smith himself says little that cannot be accommodated by an exhaustive naturalism.[24]

The evidence from his library, moreover, suggests that Smith had little interest in theological issues.[25] There is no sign of any important work of European Protestant theology—Calvin, Bullinger, and the Puritans do not feature. Nor do we find much in the way of eighteenth-century apologetic works such as Joseph Butler's *Analogy* or George Campbell's *Dissertation on Miracles*. While, of course, Hutcheson and Hume feature prominently, the exponents of the Protestant faith of his native land are largely conspicuous by their absence. It is almost as if Smith's library had been purged of all such work. The impression of a deep ambivalence around the Christian religion in Smith is hard to avoid, perhaps confirmed by the sense among his some of his contemporaries that he was not quite sound. Phillipson quotes an anonymous writer in 1791: "In many respects, Adam Smith was a chaste disciple of Epicurus, as that philosopher is properly understood. . . . O venerable, amiable, and worthy man, why was you not a Christian?"[26]

---

23. TMS VI.iii.25.

24. In my judgment, Smith's occasional references to an "invisible hand" incline toward a more naturalist reading. Although he would be fully aware of the theological associations of this metaphor, he uses it infrequently and never develops it along familiar theological lines. It is more easily read as a description of natural effects. While one might readily locate this within a theory of general providence, Smith offers little encouragement to do so. But for an excellent discussion of the provenance of the notion and a stronger reading than the one I offer, see Peter Harrison, "Adam Smith and the History of the Invisible Hand," *Journal of the History of Ideas* 72, no. 1 (2011): 29–49. This reading is also preferred by Paul Oslington, "God and the Market: Adam Smith's Invisible Hand," *Journal of Business Ethics* 108, no. 4 (2012): 429–38.

25. See Hiroshi Mizuta, *Adam Smith's Library: A Catalogue* (Oxford: Clarendon Press, 2000).

26. Phillipson, *Adam Smith: An Enlightened Life*, 281.

Further Problems of Smith Interpretation

How might these comments impact upon the wider issues in the interpretation of Smith? In conclusion, I raise three of these to assess how this ethical context might be relevant for his economics:

1. *"Das Adam Smith-Problem"* emerged in nineteenth-century Germany as a conundrum about the mismatch of his two key texts—*The Theory of Moral Sentiments* and *The Wealth of Nations*.[27] In discussing the human agent in these works, commentators remarked upon the sympathetic moral agent of TMS against the acquisitive *homo economicus* of WN. The dutiful and benevolent person of the earlier work seemed to be displaced by the self-centered and wealth-seeking individual of the marketplace. This is best illustrated in the famous passage: "It is not from the benevolence of the butcher, the brewer, or the baker, that we expect our dinner, but from their regard to their own interest."[28] According to some commentators, this apparent shift in perspective was to be explained by a sudden turn in Smith's thought toward a French materialism in which he abandoned the religious and Stoic orientation of his earlier work. But this hypothesis of "two Smiths" is now widely rejected. The problem can readily be resolved without resort to such a radical hypothesis. Although the focus of TMS is on moral agency and the character of sympathy, Smith nowhere denies that self-love is an important motive of conduct. Indeed, he spends time extolling the importance of prudence, industry, and frugality, all of which are entirely consistent with WN. And, in writing a treatise on economics, it is not in the least surprising that the focus falls on the self-interest of the agent. But he nowhere denies that the same agent is sociable, capable of fellow-feeling or alert to the claims of justice. His account of sympathy is intended precisely to show the continuities between self-love and love of the other.[29] As Raphael notes in his introduction to TMS, Smith himself provides the strongest argument against the problem. He revised TMS shortly before his death and did so in a way that clearly signaled its consistency with the claims of WN. The providentially ordered society that Smith described was one in which self-love played its part alongside other motives for action. Love of self and love of neighbor were not mutually exclusive but correlative, even if obvious tensions could persist between these springs of conduct. But these are held together in Smith's account of the regulated life in which different virtues and practices are properly ordered.

---

27. W. von Skarżyński, *Adam Smith als Moralphilosoph und Schoepfer der Nationaloekonomie: Ein Beitrag zur Geschichte der Nationaloekonomie* (Berlin: Verlag von Theobold Grieben, 1878); Keith Tribe, *The Economy of the Word: Language, History and Economics* (Oxford: Oxford University Press, 2015).

28. WN 1.2.2.

29. Alexander Broadie, "Sympathy and the Impersonal Spectator," in *Cambridge Companion to Adam Smith*, ed. Knud Haakonssen (Cambridge: Cambridge University Press, 2006), 158–88.

2. The question of Smith's allegiance to laissez-faire economics has long divided commentators. The "problem" for German commentators arose from their skepticism about whether the pursuit of individual economic interests would result naturally in the promotion of the general good. But was this really the view of Smith himself? Certainly, in much nineteenth-century British economic thought, a confidence in market forces was upheld to the extent that interference with these could even be perceived to be against the will of God. Some passages in Smith obviously incline in this direction, particularly those that refer to an "invisible hand," though these are infrequent.

> By preferring the support of domestic to that of foreign industry, he intends only his own security; and by directing that industry in such a manner as its produce may be of the greatest value, he intends only his own gain, and he is in this, as in many other cases, led by an invisible hand to promote an end which was no part of his intention.... By pursuing his own interest he frequently promotes that of the society more effectually than when he really intends to promote it.[30]

Theological appropriations of this language are not difficult to find, particularly in the nineteenth century. An exponent of free trade, Thomas Chalmers insisted that the economic order was ordained by divine providence; if respected it would prove benevolent in its outcomes.[31] The internal order of the system constrains us to develop Christian virtues, thus demonstrating its providential worth. Other considerations were also advanced by Evangelical economists, including the thought that a population surfeit amid scarce resources would encourage emigration and so the spread of the gospel to distant places. State intervention through the Poor Laws was correspondingly criticized as destructive, inter alia, of personal initiative, philanthropic endeavor, and family ties.

But whether this reflects Smith's own position is doubtful. Free trade was undoubtedly perceived as an activity that brought many benefits to individuals and society. Yet Smith did not regard unbridled free trade as a universal panacea. In this connection, he recognized the limitations of the market and the need for state regulation and selective intervention. This applies for example to the control of interest rates where the maximum legal permitted should be set "a little above" the market rate. According to Smith, capping the interest rate ensures a more generally advantageous use of capital while also constraining those actions of "prodigals and projectors" which damage the system and bring it into disrepute.[32] Furthermore,

---

30. WN IV.2.9.

31. Boyd Hilton, "Chalmers as Political Economist," in *The Practical and the Pious: Essays on Thomas Chalmers (1780–1847)*, ed. A. C. Cheyne (Edinburgh: St Andrew Press, 1985), 141–56.

32. See Amartya Sen, "The Contemporary Relevance of Adam Smith," in *The Oxford Handbook of Adam Smith*, ed. Christopher J. Berry, Maria Pia Paganelli, and Craig Smith (Oxford: Oxford University Press, 2013), 582.

the aims of political economy are not only to ensure the subsistence of a people but also to enable the provision of public services by the state. For Smith, this included poor relief, the provision of free education, and the improvement of transport infrastructure. The case for free trade which he made, therefore, did not hinge upon a defense of a radical laissez-faire approach. A strong sense of the common good, the welfare of all, and the role of civic bodies and the state in promoting these informs his work, as one would expect given his moral philosophy. His economic theory is set within the wider context of an account of the human condition, society, and the order of nature. A vision of human flourishing informs his work—his writings on political economy should not be set apart from this.

3. The question whether Smith was optimistic or pessimistic about the outcomes for political economy has also received contradictory answers.[33] Excessive appeal to the "invisible hand" passages might suggest that social and economic progress are inevitable over the course of time. If there is an inherent order in the cosmos to which we are bound, then this might be expected to prevail in ways that are providential. The ends of nature—self-preservation, procreation and happiness—best prevail in a free trading, commercial society. Here much of Smith's work resonated with the optimistic spirit of the following century. Yet against this there are many more cautionary and somber elements in his work. Commercial society is neither inevitable nor permanent, and even where it flourishes it does so amid conflict and tension. Class envy, excessive materialism, manipulation of government by powerful elites, and the urge to dominate other peoples—all these forces and problems threaten the *telos* of a commercial society. Given the textual evidence for both positions, this tension in Smith seems unresolved. It is inherent rather than apparent. He remains a "sober optimist" or a "hopeful pessimist" held captive by the different tendencies in his thought. But, in this respect at least, he may be regarded as belonging to the religious ethos of moderate Scotland and its realism about human nature. Confident of economic and social progress, it had moved beyond the religious violence, impoverishment, and intolerance of the seventeenth century. Yet the Reformed theological tradition, with its somber estimate of human capacities, continued to exercise a refracted influence among the Moderates. In this intellectual setting, Smith's ambivalent approach to human nature and society makes good sense.

---

33. James Alvey, *Adam Smith: Optimist or Pessimist* (Aldershot: Ashgate, 2004).

Chapter 10

NATURAL THEOLOGY AFTER DARWIN

Types of Natural Theology

The term "natural theology" typically describes that branch of the subject that appeals to evidence for the existence and character of God from sources available to all rational beings. These include observation of the natural world as well as universal patterns of human experience whether moral, aesthetic, or religious. Excluded are appeals to particular sources of divine revelation, whether sacred texts, religious institutions or single historical events. A methodological distinction is thus generated between a natural theology appealing to universally accessible phenomena and a revealed theology that deals with Scripture, tradition and miracles. From the early church onward, there is a tacit assumption that these two sources of knowledge, however configured, are complementary. Each supports the other, and together they offer a persuasive account of the being and action of God in relation to the creation. This yielded the famous metaphor of the two books—the book of nature and the book of God, their stories being combined to form a single, coherent narrative. In this way, it was generally assumed that scientific observation could support and confirm the fundamental convictions of faith, though we should beware of assuming anachronistically that these modes of reflection always represented clearly differentiated disciplines as in the modern academy.

This stock description of natural theology will be familiar to most readers, and on the whole it is uncontroversial. Yet it conceals significant differences of approach and context. Natural theology has been used in a variety of ways at different periods in the history of theology. By my reading of the subject, there are at least five forms, and even some of these may be liable to sub-division. These range from stronger to weaker forms of approach. What is interesting is that each has a particular historical context, conditions under which a strategy typically flourished as a response to various challenges and opportunities.[1]

---

1. I have borrowed this typology from an earlier essay, "Types of Natural Theology," in *The Evolution of Rationality: Interdisciplinary Essays in Honor of J. Wentzel Van Huyssteen*, ed. F. Le Ron Shults (Grand Rapids: Eerdmans, 2006), 380–93.

1. First, we might cite the strong deist conviction that natural theology is a more reliable and less provincial guide to knowledge of God. A cause of much early modern conflict, claims based upon special revelation were perceived to be partial and divisive. Their epistemological status was less persuasive to an age increasingly impressed by the accessibility and universality of scientific claims. Hence we find a commitment to the priority of natural theology over revealed theology in writers such as Matthew Tindal at All Souls, Oxford. He argues for the superiority of natural theology. Scripture is to be assessed for its capacity to teach and conform to what we know on prior and independent grounds; at best, it contains a "republication" of the truths known to reason.[2] The existence of God, the providential ordering of the world, and the moral truths which regulate our conduct can all be discerned by reason without reference to Scripture or the teaching of the church. Indeed, much historical religion is here viewed as a corruption of an earlier and purer natural religion based upon reason and intuition. The valorizing of natural theology in deism is intended as a means of criticism of revealed religion. In this respect, it has a radical edge through much of the eighteenth century.

2. A second type of natural theology is less skeptical of revealed theology but it regards the former as necessary to establish the reliability of the latter. In other words, natural theology functions as a necessary preliminary activity upon which the claims of revelation can subsequently be founded. This role is one that is sometimes found in modern epistemological projects. In an oft-quoted essay, Nicholas Wolterstorff detects this approach in Locke's claims for the reliability of Scripture.[3] These are based upon the manner in which belief-claims more generally are to be justified. Hence a commitment to the truths contained in Scripture must be grounded upon the justification of the credibility of the biblical writers. This is achieved, it seems, by reference to considerations about the veracity of testimony. Only insofar as the witness of Scripture can be judged reasonable are we

---

2. "I desire no more than to be allow'd, that there's a Religion of Nature & Reason written in the heart of every one of us from the first Creation, by which all Mankind must judge of the truth of any instituted Religion whatever: and if it varies from the Religion of Nature and Reason in any one particular, nay, in the minutest circumstance, that alone is an argument which makes all things else that can be said for its support totally ineffectual." Matthew Tindal, *Christianity as Old as the Creation or the Gospel a Republication of the Religion of Nature* (London, 1731), 52.

3. Nicholas Wolterstorff, "The Migration of the Theistic Arguments: From Natural Theology to Evidentialist Apologetics," in *Rationality, Religious Belief and Moral Commitment*, ed. Robert Audi and William J. Wainwright (Ithaca: Cornell University Press, 1986), 38–81.

entitled to adhere to the distinctive truth claims of revealed theology. The particular and essential commitments of Christian faith are grounded therefore upon more general arguments for the divine existence together with the attendant signs and wonders that accompany Scripture.[4] In this context, the design argument and the appeal to miracles play an important role in establishing the truth and excellence of Christian religion. With the necessary epistemic justification in place, we can then turn to the detailed teaching of the Bible assured that it will furnish us with further information about the works of God. Revelation can be believed as a source of knowledge not otherwise accessible, but only at the bar of reason. For Locke, this excluded the deplorable fanaticism and dangerous certitude of splinter groups.

3. A third type might be discerned in the work of Thomas Aquinas, although here interpretations vary. There are some truths about God which, although presented and known through Scripture, can also be attained by the use of human reason. Aspiring to such truth, the mind can comprehend in relative detachment from Scripture a knowledge of the existence and unity of God. This is a divinely ordained goal of the human intellect even if not all human beings have the inclination, opportunity and capacity to attain it. For Aquinas, such knowledge does not precede Scripture in any kind of epistemological priority nor does it make Scripture redundant. In this respect, natural theology performs a different function from the previous two types. Yet it appears to be a capacity of the human mind to reason from the world to God, at least in some rather limited ways. This function of natural theology can be found in the *Summa Contra Gentiles* alongside the apologetic task which is the next type. "Yet it is useful for the human reason to exercise itself in such arguments, however weak they may be, provided only that there be present no presumption to comprehend or demonstrate. For to be able to see something of the loftiest realities, however thin and weak the sight may be, is . . . a cause of the greatest joy."[5]

Nevertheless, much recent interpretation of Aquinas understands the role of philosophical reason here neither as preparatory nor semi-independent, but as set firmly within the context of faith. The limits of reason are constantly stressed by Aquinas, while even the much-discussed Five Ways may be regarded as deflationary arguments to curb human pretension and idolatry. God's existence is not self-evident, and even the

---

4. The appeal to the miraculous events accompanying the writing of Scripture was long used as a supplementary mark of its divine authority. But for Locke it provides the rational warrant for believing Scripture to contain divine revelation. In this respect, revelation is epistemologically dependent upon the correct exercise of our natural reason. Cf. *An Essay Concerning Human Understanding*, Book IV, Chapter 19.

5. *Summa Contra Gentiles* Book One, 8.1.

hard-earned conclusions of rational argument do not take us very far.[6] In this setting, natural theology has a legitimate, but clearly subordinate and circumscribed role; it is not an independent, autonomous source and norm for the knowledge of God. Aquinas is not a forerunner of Locke or the deists.

4. A further function of natural theology is the more apologetic task of defeating the strongest objections leveled against some or all aspects of the Christian faith. In this respect, natural theology might include arguments against the eternity of the world, socio-biological explanations of morality, the claim that religion is a form of false consciousness under the oppressive conditions of capitalism, and the thesis that the freedom of the will is an incoherent notion. Although one can find arguments of natural theology in the early and medieval church performing this role, it becomes more prominent under the conditions of modernity where belief in God is no longer a given. However, its function here is mainly negative. The task of the natural theologian is primarily to "defeat the defeaters," to use Alvin Plantinga's expression. Attempts to convict believers of inconsistency, irrationality, or sheer wishful thinking need to be confronted and rebutted. In this project, natural theology may have a role but it is clearly a defensive and subsidiary one, rather than a foundational or preparatory one.

5. Finally, a fifth task of natural theology might be discerned in the perceived need to display the ways in which the essential claims of revelation can coexist in positive relation to the best insights available from other disciplines and fields of knowledge. Although closely related to the apologetic function, it has a more positive role in showing the consistency of theology with other important forms of inquiry, for example, natural science and history. In this respect, natural theology remains a modest, *ad hoc* type of enterprise in seeking to show the capacity of faith to coexist with what we know of the world, its history and forms of life from other fields of inquiry not directly related to Scripture or the church. In this last respect, natural theology may actually be viewed as an important pastoral and educational function of the church. Active in many important secular activities—science, medicine, and technology—the members of the church seek to relate the knowledge and insights of the workplace to those of the faith communities to which they belong. They deserve all the support available to them.

---

6. "The point of insisting that arguments for God's existence is required is, then, not to convince hypothetical open-minded atheists, or even to persuade 'fools', so much as to deepen and enhance the mystery of the hidden God. From the start, the 'theistic proofs' are the first lesson in Thomas's negative theology. Far from being an exercise in rationalistic apologetics, the purpose of arguing for God's existence is to protect God's transcendence." Fergus Kerr, *After Aquinas: Versions of Thomism* (Oxford: Blackwell, 2002), 58.

Given these different approaches to the function of natural theology, it is hardly surprising that its content should vary considerably also. What passes for "natural theology" may include a wide range of claims, some more modest in scope than others. Deistic and Lockean arguments will typically make strong claims about the divine existence and nature which either precede or exercise their validity independently of Scripture, faith and the church. A natural theology that reflects the divinely bestowed powers of reason will tend to be determined by estimates of the strength and virtues of the human mind outside the visible church. On one recent reading of Aquinas, noted above, natural theology may actually attain relatively little in this respect. Similarly, while Calvin attached some significance to the *sensus divinitatis* and classical arguments for God's existence, these were of minor significance compared to the theological tasks with which he was confronted. And the authority of Scripture is confirmed not so much by its felicity, coherence, and attendant miracles as by the internal testimony of the Holy Spirit. Clouded by the insidious effects of sin, our reason and judgment are unreliable without the guidance of Scripture and mother church. When we come to the more defensive role of natural theology (type four), we find that it is largely set by secular forces, these being combated by negative arguments to defeat the defeaters. Hume, Darwin, Marx, and Freud presented challenges to theology that have been met in different ways, all of which were largely reactive. Yet, whether the outcome of this exercise leaves faith exactly where it was is doubtful. Its historical mobility and capacity to adapt under shifting intellectual conditions is not entirely captured by the language of defeat. Moreover, the ineluctable vocation of attesting that Christian faith can coexist with the best insights from other fields of knowledge may largely be an "*ad hoc*" task, driven by the social and institutional context of the theologian.[7] In short, what we find is that the term "natural theology" has been stretched to comprehend a wide variety of theological tasks that cannot be reduced merely to a reformulation of the traditional philosophical arguments for God's existence. It is regrettable that the way in which the proofs are frequently taught in school and university syllabi tends to obscure these important shifts in context and function.

The Impact of Darwinism

Published in 1859, *The Origin of Species* is often represented as a watershed in the history of relations between science and religion. With the explanatory mechanism of natural selection, it was argued, much that had previously been attributed to the operation of divine design could now be explained by purely natural causes. Almost overnight, God had become redundant. Although not put about by Darwin

---

7. The term is borrowed from Hans Frei's justification of "*ad hoc*" apologetics and correlationism. See *Types of Modern Theology* (New Haven: Yale University Press, 1992), 70-91.

himself, this view was encouraged by some of his followers, most notably T. H. Huxley, famously dubbed "Darwin's bulldog." For Huxley, the teleology favored by Archdeacon Paley in the early nineteenth century could now be given natural explanation. The adaptation of means to ends throughout creation no longer required to be attributed to design. Organs had evolved with greater complexity, species had adapted to the environment, and changes had taken place in life forms under the pressure of natural selection rather than divine design. According to Huxley, what theology called providence, science perceived only as natural order.[8] This fundamental opposition was also affirmed by voices on the theological side.[9]

We find echoes of this dialectical opposition of scientific and religious explanation in much of today's New Atheism. It is admirably captured in Daniel Dennett's metaphor of cranes and sky hooks.[10] As the power of nature's cranes becomes better understood with the march of science, so the need to appeal to a sky hook recedes. Here the assumption is that science and religion occupy common ground in their explanatory accounts of nature. At earlier stages in the history of ideas, large and incomprehensible gaps in our understanding of nature were filled by recourse to a divine skyhook. However, as these gaps diminish so the cranes start to do the heavy lifting, with the result that religious explanation fades in significance. Richard Dawkins is the most strident exponent of this view today. Once upon a time natural theology had sought to explain the appearance of complex organs such as the eye, as well as the extraordinary adaptation of species to environment. But now a neo-Darwinian account of genetic mutation and natural selection can offer a powerful story of how this all came to be. Darwin's brilliant idea works like a powerful acid upon earlier forms of theological reflection. Instead of a worldview dominated by the hypothesis of intelligent design, we now have a naturalist outlook in which God lacks any substantial explanatory role. Nevertheless, despite its powerful advocates, this view is neither historically nor philosophically compelling. Soon after the appearance of *Origin of Species*, Christian theologians showed themselves both persuaded by the force of Darwin's science and ready to offer it theological accommodation. Many of their arguments adumbrate positions adopted by scientists and theologians today in relation to evolutionary theory.

Given the ways in which Darwin's theory of evolution built upon a significant body of scientific discovery in the first half of the nineteenth century, we should not be surprised to discover that theologians were already somewhat prepared for the subsequent debate. Charles Lyell's work in geology had persuaded many that the earth must be millions of years older than the traditional dating of 4004 BCE proposed by Archbishop Ussher on the basis of the biblical record. By the early nineteenth century, geologists could show that through "uniformitarian" processes

---

8. Cited by David N. Livingstone, *Darwin's Forgotten Defenders: The Encounter between Evangelical Theology and Evolutionary Thought* (Grand Rapids: Eerdmans, 1987), 49.
9. For example, Charles Hodge, *What Is Darwinism?* (London: Nelson, 1874).
10. Daniel Dennett, *Darwin's Dangerous Idea* (New York: Touchstone, 1995), 136.

the formation of rocks and changes to the earth's surface could be explained by natural causes such as volcanoes, glaciers, sedimentation, and erosion by water. These processes, however, required a great deal of time and only a much older universe than the one posited by Ussher would fit the bill. From about 1820, therefore, we find many theological writers denying a young universe that had been decisively shaped by a catastrophic event such as the flood. The capacity to interpret Genesis 1–11 in nonliteral ways was already apparent, as it was in the exegesis of the early church fathers.[11] As always, the intellectual causes for a sudden shift in perspective are complex and multiple. Why then did Darwin's theory seem to cause such an intellectual upheaval for religion? At least four reasons are apparent; each will be explored.[12]

1. *God now appeared to be remote from the cosmos.* The natural theology that had dominated British theology until the early nineteenth century was epitomized by William Paley. Here the evidence of divine design seemed everywhere manifest, so much so that little credence was given to Hume's skepticism. While the arguments of Philo in Hume's *Dialogues* may have appeared unassailable to later analytic philosophers, for much of the nineteenth century they were regarded as overblown and fanciful. The evidence of design was too compelling to sustain such skepticism. Successive contributions to the Bridgewater Treatises, including that of the Evangelical theologian Thomas Chalmers, confirmed this confidence in the design argument.[13] So much of the natural world was inexplicable without appeal to the God-hypothesis that it was assumed that a greater understanding of its workings would only confirm the intuitive impression of design. But if natural selection could explain what had formerly been assigned to the mechanism of supernatural design, would the latter then become redundant? This was undoubtedly a fear in some theological quarters matched by the hopes of Huxley et al. Yet, this making God otiose proved too hasty. Since at least the time of Newton, scientists and theologians, impressed by the explanatory power of scientific law, had seen its rational operation as evidence of the majesty of the Creator. If the laws of nature could explain the formation of rocks, then this merely registered the

---

11. Symbolic readings of the Genesis story were commonplace in the early church, as is evident in Augustine's *Confessions*.

12. In what follows, I have drawn from an essay on "Providence after Darwin," in *Theology After Darwin*, ed. Michael Northcott and R. J. Berry (Milton Keynes: Paternoster, 2009), 73–88. For a much fuller historical discussion see David Livingstone, *Dealing with Darwin: Place, Politics and Rhetoric in Religious Engagements with Evolution* (Baltimore: Johns Hopkins University Press, 2014).

13. Thomas Chalmers, *On the Power, Wisdom, and Goodness of God as Manifested in the Adaptation of External Nature to the Moral and Intellectual Constitution of Man*. 2 vols (London, 1833).

power of the Creator who had ordained those laws.[14] God was not required occasionally or frequently to intervene in the cosmic process in order to achieve the intended results. Instead, the way the world had been established under the general working of natural law was itself sufficient to realize those creaturely states and entities desired by God. Not surprisingly, this move was to become a stock response to Darwinian theory. If evolution is how states of greater complexity emerge in the history of the cosmos, then it is open to the theologian to claim that this is how God does it. In his 1884 Bampton Lectures, Frederick Temple adopts this strategy. God "did not make the things, we may say: no, but He made them make themselves."[15] This was teleology at one distance removed and offered a different account of design to Paley. Indeed, in an important respect, Temple sees his view as improving upon Paley. Instead of an Artificer who has to interject at regular intervals to bring about the intended effects in the production of life forms, we have a Creator who has from the very beginning endowed the creation with sufficient natural powers to evolve as intended.

This argument was already employed by Principal Robert Rainy in his inaugural address at New College, Edinburgh in 1874.[16] According to Rainy, all that has changed is our conception of a world that was originally endowed with sufficient fruitfulness to yield emergent patterns. Rainy notes that there may be some loss "of the argumentative benefit of pleading earlier interpositions as analogical instances" of divine revelation in history. A God who regularly intervenes to direct the course of history might be expected to do the same in the natural world. However, this assumption can be yielded in favor of an evolutionary worldview. While expressing some reservations about Darwinism, he seeks to distinguish the approach of the natural scientist from that of the theologian. These different forms of understanding occupy separate domains allowing a relative independence within each but a complementarity when viewed in conjunction. One upshot of all this is the clearer recognition of the disciplinary boundaries between theology, philosophy, and the natural sciences. Theology is now positioned less as a discipline that encroaches upon and supplements the descriptions of the natural scientist; set apart and with its own subject matter, increasingly it seeks a complementary alignment rather than filling any intermediate gaps in scientific explanation.

Embedded in this approach is the correct response to creation science and intelligent design theory. An evolving world, as described by the natural sciences, can equally well be viewed as the outcome of divine design. We do not need to seek gaps in scientific explanation in which to interject the

---

14. See the argument of John Hedley Brooke, "Natural Law in the Natural Sciences: The Origins of Modern Atheism?," *Science and Christian Belief* 4, no. 2 (1992): 83–103.

15. Frederick Temple, *Religion and Science* (London: Macmillan, 1884), 115.

16. Robert Rainy, *Evolution and Theology* (Edinburgh, 1874).

agency of God. By allowing these spaces to be filled by subsequent scientific research, we can concede this domain of explanation to the natural sciences. At the same time, the theologian can insist that God has endowed the creation with the capacity to evolve increasingly complex patterns of life forms.[17] To appeal to divine intrusion at the point when the latest scientific explanation falters is to give hostages to fortune. As science progresses so the gap is closed. In any case, such defensive strategies fail to recognize the different and complementary levels at which physical and theological explanation operate.[18]

2. *The role of chance and loss of providential control.* Much theological anxiety can be detected around the role assigned to "chance" by Darwinian science. Even among writers in search of an alliance with evolutionary theory, we find attempts to replace the function of chance with a more deterministic mechanism. Of course, for Darwinian theory "chance" does not refer to the inexplicable or the uncaused. Instead, it is the denial of a single deterministic trajectory followed by the evolution of life forms. There seem to be two types of process that are characterized by the language of chance. One of these concerns the minor physiological variations that are evident through the reproduction of species, and the other is in the intersection of unrelated causal systems, for example, the impact of a sudden change in climate upon the development of species in a hitherto stable ecological niche. The mechanism governing physiological variation was not understood until the later development of genetics; informed critics of Darwin in the nineteenth century recognized this *lacuna* in his theory. This was eventually filled by developments in genetics, thus allowing the neo-Darwinian synthesis with its twin principles of natural selection and genetic mutation to dominate explanatory theories.

Yet it was the random course of evolution, as described by Darwin, that most offended Charles Hodge in Princeton. He regarded this as practically atheistic since there could be no governing purpose or overriding control exercised over the direction of nature. What was under threat here was not so much the doctrine of creation from Darwinian evolution—a transcendent origination of the whole scheme could still be conceived—as the doctrine of providence. Hodge could concede that a process of evolution was consistent with theism. However, the particular account offered by Darwin with its stress on natural selection led him to believe that it was metaphysically inconsistent with the teleological principle that belonged both to revealed and natural theology. If God were no longer in control of the course of life on earth, then it could not be perceived as proceeding toward an appointed

---

17. See Howard van Til, "The Creation: Intelligently Designed or Optimally Equipped?," *Theology Today* 55 (1998/9): 344–64.

18. This is eloquently argued by Francis Collins, *The Language of God: A Scientist Presents Evidence for Belief* (New York: Free Press, 2006).

end. For a Reformed theologian such as Hodge, this was tantamount to a practical atheism.

Nevertheless, within that same tradition others reached different conclusions by placing evolution within a wider context that was perceived to be providentially ordered. Asa Gray, the Harvard botanist, replied to Hodge. His difficulty with Darwin, Gray claimed, arose out of an unduly restricted account of how divine teleology works. The Creator can endow nature and organisms with the powers of evolution into states of greater complexity. Hodge simply begs the question against this type of teleology with its commitment to an older, Paleyian type of strategy. This was also the line taken by Robert Flint in his Baird lectures on *Theism* that went through numerous editions during the late nineteenth century. Here his interaction with Darwinism offers a set of responses that have become standard in theological appropriations of evolutionary science. The development from lower to higher organisms can be explained as a mark of design. The tendency toward improvement and progression requires explanation. Evolutionary process can be envisioned as a vast scheme of order and beauty, rather than a grim arena of conflict and waste. This more positive vision of evolutionary complexity would be developed subsequently by writers such as J. Arthur Thomson and Patrick Geddes in their 1912 study of evolution.[19] Later in Princeton, Alexander Hodge and B. B. Warfield would make their peace with Darwinism, arguing that it was both scientifically sound and consistent with an account of divine providence.[20]

Other theological responses after the publication of *Origin* offered a more immanent account of divine involvement in the evolutionary process. In his essay in *Lux Mundi* (1889), Aubrey Moore wrote in a celebrated passage:

> The one absolutely impossible conception of God, in the present day, is that which represents him as an occasional visitor. Science has pushed the deist's God further and further away, and at that moment when it seemed as if He would be thrust out all together Darwinism appeared, and, under the disguise of a foe, did the work of a friend.[21]

Moore's claim is that Darwinism affords a positive opportunity for Christian theology to reaffirm its commitment to a perpetual involvement

---

19. J. Arthur Thomson and Patrick Geddes, *Evolution* (London: Williams & Norgate, 1912).

20. This also reveals how Darwinism could be interpreted in a wide variety of ways. James Moore, biographer of Darwin, argues that in the 1860s there were as many as five different types of Darwinism, each contending with one other. See "Deconstructing Darwinism: The Politics of Evolution in the 1860s," *Journal of the History of Biology* 24 (1991): 353–408.

21. Aubrey Moore, "The Christian Doctrine of God," in *Lux Mundi*, ed. Charles Gore (London, 1889), 99.

of the divine spirit in the natural world. Instead of the more remote and disengaged God of deism, we now have an immanent divine presence that is at work in the creative and open-ended processes of evolutionary history. Rather than posing a threat, therefore, the apparently free movement of natural forms is consonant with a God who is present and active within the creative process. This model of divine engagement resonated with the kenotic theologies that flourished around the same time. The model here is of God's "letting the world become itself," not in such a way as to abandon it but in the interests of a patient accompanying that seeks to work within and alongside creative processes. Again, science is used not so much to demonstrate theological conclusions but rather to show the consonance or fit between evolutionary theology and a kenotic doctrine of God. A more modest approach of discerning a possible harmony of understandings is typically pursued.

While Paley's teleology did not reflect a commitment to deism, its model of the God–world relationship seemed to lean in that direction with the notion of a perfectly ordered world in little need of repair or further development. After Darwin, however, theologians could see the world of nature as having a history, as being constantly in the process of making. Its narrative shape could increasingly be detected by advances in the natural sciences. Like history, therefore, nature was a work in progress, a construction site on which God could be seen as a sustaining, creative, guiding presence. Despite the attractions of a divine accompanying of the evolutionary process, problems remain over the mode and efficacy of this divine agency. An account of a sustaining presence can coexist with scientific explanation, but does God actually make a difference to outcomes beyond the initial endowment of matter with its evolutionary possibilities? This problem was hardly addressed by Aubrey Moore and persists for anyone advocating his more immanentist solution.[22]

3. *The intensification of the problem of evil.* A further recurrent concern in the theological reception of Darwin concerns the problem of evil. This was hardly a new challenge to confront Christian theology. The Book of Job already reveals a long history of reflection on this in Jewish traditions. And, in any case, the facts of predation, disease, suffering, and death were manifestly visible before any theory could explain their contribution to the evolutionary story. But what was striking in Darwin's description of evolution was the extent to which suffering, waste and the competition for survival were the drivers of evolution. These were part of the "design" that enabled the emergence of species, including human beings. Instead of Paley's notion of creatures living always in a state of equilibrium, their prosperity secured by a single divine blueprint, theologians now faced a

---

22. I have discussed this in *The Providence of God* (Cambridge: Cambridge University Press, 2018), 217–40.

bleaker scenario in which earlier species were driven to extinction in a perpetual warfare of life forms. How could this suggest a divine providence? If predation and extinction are constitutive features of the natural world, then it becomes progressively harder to view natural evil as a dysfunctional element in an otherwise well-regulated system.

One type of theodicy that confidently took Darwinian explanation on board argued, more or less, that the end justifies the means. Since evolution produced fitter and more advanced species, particularly *Homo sapiens*, we could conclude that the laws of evolution were all part of a benevolent divine plan. The production of better-adapted forms of life could thus be seen as an outworking of an overall teleology. This was the strategy pursued by the aforementioned Duke of Argyll, Henry Drummond, and Temple in his Bampton Lectures.[23] At the same time, these writers sought to introduce a different set of metaphors to overcome the prevailing sense of waste and random, meaningless suffering. Attention was drawn to the interdependence of species, the unity of the natural world, the long periods of relative equilibrium characterized in large measure by the enjoyment of life, and the beautiful harmony of flowers and insects.[24]

Others would point to patterns of self-sacrifice in nature that adumbrated later Christian moral ideals. In his study *Christianity and Evolution*, James Iverach noted that the individual often sacrifices itself for the well-being of the species to the extent that something like a virtuous family life emerges naturally.[25] The risk again is in presenting this as an implausible justification for violence and loss. Undoubtedly, evolution has its upside, yet in pointing to this we have not resolved the problem of suffering. If nature discards the weak and the unsuccessful, is this so that fitter and better-adapted species may emerge? The ends of evolution then enable us to explain why the system is one in which much is discarded as unfit, superfluous and disposable. This could tilt in dangerous directions particularly as human evolution came into focus. Should social policies be developed that artificially selected the fittest for reproduction?[26]

Nevertheless, by the later nineteenth century, this rather confident style of theodicy was being replaced by more reserved approaches to the problem of suffering. While a divine plan may be in a process of outworking, its meaning and significance are not yet discernible from a human vantage point. We simply cannot speculate on what purpose long eons of animal

---

23. See the discussion in James C. Livingston, *Religious Thought in the Victorian Age* (London: T&T Clark International, 2006), 69ff.

24. Temple, *Religion and Science*, 122.

25. James Iverach, *Evolution and Christianity* (London: Hodder & Stoughton, 1894).

26. For further discussion see Diane B. Paul, "Darwinism, Social Darwinism and Eugenics," in *Cambridge Companion to Darwin*, ed. Jonathan Hodge and Gregory Radick (Cambridge: Cambridge University Press, 2003), 214–39.

suffering may serve. Again, however, a virtue can be made out of a necessity. The theologian has no business reading off the details of divine design from the pages of natural history. The only index to providence is that of faith in Christ—more speculative and comprehensive accounts should be eschewed. At the same time, Darwinism may also helpfully save the theologian from embracing too narrow an anthropocentrism. Given the relatively late emergence of human beings and the extent to which animal life has evolved for much of the time with no reference to ourselves, we cannot assume that God's purposes are solely directed toward our own species. God must have more in mind than the evolution of humankind. [27]

4. *The perceived threat to human significance.* This last point leads to another hotly debated topic emerging from Darwinism, namely the significance of human beings in creation.[28] To a large extent, the greatest fear surrounding evolutionary theory was that it threatened to undermine our most fundamental convictions about the intellectual, moral, and spiritual distinctiveness of human beings. This was expressed immediately after the publication of *Origin of Species* in 1859 and before the appearance of the *Descent of Man* in 1871. The same anxiety continues to infect much of the debate today. If human beings emerged from other mammals over millions of years of evolution, is their uniqueness thereby compromised? Once more, a religious accommodation with Darwinism was proposed by successive writers, while also maintaining a traditional commitment to human distinctiveness. Scholars like Rainy and Temple argued again for a complementarity of explanations. The scientist could describe how human beings had emerged from other primates while also displaying significant similarities to other species. Yet the theologian could appeal to phenomena such as consciousness, our moral capacities and spiritual discernment that demand different forms of explanation and understanding from those available to the natural sciences. Here the natural theologies of the late nineteenth and early twentieth centuries inclined in a Kantian direction with their preoccupation with moral phenomena. This is evident in the arguments for a moral theism in some of the early Gifford lecturers.

Conclusion

Evolutionary theory did not sound the death knell for natural theology. Around the time of Darwin's death, Lord Gifford was preparing his last will and testament that would ensure that natural theology was studied and defended before public audiences in each of the four ancient universities of Scotland. The history of the

---

27. Moore, "The Christian Doctrine of God," 108f.

28. See Wenztel van Huyssteen, *Alone in the World? Human Uniqueness in Science and Theology* (Grand Rapids: Eerdmans, 2006).

Giffords points to the vitality of the subject and its capacity to flourish under shifting intellectual conditions.[29] While Darwinian science rendered one version of the design argument redundant, physicists soon became fascinated with instances of so-called fine-tuning which suggested that ours is a universe with an anthropic bias. These debates continue with intense discussion of the multiverse concept.

The revival of the philosophy of religion in analytic circles, championed by scholars such as Swinburne, Stump, and Plantinga in their different ways, has occasioned greater confidence in some of the standard arguments of natural theology. Apologists argue (too?) confidently that Big Bang cosmology confirms the ancient *kalam* cosmological argument that the universe must have had a temporal beginning, this being the consequence of a divine creative act. At the same time, the emergence of comparative theology has drawn attention to the ways in which exponents of each of the Abrahamic faiths have tended to adopt similar arguments and strategies in defending the convictions of their communities.

Much of this revitalized natural theology has viewed science and theology as complementary forms of understanding, not competing with each other to explain the phenomena but respecting the particular questions, domains and procedures of these different forms of inquiry. This clearer differentiation of disciplines was in part an outcome of the engagement with Darwinism. Increasingly, theologians recognized that it was futile to attempt to contest scientific explanation in order to save the day for God.

Finally, what of the total resistance to natural theology on the part of Karl Barth and many of his acolytes? His rejection of the discipline continued a long history of Germanic skepticism toward natural theology dating back to Kant and Schleiermacher who regarded the standard proofs as both unconvincing and anthropomorphic. This hostility was shared by the liberal school of Albrecht Ritschl which viewed *history* as the locus of divine activity rather than *nature*. Metaphysical speculation was eschewed in favor of historical study and the interpretation of the distinctively ethical dimension of human existence. Emerging from out of this tradition but turning against it, Barth launched a positive theological attack on natural theology. Instead of ignoring it or treating it skeptically, he denounced its idolatrous tendencies. The proofs were a decidedly bourgeois exercise that could yield only a God in our own image, belief in whom was a form of self-aggrandizement and acquiescence in the status quo. Much of this, especially his famous "*Nein*" to Brunner, was played out in the heat of the German church controversy in the early 1930s. Natural theology leads us astray from proper obedience to the one Word of God who is Jesus. The only God who is self-disclosed in a determining act of revelation is the God and Father of Jesus.[30]

---

29. See Stanley Jaki, *Lord Gifford and his Lectures* (Edinburgh: Scottish Academic Press, 1995).

30. See Alister McGrath, *Emil Brunner: A Reappraisal* (Oxford: Wiley Blackwell, 2015), 90–132.

Barth's theology clearly excludes some types of natural theology, particularly those that assign it a foundational, indispensable, or controlling function. But whether it completely forbids the more modest strategies of defeating the defeaters or showing the compossibility of theological with other forms of knowledge remains an open question. In the work of T. F. Torrance, his leading British pupil and commentator, we find an attempt to revive natural theology by integrating and subordinating it to the claims of positive theology.[31] And in Barth's own later writings, his discussion of the "little lights of creation" may offer possibilities of more nuanced interpretation of his prohibition of natural theology.

Where does this leave us? Increased awareness of the contextual setting of all natural theology, together with our greater sense of the disciplinary discreteness of science and religion, must render it a more modest type of inquiry than that supposed by either the deists or Archdeacon Paley. Natural theology takes place within a setting of presuppositions and particular problems requiring to be addressed. Its shifting contexts suggest that it has a more *ad hominem* character in intellectual debates than was often acknowledged. At the same time, a recognition of science and religion as offering complementary forms of understanding should caution against any assumption that there is a direct argumentative line from scientific premises to theological conclusions. This should also ensure that natural theology assumes a more modest and deflated character. In any case, we need to concede that faith is not so much the result of a particular propositional state generated by an argument. A wide-ranging commitment of a practical, affective, and intellectual nature, faith is embraced as a result of diverse considerations not readily capable of precise theoretical expression.

The issue of the relationship of faith to reason greatly exercised John Henry Newman in his *University Sermons* and later in the *Grammar of Assent* around the time of Darwin's scientific discoveries. Pointing to the practical character of religious belief, he claims that faith is mainly swayed by "antecedent considerations." These are its "previous notices, prepossessions, and (in a good sense of the word) prejudices."[32] Preaching in 1839 on the text that God has chosen the foolish things of the world to confound the wise, Newman compares the judgments of faith to the wisdom of a great general who "knows what his friends and enemies are about, and what will be the final result, and where, of their combined movements." Yet when asked to argue in word or on paper, the same general may find all his conjectures and reasonings to be less than adequate. By analogy, he speaks of

> faith (as) a process of reason, in which so much of the grounds of inference cannot be exhibited, so much lies in the character of the mind itself, in its general view of things, its estimate of the probable and the improbable, its impressions concerning God's will, and its anticipations derived from its own inbred wishes,

---

31. T. F. Torrance, *Karl Barth: Biblical and Evangelical Theologian* (Edinburgh: T&T Clark, 1990).

32. John Henry Newman, *University Sermons* (London: SPCK, 1970), 187.

that it will ever seem to the world irrational and despicable—till, that is, the event confirms it.[33]

Natural theology may have a place in this scheme of things, but it will tend toward a subordinate role in relation to the wider judgments of faith, and may be none the worse for that.

In terms of my initial typology, the first two types may now be excluded whereas the latter two exercise, *pace* Karl Barth, a significant auxiliary role in defending, declaring, and understanding the faith. The third type too may have its place— people who sit quite lightly to any faith community or tradition will continue to inspect and sometimes to rehearse the arguments of natural theology, finding these plausible in some measure.

Neither Darwin nor Barth in their different ways succeeded in killing off natural theology; perhaps it was only particular historical manifestations that aroused skepticism in the former and anger in the latter. Given the variety of types of natural theology and its adaptation to different historical contexts, its constant capacity to mutate should not surprise us.

33. Ibid., 217–18.

Part Three

CHURCH

Chapter 11

THE THEOLOGY OF WORSHIP

A REFORMED PERSPECTIVE

The theology and practice of worship have generated more attention in recent years. In the work of Geoffrey Wainwright an entire systematics is constructed from the perspective of worship.[1] There may be several reasons for this resurgence in interest in the subject; by inspecting these under four headings—history, philosophy, ethics, and ecumenism—some initial insight into the theology of worship can be gained. From there, I proceed to outline Reformed approaches by examining the two characteristic notes or marks of the church.

The Study of Doctrine in the Context of Worship

History. The study of the history of doctrine reveals the way in which doxological practices preceded and shaped the formation of dogma. Without asserting an absolute priority of doxology over dogma, we can observe the importance of worship in shaping Christian belief. This is already evident in Hebrew religion where, in the Psalms, the celebration of salvation history, law, divine rule and wisdom all contribute to the shaping of Israel's faith. Similarly, the elaborate sacrificial system and holiness code reveal long-standing practices which, for example, condition faith and belief in atonement for sin. New Testament scholarship has also explored those creedal fragments in the letters of Paul and elsewhere which reflect liturgical usage in early Christian worship, for example the Christ-hymn in Philippians 2:5-11.[2] Theology was decisively shaped by a range of practices such as praying to Jesus, baptism in the threefold name, and the celebration of the Lord's Supper as recorded in 1 Corinthians 11. In the patristic period, the development of dogma was similarly influenced by established practice.[3] Thus in the Arian controversy,

---

1. Geoffrey Wainwright, *Doxology: A Systematic Theology* (London: Epworth, 1980).
2. For discussion of the significance of worship in the New Testament see Larry Hurtado, *At the Origins of Christian Worship* (Carlisle: Paternoster, 1999).
3. This is shown repeatedly in Jaroslav Pelikan, *The Emergence of the Catholic Tradition (100–600)* (Chicago: University of Chicago Press, 1971).

Athanasius could appeal to the widespread practice of addressing prayer to Jesus. Against Pelagius, Augustine could cite the practice of baptizing infants for remission of sin. Anselm's theory of the atonement invoked the categories of the church's penitential system, while eucharistic controversies in the Middle Ages were determined by the language of the liturgy. One would also have to view Mariology and the subsequent dogmatic definition of the Immaculate Conception and bodily Assumption of Mary in light of long-standing practices of devotion that first emerge in the patristic period. In all this, however, it is not merely a matter of doctrine tracking widespread practice. Critical doctrinal reflection can act as a corrective upon our doxological habits.[4]

Philosophy. The work of the later Wittgenstein has been interpreted and deployed by theologians in a range of ways, not all of which are consistent. But one widely recognized contribution of Wittgenstein is the stress on practice and forms of life in the acquisition of meaning. When a builder shouts, "Slab," to his colleague he is not engaging in a simple act of naming, as earlier theories of meaning suggested.[5] Instead he is issuing an instruction about how and when to deliver the next slab to his colleague who is laying them in a particular order. The salient point of this illustration is that meanings are only acquired through initiation into the practice and forms of life that shape the world of the building site. Words are not learned by looking out at the world and receiving examples of how to label the objects of experience. Learning takes place through action, exchange, and participation in a complex set of rule-governed practices. Instead of a detached visual recognition, meaning is grasped through touch and sound in complex, communal activity.

These observations about meaning are significant for an account of theological knowledge. We know God not so much by attaching labels to experiences, events, or phenomena but through participation in a range of rule-governed practices and forms of life. An alternative way of expressing this is to say that we can only speak of a knowledge of God in terms of exposure to and immersion in the life of the community. This will typically require catechesis, baptism, regular participation in worship, daily prayer, and the disciplined practice of loving God and one's neighbor.

On this account of meaning, we now become better placed to appreciate the integral connection of worship to a practical knowledge of God. The worship of the community informs our knowledge of God. We are initiated into ways of seeing the world, ourselves, and other people that are theologically significant. Without the regular patterns of worship, the language of faith and its modes of perception

---

4. The *lex orandi, lex credendi* principle has some traction but can easily be overstated. See James Kay, "The Place of Prayer in Theological Method: A Conversation with Sarah Coakley," in *Schools of Faith: Essays on Theology, Ethics and Education in Honour of Iain R. Torrance*, ed. David Fergusson and Bruce L. McCormack (Edinburgh: T&T Clark, 2019), 117–28.

5. This example is drawn from Ludwig Wittgenstein, *Philosophical Investigations* (Oxford: Blackwell, 1953), 8–10.

will make little or no sense to us. This is a central theme of George Lindbeck's *The Nature of Doctrine*.[6] We learn faith in a way analogous to a child learning its first language. Experience and belief, too long abstracted from worship in theology, are now perceived to repose upon the practices of the worshipping community.

Ethics. Recent return to Aristotelian virtue ethics in both philosophy and theology has brought a renewed stress upon the importance of habit in the moral life. We act well typically through the development of good habits. These require formation through acknowledgement of the texts, authorities, traditions, and practices of the Christian community. The most important single voice here is that of Stanley Hauerwas. Training in the Christian life, he argues, requires induction into the practices of worship, familiarity with the examples and stories of the saints, and the reorientation of one's life by the claims of Christ and his church. This is stressed in a countercultural spirit. The distinctiveness of Christian living requires attention to the ways in which the worship, fellowship, belief, and moral witness of the church reshape our lives.

A common observation is that there is a Catholic moment in the ethics of Hauerwas. The attention given to the authority of the church, the lives of the saints and the Aristotelian-Thomist tradition positions in this style of Christian ethics sits much closer to Roman Catholicism than the neoliberal Protestant views it typically criticizes. On the other hand, his writings should also be interpreted in the context of Reformed emphases upon personal holiness, the Christian life, the discipline of the church community and the transformation of society. Many of Hauerwas's essays are published sermons. These reflect a commitment to the power of the preached Word to change the lives of its hearers. Through the regular practice of communal worship we are trained to live as God's people in the world. "Our Sunday worship has a way of reminding us, in the most explicit and ecclesial of ways, of the source of our power, the peculiar nature of our solutions to what ails the world."[7]

The work of Hauerwas should be viewed in the same post-liberal paradigm as Lindbeck. This is developed by others from different perspectives. In a discussion of pastoral care, Willimon points to the importance of worship in consoling, healing, and renewing us amid the crises of life. He appeals to worship as central to what distinguishes Christian pastoral care from secular forms of counseling and therapy.[8] Miroslav Volf speaks of belief-shaped practices and practice-shaping beliefs to describe the integrity of doing and believing in the Christian life.

---

6. George Lindbeck, *The Nature of Doctrine* (London: SPCK, 1985).

7. Stanley Hauerwas and William H. Willimon, *Resident Aliens* (Nashville: Abingdon, 1993), 171. In a similar vein, Sam Wells has sought to describe the range of ways in which worship is ethically formative. "How Common Worship Forms Local Character," *Studies in Christian Ethics* 15 (2002): 66–74.

8. William Willimon, *Worship as Pastoral Care* (Nashville: Abingdon, 1979).

"Christian practices have what we may call an 'as-so' structure: *as* God has received us in Christ, *so* we too are to receive our fellow human beings."[9]

Ecumenism. The ecumenical movement has also made a contribution to the renewed sense of the importance of worship for Christian doctrine. Through study of shared practices, a greater sense of ecumenical convergence has been achieved, even where there this has not yielded structural unity. This has been fostered by biblical scholarship and historical study of church traditions.

The process leading to the formulation of "Baptism, Eucharist and Ministry," the Lima document of 1982, is instructive. In particular, the section on the Eucharist makes significant ecumenical progress by shifting attention away from rival theories of the real presence by focusing on the wider context of eucharistic worship. This was achieved in part through the liturgical reform movement and the creation of an ecumenical liturgy for sacramental celebration. The Eucharist contains most, if not all, of the following elements: praise; confession of sin; declaration of pardon; proclamation of the Word; confession of the faith; intercession for church and world; words of institution; *anamnesis*; *epiklesis*; commemoration of the faithful departed; prayer for the coming of the kingdom; the Lord's Prayer; the sign of peace; praise; blessing and sending. The stress on the ecumenical sharing of these aspects of eucharistic worship has contributed to a process in which historical differences are minimized, though not overcome.

Theological Description of the Forms of Worship

Attempts to define worship as if it were one single thing or activity, and then to organize everything else around this, are liable to cause distortion. This is a mistaken "essentialist" strategy which will tend to miss vital elements. Instead, the task is better conceived as offering a description of worship which is informed both by its centrality for Christian belief and practice, and by the central creedal affirmations of the faith. We should think in this context of "description" rather than "definition."

Attention to linguistic study of the various terms for "worship" in its biblical and post-canonical usage is necessary but not sufficient for the construction of a theology of worship. The Hebrew verb *shachah* is most commonly used to describe the activity of divine worship. It refers to the act of bowing down or rendering obeisance to whom it is due. In the Greek New Testament, the verb *proskuneo* is used in many places with much the same sense of bowing down. *Latreuo* is also employed several times for public worship, and denotes the idea of offering service. Church worship is thus described as service; we continue refer to the "church service" in English or the *Gottesdienst* in German. The English term "worship"

---

9. Miroslav Volf, "Theology for a Way of Life," in *Practicing Theology*, ed. Miroslav Volf and Dorothy C. Bass (Grand Rapids: Eerdmans, 2002), 250.

itself derives from an Anglo-Saxon word for "honor" (*weorthscipe*) suggesting again that worship is an action of honoring one who is worthy. The same descriptor can be used of persons other than God in different contexts. Thus, using archaic English, we might address "the Worshipful the Mayor." A more familiar example is found in the order for the solemnization of matrimony in the Book of Common Prayer (1662). "With this ring I thee wed, with my body I thee worship, and with all my worldly goods I thee endow."

In much confessional writing, the biblical sense of honoring the divine majesty is prominent. "To (God) is due from angels and men, and every other creature, whatsoever worship, service, or obedience he is pleased to require of them."[10] In Reformed criticism of idolatry, the honoring of God alone is frequently stressed in the exposition of the first table of the Decalogue. Hence the Westminster Shorter Catechism informs us that "The First Commandment forbiddeth the denying, or not worshipping and glorifying, the true God as God, and our God; and the giving of that worship and glory to any other which is due to him alone" (Answer 47). All this must find a place in a theology of worship, yet the honoring of God is neither a necessary nor a sufficient condition for an adequate description of worship. There are several reasons for this. We can honor and acknowledge God in ways that extend beyond worship, for example in our daily work, in the life of the household, in political and social activity. The doxological form of this honoring requires articulation in a theology of worship. Worship, moreover, involves a wide range of activities not all of which are entirely captured by the notion of acknowledging or honoring God. The range of forms cited in the New Testament recalls us to this diversity, as does the practice of the synagogue. Indeed, the Psalms already attest the variety of functions fulfilled by public worship; these include praise, thanksgiving, celebration, recounting, proclamation, confession, petition, instruction, and lament. While Christian practice has sometimes found difficulty in accommodating lament and complaint, all these other themes are generally present in the worship of the church.

Worship as an Action in Which God Is Both Subject and Object

As an event in which God is not merely a passive recipient of our praise, worship creates an exchange between the divine and the creaturely in which God is the subject as well as the object of worship. This dramatic character of worship has often been portrayed by Protestant accounts of preaching and by Catholic descriptions of the Eucharist. The preaching of the Word is an event in which not only the preacher speaks but God addresses the people. It is this that bestows upon worship both its gravity and joyfulness. In the medieval and Tridentine doctrine of transubstantiation and its accompanying account of ordination, the description of the fraction at the altar affords an acute sense of the continual action of God in the

---

10. *The Confession of Faith* (Edinburgh: Blackwood, 1957), III.2, 8.

regular worship of the church across space and time. Christ is represented to his people each time the sacrament of his body and blood is celebrated. Similarly, note should be made of the action of the Spirit in public worship in recent charismatic traditions. The criticism that mainstream Western theology has been too binitarian is not without force at this point. A fuller account of the person and work of the Spirit should enhance the sense that the Spirit is active in prompting, guiding, and enabling worship in all its dimensions. The churches of the Global South attest a keen sense of spiritual power often articulated by reference to the continual action of the third person.

Worship might be described as a performative action in which both the church and God participate. This is not merely a human acknowledgement of who God is or what Christ has done. Worship is an event by which God is known and Christ communicated; it is not of our own making for it is dependent upon the grace of God. In this regard, the act of worship is not only a human recollection or bearing witness although it includes these elements. Worship is also an event in which God's grace works for us in repeated, regular, and dependable ways, albeit in a manner that references the once-for-all action of Christ. Appeal can be made in this context to the priestly theology of the Hebrews and the claim that the ascended Christ is seated at the right hand of the Father. Though difficult to formulate conceptually, this language implies that Christ continues through the Spirit to intercede on our behalf. He continues to pray for and with us, even as we pray through him and in him. Worship here becomes the coincidence of divine and human action together.[11]

This can be a powerful and liberating insight, particularly at those moments when faith falters and prayer becomes fitful. Simon Peter is told that though his faith will fail, Christ has prayed for him. And the ascended Christ continues through the Spirit to intercede for us. The awareness of Christ as the one who perpetually prays for us and also of the company of the faithful who surround us is a source of pastoral encouragement and liturgical strength. In reflecting upon the theology of Easter Saturday in the midst of his own terminal illness, Alan Lewis penned these moving words.

> We face suffering, distress, and death with courage, faith and trust, not by maintaining serenity of psyche or buoyancy of soul within, but precisely by casting ourselves in all the times of emptiness, aridity, and wordlessness—as well as those still more spiritually dangerous times of optimism or elation—upon the gift of grace outside us and around us. God promises to do what we cannot do, and go where we need not go, to enter the dark valley ahead of us and defeat on our behalf the frightening foe. And the Spirit undertakes to pray for us, and stirs others to intercede on our behalf, just when we feel awful, overwrought in body

---

11. This is developed by James B. Torrance, *Worship, Community and the Triune God of Grace* (Carlisle: Paternoster, 1996).

or in spirit, when faith eludes intellect or consciousness and our tongues have lost all utterance.[12]

In stressing the ongoing action of the Spirit in relation to the priestly office of the ascended Christ, the church understands worship as God's action in our midst. Yet, in pressing this point, however, we should not overstate it so as to present worship as something that we do not do. Worship is not an intra-Trinitarian transaction that takes place over our heads, unrelated to the practices of the visible, empirical congregations to which we belong. An over-stretched christomonism will lead to the enervating and implausible conclusion that in worship there is nothing much left for us to do.

To illustrate the performative character of worship, we might consider again the Psalms. These are generally assumed to have been memorized and recited in worship before being committed to their present literary form.[13] In celebrating the kingly rule of God, the Psalms not only attest that rule but also contribute to it and participate in it. Through the praise of Israel, God's rule over creation is celebrated. Through a covenant partnership, expressed in the forms of worship, God wills to be known and obeyed. In Psalm 24, though the ark of the covenant is no longer present, the enthronement of God in the praise of the post-Exilic people is enacted. Here we see why worship must have a public character. Israel and the church are called into covenant partnership with God not as an aggregate of disconnected individuals, but as a people who, in their corporate, social existence, worship together. This does not exclude private acts of worship and devotion, but it seems to demand the centrality of the regular, public diet of worship on the Lord's Day in fulfillment of the fourth commandment. This public event has a dramatic quality by virtue of its character as both a divine and a human action. In his Aberdeen Gifford lectures, Barth once insisted that "the church service is the most important, momentous and majestic thing which can possibly take place on earth, because its primary content is not the work of man but the work of the Holy Spirit and consequently the work of faith."[14]

Reformed Exposition of Worship under the Rubrics of Word and Sacrament

In much Reformed writing, the topic of worship is dealt with by reference to the two "notes" of Word and sacrament. What takes place in worship is expounded by reference to the reading and preaching of God's Word and the right administration of the sacraments.

---

12. Alan E. Lewis, *Between Cross & Resurrection: A Theology of Holy Saturday* (Grand Rapids: Eerdmans, 2001), 430–1.
13. E.g. Claus Westermann, *The Living Psalms* (Edinburgh: T&T Clark, 1989), 4.
14. Karl Barth, *The Knowledge of God and the Service of God* (London: Hodder & Stoughton, 1938), 98.

Set out in confessions, catechisms and theological textbooks, much of the exposition is located within an initial context of sixteenth-century polemics. The need to reform the life of the church according to the Word of God entailed a good deal of attention to the range of activities that took place in worship. Thus Bullinger's *Second Helvetic Confession* engages in a patient description of the tasks of the minister, the sacramental relation, baptism and the Lord's Supper, religious meetings, church architecture, the language of prayer, singing, canonical hours, holy days, fasts, catechizing, pastoral care of the sick, burial of the dead, ceremonies, rites, and *adiaphora*—the things of indifference. In his *Second Helvetic Confession*, we have something akin to a comprehensive description of worship.

> Although it is permitted all men to read the Holy Scriptures privately at home, and by instruction to edify one another in the true religion, yet in order that the Word of God may be properly preached to the people, and prayers and supplication publicly made, also that the sacraments may be rightly administered, and that collections may be made for the poor and to pay the cost of all the Church's expenses, and in order to maintain social intercourse, it is most necessary that religious or Church gatherings be held. For it is certain that in the apostolic and primitive Church, there were such assemblies frequented by all the godly.[15]

Although this is a rather low-key and urbane account of worship, its attention to detail and strong sense of the local, empirical, and visible congregation are commendable. Its broader setting contrasts with other Reformed accounts of worship which focus more exclusively on Word and sacrament. These require some comment.

The attention to the preaching of the Word reflects several features of Lutheran and Reformed worship. These include the return to Scripture alone over against tradition as the supreme rule of faith and life; the importance of a right understanding of the faith, reflected also in the translation of the Bible and the liturgy into the vernacular; the commitment to education shared with Renaissance humanism; and also a polemic against the medieval notion of the sacraments as effective *ex opere operato* (by the sheer performance of the act) without reference to the faith of the recipient. In the response to all these concerns, the regular preaching and hearing of the Word became of paramount importance. In much Reformation theology, preaching is characterized in sacramental language. For Luther, the Word of God could be described as present in, with, and under the words of the preacher. Within the Reformed tradition, the relationship is not described in terms of a consubstantiation but in terms of the capacity of the Spirit to speak through human words that have been properly applied to the proclamation of the Scriptures. Here there is an indirect identity of human and

---

15. "Second Helvetic Confession" (1566), Chapter 22 in *Reformed Confessions of the Sixteenth Century*, ed. Arthur C. Cochrane (London: SCM Press, 1966), 288–9.

divine speech in a manner that again recalls sacramental language.[16] By contrast, the Roman Catholic tradition has historically tended to construe the sermon more as a homily, a piece of instruction, subsidiary to the celebration of the Mass.[17]

While Lutheran and Reformed accounts of preaching often drew upon images of sacramental grace to describe its significance and efficacy, there was simultaneously a move in the opposite direction that further reinforced the centrality of the preached word.[18] The sacraments themselves became annexed to the proclamation of the Word so that their efficacy was derivative from and subordinate to the latter and its proclamation. Here attention was given to Augustine's notion of a *visibile verbum* whereby the sacraments were described in terms of their representation to the other senses of what was heard through the reading and preaching of the Word. This supra-sacramental account of preaching resulted in the widespread Protestant practice of centralizing the sermon in the weekly diet of worship. It finds its roots in the ministry of the prophets and Jesus, and in the New Testament imperative to declare the gospel, an action that itself could simply be described as "the Word of God." Hence Bullinger's famous dictum that "the preaching of the Word of God *is* the Word of God." This was a marginal note added to the text of the *Second Helvetic Confession—praedicatio verbi Dei est verbum Dei*—reflecting Bullinger's belief in the power of the proclaimed message, even when announced by unworthy ministers.[19] This message, however, always has a derivative and dependent status in relation to Scripture. In interpreting the message of the Bible for a given time and place, the sermon becomes again the Word of God.

Expounded in Bullinger's *Decades*, this became something like the standard Reformed view. Both the centrality of proclamation in the life of the church and its subordination to the written Word are established.[20] Scripture requires regularly

---

16. See, for example, R. S. Wallace, *Calvin's Doctrine of the Word and Sacrament* (Edinburgh: Oliver & Boyd, 1953).

17. More recently, post-Vatican II pneumatology has stressed the importance of preaching and the need publicly to invoke the Spirit at its outset.

18. This is explored by Alan Lewis, "Ecclesia ex Auditu: A Reformed View of the Church as the Community of the Word of God," *Scottish Journal of Theology* 35 (1982): 13-31.

19. Here I am following the interpretation of Bullinger in E. A. Dowey, "The Word of God as Scripture and Preaching," in *Later Calvinism: International Perspectives*, ed. W. Fred Graham (Kirksville: Northeast Missouri State University 1994), 5-18. See also James Kay, *Preaching and Theology* (St Louis: Chalice Press, 2007). The alleged differences between Calvin and Bullinger perceived by T. H. L. Parker seem to me largely over-drawn. See *Calvin's Preaching* (Edinburgh: T&T Clark, 1992), 22. With their claims for the centrality of preaching in the church yet as subordinate to Scripture, there is an important consensus between the two Reformers.

20. In the Lutheran tradition, by contrast, there tends to be an assimilation of the promise of the gospel announced in Scripture with its repetition in the declaration of the preacher. One recent commentator remarks that "preaching in a sacramental fashion

to be interpreted and applied to the situation of the congregation. This task assigns to preaching not only a singular character in terms of its initial announcement of the gospel but also an ongoing, repeatable, and regular function within the community of faith. Preaching is neither a monotonous action that simply repeats in timeless fashion a single message, nor a paraphrase of the Scriptural passages that have already been read. We might liken it to the different performances of a single musical score, or variations on a theme. Always there is a return to what has been composed; this continues to control what is said. Yet the performance will vary according to the needs, capacities, and situation of the hearers. The preaching of God's Word is facilitated both by Scripture and the ongoing action of the Spirit. We find this position elegantly stated in the *Larger Catechism*.

> They that are called to labour in the ministry of the word, are to preach sound doctrine, diligently, in season and out of season; plainly, not in the enticing words of man's wisdom, but in demonstration of the Spirit, and of power; faithfully, making known the whole counsel of God; wisely, applying themselves to the necessities and capacities of the hearers; zealously, with fervent love to God and the souls of his people; sincerely, aiming at his glory, and their conversion, edification, and salvation.[21]

This account of the Word contributed greatly to the dramatic and performative character of worship. Where the preacher speaks, there God too will address us. This attaches to preaching, together with the training and preparation invested in it, the highest seriousness.

We find Scriptural support for preaching in the prophets, in the ministry of Jesus himself and in his command to preach the gospel. Yet the isolation of the sermon from other forms of oral communication has become problematic in Reformed worship. In particular, the relative loss of both instruction and discussion has caused an undue constriction of worship, and an isolation of the preaching of the Word that does it no service.[22] From the beginning of its history, instruction in the faith was important for new converts. The risen Christ bids his disciples not only to preach but to teach all that he commands. Jesus himself had been called a teacher, a rabbi, by those around him. And this didactic task was taken seriously by the early church in instruction about the foundational events of the faith and the catechizing of candidates for baptism. Instruction never assumed sacramental status, yet it is as prominent in the New Testament as either baptism or the Lord's Supper. Whether it takes place in or alongside the weekly diet of worship, it is closely associated with the upbuilding of the community. Similar remarks can be

---

is doing to the hearers what the text authorizes you to do to them." Gerhard Forde, *The Preached God: Proclamation in Word and Sacrament* (Grand Rapids: Eerdmans, 2007), 91.

21. "The Larger Westminster Catechism," in *Confession of Faith*, 159, 99.

22. Here I am indebted to Hendrikus Berkhof, *Christian Faith* (Grand Rapids: Eerdmans, 1979), 352ff.

made with respect to discussion. Conversation is a means of grace in the ministry of Jesus. One thinks of his private exchanges with the disciples, Nicodemus and the Samaritan woman. Moreover, empirical research suggests that many more people come to faith through personal conversation, discussion and exchange than through listening to sermons.[23] In this respect, we ought not to discount the role of para-church organizations where the faith was actively discussed. These complemented and enriched the preaching of sermons. Their decline in some quarters should be viewed with some concern, particularly at a time when we have become conscious of the countercultural significance of Christian formation. The ministry of the Word needs to be set within wider patterns of communication in the church.

The necessity and nature of preaching can also be elucidated by parallels with the interpretation of the Hebrew Bible in rabbinic Judaism. With the closing of the canon, there could be no new or additional works that became part of the Tanakh. On the other hand, it was believed that God could speak in new and relevant ways through the canon of Scripture. This required an interpretive act by the teacher within the synagogue. The very nature of a completed canon had as its necessary accompaniment in the community of faith a procedure for its interpretation and application to the lives of contemporary readers and hearers. Michael Fishbane speaks about the singularity of Scripture residing in "the depth of possibilities for true teaching, the legal and theological experience, latent in the text." He quotes the words of one midrashic commentary: "When the Holy One, blessed be He, gave the Torah to Israel, He only gave it as wheat from which to extract flour, and as flax wherewith to weave a garment."[24] The critical and creative discernment of the interpreter is a corollary of there being a sacred text at all. This work, moreover, takes places within a community of practice. So key passages of the Hebrew Scriptures are used as lectionaries for Sabbaths, as recitations for festivals and fasts, as the focus of public expositions and sermons, and in the reading and praying of the Psalms. These activities all regulate the use and function of Scripture in the synagogue, while also highlighting the importance of a liturgical calendar, the seasons of which frame the central themes around which the faith is to be interpreted.

For the Christian as well as the Jewish expositor, a central act of weekly worship is the interpretation of Scripture, not as mere repetition or explanation but as an appropriation and unfolding of its meaning for a particular context. Given the character of the Scriptures of the Old and New Testaments with their reference to Christ in the form of promise and fulfillment, this act of interpretation also has the character of witness, as an ongoing attestation of the presence and significance of Christ for the church. Yet this is not a single, monotonous message—different forms

---

23. For example, John Finney, *Finding Faith* (Swindon: British and Foreign Bible Society, 1992).

24. Michael Fishbane, *The Garments of Torah* (Bloomington: Indiana University Press, 1989), 37–8.

include celebration, upbuilding, teaching, challenging, rebuking, comforting, fortifying, and inciting to good works. Understood in this way, we can assign to preaching an abiding importance but one that belongs to the wider and varied contexts of the church in the world. This must also include a close relationship to the sacraments, as the Reformers' switching of terms from one to the other suggests. The relationship of Word to sacrament, however, remains problematic in practice, if not in theory, for the Reformed churches.

In the traditional exposition of the sacraments in confessions and catechisms, we frequently find a generic definition of a sacrament followed by exposition of baptism and the Lord's Supper. A sacrament is first defined, followed by an account of the different senses in which both baptism and the Lord's Supper conform to the definition. Despite their lucidity and precision, these statements also have their drawbacks. The generic account of a sacrament tended to emerge from eucharistic controversies about the nature of the real presence. The effect was somewhat Procrustean when baptism was presented as another species of the genus. Here, despite disclaimers, the effect of baptism was too tightly tied to the action of immersion or sprinkling in the threefold name. Thus the act of initiation became too easily detached from the context and subsequent activities which also mediated divine grace and without which the language of baptism made little sense.

In the case of the Lord's Supper, attention to and disputes over the sacramental nexus also contributed to a loss of the wider ethical significance of the sacrament, the "as-so" connection described above. The regular reception of God's hospitality in the Supper is closely linked in the New Testament to the hospitality that we are called to display toward others. Though this link between eucharistic celebration and *diakonia* was arguably obscured in formal accounts of worship, it is robustly present in works such as Wolterstorff's *Until Justice and Peace Embrace*.[25] A narrowing of sacramental focus may have been compounded by the tendency toward infrequent celebration of the Lord's Supper, the arguments of Calvin and others notwithstanding. This has led arguably to a situation of sermonic isolation where the preached word remains as the focal point of the service but often without its prescribed link to the sacraments and remote from other forms of education and instruction. Since at least the late nineteenth century, a body of scholarship has urged the need for more frequent celebration of the Lord's Supper both in faithfulness to the convictions of Calvin and, even more importantly, to the wider ecumenical traditions of the church catholic. The inertia of the Reformed churches in relation to this theological consensus requires some explanation. In the twenty-first century, this remains unfinished business.

---

25. Nicholas Wolterstorff, *Until Justice and Peace Embrace* (Grand Rapids: Eerdmans, 1987).

Chapter 12

REFORMED THEOLOGY AND VISUAL CULTURE

Throughout the most recent phase of his academic career, Gordon Graham has done much to promote the intellectual commerce between Princeton and Scotland. Begun in Aberdeen, his leadership of the Centre for the Study of Scottish Philosophy has flourished from its Princeton base during the last decade. A plethora of conferences, publications and the consolidation of a scholarly journal dedicated to the subject have followed. And through his occupancy of the Chair at Princeton Theological Seminary, he has expertly combined the study of religion, philosophy and the arts with his characteristic vision, intellectual acumen, and indefatigable enthusiasm. In honoring a former colleague and valued friend, I am pleased to offer these modest reflections on the Reformed churches and the arts.

Blasting the Past

The Reformed tradition has often been charged with an aesthetic deficit. Given the destruction of images, paintings and stained glass in churches after the Reformation, we stand guilty as charged. Allied to this is a series of theological attacks on images among several of the leading Reformed theologians. Despite some exceptions, this iconophobia was not matched by Lutherans or Anglicans. A visit to the town church of Wittenberg affords a striking view of Lukas Cranach's altar triptych depicting Luther preaching to a small congregation that includes his wife and family, his students, colleagues and fellow townspeople. Installed in 1547 after his death, Luther is depicted here pointing to the figure of the crucified Christ, whose loin cloths blowing in the breeze symbolize the power of the Spirit moving among the people of this small church.[1] Calvin, by contrast, would never have tolerated such representation in the church. His self-effacing style was carried to the grave with the instruction that there was to be no tomb or stone to mark his last resting place.

In their reluctance to admit images into the sanctuary or to acknowledge the contribution that these make to the understanding and internalizing of the

---

1. This represents the beginning of a new Protestant iconography. See William A. Dyrness, *Reformed Theology and Visual Culture: The Protestant Imagination from Calvin to Edwards* (Grand Rapids: Eerdmans, 2004), 55–7.

Christian faith, the Reformed churches have generally been perceived as more austere. Attitudes to the theatre and dancing have often been censorious. In 1649, an Act of the General Assembly Act in Scotland condemned the practice of "promiscuous dancing" at penny weddings. When a man died as a result of dancing at his own wedding celebration, this was viewed by the Presbytery of Duns as signaling "the displeasure of God against the form of his marriage."[2] Regarded as a sensuous stimulus, dancing was feared for generating a loss of inhibition and instilling of lewd and licentious habits. Perhaps it did sometimes. But doubtless all this has contributed to the stock criticism that Reformed culture has been repressive in the ways in which it has enthralled not only congregations but entire societies. Three brief examples of this trend toward blanket criticism may suffice.

Iain Crichton Smith's haunting rejection of his Presbyterian upbringing in the west highlands of Scotland scarcely conceals the anguish that this could produce. Recalling the black-hatted and white-collared ministers of Lewis, he remarks that "with their tight-lipped brilliance, they have suppressed the magic of the theatre."[3]

In his reflections on Scottish paining, J. D. Fergusson, the celebrated Scottish colorist, presents Calvinism as a cipher for everything that is detrimental to the flourishing of the arts, national self-esteem, and the liberation of the human spirit. His entertaining study is not prone to scholarly scruples and Fergusson admits that he doesn't know much about John Knox. But Calvinism is still accredited with all that is bleak and grim in Scottish society.

> [T]he Calvinist . . . revels in the enjoyment of seeing people stopped, frustrated, deprived. He can do with little food, without alcohol, without theatres, dance halls, cinemas and other abodes of the devil: with plenty of strong tea, bread and jam, the exultation of seeing someone fail in the attempt to get some joy out of life, and the conviction that Calvinism is Christianity.[4]

More recently, Richard Williams has argued that the Victorian architecture of Morningside in Edinburgh betokens the sexual repression of Presbyterian culture in Scotland's capital city. Its elegance notwithstanding, the rows of buildings on this south side district lack a fully expressive force in their restraint, concealment, and austerity. With a clear divide between the public and private faces of these dwellings, an outward propriety is maintained at all costs, further reinforced by the crowds who attend the sundry local churches at "Holy Corner." Williams's

---

2. Presbytery of Duns, January 3, 1721. Quoted by Ralph E. Graham, *Ecclesiastical Discipline in the Church of Scotland, 1690–1730* (University of Glasgow, PhD thesis, 1964), 137. See also Henry Grey Graham, *The Social Life of Scotland in the 18th Century* (London: A&C Black, 1899), 327–8.

3. Iain Crichton Smith, *Murdo: The Life and Works* (Edinburgh: Birlinn, 2001), 227.

4. J. D. Fergusson, *Modern Scottish Painting* (Glasgow: Luath Press, 2015). The work was first published in 1943.

thesis is provocative and challenging, even though the property market suggests that Morningside houses remain an excellent investment.[5]

This relentless castigation of Calvinism needs to be balanced by a more positive reading of the influence of the Kirk on Scottish society. The achievements of the Scottish Enlightenment suggest a cultural flourishing that was facilitated rather than obstructed by the educational system promoted by the Kirk with high standards of literacy attained across society. Throughout the nineteenth century, this was often matched by the work of scientists, philosophers, novelists, theologians, missionaries and environmentalists whose contributions now seem disproportionate to the size of the country that produced them. The recent commemorations of the Reformation have pointed toward a release of energy in the secular world that so often seemed to accompany Protestantism, though doubtless allied to other forces.[6] While this does not negate necessary criticism, it signals the need for a more balanced assessment. At the very least, we should cease adopting the term Calvinist as a proxy for all our psychological and social ailments.

Artistic suppression often resulted more in refraction than in the extinguishing of activity. Architecture, portrait painting, and literature flourished in different ways, often outside the immediate environs of the church. With the emergence of Enlightenment ideals, often promoted by theologians and preachers, these spheres of activity flourished, especially from about the middle of the eighteenth century. The original design of Edinburgh New Town by James Craig, the subsequent buildings of Adam and Playfair, the poetry of Fergusson and Burns, the painting of Raeburn and Wilkie—all provide striking examples of cultural flourishing in Presbyterian Scotland. Around the same time, philosophers such as Hutcheson, Hume, and Reid offered important reflections on the nature of aesthetics.

The place of music within the Reformed tradition has often been studied. There is little doubt that the internalizing of the faith was aided by the memorizing and regular singing of metrical psalms, and later by paraphrases and hymns. Uncluttered and simple, church buildings came to express grace, mercy, and light.[7] Within the

---

5. "Morningside's very architecture seemed to be repression written in stone. . . . The repression I thought I saw in the everyday architecture of the city was only underlined further by the density of the churches in the area, not abandoned as they would be in any sensible secular city, but thronged every Sunday, each one offering its own unique proscription of the libido." Toward the end of his study, he concedes that much of this reaction is his own negative projection. Richard Williams, *Sex and Buildings: Modern Architecture and the Sexual Revolution* (London: Reaktion, 2013), 8.

6. See for example Alec Ryrie, *Protestants: The Radicals Who Made the Modern World* (London: Collins, 2017).

7. Lee Palmer Wandel shows how this generated a different aesthetic rather than the absence of one. See *The Reformation: Towards a New History* (Cambridge: Cambridge University Press, 2011), 202.

printed Bible, numerous illustrations of figures and scenes were included. The setting apart of sanctuaries for weekly worship, civic occasions and important rites of passage ensured that the shape and furnishing of a building would have a profound impact upon its users. Ensuring that it was painted, varnished, and regularly cleaned reflected a commitment not only to its utility but also its beauty. Church furnishings were valued and wooden carvings appreciated, while stained glass and pulpit falls would become later objects of intense interest and pride.

Why then did the impression arise that the Reformed tradition was hostile to visual images? The sources of this antipathy are readily traced in several leading figures of the sixteenth century. In what follows, I inspect these arguments for the sake of assessing their validity, before offering some musings on where the Reformed tradition should proceed from here.

Sixteenth-Century Iconophobia

Luther appears to have moved from a position of indifference to the presence of visual images in church to a recognition that they can have a useful subordinate role in illustrating the stories of Scripture and in highlighting the two notes of the church—the proclamation of the Word and the administration of the sacraments. By contrast, for Zwingli, the sovereignty of God, the uniqueness of Christ, and the necessity of faith tend to exclude the traditional role of visual images. Christ is mediated, but only by the written and preached Word. This must be received in faith. Hence the external contemplation of an image cannot substitute for the inward act. In dichotomizing the subject in this way, Zwingli inclines toward a series of dualisms between inner and outer, faith and sensory perception, the spiritual and the physical. And, as a consequence of these binary distinctions, visual images belong on the wrong side with a tendency toward idolatry, loss of comprehension, and false works.[8] Is this fair?

The abuse of material objects can no doubt result in superstitious habits. The contemplation of an image or the touching of a relic do not put one right with God or secure some special protection from harm. Here some protest requires to be registered, though we might also admit that Protestants have generated their own peculiar forms of superstition.[9] So far, so good. But might not images serve some useful function in the promotion of faith, as Luther seemed to recognize?

---

8. For further discussion of the Reformed "iconophobes" see Sergiusz Michalski, *The Reformation and the Visual Arts: The Protestant image question in Western and Eastern Europe* (London: Routledge 1993), 43–74.

9. I am thinking here of the tendency to decode every circumstance in one's life as if it were a sign from God attesting some blessing, reproof, warning, or correction. See Alexandra Walsham, *Providentialism in Early Modern England* (Cambridge: Cambridge University Press, 1998).

Zwingli's own German treatise on the Lord's Supper carries a title page with four woodcut images depicting a Passover meal, the provision of manna in the wilderness, the feeding of the five thousand, and the Last Supper.[10] These illustrations explain the way in which the practice of communion should be understood by the people of Zürich. The recourse to such images points to the inherent weakness in the Reformed position. As sensory beings, we are reliant upon the deliverances of sight, sound, touch, scent, and taste to know the world. And our knowledge of God no less relies upon such forms of mediation. Given that the Reformed churches recognized this with respect to hearing, speaking, and singing, we must ask whether the hyper-allergic condemnations of images were an over-reaction resulting in some significant losses that we have been slow to recover. Assuming their usefulness, one might ask why images should not be placed in the sanctuary to assist the true worship of God. Are we so prone to distraction, so susceptible to abuse that these require altogether to be prohibited? Zwingli believed that this was the case with respect to representations of the human Christ in the church. "I have never seen in churches a cross displayed without one making it into an idol."[11] Here the object of attack is the crucifix, which Zwingli viewed as generating a slippery slope toward idolatry. Elsewhere, however, he can contemplate the use of visual representations of Christ, provided that these are historical depictions, in domestic settings. In this context, they serve a pedagogical function in pointing toward Jesus as he is attested in the gospels. When restricted to this illustrative function, the tendency toward idolatry was apparently checked.

Calvin's rejection of images shows more subtlety, developing further consideration of the ways in which God is mediated to us in the world.[12] The notion of an image is not itself faulty. Without images, we cannot apprehend God. But, for Calvin, the imperative is to consider those images by which God accommodates the divine being. This notion of "mediated immediacy"[13] is vital to his theological epistemology. In revealing the divine self to embodied humans, God must adapt creaturely materials. These mediate both the divine majesty and condescension. Unless we capture this dynamic, we fail to understand the central conviction of Calvin's theology.

Although the language of accommodation is applied more extensively, in the context of understanding his critique of visual images, three media are significant. These are the created world, our neighbors and the two sacraments. The entire cosmos attests the glory of God. With his love of astronomy, Calvin was profoundly

---

10. See Dyrness, *Reformed Theology and Visual Culture*, 59–61.

11. Quoted by Charles Garside, *Zwingli and the Arts* (New Haven: Yale University Press, 1966), 171.

12. For his criticism of images see *Institutes* 1.11. Further discussion is offered by Dyrness, *Reformed Theology and Visual Culture*, 62–89, and Randall Zachman, *Image and Word in the Theology of John Calvin* (Notre Dame: University of Notre Dame Press, 2007).

13. John Baillie, *Our Knowledge of God* (Oxford: Oxford University Press, 1938?), 178–98.

aware of how the stars and planets convey a sense of divine majesty. Other people, moreover, bear the image of God. This is one reason why poverty is offensive to God and to be ameliorated by a more equal distribution of material goods. And, third, we do not require visual images in church to communicate a sense of God's grace, since we have been given by Christ himself the water of baptism and the elements of bread and wine for sacramental use. These physical images should be sufficient for us in reinforcing the message of the Word of God which is the primary means of divine revelation. "By these our eyes ought to be more steadily fixed, and more vividly impressed, than to require the aid of the images which the wit of man may devise."[14] Hence in stripping churches bare, Calvin believed (wrongly) that the Reformed churches were returning to the universal practice of the church during its first five hundred years.

Registered in Calvin's theology, these shifts in understanding oppose any sense of the divine presence being concentrated in a particular object or place—this is reflected also in his discouraging the practice of visiting the sanctuary for acts of private devotion outside services of public worship. The glory of God is everywhere apparent to the eye of faith. By reposing upon the Word alone, we can discern God in our world and in other people. Yet, when introduced to the church, human works of art are judged an obstacle to such perception rather than an aid. Does this merely reflect Calvin's own context or should it function as a universal prescription?

Bullinger Assessed

A clear and concise summation of the Reformed position can be found in Heinrich Bullinger's Second Helvetic Confession (1566), Chapter 4.[15] Images of God are to be forbidden on the basis of the second commandment. In essence invisible, God cannot be represented by a visual image—any attempt to depict God in visual form will be misleading and deceitful. Although Christ assumed our human nature, "he did not on that account assume it in order to provide a model for carvers and painters." Bullinger takes the view that Christ's bodily presence is not profitable for the church—what matters is that he abides in us by his Spirit. And since the saints forbade worship of themselves while on earth, we should not perpetuate this practice now that they are in heaven. Since their adoration is particularly abhorrent, we should forbid such depiction. Having thus argued for the prohibition of images on account of their negative effects, Bullinger proceeds to offer more positive considerations against their use. Christ has commanded the preaching of the gospel, not its painting, he asserts. And in establishing the two sacraments, he has provided us with images that can signify this same gospel. Finally, in the case of the saints, we are surrounded by the witness of our fellow believers who should

---

14. *Institutes* 1.11.13.

15. See Arthur C. Cochrane, *Reformed Confessions of the 16ᵗʰ Century* (London: SCM, 1966), 229.

present a more vivid impression of the gospel than depictions of those long dead. Each of these arguments can be contested in sequence.

1. When Michelangelo depicted the finger of God reaching out to Adam on the ceiling of the Sistine Chapel, did he assume that that his viewers would assume that God was an old man in the sky? That seems unlikely. Most would have recognized this as a symbolic representation of an imperceptible event, namely the creation of the first human being as narrated in the opening chapter of Genesis. A similar meaning would readily be attached to Blake's *Ancient of Days* or to Rublev's celebrated icon of the Trinity as the three men by the oaks of Mamre. These obviously human depictions of God might in themselves be seen as acknowledging the impossibility of seeing the divine with one's eye. With their unabashed anthropomorphism, they concede the point that of course God cannot be visualized. The representation is instead an arresting image that provokes further thought and sensibility, or in the case of the icon focuses prayer and devotion in relation to an invisible and ineffable reality.
2. Even more problematic is the claim that Christ's bodily presence is not profitable for the church. This seems to run counter to the logic of the Incarnation. The appearance of the Word in flesh is precisely for our benefit. "We declare to you what was from the beginning, what we have heard, what we have seen with our eyes, what we have looked at and touched with our hands, concerning the word of life" (1 John 1:1). Bullinger's point seems to be that following the ascension of Christ, the church is no longer dependent upon his bodily presence but rather knows him through the power of the Spirit. This seems correct insofar as it goes, yet one wants to ask whether the gospel stories (as the oral and written record of his incarnate life) might not be illustrated and represented by works of human art. Can their significance for each generation not be artistically translated? One might even venture the claim that this is a responsibility rather than merely an open possibility.
3. Representations of the followers of Christ are also to be prohibited. Bullinger assumes that the practice of the veneration of the saints will quickly transition into outright worship and idolatry. Although there may have been legitimate contextual reasons for diminishing the significance of the saints as intermediaries who derogate from the authority of Christ, this now appears less plausible as a permanent proscription on any visual representation of the followers of Christ. The celebration of heroic examples of faith became a key source of Protestant inspiration, for example in Foxe's *Book of Martyrs* (1563) which included over sixty woodcut illustrations and went through numerous editions. The historical realism of these images was in part intended to avoid replicating the cult of the saints but the use of visual imagery promoted a distinctively Protestant iconography that requires some nuancing of the standard arguments against imagery. In any case, Catholic depictions of the saints can themselves overcome the standard Protestant complaint. In discussing El Greco's "saintly" pictures, Gordon Graham notes

that their "otherworldly" characteristics are intended to inspire the faithful here and now. As images of hope for mundane lives, these are "visually aspirational" in encouraging people to seek a spiritual realm they inhabit, but often fail to recognize.[16]

4. Preaching and teaching of the faith assume a priority by virtue of Christ's command to his disciples in Matthew 28:19-20. In one respect, Bullinger is correct. There is no injunction to paint or sculpt in the words of the risen Jesus. But nor is there any prohibition, which leaves us with the possibility that artistic representation of Christ, the church or the world may assist rather than displace the dominical command. The concession to historical paintings of Scriptural stories for domestic use seems to admit this possibility. And the presence of illustrative images in printed Bibles is surely to be understood in similar terms as an auxiliary device for complementing the written Word.

5. The sacraments offer visible and tangible signs of God's promise to us. Instituted by Christ, do they not suffice for faith? The focus on Word and sacrament suggests that the simplicity of a small meeting house is in no way disadvantaged by contrast with a finely adorned cathedral as a place of true worship. Although this may be one of the enduring insights of the Reformation, it does not negate the additional benefit of visual imagery in the sanctuary or its use to assist the preaching of the Word any more than singing or unaccompanied music do. Consider the following example. The reappearance of stained glass in Scottish Presbyterian churches in the middle of the nineteenth century signalled a recovery of a practice that had disappeared after the Reformation. If the commissioning of such work appeared controversial in 1856 when the first stained glass window was installed at Greyfriars Kirk, the practice soon become widespread. While these windows were intended to offset the austere and monochrome appearance of Reformed sanctuaries, they also served a pedagogical purpose in drawing attention to biblical characters and stories.[17]

6. This last point may also provide a corrective to the final argument advanced by Bullinger. Recalling and depicting the saints of the church may have led to the excesses and distractions apparent in his own day. But whether this need always be the case is doubtful. Protestants soon developed their own roll-call of inspiring examples of faith. These became appropriate subjects for instructing and encouraging others to do likewise. Where his argument has some purchase is its eschewal of any binary division between those set apart as saints of the church and the ordinary Christians who surround us in our own churches. But we do not require to neglect the saints of yesterday

---

16. Gordon Graham, *Philosophy, Art and Religion: Understanding Faith and Creativity* (Cambridge: Cambridge University Press, 2017), 71.

17. See for example Michael Donnelly, *Scotland's Stained Glass: Making the Colours Sing* (Edinburgh: Historic Scotland, 1997).

to do justice to those of today. The recent representation the life of Jane Haining, the schoolteacher who followed her Jewish pupils from Budapest to Auschwitz, is a powerful witness to the ways in which ordinary Christians from our midst have served God with selfless courage and steadfastness.[18]

Conclusion

The marks or notes of the church in Word and sacrament may be exclusive, but these should not discount the complementarity of visual images and material objects. The theological and ethical priorities of the Reformed tradition may provide directionality for the appropriate use of the visual arts in the life of the churches. These may often result in aesthetic forms such as simplicity, sobriety, and order.[19] But a greater sensitivity to the ways in which the visual arts can assist faith and worship may be now required of the Reformed churches as a further manifestation of the *semper reformanda* principle. Given the undisciplined appearance of PowerPoint in worship, together with the visual images that populate church websites and social media, this may be an opportune moment carefully to reappraise the tradition. If this involves a greater appreciation of Orthodox, Catholic, Lutheran, and Anglican uses of art, then so much the better for receptive ecumenism.

---

18. In 1948, two stained glass windows in memory of Jane Haining and her Jewish pupils were dedicated at Queen's Park Govanhill Church, Glasgow.

19. I have reflected further on this in "Aesthetics of the Reformed Tradition," in *Worship and Liturgy in Context: Studies of Theology and Practice*, ed. Duncan B. Forrester and Douglas C. Gay (London: SCM, 2009), 23–35.

Chapter 13

MAPPING THE CHURCH

CURRENT CHALLENGES OF HISTORY AND MISSION

The Church as a Necessary Condition of Christian Faith.

From my time as an undergraduate in the 1970s, I recall a talk by Professor Murdo Ewan McDonald in Glasgow. He tackled the claim by Malcolm Muggeridge that we should dispense with the church and concentrate on Jesus only. Provoked by this suggestion, Murdo Ewan wanted to engage Muggeridge in public debate. He indicated that he would put two points to him. Did not Jesus gather around himself a group of disciples who were the harbingers of the church? The formation of a body of followers was surely integral to Jesus' ministry—any attempt to separate these is anachronistic. His second claim was that the only way in which the story of Jesus could be transmitted is through the medium of the church. The gospels themselves are the product of the early church and without the sustained witness of the institution through the centuries neither he nor Muggeridge would have received the faith. These two points remain fundamentally correct in my opinion and provide an argument for the necessity of the church. But there is a third claim that also needs to be articulated which is part of the case against any separation of Jesus from the church. As the body of Christ, the church is the community in which Christian faith is experienced, nurtured, and celebrated. The Christian life may not be confined to the church, but it cannot be lived except in this communal setting with other Christians. Its significance is not merely instrumental. There are, of course, examples of people who have managed to keep the faith while separated from the church. Confined to his prison cell, Bonhoeffer is one heroic case. Yet his separation from fellow Christians was a constant source of lament, especially on Sundays when he was acutely conscious of his absence from the worshipping community. In a seminal essay, Andrew Walls has written,

> [T]he first effect of Christian expansion is not the production of saved or enlightened individuals, but of congregations. . . . The influence of Jesus not only produces group response; it works by means of groups, and

is expressed in groups. The influence of Jesus, that is, operates in terms of social relations.[1]

The sacrament of baptism is relevant in this respect. As a mark, recognized by the ecumenical church, it signals not only a commitment to Christ but membership of his body, the church. These remain inseparable. Calvin is insistent on this point, repeating Cyprian's claim that you cannot have God as your Father if you do not have the church as your Mother.[2]

Inflecting Traditional Ecclesial Dicta

In one sense, there has always been a doctrine of the church, if we intend by this a substantial body of theological literature that reflects upon the church as both a divine creation and a human institution. And there have been some notable contributions to this in recent years, not least by Tom Greggs.[3] At the same time, we should note Pannenberg's observation that the church was not a subject of sustained theological investigation until relatively late. He points out that the *doctrine* of the church did not become a separate locus of theological study until the late Middle Ages and the Reformation.[4] While theologians wrote about the church, especially Cyprian and Augustine, they did so in occasional ways, often in other contexts and drawing upon a multiplicity of images. Despite some schisms, notably that of the Donatists in Augustine's time, the doctrine of the church remained underdeveloped because it was not the site of major ecclesiastical division. The claim that the church was one, holy, catholic and apostolic was made in Cyril of Jerusalem's *Catecheses* (c. 350), these four adjectives later appearing in the Nicene Creed (381). Yet, notwithstanding this body of work, Pannenberg maintains that the Reformers were the first to introduce the church as a discrete dogmatic theme, for example in the final edition of the *Institutes* (1559) with Calvin's extended treatment of the true church, its marks, offices, and sacraments. The task here was not to defend innovation but to indicate continuity with and recovery of apostolic themes.

Despite the historical consensus, some of the better-known slogans in ecclesiology have recently been problematized and in need of some restatement,

---

1. Andrew Walls, *The Cross-Cultural Process in Christian History* (Edinburgh: T&T Clark, 2002), 10–11.
2. John Calvin, *Institutes*, trans. Ford Lewis Battles (Philadelphia: Westminster Press, 1960), IV.1.1, 1012.
3. Tom Greggs, *Dogmatic Ecclesiology Vol. 1: The Priestly Catholicity of the Church* (Grand Rapids: Baker, 2019).
4. Wolfhart Pannenberg, *Systematic Theology*, Vol. 3 (Edinburgh: T&T Clark, 1998), 21–7.

if not discarding. The aforementioned Nicene Creed speaks of the church as one, holy, catholic, and apostolic. This has been widely accepted throughout the ecumenical church, though questions were raised in the sixteenth century about where it was to be located and how it was to be recognized. The marks or notes of the church in the Reformed confessions were an attempt to address this problem. The church was visible through Word and sacrament—the preaching of the Word of God and the correct administration of the two sacraments. The ecumenical advantage of this claim lay in part in its minimalism. The *satis est* of the Augsburg Confession enabled recognition of any church where Word and sacrament could be discerned.[5] This enables us to view different churches, despite still lacking full visible unity, as making a vital contribution to the wider body of the universal church. In our own time, the project of receptive ecumenism seems to be governed by this assumption.[6] Notwithstanding the failure of ecumenical aspirations in the late twentieth century, the need for greater visible unity remains a Scriptural and missional imperative.

The Augustinian distinction between the visible and invisible church was frequently employed at the Reformation. By separating these, one could distinguish the invisible company of the elect through the ages from the visible church into which entire populations were baptized. The visible church could thus remain an authentic church of Word and sacrament, even though not all its adherents belonged to the elect. One could also hold that the elect might include some not adhering to the visible church through the mark of baptism, though this remained a point of division among the Reformers.[7]

With the tendency in modern theology to reconfigure the relationship between the church and the world, the distinction between the visible and the invisible church has had to be recast, both in Catholic (Vatican II) and Protestant theology.[8] If the church is witness, foretaste, and sign of the coming kingdom of God, then its fundamental identity is visible.[9] A purer invisible church requires a doctrine

---

5. Augsburg Confession VII.

6. Paul Murray (ed.), *Receptive Ecumenism and the Call to Catholic Learning: Exploring a Way for Contemporary Ecumenism* (Oxford: Oxford University Press, 2008).

7. These ecclesial distinctions were not without their practical tensions after the Reformation. Was the church a national institution into which everyone was to be baptized or a gathered company of those adhering to the true faith? See Scott Spurlock, "Boundaries of Scottish Reformed Orthodoxy 1560–1700," in *History of Scottish Theology, Vol. 1; Celtic Origins to Reformed Orthodoxy*, ed. David Fergusson and Mark W. Elliott (Oxford: Oxford University Press, 2019), 359–76. On the salvation of those outside the church, Zwingli's inclusion of the virtuous pagans was rejected by later Reformed theology, for example in the Westminster Confession, 10.4.

8. For example, Karl Barth, *Church Dogmatics* IV/3 (Edinburgh: T&T Clark, 1962), 722–55.

9. George Lindbeck points out that there was never a doctrine of the invisible Israel. "The Church," in *Keeping the Faith: Essays to Mark the Centenary of Lux Mundi*, ed. Geoffrey Wainwright (Philadelphia: Fortress Press, 1988), 179–208.

of election that stresses a decreed and final separationism. This has generally not commended itself to modern ecumenical theologians. Yet the visible-invisible distinction does not need to be abandoned entirely. If the notion of an invisible church can provide us with a keen sense of our links in the *communio sanctorum* to the church across space and time, then it continues to serve a useful function. This need not be tied to earlier assumptions about the nature of Christendom and the doctrine of election.

A further difficulty with characterizing the visible church in terms of its two marks is the lack of sufficiency in the definition. Word and sacrament are necessary but what about church order, offices, oversight, government, and forms of historical continuity? Such concerns moved Bucer and the authors of the Scots Confession to add a third mark, namely that of pastoral discipline. Today we are nervous around this supplementary note, partly owing to its subsequent preoccupation with sexual morality. Yet its intention was to underscore the importance of order, justice, and the common good of both church and society.

Problems around the sufficiency of any one definition of the church have led to contrasting approaches that are shaped by a series of models; these have roots in the multiplicity of Scriptural images of the church. This has obvious advantages. A plethora of images in the New Testament is evident, for example, the body of Christ, the household of God, the creation of the Holy Spirit, the people of faith, the called and the elect. Other notions such as the vine, the bride, and the flock illustrate both the relationship of church to Christ and of the members to one another. Paul Minear discerns a startling ninety-six images.[10] The unity of the church, the diversity of gifts and ministries distributed by the Spirit, the equality of the members, the emergence of disparate offices and the need for order: these are all important and reflect various crises during the apostolic age. Given its complexity, we need images rather than an Aristotelian definition to capture the richness and multi-dimensionality of the church. There is a danger of essentializing it with one single image or account of order, thus missing its diverse expressions by excluding all but one form. This recognition is an ecumenical breakthrough.

Avery Dulles's treatment of the models of the church has become something akin to a modern classic. He distinguishes six models, while exploring the value and limitations of each. His argument is that all are needed to generate a balanced and rounded ecclesiology that avoids an over-determination of one perspective or set of actions. His six models comprise the church as an institution (a traditional Catholic notion), the church as a mystical body (including the body of Christ and people of God), the church as a sacramental sign (reflecting the Vatican II notion of "sign"), the church as herald (a more Protestant notion of witness), the church as servant (a greater stress on the diaconal role of the church to the world is provided here), and as community of disciples (the links

---

10. Paul Minnear, *Images of the Church in the New Testament* (Louisville: Westminster John Knox Press, 2004).

to Jesus' calling of the twelve are explicit here). Dulles registers some telling criticisms of each but acknowledges that there should be room for all in tackling an agenda of contemporary problems. His last model was added to the 2002 edition of the work in an attempt to find a setting in which the other five can be anchored.[11]

Two additional problems can be detected in the classical Reformation statement of the dual marks of the church, and these will form the bulk of what remains in this essay. One concerns history and the other mission. The historical problem is already evident in what became known as the "Protestant time warp." With the perceived need to secede from the Roman Catholic Church, the Reformers faced the dual challenge of establishing their links with the apostolic church of the New Testament and the early centuries, while simultaneously so stressing the corruption of the institution that was being abandoned that its continuity with the apostolic church could be contested. This generated a vague sense that a thousand years of church history were a dark age that had now been corrected by a sudden return to a purified church. Although this is a caricature when we consider the liturgical, theological and legal continuities with the late Middle Ages, nevertheless elements have persisted in the Protestant mindset. No doubt that has often been encouraged by a theological curriculum which too quickly jumped from Augustine to the Reformers in its attention to doctrinal matters.

But the problem of church history runs deeper today. To make sense of the church, we have to tell a story about ourselves. (This applies *mutatis mutandis* to other institutions too.) The story requires to be positive and to have a measure of plausibility under the scrutiny of the historian. In the case of the church, there are strong theological reasons for assuming that the emergence of the Christian faith made a difference both to its adherents and to the wider world. The transformative potential of the gospel in the lives of the followers of Jesus confirms its claims. A constitutive feature of Christian faith is that the appearance of a new and unique society of believers in the first century, together with its many subsequent expressions, made a positive difference. These claims are already ventured in the New Testament, particularly in the first attempt to write a history of the church in the Acts of the Apostles. From this inheritance, our own practice of the faith is enriched and connected with that of the ecumenical church. Yet the problem today is that such claims are the target of a relentless hermeneutics of suspicion with the exposure of dubious practices, mixed motives and shameful episodes; these then fuel secular narratives about shaking off the yoke of traditional faith claims. Nietzsche got there before the New Atheists with his oft-quoted remark: "Better songs they will have to sing for me before I learn to believe in their redeemer; more redeemed his disciples would have to look."[12]

11. Avery Cardinal Dulles, *Models of the Church* (New York: Image Books, 2014).
12. Friedrich Nietzsche, *Thus Spoke Zarathustra*, ed. Adrian Del Caro and Robert Pippin (Cambridge: Cambridge University Press, 2005), 71.

A further *lacuna* is that the two marks make no reference to mission, a subject that has become central to many recent theological descriptions of the church, not to mention policy shifts regarding the deployment of resources. Why the Reformers did not regard mission as significant and when this shifted in the Protestant mindset are interesting historical questions on which more work is needed.[13] No doubt, the priority of reforming the church rather than extending its reach is part of the story. But the apparent absence of mission from the *notae* counts as a serious omission for many today. Is the church now to be defined in terms of mission, perhaps proceeding from the *missio Dei* as its ground? Or does this suffer too from the narrowing of purpose, form and activity that afflicted earlier approaches?[14]

Dismal Stories?

An underlying meta-narrative of the secular age is that we have now broken free from the irrational and damaging hold of religion upon our society. We have entered, so the narrative continues, a new age of liberation, peace, sexual freedom, and individual rights. I take this to be a historical story (as opposed to a philosophical or scientific claim) which underlies skepticism, New Atheism, and a more diffused secular antipathy toward the church. The narrative features some shameful examples (the Crusades, the Inquisition, sectarianism, violence, burning of witches and recent exposure of chronic child abuse—admittedly, these are not difficult to find) and tends to view these as indicative of the practical effects of Christian faith across the ages. Hence the triple claim that religion is irrational, damaging, and inhibiting is supported by a historical story that we have now internalized as a culture. This has particular appeal in the secular West—the examples indeed are largely drawn from Western history. Since the 1960s, the rapid process of secularization has confirmed the plausibility of this new meta-narrative for many of our fellow citizens. It enables critics to castigate Christian attitudes as "medieval" and to view its rejection as accompanied by greater freedoms, the end of a cramping institutional authority, and life-enhancing practices.

I offer three types of response to this story of liberation from the "dark ages" of Christianity:

1. Repentance is required of the churches for previous abuses of faith and power. This is needed for the purification of memory and for the constant

---

13. David J. Bosch points out that Anabaptist missions provided an exception. See *Transforming Mission: Paradigm Shifts in Theology of Mission* (Maryknoll: Orbis, 1991), 246.

14. For discussion of Reformed attitudes to mission, see Darrell L. Guder, "Reformed Theology, Mission and Ecumenism," in *The Cambridge Companion to Reformed Theology*, ed. Paul T. Nimmo and David A. S. Fergusson (Cambridge: Cambridge University Press, 2016), 319–34.

task of reformation in our own age. Humility is the first flower that grows at the foot of the cross. We should also acknowledge that the secular world may have much to teach us. In the past, the churches have often been too slow to appreciate the importance of democracy, the equality of the sexes, tolerance, the provision of legislation for divorce and remarriage, and human rights, even though resources within the tradition can be deployed to support these. Some forms of secularism offer a blanket condemnation of Christianity. But we should not repeat the same mistake by making a blanket judgment about secularism, as if its benefits must be entirely deleterious.

The representatives of any contemporary institution have a responsibility to reckon with its history. In belonging to the church, we position ourselves *a fortiori* in continuity with those who preceded us and invested in its practices and beliefs. Implicit in the belonging is a claim about institutional origins and standards, and our alignment with these. Edmund Burke famously stated that if an institution is worth preserving, we should be prepared to reform it. The converse also holds. If an institution is worth reforming, we must be ready to defend its preservation. This will involve a reckoning with the past and a readiness to admit its defects and lapses. The act of reforming should be accompanied by an appropriate acknowledgement of where we and our predecessors went wrong. That may involve apology or reparations to other groups or individuals who have been harmed, sometimes grievously, and honest historical excavation of the past, both remote and recent, and what was undertaken in the name of the institution. Repentance may take different forms, depending on time and circumstance, but it is a prerequisite for the work of preservation and reform. Though its roots are medieval and catholic, the ancient slogan of *semper reformanda* is often associated with the Reformed churches. If we always need to be reformed, then we must stand in a dialectical relationship to the past in both interrogating its failings and lauding its achievements.[15] The Christian mediocrity of which Augustine spoke constantly afflicts the life of the church. Diarmaid MacCulloch's verdict is therefore unsurprising. Christian faith "has brought human beings to acts of criminal folly as well as to the highest achievements of goodness, creativity, and generosity."[16]

2. Nevertheless, a close scrutiny of the historical evidence reveals that much of the contemporary secular narrative is unbalanced—the entries are mostly in the debit column. Yet the early Christians were critical of the violence and corruption of the Greco-Roman Empire. They espoused high standards, as many of their opponents conceded. Despite popular caricatures, the Middle

---

15. For discussion of the slogan see Leo J. Koffeman, "'Ecclesia reformata semper reformanda': Church Renewal from a Reformed Perspective," *HTS Teologiese Studies/Theological Studies* 71, no. 3 (2015): 1–5.

16. Diarmaid MacCulloch, *A History of Christianity* (Harmondsworth: Penguin, 2009), 13.

Ages were a time in which monasteries and cathedrals were built, schools and universities founded, patterns of commerce developed, and care for the sick and poor practiced. The just war theory and popular concepts of political authority were articulated by medieval scholars. And, after the Reformation, the case for freedom of conscience and religious tolerance was argued forcefully by dissident Protestant groups, particularly in England, before secular arguments for autonomy emerged. Newton, Kelvin, and Clerk Maxwell saw no conflict between their faith and their science. The oft-quoted cases of Galileo and Darwin were never a simple clash of a recondite religion with an enlightened science.[17] In modern times, Christians have also been involved in reform movements, in political radicalism, in making the case for social welfare and in supporting education and health care provision wherever the church spread in the world. We need to tell these stories. And despite developments surrounding marriage, it remains a surprisingly persistent institution that has been adapted rather than abandoned by our contemporaries. Meanwhile, the record of atheist regimes in the twentieth century and since has often been murderous.

Except in a piecemeal way, the challenge of offering a more positive narrative of the church has not generally been met by theologians and church historians. This remains an important apologetic task, though it has not been pursued with the same vigor as have responses to scientific and philosophical challenges. One notable exception is Rowan Williams's measured analysis in *Why Study the Past?*[18] Here Williams identifies the need to move toward a post-critical reading of church history to find a way of understanding the institution to which we belong without evading necessary critical questions. We must shun both a progressivist account in which we see ourselves as improving steadily upon the past and also the claim that there was once a pristine age of the church which has been lost but now recaptured in some fresh way. Yet monotonous deconstruction will cause fatal damage to our sense of belonging to the body of Christ.[19] Proper criticism must be combined with an appreciation of the past. Further support has arrived from less likely quarters, for example, in the recent work of Tom Holland which sees the treasures of the Enlightenment not as a release from the inheritance of Christianity but as reposing upon it.[20]

---

17. See Ronald L. Numbers, *Galileo Goes to Jail and Other Myths about Science and Religion* (Cambridge, MA: Harvard University Press, 2010).

18. Rowan Williams, *Why Study the Past? The Quest for the Historical Church* (London: Darton, Longman and Todd, 2005). For a robust set of responses to recent criticism see also David Bentley Hart, *Atheist Delusions: The Christian Revolution and its Fashionable Enemies* (New Haven: Yale University Press, 2010).

19. Williams, *Why Study the Past?*, 27.

20. Tom Holland, *Dominion: The Making of the Western Mind* (London: Little, Brown, 2019).

3. Much Christian service takes places in local and concealed ways that are not immediately evident in the textbooks of historians. In his 1949 study of *Christianity and History*, Herbert Butterfield wrote of how the standing work of the churches through the ages among local communities has made an incalculable practical change to the quality of life. But he then immediately acknowledged how difficult it can be for historians to factor into their work the inner spiritual life of the church and its parochial activities. This may be the most important way in which the meta-narrative of secularism can be contested. Today we speak of the social capital generated by faith communities with their resilience and positive significance. Throughout our country, Christians quietly visit the sick, run food banks, establish credit unions, maintain youth organizations, raise, money for work overseas and support refugees. This requires to be taken into account as a pointer to a very different story that undergirds faith. If we cannot overturn the mind-set of our age with immediate effect, we can at least find ways of contesting it both intellectually and practically.

In their study *American Grace*, Robert Putnam and David Campbell suggest that those frequenting a church or synagogue are more likely to do voluntary work for a charity and offer multiple forms of support to those in need. Frequent, rather than occasional, worshippers are significantly more active citizens. This is practice, not belief. Taking part is what counts, rather than giving intellectual assent to a creedal position. Putnam and Campbell "speculate that an atheist who went regularly to church (perhaps because of a spouse) would be more likely to volunteer in a soup kitchen than a believer who prays alone."[21] These actions of the church tend to be local, individual and seemingly modest in their impacts. Yet their cumulative effect, when assessed in such studies, is striking. Much of this activity does not make for a headline story or a single episode available for historical scrutiny, yet its persistence is remarkable in its own way.[22]

Mission in Perspective

A stress on the local provides a salutary reminder of the multiple forms of social engagement that take place in most Christian congregations. This is not the privileged domain of so-called national churches but is apparent in many other

---

21. Robert D. Putnam and David E. Campbell, *American Grace: How Religion Unites and Divides Us* (New York: Simon and Schuster, 2010), 427–8.

22. Jeffrey Stout's study, *Blessed Are the Organised: Grassroots Democracy in America* (Princeton: Princeton University Press, 2010) similarly demonstrates the ways in which local activism is necessary for the preservation of a democratic culture. This again may illustrate ways in which Western democracies remain more indebted than is often recognized to the faith communities that they host.

traditions and increasingly in other faith communities. To defend a national church on the grounds that it cares for everyone in its parish and not only its own members is a misrepresentation of other groups that are equally impressive in their outreach, witness, and generation of social capital.

Nevertheless, one of the frequent complaints of those who advocate mission as the central component of ecclesial strategy is that this has been neglected throughout much of our history. In transitioning from a maintenance model of church life to a missional one, the church is urged to adopt a strategy that has mission at the heart of everything it does. Nevertheless, while the discourse of mission does not feature much in early Reformed texts, much of what might count as mission today has been exhibited for many centuries. Although the term "mission" was not in common currency, the aim of social transformation runs deep in the Reformed churches. These were concerned with the shaping of society and not merely the church. The ideal of a "godly commonwealth" became a powerful expression of the importance of Christian transformation, as did its predecessor concept of the "common good" in medieval thought. To this extent, the church maintained an outward focus beyond its walls. Its members were sent into the secular world to suffuse it with their Christian standards, while the church itself sought to enter into a partnership with the political state.[23]

To cite my own Scottish context, our nineteenth-century predecessors were also heavily engaged in forms of mission—church planting, education of the people, foreign missions, and forms of social service and health care. Having suffered the trauma of the Disruption in 1843 in which it lost one-third of its ministers and one half of its members, the Church of Scotland recovered largely through this concerted missional effort. By the end of the century, it had become the largest Presbyterian grouping. This renewal took place partly through the work of Evangelicals who remained within the ranks of the Kirk, but also by a broader church party that was persuaded of the value of an established parish church. By the time of the 1929 reunion, the Auld Kirk was almost twice the size of the United Free Church. Its commitment to education, liturgical reform, new church development, overseas work, social outreach, and uniformed organizations was central in this process of recovery. The base from which these activities emerged was the local parish church, which transmitted the faith to new generations and generated the human and financial resources for the accomplishment of its work.

Also worth pondering are the innovations of the twentieth century, many of them undertaken by some of the most gifted people that the Scottish churches have produced. When we consider the array of new ideas and initiatives that produced the Iona Community, counseling services, Christian education, Tell Scotland, and Scottish Churches House, we realize that fresh expressions were

---

23. Luther's secularization of vocations is an important element of this outward focus and provides a stronger social theology than is sometimes recognized. See Michael Richard Laffin, *The Promise of Martin Luther's Political Theology: Freeing Luther from Modern Political Narrative* (London: Bloomsbury, 2016).

already developed by earlier generations.[24] We continue to learn from these creative initiatives and movements. Although the second half of the twentieth century was a time of church decline, these innovations reveal impressive work that was undertaken. The history of the Scottish churches in the twentieth century has yet to be written, but these initiatives will surely feature.

Why then has the language of mission suddenly attained such prominence? Much of this has its roots in the *missio Dei* theologies of the twentieth century.[25] With the spreading of the Christian faith to the Global South, mission assumed a new salience that had not characterized Western church life at earlier periods. The stress on God's mission, moreover, enabled a keener sense of the distinction between the kingdom of God and the work of the church. God intended not only a church. Rooted in the teaching of Jesus, the kingdom, or commonwealth of God provided a more capacious concept with universalist and eschatological aspects. The sending of the church, therefore, was for the wider purpose of witnessing to and working for the kingdom. This enabled the language of mission to assume a more critical sociopolitical edge. As theologians developed the *missio Dei*, an important Trinitarian inflection was discerned. The mission of Christ upon which the church reposed was generated by the missions of the triune God in the *opera Trinitatis ad extra*. The sending of the Son and the Spirit into the world reflected the eternal begetting and the eternal proceeding of their persons in the life of the Trinity.[26] For this reason, the entire economy of creation and salvation could be characterized in terms of mission, a going-forth of God to make and save the cosmos. With the renaissance of Trinitarian theology, this wider hermeneutical context has resulted in an inflation of missiological discourse.

Yet a more proximate cause for the predominance of the language of mission in contemporary ecclesiastical strategies is surely the sudden loss of Christendom status in the West. As parish churches have declined and large swathes of the population have become disconnected from the Christian faith, a rapid move from maintenance to mission seems required of the contemporary church. At times, it is difficult not to feel a sense of anxiety creeping into the rhetoric of mission. Unless we mend our ways, extinction threatens. Church strategy needs to be driven by missional priorities.

First developed within the Church of England, the "five marks of mission" are worth considering[27]:

---

24. Alexander C. Forsyth, *Mission by the People: Re-discovering the Dynamic Missiology of Tom Allan and his Scottish Contemporaries* (Eugene: Wipf and Stock, 2017).

25. See Bosch, *Transforming Mission*, 389–92.

26. For discussion of how the *missio Dei* became the *missio Trinitatis* see John Flett, *The Witness of God: The Trinity, Missio Dei, Karl Barth and the Nature of Christian Community* (Grand Rapids: Eerdmans, 2010).

27. "Microsoft Word—CoE Web MISSION template five marks of mission WORD version.docx" (churchofengland.org) accessed on November 3, 2023.

To proclaim the Good News of the Kingdom.
To teach, baptise and nurture new believers.
To respond to human need by loving service.
To seek to transform unjust structures of society, to challenge violence of every kind and to pursue peace and reconciliation.
To strive to safeguard the integrity of creation and sustain and renew the life of the earth.

These have evolved since 1984, the fourth one being most recently expanded. The breadth of missional work is apparent here from proclamation and conversion through to sociopolitical activism and ecological preservation. Undoubtedly, there is Scriptural support for grouping these actions of the church under the banner of mission. Jesus sends out the twelve and the seventy to proclaim. At the close of Matthew's Gospel, the church is commissioned to teach and baptize the nations. In John, the disciples are to follow the example of Jesus in loving service. "As the Father has sent me, so I send you" (John 20:21). The commitment to justice and cosmic wholeness is also deeply embedded in the Psalms, the Law, the Prophets, and the teaching of Jesus. The apocalyptic vision that concludes the New Testament is one that encompasses the nations and transforms social life.

Yet the five marks are not comprehensive. Perhaps most surprisingly, the name of Jesus is never mentioned though doubtless it is implicit in marks one and two. Other actions of the church seem to be missing. Worship as the glorifying of God, the pastoral care of its members, Christian education, and the Eucharist do not feature explicitly in the five marks. What this suggests is that though the five marks may be useful for benchmarking the work of congregations, they are not intended to provide a comprehensive list of essential activities, an ordered set of priorities or a menu from which only some may be selected.[28] The raison d'être of the church is not exhausted by their iteration. The focus on "sending" in missional theology becomes Procrustean when the entire range of ecclesial action is grouped under this one heading.

Once again, the necessary multiplicity of ecclesiological models may prove relevant here. In the 2002 edition of his work, Dulles introduced the model of the community of disciples which he argued could ground the other five models.[29] This had the advantage of being close to the experience of Christians and readily assimilated in their understanding. Within this foundational model, he sees both assembling and sending as activities that should be inter-related.

---

28. Jesse Zink, "Five Marks of Mission: History, Theology, Critique," *Journal of Anglican Studies* 15, no. 2 (2017): 144–66. Zink suggests that such lists have a useful function in uniting the ecumenical church and in balancing local with global concerns. But their shelf life is likely to be not much more than ten to twenty years, after which they will be supplanted.

29. Dulles, *Models of the Church*, 195–217.

The church is never more church than when it gathers for instruction and worship. On such occasions it becomes most palpably the "the sacrament of Christ" as proposed in the third model. But it would not be completely church unless it went forth from its assemblies to carry on Christ's work in the world. The church's existence is a continual alternation between two phases. Like systole and diastole in the movement of the heart, like inhalation and exhalation in the process of breathing, assembly and mission succeed each other in the life of the church. Discipleship would be stunted unless it included both the centripetal phase of worship and the centrifugal phase of mission.[30]

This insight has some practical outcomes for the contemporary church. The over-determining of mission may be just as bad as neglecting it. The church has many functions—the glorifying of God in its worship, the education and nurture of its people, the pastoral care of the sick and the dying, and the bearing witness to the gospel in the life of the world. These activities of the church are necessarily plural, even as we affirm that there is one faith and one Lord. Yet none of this is to imply that the church does not find itself today in a very different historical position. If we begin with a sad lament for its former status, then we will tend to present the solution as merely reversing that decline with mission becoming a project of restoration. Yet this neglects the way in which we have shifted from a culture of obligation to one of consumption, the ways in which people increasingly choose their religion or spirituality and function as seekers rather than dwellers.[31] There is plenty of sociological evidence and analysis to support these conclusions. Secularization is not the fault of the church—this is simply where we find ourselves. Our post-Christian setting is a new one in the history of the church. We have to opt in rather than opt out. For most, the default setting is one of market choice rather than cultural obligation. This entails that churchgoing and religious observance must compete with a range of other leisure-time pursuits—hence the difficulty in attracting and retaining young people. Vicarious religion, sympathetic indifference, forms of Christian affiliation outside the institutional churches—these are novel features of our condition that we have not hitherto experienced as a society. Other Western European societies are experiencing similar shifts, and the United States may not be so far behind, despite earlier claims for its exceptionalism.

The future of the church in our society is likely to be one in which it is smaller. Predictions of transformational events are notoriously imprecise and uncertain. Who predicted the collapse of Communism and the Berlin Wall, 9/11, the credit crunch in 2008, and Covid-19? Our pollsters could not even foresee Brexit and the election of Donald Trump. Forecasting is a hazardous business. Maybe we will be surprised by the sudden revival of the churches when it happens, as well as by its causes. But, for the moment, the church needs to recognize that it will be much smaller in the coming generation and to figure out how to function effectively

---

30. Ibid., 211.

31. Grace Davie, *Religion in Britain: A Persistent Paradox* (Oxford: Wiley Blackwell, 2015), 133–74.

with its reduced capacity. A missional strategy that is based upon returning to a position of cultural pre-eminence is profoundly mistaken. We need to become a humbler church, recognizing that we have lost our cultural standing to a significant degree. This will mean fewer buildings and congregations. People may need to travel a bit further to attend church. But some consolidation is inevitable and hard decisions about finance and fabric are necessary. In particular, we need to concentrate on buildings and worship to provide a transformative experience on a Sunday morning and at other times in the week, from which further activities can then follow. Liturgical reinvigoration, not least through church music, may be vital to our missionary strategy. People should leave church feeling much better than when they entered, not merely relieved that an act of observance is over for another week.

We should also be realistic in what we can expect, and ready to accommodate those who want to attend only occasionally without generating too many obligations. Perhaps this is why Saturday night Mass is popular in many Roman Catholic churches and why cathedral worship has grown significantly in England. In this context, to impose too many missional obligations on the church may actually be to its detriment.

Within our town and cities, we should offer greater variety to people in terms of styles of worship, theology, and outreach. The Church of England may be rather better at this than the Church of Scotland. Spirituality and religion will not be provided wholesale to an entire population. Different products and retail outlets will be required for people who are increasingly educated, selective, and mobile in relation to institutions. Large evangelical churches should be allowed to flourish with a greater degree of autonomy, as should cathedrals and other historic buildings that offer more traditional patterns of worship. We need to encourage local initiatives and diversity at grass roots level. Let's give our declining congregations a menu of options and encourage them to assess what might work best for them. Many of the churches that continue to flourish are those with strong connections to their surrounding communities, and are able to offer lively worship and a range of activities for people of all ages. This embeddedness of churches in their localities is what earns them respect, especially where this is evident in forms of service and support to hard-pressed people. The parish model continues to have traction in different places.[32]

The saddest element in recent research about leaving the church are the stories of those who did not find friendship and love or were not allowed to express their doubts and lack of conviction.[33] Feeling pressurized to conform, they became

---

32. For a missiological defense of the parish model, see Lesslie Newbigin, *A Word in Season: Perspectives on Christian World Mission* (Grand Rapids: Eerdmans, 1994), 48–65.

33. Steve Aisthorpe, *The Invisible Church* (Edinburgh: St Andrew Press, 2016); Robin Stockitt and S. John Dawson, *Leaving Church: What Can We Learn from Those Who Are Done with Church?* (Cambridge: Grove Books, 2020).

impatient with the persistent refusal to embrace change and grew weary of ever-increasing demands. Any missionary strategy for the future needs to be alert to problems that produce alienation within the body of Christ itself.

But in permitting diversity and enabling local initiatives, by adopting a more humble posture and a realistic recognition of what can be expected of people, we may arrive at a place where the Spirit surprises us. This is by no means to forsake mission, especially the obligation to transmit the faith to those who come after us. But we should release ourselves from unrealistic burdens and expectations in order to serve God as best we can in our own day. Freed from strategic postures induced by either panic or denial, we can better appreciate and be grateful for the multiplicity of ways in which the church continues to live and act in the name of Christ.

Chapter 14

THE BIBLE IN MODERNITY

The Centrality of Scripture in the Life of the Church

The centrality of Scripture in the life of the church is a vital element for any account of its authority. Theology, worship, proclamation and ecclesial self-understanding entail repeated reference to Scripture.

In seeking to describe the theological significance of Scripture, one might start by noting its functional centrality in the life of the church. Confessional traditions, whether Catholic, Orthodox, Anglican, or Reformed, owe allegiance to the authority of Scripture, despite some competing accounts of the nature of that authority and its relationship to the church, or more specifically its councils and magisterial offices. Yet the Bible is revered everywhere across the ecumenical church, its presence in each act of worship being accompanied by appropriate symbolic gestures. Our liturgies too are deeply informed by the language of Scripture, especially the Psalms and the Gospels, while the reading and preaching of the Word of God are central to most diets of worship including celebration of the Eucharist. This dependence of the church upon Scripture is not an accidental or external feature of its existence. To that extent, it is impossible for the church to evade or diminish the endless task of reading, interpreting, arguing, and receiving the meaning of the Bible. In part, this is an inevitable outcome of a faith that attaches normative significance to a sequence of historical events and understands its identity by reference to the past. The "scandal of particularity" requires a canon of authoritative witnesses as its necessary condition. What happened once upon a time determines the meaning of the present and the future. This applies not just generically to traditions of thought and practice but to the particular history of Israel, the life of Jesus and the birth of the church. Later I shall advance further Christological reasons in support of this claim about particularity. At the outset, however, it is worth recalling the ways in which the Bible is embedded in the theology and practice of our churches. This context has remained largely constant despite the disputes that have surrounded the nature, authority, and interpretation of Scripture in modernity.

Gains and Losses of the Reformation

The translation of the Bible into the vernacular and the appeal to Scripture over church teaching ensured from the sixteenth century onwards that Scripture became the focus of intense enquiry. However, lack of consensus about its meaning led to the fracturing of Protestantism.

The Protestant Reformation of the sixteenth century generally appealed to the authority of Scripture over against the teaching of the church. The practice of the church was normed by Scripture, which meant that the activity of the church required constant correction in light of the teaching and preaching of the Word of God. This process was never complete but required to be undertaken in every generation—*ecclesia reformata sed semper reformanda*. According to this slogan, which is medieval in origin, the church is never immune from further reform but is always requiring to be reformed according to the Word of God. As a principle this seemed clear, but in practice *sola Scriptura* was seldom straightforward. Against the individualism and anarchy of some elements of the Reformation, Calvin insisted that the reading of Scripture was most profitably undertaken by a community of persons who collectively sought the wisdom of the Spirit.[1] For this reason, the teaching of church councils, if not infallible, was nevertheless to be accorded a high respect and generally allowed to guide one's understanding of the text. Despite this ideal, the fractured outcomes of the Reformation illustrated the Achilles' heel of its appeal to Scripture over the church. There was no emerging consensus among Protestant groups on the correct interpretation of the Bible with respect to a range of issues, for example, predestination, the real presence of Christ in the eucharistic elements, the validity of infant baptism, patterns of worship, Sabbath observance, the authority of the civil magistrate, forms of church government, and even the doctrine of the Trinity. Ironically, it was precisely those disagreements about the interpretation of Scripture that contributed to the emergence of the ideals of religious toleration and diversity in early modern England, an ideal that was presented not so much on secular grounds but rather as one that was implicit in the New Testament itself.[2] Yet this too was contested as a reading of Scripture, particularly in Scotland where appeals to the unitary religious character of biblical Israel persisted well into the eighteenth century.

Unquestionably, the Reformation raised the profile of the Bible in Europe. It derived in part from late medieval and Renaissance efforts to translate the Bible into modern European languages; hence, it became more widely available

---

1. *Institutes*, Book 4, Chapter 9.
2. This is explored by John Coffey, *Persecution and Toleration in Protestant England 1558–1689* (Harlow: Longman, 2000).

to populations at large. Tyndale's vision of the ploughboy reading the verses of Scripture was accomplished, at least in part, by the eighteenth century with higher literacy levels and the saturation of our culture with biblical stories, precepts, and images. The quatercentenary celebrations of the King James Bible reminded us of this, not least through recalling the number of metaphors and sayings in common currency that have their provenance in the 1611 translation. Nevertheless, the respect for and awareness of the Bible was not accompanied by agreement on its correct interpretation, and this despite the centuries-long dominance of one single translation in the English-speaking world. If anything, the circulation of the text in the vernacular contributed to greater disagreement and division than had characterized the pre-Reformation era. Perhaps this confirmed Catholic fears about too much biblical literacy. Thomas Forret, vicar at Dollar, was condemned by George Crichton, the Bishop of Dunkeld, for teaching his parishioners the English Bible and preaching on it every Sunday. Forret was subsequently executed in 1538. Crichton declared, "I thanke God, that I never knew what the Old and New Testament was."[3]

Problem A: The Significance of Historical Criticism

Historical criticism induced uncertainty surrounding the reliability of Scripture, as is evident from deism. However, its questions and findings have been diverse and remain a necessary though insufficient element in the interpretation of the Bible today.

If the Reformation brought disparity over the right interpretation of Scripture, the early modern period began the process of historical criticism that continues unabated to the present day as a major research industry in our universities. We sometimes assume that the application of higher criticism to Scripture was a nineteenth-century phenomenon. However, while many significant advances were made at this time and there were several high-profile church controversies, we should not forget that the project had commenced much earlier in the work of Spinoza, Hobbes and others in the seventeenth century.

According to Jowett's dictum, the work of higher criticism treats the books of the Bible like any other ancient text for the sake of historical investigation.[4]

---

3. Quoted by David F. Wright, "'The Common Buke of the Kirk': The Bible in the Scottish Reformation," in *The Bible in Scotland's Life and Literature*, ed. David F. Wright (Edinburgh: St Andrew Press, 1988), 155–78 (162).

4. Benjamin Jowett, "On the Interpretation of Scripture," in *Essays and Reviews*, 3rd ed. (London, 1860), 330–433 (377). However, when it is assumes the status of a dominant methodological axiom, the dictum "like any other book" becomes highly problematic. See

This includes the following: study of the different contexts in which the texts were written and edited; the religious, political, and ethical tendencies of the authors; likely processes of transmission and adaptation prior to the text reaching its final form; and the reconstruction of the historical events to which they refer. As higher criticism delivered its historical hypotheses, some troubling considerations presented themselves for the believing community. Moses did not write the Pentateuch. The gospel narratives contain contradictory elements that may reflect the different interests of the early Christians and the Evangelists—these are to be explained by the creative function of the tradition rather than the complementary perspectives of eyewitnesses. Different theologies are at work in Scripture. There are mythological elements and miraculous stories that seem more consonant with other ancient texts than with the writings of a modern historian.

In part, this growing skepticism about elements of Scripture contributed to the rise of deism in Europe and North America. Deism takes different forms, and it should not be assimilated to a single monolithic system of thought. At one end of the spectrum, it represents a modification of Christian orthodoxy while at the other it shades into agnosticism, scepticism and atheism. Nevertheless, one of the unifying features of deism is that the power of natural reason tends to be privileged over the authority of Scripture. According to Matthew Tindal, at All Souls College, the most that Scripture can offer is a republication of the tenets of natural religion. These are established primarily by reason and only secondarily by reference to the Bible. Somewhat ironically, it was historical investigation also that undermined deism. Its characteristic claim that at the root of all human culture there was a simple natural religion, which was both intellectually credible and morally worthy, proved untenable. The varieties of religion could not be distilled to a single essence. These were variable, context-dependent, and not readily conformable to the philosophy of the early Enlightenment.[5]

Nevertheless, historical criticism of the Bible continued apace, being conducted on an increasingly sophisticated basis. Its exponents did not hesitate to describe its methods as scientific. Its focus was on the supernatural character of events recorded in Scripture, especially miracles, and also the historical reliability of the stories of Israel, Jesus and the early church. The first of these twin *foci* was significant given the ways in which miracles had functioned through much of the early modern and Enlightenment periods as proofs for the distinctive truth claims of Christianity, for example in the philosophy of John Locke. In ways that now seem quaint and misplaced, much critical effort was expended in offering natural explanations of seemingly miraculous stories.

R. W. L. Moberly, "'Interpret the Bible Like Any Other Book?' Requiem for an Axiom," *Journal of Theological Interpretation* 4 (2010): 91–110.

5. See for example the account of religious diversity in David Hume, *The Natural History of Religion* (1757).

Perhaps most unsettling of all was the quest for the historical Jesus. If too much was ascribed to the creative power of the early community, the formative role of church history, and the different perspectives of the Evangelists, could we be sure that Jesus said and did most of what is attested of him in the four gospels? So, for example, the investigations of David Friedrich Strauss suggested that the divine Saviour who performed miraculous work was largely a mythological construct that reflected the faith of the first Christians rather than the history of Jesus of Nazareth. The dawning conviction that the Fourth Gospel represented a theological reflection upon the significance of the historical Jesus set it apart from the Synoptic Gospels. This almost exactly reversed the position of Schleiermacher who had been drawn to the opposite conclusion. For him, the Christ of the Fourth Gospel was authentic. The unity and force of Jesus' depiction in John must have derived from the spiritual influence of a historical personality. Since Strauss, however, biblical criticism has tended to lean in the opposite direction.

Some have declared the quest to be historically impossible and others theologically unnecessary.[6] One might even hold both of these propositions together. What is clear, however, is that despite attempts to declare a moratorium, it has continued unabated into the present day with contrasting portraits of Jesus offered by Marcus Borg, Dominic Crossan, Dale Allison, et al. The field has been occupied not only by revisionists and skeptics, but also by scholars with strong faith convictions who maintain that historical investigation can confirm the reliability of the gospel witness. There is a long tradition of what has been called "believing criticism" that includes scholars such as Vincent Taylor, C. H. Dodd, William Manson, and, in our own day, N. T. Wright. A notable recent attempt to defend the historical reliability of the gospels has been Richard Bauckham's *Jesus and the Eyewitnesses*.[7]

The historical-critical method has come under concerted attack in recent times, both from postmodern literary criticism and from within Christian theology. It is criticized for being spuriously objective and value-neutral, thus concealing a nest of ideological assumptions. The "view from nowhere" is a delusion, since each act of interpretation inevitably reflects the interest, concerns, and perspectives of the interpreting subject. Indeed, a historical survey of the application of the historical-critical method itself will tend to confirm the ways in which different readings of Scripture have their own distinctive cultural and ecclesial location.

Theological critics of the method have also complained that it has a tendency to silence the text as the Word of God. It yields historical findings yet the capacity

---

6. I have sought to explore this more fully in "Jesus and the Faith-History Problem Today," in *Jesus Christ Today: Studies of Christology in Various Contexts*, ed. Stuart G. Hall (Berlin: Gruyter, 2009), 265–82. For a survey of recent quests see Helen K. Bond, *The Historical Jesus: A Guide for the Perplexed* (London: T&T Clark, 2012), 19–36.

7. See Richard Bauckham's *Jesus and the Eyewitnesses* (Grand Rapids: Eerdmans, 2006). Bauckham extends his argument to the Fourth Gospel, hanging much on the significance of the "beloved disciple" in John 21 whom he identifies with John the Elder, a Jerusalem follower of Jesus.

of Scripture to address, even assail, the Church is lost by too heavy a concentration on the typical questions posed by historians. Are the interminable debates about the different source traditions embedded in the Pentateuch or the Gospels of much relevance to church or society today? Are these questions that only preoccupy an increasingly inward-looking scholarly guild? The fear of a bracketing of the important moral and religious issues raised by the canon of Holy Scripture has led to some outright hostility to historical criticism.

Nevertheless, this appears to be an objection not so much to biblical criticism itself as to the privileging of some questions and methods of study to the exclusion of others. The complaint is best interpreted as one about a narrowing of the field rather than the methodological impropriety of types of criticism. In any case, the questions of historical criticism and the answers offered in response tend to be more heterogeneous that this frontal attack implies.

The sheer diversity of findings by biblical critics is in itself positive, for it militates against the charge that the method of historical criticism is ideologically loaded in ways that disadvantage the claims of faith. Historical criticism has more often than not been pursued by believing critics who have produced works that seek to shed light on the text for the edifying of the church. This has often been an aim of commentaries series or one-volume encyclopedic works. They are written not merely for other scholars but also for preachers who wish to harness the best insights of biblical criticism for their work. Biblical criticism has thus been more varied in its findings and more frequently directed toward the needs of the church than some wholesale objections permit.[8] Insights into the historical context of first-century Palestinian Judaism and the *Sitz im Leben* of the early church will facilitate understanding of the New Testament texts; these are necessary tools for their contemporary appropriation by preachers and educators.

John Barton has pointed to the variety of questions pursued by biblical critics and to the kinds of skills that are required for this task. This tends to undermine the notion that there is one single method that is applied with relentless ideological force by historical critics. He claims that the work of critics is typically characterized by three central features. These are:

1. Attention to semantics, to the meaning of words, phrases, sentences, chapters and books.
2. Awareness of genre.
3. Bracketing-out of questions of truth, these belonging to the domain of theology rather than biblical criticism.[9]

---

8. This is largely borne out by John J. Collins's study in which he argues that the significance of postmodernism resides primarily in affording a wider diversity of interpretive voices within biblical criticism. See *The Bible After Babel: Historical Criticism in a Postmodern Age* (Grand Rapids: Eerdmans, 2005).

9. John Barton, *The Nature of Biblical Criticism* (Philadelphia: Westminster John Knox, 2007), 58.

I return to this last point later, but here it is sufficient to note the range of questions and the typical approaches adopted by modern critics. These often yield valuable insights and, as an approach to the text, historical criticism is a necessary accompaniment of any act of interpretation. So, for example, theological efforts to understand and appropriate the notion of the *imago Dei* in Genesis 1:26-27 will need some account of the significance of the Hebrew words *tselem* and *demuth* in the Old Testament, what range of meanings these might have had for ancient Israel, how the (Greek) New Testament advances a more Christological reading of the *imago Dei*, and how all these notions have been interpreted (or misinterpreted) in the history of the church. The task may not be exhausted by biblical criticism, but it cannot be undertaken without it.

Furthermore, there is a sense in which the enterprise of higher criticism, whatever its outcomes, must inevitably adjust one's understanding of the content of Scripture. We cannot return to a pre-critical phase of interpretation and assume with earlier commentators that the stories happened much as they are narrated or that the different accounts of the same events can readily be harmonized. None of this is to say that pre-critical readings have nothing to teach us—far from it—but there is no escaping the issues that have been raised for modern theology by the work of biblical historians or the enrichment that they offer for contemporary readings of Scripture. If one allows for the possibility of creativity, editorial redaction, adjustments in the process of transmission, and so on, then pre-critical understandings of Scripture will need to be adapted. This has been part of the staple diet of theological education for several generations now, although whether it has reached the wider Christian community, let alone the general public, is questionable.[10]

Problem B: The Moral Ambiguity of Scripture

The "hermeneutics of suspicion" should be acknowledged and accommodated in the task of appropriating Scripture today.

A related set of anxieties to those generated by historical criticism surrounds the moral ambiguity of portions of Scripture and their use in the church. Historians have applied a hermeneutic of suspicion to the interpretation of the Bible in the church. There are some uncomfortable findings about its role in legitimizing the treatment of heretics, witches, and slaves. It has been used at times to authorize oppressive forms of government, the subordination of women, the waging of war and imperial expansion. Adrian Thatcher's *The Savage Text* (2008) chronicles the abuses of Scripture in ways that are unnerving, at least at first sight, whether these be with reference to homophobia, racism, slavery, anti-Semitism, or misogyny. Of course, the narrative of suspicion needs to be balanced by other stories of how the

---

10. Some of the recent writings of the "New Atheists" mistakenly assume that most Christians and Muslims must be naively literalist in their approach to their sacred texts.

Bible has functioned positively in restraining, liberating, and reforming attitudes. Scripture has also been an agent of change in promoting religious tolerance, the abolition of slavery, the freedom of the oppressed, and advocacy of civil rights, peace, and social justice. But the way in which Christian expositors can be lined up on both sides of these debates again illustrates the point about the contestation of meanings as integral to the church's life.[11] This also raises major problems for a flat inerrancy theory which views each statement of Scripture as divinely inspired in the same way and by the same means of delivery through the Holy Spirit.

Readings of the Bible from other parts of the world have also drawn attention to the somewhat provincial nature of those historical questions that have preoccupied Western scholars for two centuries. This is a repeated complaint of scholars from Asia, Africa, and Latin America, even if it not a majority position among Christians in the Global South. R. G. Sugirtharajah points to ways in which postcolonial exegetes have become sensitized to the multiple oppressions depicted in Scripture.[12] Unlike the more binary approach of liberation theology which sees the Exodus as its paradigm, a postcolonial reading of the text will be alert to the situation of the Canaanite peoples who are conquered at the culmination of that historical sequence. Perhaps there are ways to handle the conquest narratives of Joshua more subtly, but the need to depart from earlier treatments of these texts has been raised by the perspective of Palestinian Christians and others today.[13]

Nevertheless, the hermeneutics of suspicion, if not accompanied by a strong confidence in the capacity of the Word of God to illumine, instruct and inspire, can readily undermine confidence in Scripture, especially the Old Testament, which remains deeply problematic to many people in our congregations. Its seemingly violent episodes, demands for retribution, and vituperative language make it difficult to appropriate for devotion, instruction and constructive Christian living. It requires critical and trained interpretation, subject to a plurality of voices within the church and sensitized to harmful constructions of the text. This is probably a greater difficulty for the laity, especially at a time of shrill secular criticism of sacred writings. By contrast with the moral problems of Scripture, historical challenges may be less unsettling.

Problem C—the Plurality of Sacred Texts

The plurality of sacred texts in the religions of the world has generated an argument against any single authority. This works against some constructions

---

11. A fine example is Mark Noll's handling of the Bible and slavery in *The Civil War as a Theological Crisis* (Durham: University of North Carolina Press, 2006).

12. R. G. Sugirtharajah, *The Bible and the Third World* (Cambridge: Cambridge University Press, 2001).

13. For a reading of Joshua 22 that points to the ways in which the text itself invites deconstruction see Graeme Auld, "Pluralism Where Least Expected: Joshua 22 in Biblical Context," *Expository Times* 122, no. 8 (2011): 374–9.

of the authority of Scripture, while also confirming the need for a clearer understanding of the relationship of Scripture and church.

A greater awareness of the different scriptures of the world religions has raised questions about their absolute or relative authority. David Hume once argued that reports of miracles in the different religions of the world tend to cancel out one another and thus to elicit a universal skepticism surrounding such stories.[14] A similar skeptical induction is rehearsed by critics of religion today. Each faith asserts that its own sacred writings are uniquely inspired and authoritative. These claims clash and compete with one another in ways that compel us to the conclusion that probably they are all wrong in some measure, each single claim requiring extensive revision in light of the others. Nevertheless, despite its *prima facie* appeal, this argument looks less formidable upon closer inspection largely because sacred texts function in different ways for different faiths. The Qur'an, for example, does not have an identical character and authority for Muslims to the understanding of the Bible for Christians, and the authority of Torah has been differently related to oral tradition within Judaism than in Christianity.[15] The role and content of a sacred body of literature in the religious community will determine the kind of authority that it assumes for practitioners. An understanding of the status assigned to a set of texts cannot be given except by reference to its function for the faith community, judgments about its content, and accounts of its origin. In addressing these questions, we come to realize that the distinctiveness of another faith is closely aligned to its sacred scriptures and the ways these are read and understood by practitioners.

This topic is still significantly underdeveloped in the scholarly literature but it includes the following three issues. First, what does the Bible itself have to say about other faiths and their sacred texts? Here we are faced with a multiplicity of approaches ranging from "neighborly pluralism" to "cosmic conflict." These provide rich material for reflection, although they tug in different directions.[16] There is awareness of other gods and faiths, and an acceptance of the loyalty of foreign peoples to these in ways that do not compromise the sovereignty of Yahweh or the covenant with Israel. After the healing of Naaman, the Syrian commander, Elisha accepts his need to return to the worship of a foreign god (2 Kings 5:19). Jonah's mission to Nineveh results in repentance and a renewed faithfulness, but this is a foreign city where people are not required to convert to Judaism. However, there are also contests in which Yahweh must prevail and other gods who must be

---

14. Essay on "Miracles," *Enquiry Concerning Human Understanding* (1748), Part 10.

15. See for example Edward Kessler, "Judaism," in *The Blackwell Companion to the Bible and Culture*, ed. John Sawyer (Oxford: Wiley Blackwell, 2006), 119-34.

16. See, for example, Wesley Ariarajah, *The Bible and People of Other Faiths* (Geneva: World Council of Churches, 1989), Robert Goldenberg, *The Nations that Know Thee Not: Ancient Jewish Attitudes Towards Other Religions* (Sheffield: Sheffield Academic Press, 1997), and "Review Essay" by Gerald R. McDermott in *Pro Ecclesia* 14 (2005): 487-93.

defeated. In the story of Elijah and the prophets of the Baal (1 Kings 18), the false prophets are routed. Their gods are silent, inactive and powerless by contrast with Elijah's. In Paul's more eschatological remarks about the triumphal procession of Christ (Colossians 2:15), we encounter claims about the decisive defeat of other forces and powers in the cosmos. Nevertheless, the record of Paul's preaching in Acts 14:15-17 and 17:23-31 also suggests a general revelation of God in other faiths and philosophies; this offers a point of contact for the preaching of Christ. These views were held together with the conviction, decisively confirmed in the struggle with Marcionism, that the Hebrew Bible remained canonical for the church, albeit in a different ordering of its books.

Second, a related conviction, found already in Justin Martyr and other writers of the early church, is that the ancient texts of other traditions may contain much wisdom that can usefully be appropriated by the church without compromising its commitment to the distinctiveness and authority of the Bible. We find this view adopted with respect to pagan philosophy but, in principle, there is no reason why it cannot be extended to the most revered texts of other religions. Different metaphors have been employed to express a relationship that is positive but asymmetrical, for example, spoiling the Egyptians, Christians before Christ, sparks of the Logos, the handmaid of theology etc.

Third, there is a recognized commonality among the Abrahamic faiths as "people of the book" united by the commands to love God and one's neighbor. Particularly since the publication of *Common Word*, this has resulted in a greater willingness among Jews, Christians and Muslims to explore the similarities and differences between the content, function and status of their sacred scriptures.[17] This requires a theological space which can recognize the authority that texts have in the life of a faith community but without either privileging one to the extent of excluding the contribution of others or of establishing a parity between all texts that effectively flattens the particular understanding that each has for its adherents. This theological space requires much work—its excavation is mostly quite recent—but it does suggest a way ahead which avoids the siren prospects of either absolutizing one or relativizing all scriptures. Establishing a theological view of other sacred scriptures that itself is informed by the Bible is a pressing challenge for Christian theology today.

How to Discern the Meaning of Scripture

Argumentation about the meaning of Scripture is an integral activity of the church. This process is already underway in the Bible itself and is not negated by the contested notion of "perspicuity".

---

17. See Miroslav Volf and G. Talal (eds.), *A Common Word: Muslims and Christians on Loving and Neighbour* (Grand Rapids: Eerdmans, 2010).

In surveying the history of the interpretation of Scripture, one becomes increasingly conscious of the way in which the reading of the text has always been a contested matter. This may already be the case within the Hebrew Bible with its different estimates of kingship and readings of the history of Israel. Its rendering in the Greek Septuagint may reflect the concerns of Jews living in the Diaspora—even the translation itself is an interpretation of sorts. The new and dramatically divergent readings of that same text in the early church reflected the Christological convictions of the new faith and the emergence of a Gentile Christianity. In contending with Marcionism, the church determined in part the delineation of the canon of the Christian Bible, while in succeeding centuries the most intense theological and ethical debates raged around the correct interpretation of the text. Fidelity to the Word of God, it seems, requires commitment to an intense process of interpretation in each generation rather than a simple adherence to a creed, code of conduct, or set of immobile theological propositions.

Although we take it almost for granted, the presence of a fourfold gospel at the center of the Bible represents a view about the necessity of different renditions of the story of Jesus. A decision in favor of one of those, to the exclusion of the others, was never taken. Four were preferred to reflect a plurality of perspectives and interpretations although this was a constrained plurality determined by notions of apostolicity. Describing Irenaeus's defense of four gospels, Francis Watson has written,

> Irenaeus finds himself advocating a form of relativism or perspectivism in which the reality transcends the individual text and yet is truly if partially and provisionally attested in it. In their fourfold canonical form, the Gospels relativize each other and at the same time affirm each other in their relativity.[18]

Bauckham points out that this pattern of structured plurality is also present elsewhere in Scripture, for example, in readings of the history of Israel in the Old Testament.[19]

The Reformed tradition stressed the perspicuity of Scripture as one of its marks. This has been invoked recently in the context of debates about gay clergy. Opponents of their ordination state that the Word of God is quite clear and unequivocal on this matter. As such, it is claimed that this provides us with an illustration of the perspicuity and sufficiency of divine revelation. However, the history of the interpretation of Scripture suggests that such constructions of clarity are problematic. The notion of perspicuity initially represented an attempt to wrest the Bible from the control of elitist groups or a cadre of professionals whose task it was to determine the meaning of the text for everyone else. To that extent, it permits and indeed requires a listening

---

18. "Are There Still Four Gospels?" in *Reading Scripture with the Church: Towards a Hermeneutic for Theological Interpretation*, ed. A. K. M. Adam, Stephen E. Fowl, Kevin J. Vanhoozer, and Francis Watson (Grand Rapids: Baker, 2006), 108–9.

19. Richard Bauckham, "Reading Scripture as a Coherent Story," in *The Art of Reading Scripture*, ed. Ellen F. Davis and Richard B. Hays (Grand Rapids: Eerdmans, 2003), 42–3.

to the readings of a diversity of people and groups within the church. Yet the assertion of the clarity of Scripture was never intended to relieve the people of God from the burden of a careful reading of the whole text, conducted within the church, in conversation with others who read differently, and in utilizing the best insights of scholarship. Above all, clarity is not an intrinsic property of each verse, but resides in the self-revealing capacity of God's Spirit as we encounter it through the Word. The theory of perspicuity was thus historically combined with the recognition that parts of Scripture were obscure and their interpretation contested (which could also generate disagreement about which parts were clear and in what ways). In discussing the clarity of Scripture, C. G. Berkouwer examines some of the problems around the concept of perspicuity, pointing out that it was a notion historically designed to express the *accessibility* of Scripture. This is not a concept about simplicity; still less does it negate the importance of study, interpretation, and discussion. In conclusion, he notes that the discovery of Scriptural clarity is generally accompanied by gratitude and amazement in the church.[20]

This raises a further question, however, of the extent to which the fruits of biblical scholarship inform the hearing and reading of the text in our churches. How many people in our congregations would know that Mark was the earliest of the gospels and functioned as the primary source for Matthew and Luke, or that the Fourth Gospel should be handled differently from a historical perspective? The part of the Bible that is probably best known to our society is the Christmas story as recounted by Matthew and Luke—the Annunciation, the virginal conception, the census, the birth at Bethlehem, shepherds, and wise men. Yet some of the details of these stories are among the least historically secure in the gospels. This of course does not empty them of meaning—they may be replete with evangelical significance when read in light of the subsequent gospel story—but we still tend to preach and teach them as if they offer the kind of account that one might read in a newspaper. Much of this is borne of a desire to avoid controversy and unnecessary anxiety on the part of the faithful, especially at a time of year when celebration, goodwill, and children are much to the fore. But it does attest something of the gap between church and academy that has not yet been successfully bridged in most quarters. Only a concerted program of adult Christian education can successfully address this issue.

Theology and Exegesis—the Need for Dual Practice

A dual practice of theology and exegesis is required to overcome the division of academic labour that has emerged in modernity. There are some signs that such dual practice is emerging in recent projects.

---

20. See C. G. Berkouwer, *Holy Scripture* (Grand Rapids: Eerdmans, 1975), 267-98. John Webster offers a similarly holistic account of perspicuity. "Scripture is clear because of the Spirit's work in which creaturely acts of reading are so ordered towards faithful attention to the divine Word that through Scripture the light of the gospel shines in its own inherent splendour." *Holy Scripture: A Dogmatic Sketch* (Cambridge: Cambridge University Press, 2003), 94.

In an important though neglected sense, theology is needed for the reading of the Bible. We might have figured this out from the necessary role played by the *regula fidei* (rule of faith) in the early church. The interpretation of Scripture always takes place out of some pre-conception of the relationship between its parts and whole, a judgment about the function, and content of the Bible for the faith community. The discernment of how an individual passage coheres with and extends a story line; the way in which a portion of the text contributes to an understanding the world in relation to God; the reading of a verse or chapter as an aspect of a wider account of a process of divine self-revelation: these are typical of the ways in which theologians have handled the text. Of course, the characterization of the whole can be challenged and adjusted according to fresh readings of the text—there is a hermeneutical circularity here—but the need for some prior theological understanding of what the text means remains unavoidable.

The necessity of a theological pre-understanding demands some reappraisal of the practices of biblical criticism and systematic theology. Too often commentaries have suffered from a reluctance to enter into wider questions of meaning and truth with a view to hazarding some theological judgment about the text. At the same time, theologians have frequently used the text merely as a point of departure, paying token or scant attention to the work of biblical critics. No doubt most of us have fallen into this trap in our teaching and writing—the academic division of labor, our separate scholarly guilds, and our curriculum have all contributed to a disjunction of agenda. However, one recent development in the academy has been the emergence of attempts from both sides to achieve greater integration and also the appearance of several commentary series in German and English that seek to combine historical criticism, theological interpretation, and homiletic appropriation of the books of the Bible. Barton's aforementioned bracketing-out of questions of truth in favor of meaning alone seems to have been abandoned in some quarters.[21] A notable attempt at integration is the posthumously published commentary on *Mark* by Bill Placher.[22] This commentary, however, could only have been written by a theologian who took his time to read the work of historical critics and also to understand the reception of the text in the history of the church. Miroslav Volf has remarked that this integration of Bible and theology should be viewed as the most important turn in contemporary theology. It might just succeed at overcoming some of the divisions in the curriculum—only time will tell.

> In my judgment, the return of biblical scholars to the theological reading of the Scripture, and the return of systematic theologians to sustained engagement with the scriptural texts is the most significant development in the last two decades.

---

21. In any case, if knowledge of the meaning of a statement is determined by awareness of what would make it true (as in Frege's truth conditions theory of meaning), then it is not clear how an interpreter can successfully divorce questions of meaning from judgments about truth, as if meaning could be established in advance of any considerations about truthfulness.

22. William Placher, *Mark* (Louisville: John Knox Press, 2010).

Even if it is merely formal, it is comparable in important to the post-World War I rediscovery of the Trinitarian nature of God and to the resurgence of theological concern for the suffering and the poor in the late sixties of the past century.[23]

Revisiting Theories of the Authority of Scripture

Questions surrounding the authority of Scripture require to be revisited. An account that understands biblical authority by reference to its function of witness is required, although this needs qualification by reference to the multiplicity of texts and voices, and the ongoing role of the Bible in the life of the church.

The integration of Bible and theology will also require further attention to older and divisive questions about the theological status of the text. Why does the Bible merit such a status in the church? What sort of authority attaches to it? We might even want to ask whether it should be accorded the status traditionally ascribed to it in the church's theology. Has the Bible become an unwelcome burden to sections of the church that have grown weary of having ancient texts cited in support of positions from which they have long departed? It may be as well to admit that this is where many Christians now find themselves. Indeed, in the aforementioned study, Adrian Thatcher has called for a diminution of Scriptural authority and a deliberate eschewal of the claim among Christians to be a people of the book. This is equally an issue for biblical scholars who need to justify the professional attention that they devote to the text of Scripture which far exceeds the study of any other set of ancient documents.

At the time of the Reformation, an alternative account of the authority of Scripture emerged somewhat polemically in the writings of Luther. His appeal to the doctrine of justification, to gospel over law, to Christ over the church, had the effect of establishing a canon within the canon. One indirect consequence of this was of course his negative estimate of the Epistle of James. However, as Brian Gerrish has shown, the wider theological significance of this move was to establish the authority of Scripture not in terms of the medieval theory of verbal dictation by the Holy Spirit but in terms of its capacity to bear witness to the primary object of faith, namely Jesus Christ.[24] While both of these approaches can be conjoined, the possibility was now created of providing an alternative account of authority in circumstances where a theory of verbal dictation had collapsed. This move was made by biblical critics in the nineteenth century seeking to offer a theological defense of their practice. The text derives its authority primarily from its witness to Christ and his gospel. This leaves the historical critic free to ply his or her trade without compromising the theological character of Scripture. In the

---

23. Miroslav Volf, *Captive to the Word of God: Engaging the Scriptures for Contemporary Theological Reflections* (Grand Rapids: Eerdmans, 2010), 14.

24. Brian Gerrish, *The Old Protestantism and the New* (Edinburgh: T&T Clark, 1982), 51–68.

following century, this approach was most closely associated with Karl Barth and his stratified account of the threefold form of the Word of God. Its preached form reposes upon its written form, which in turn derives from its attestation of the one Word of God incarnate, Jesus Christ.[25]

The move toward a more functional theory has the virtue of combining an account of the authority of Scripture with a claim about its distinctive content. It is by virtue of its capacity to refer to Christ that the Bible is authoritative. This capacity, however, requires also some account of the activity of the Spirit here and now upon the reader of the text. God continues to speak to the church in and through the words of the Bible.[26] The Christological character of Scripture, moreover, provides a criterion of interpretation. The center-piece of the canon is the four gospels for it is the person and work of Christ which provide a standard by which the various parts of Scripture are to be read and understood. Thus authority, content, and interpretation can be integrated in ways that tend to elude other theories, for example, B. B. Warfield's doctrine of plenary inspiration.

A commitment to a position something like this can be found not only among the followers of Karl Barth but in much church life today. However, while it is broadly correct, indeed almost unavoidable in my opinion, it may have to be nuanced and developed in important ways:

1. To speak only about the Bible and Jesus Christ is to risk neglecting the place of the church. The story of Israel and Jesus leads to the story of the church, and the church's relation to its Scriptures is therefore an internal one. The Bible gives us an account of the church, including how it is constituted by virtue of its relationship to Christ, and the faith that is exclusively delivered to it. In this respect, the church makes no sense without that Bible, its very character requiring a constant return to those books that it set apart as canonical for its subsequent existence. The interpretation of Scripture is therefore a necessary task, both liberating and burdensome, that is placed upon the church. Without it, the church would cease to be itself. At the same time, while the church reposes upon Scripture, there is also a sense in which the Bible is the work of the people of God. In the case of the New Testament, the books that are acknowledged as canonical are the writings of the first generations of Christians. Hence any providentialist account of the formation and preservation of Scripture will also require a related account of the church.

---

25. Karl Barth, *Church Dogmatics* I/1, trans. G. T. Thomson (Edinburgh: T&T Clark, 1969), 98–140. Barth's later theology has a looser relationship between these forms, perhaps through anxieties around overestimating the position of the church in relation to Christ. See Thomas Christian Currie, *The Only Sacrament Left to Us: The Threefold Word of God in Karl Barth's Theology and Ecclesiology* (Eugene: Pickwick, 2015).

26. This is a dominant theme of Nicholas Wolterstorff's *Divine Discourse* (Cambridge: Cambridge University Press, 1995).

2. The model of the Bible as a historical witness may also obscure the ways in which it is through the text that God continues to address the church. Scripture bears witness to the past, but its role in the liturgy implies that it also speaks here and now. Hence the doctrines of Word and Spirit belong together.
3. In assigning a Christological authority and content to Scripture, there is a risk that one may also overlook the diversity of its materials, particularly within the Old Testament. This does not deny that everything in the Bible should be placed in some positive relation to the gospel of Jesus—again, that is a requirement of ecclesial existence—but we should not forget the polyvalent character of that witness. Bonhoeffer once remarked that it is not Christian to attempt to get too soon and too directly to the New Testament.[27] It may be necessary to dwell longer upon the stories of the Old Testament and not to become over-anxious about finding the quickest possible route from there to the gospels. Many sermons move too swiftly from the interpretation of one portion of Scripture to stock claims about the person and work of Jesus. The witness of much of Scripture to Jesus may be of a more indirect character than the Lutheran-Barthian model suggests.[28] If, following Colossians 2:2-3, we view Christ as the one in whom are hidden all the treasures of wisdom and knowledge, then we might find a rich diversity of material throughout Scripture that is characterized by this more indirect or concealed relation. Alternatively, one might describe Scripture as authoritative by virtue of its witness to God's wisdom, provided we can think of this wisdom as disclosed not only in nature but in history and the Incarnation. This wisdom-focused model also has the advantage of showing the practical character of Scripture for life in the church and the world today.

The Use of the Bible in the Church Today

The use of the Bible in the church today presents challenges for the cultivation of widespread Biblical literacy. These have been highlighted by the celebration of the 1611 King James Bible.

In a digital age of sound-bites, texting, and short attention spans, what are the prospects for sustained and widespread biblical literacy? The anniversary celebrations of the

---

27. "Whoever wishes to be and perceive things too quickly in a New Testament way is to my mind no Christian." Dietrich Bonhoeffer, *Letters and Papers from Prison, Collected Works*, Vol. 8, ed. John W. de Gruchy (Minneapolis: Fortress, 2010), 213.

28. See also Ellen F. Davis, "Teaching the Bible Confessionally in the Church," in *The Art of Reading Scripture*, 9-26. For an account of Barth's understanding of the authority of Scripture see Bruce L. McCormack, "The Being of Holy Scripture is in Becoming: Karl Barth in Conversation with American Evangelical Criticism," in *Evangelicals and Scripture: Tradition, Authority and Hermeneutics*, ed. V. Bacote, Lauran C. Miguelez and Dennis L. Okholm (Downer's Grove: IVP, 2004), 55-75.

King James Bible revealed a surprising resurgence of interest in the most durable English translation that we are likely to see. Oxford University Press reported that the King James Bible was its best-selling book in 2011. Nevertheless, the study of the history of this translation reveals that previous generations were immersed in the stories, teaching, and language of Scripture to an extent that is nowhere matched in Western society today. While there is a hunger for learning more about the Bible among many of the younger churches, its recovery for a generation that has gradually forgotten it seems an even bigger challenge for programs of adult Christian education today. Perhaps the external pressures of a skeptical and secular modernity will produce a counter-reaction within the church, or maybe we will have to await a more complete erasure of the memory of Scripture before a fresh curiosity emerges among a new generation. At a minimum, this will require theologians and biblical scholars together to prepare commentaries and theological handbooks that are generally more accessible than most of what is currently available.

One consequence of the demise of the King James Bible in the English-speaking world is that its stories, idioms, and sayings are no longer as resonant to contemporary audiences. It has gradually disappeared from our common consciousness. This is often lamented, not least in the teaching of English literature where the allusions tend to be missed, thus requiring new critical editions of texts that make explicit for the contemporary reader the connection to a passage of Scripture.[29] C. S. Lewis once forecast that the Bible would be read only by Christians.[30] In a post-Christendom setting, this prediction has largely been fulfilled. We can no longer expect our educational system (at least in the UK, but surely elsewhere too) to equip pupils with a general biblical knowledge. While it will remain a resource in all forms of education, an informed understanding of the text is likely to arise only through Christian nurture. As a practical problem, this may be an indirect consequence of modernity, but it is at least as significant as any of the others raised in this essay.

Today the use of the Bible in the church is faced with challenges surrounding its interpretation, validity, and authority. However we choose to characterize our social and intellectual world in relation to modernity, these problems will require to be faced, if the Bible is to maintain its position at the center of worship and witness. As a prerequisite for this task, it will need to be read and learned with renewed commitment by Christian people together.

---

29. A good example of this is Peter Garside's edition of James Hogg, *The Private Memoirs and Confessions of a Justified Sinner* (Edinburgh: Edinburgh University Press, 2002) in which the footnotes draw attention to the frequent quotation and misquotation of Scripture.

30. Quoted by Gordon Campbell, *The Bible: The Story of the King James Version* (Oxford: Oxford University Press, 2010), 257.

Chapter 15

REFORMED SOCIAL THEOLOGY

CONTEXTS AND CONSTANTS

Introduction

In what follows, I sketch in broad outline the social theology of the Reformed churches. My argument is that, while this was shaped in part by the contingent political circumstances that obtained in Europe in the sixteenth century, there are some recognizable theological constants that should be articulated and transposed to other times and places. This adaptation of theological insights to different settings is a sign of the necessary enculturation of the Christian faith across space and time, and a reminder that our traditions require retrieval and re-articulation.

The goal of social transformation through the establishment of a godly society runs deep in Reformed theology and is shared in multiple ways with other traditions from which we have much to learn. This goal generated several interconnected emphases. These remain relevant in our time of increased fragmentation, populist resurgence, and political uncertainty. Although not an exhaustive list, I shall select seven elements in an effort to demonstrate their interlocking force. Without a renewed commitment to each in our time, the social witness of the Reformed churches will be impaired.[1]

Elements of a Reformed Political Theology

a *Politics as a vocation.* In both Lutheran and Reformed theology, political office is ordained by God and necessary for the well-being of the church. For that reason, it was entirely proper for Christians to regard the holding

---

1. In this first section, I have drawn upon a more extended historical treatment in my essay "Politics, Society and Law," in *Oxford Handbook of Reformed Theology*, ed. Michael Allen and Scott Swain (Oxford: Oxford University Press, 2020), 592–608.

of such office as a calling of God. Much of this thinking can already be discerned in medieval accounts of the Christian prince, but it is emphasized in different ways at the time of the Reformation and often against the more exclusionist trends of the radicals. In Lutheranism, the concept of vocation becomes secularized. The service of God is fulfilled in the home, in commerce and in political life. Vocation is no longer confined to the cloister. Christ is to be served in the world, freely and gladly without the burden of having to perform extraordinary meritorious works. This lent a dignity and seriousness to the responsibilities of the everyday. Exercised within the secular domain, the calling of the Christian was not out of the world but within it, informed by faith and animated by love.

b *Civil resistance.* A succession of Reformed writers, including John Knox, Peter Martyr Vermigli and Theodore Beza developed arguments for civil resistance.[2] These converged upon several convictions. The power of the monarch is neither absolute nor unfettered. Kings and queens are ordained by God to serve the people and they do so in accordance with natural laws that are not of their own making. A second line of argument developed the notion of a local magistracy which had its own responsibility to act lawfully and to promote the common good. Where local rulers find themselves in opposition to national or imperial forces, they have a right, even a duty, of resistance. In doing so, they act not as private citizens but as holders of an office which carries its own responsibilities and rights. Third, Protestant theories of resistance could appeal to classical and medieval traditions of popular consent. These philosophical and theological considerations were conjoined in the seventeenth century by theologians such as Samuel Rutherford.

c *The coordination of church and state.* In the *Institutes* 4.11.8, Calvin underscores the difference between the offices of pastor and prince. These are to be neither confused nor disjoined. Both offices serve a common end under the divine rule. Together church and state are committed to a sanctified society according to the Word of God, even though pastors and politicians should not conflate their different functions. Ideally, the Church and the state should act together to fulfill the divine will in the ordering of a peaceful, just and harmonious society. This model reflects earlier Christendom notions and assumes that each citizen is to be regarded as baptized into the visible church. In sixteenth-century Geneva, membership of the church and the *polis* are notionally co-extensive. One consequence of this is that excommunication from the former would have entailed exile

---

2. See, for example, Roger Mason (ed.), *Knox: On Rebellion* (Cambridge: Cambridge University Press, 1994); Robert M. Kingdon, "Calvinism and Resistance Theory 1550–1580," in *Cambridge History of Political Thought 1450–1700*, ed. J. H. Burns (Cambridge: Cambridge University Press, 2008), 193–218.

from the latter. While this has obvious problems for modern pluralist societies, we can at least note that the recommended partnership of church and state was intended to promote social justice and order as well as undergirding ecclesiastical reform.

d *Democracy*—The Reformation is sometimes interpreted as a democratic movement. This is true only in a restricted and qualified sense. Luther accepted the right of hereditary monarchs to rule. But, as a humanist scholar and lawyer, a French refugee and citizen of Geneva, Calvin was more alert to constitutional issues. He examines these rather tentatively in the closing chapter of the *Institutes* where he expresses a mild preference for an admixture of aristocracy and democracy.

In other settings, however, Reformed theology was keenly alert to the distribution of authority and popular consent. This is apparent, for example, in church government and the public calling of ministers. Each minister is called by God, yet the ecclesiastical rite of ordination must take place always with the consent of the people. Ministerial appointment requires popular legitimation, and should not be imposed top-down by church authority. The government of the church, moreover, involves the rule of elders who function with ministers as a senate-like ruling body. These elders are described by Calvin as senior figures elected by the people. We are some way here from later democratic ideals of universal adult suffrage, but these features of Reformed polity indicate the presence of popular impulses with respect to church government and the empowering of the laity. Inevitably this would have a wider political effect, as already noted in approaches to civil resistance.

e *Law*—The third use of the law is another distinctive feature of Reformed theology. This is also apparent in Melanchthon's *Loci Communes* where he speaks about a tertiary use of the law in the lives of those who are reborn. This is given for the Christian life so that we can be constantly reminded of our continued sinfulness and the need to do God's works. The *tertius usus legis* reminds us that, even as Christians, our inner self needs to be constrained by the law of God. Since we continue to display the marks of sin, we need the law in both its primary and secondary functions. Reformed theologians, however, went beyond this by stressing the law as exercising a further positive function in relation to individual and social sanctification. For Calvin, the law is a divine gift to enable people to live together in unity with one another and in true worship and obedience of God. This is neither burdensome nor oppressive—the law properly acts for our well-being. Hence there is no enduring dialectical opposition of law and gospel in Reformed theology, but an integration of the two under the rubric of the third use.[3]

With respect to its application, however, the third use was to give rise to some tensions. How rigorously are Old Testament injunctions to be applied

---

3. See Edward A. Dowey, "Law in Luther and Calvin," *Theology Today* 41 (1984): 146–53.

to the Christian life, the church, and civil society? Are there ways in which these can be modified, mediated, and interpreted in light of changing social and political circumstances? An overly rigorous application of Scriptural precedents could result in some counterproductive measures, while also proving inadequate to growing ideals of toleration, democracy and equality as these emerged in early modern and Enlightenment Europe. And yet the fundamental impulse of Reformed theology seems right. The laws that govern civil society cannot be construed only in a negative modality as ordinances of restraint. They exist to promote social justice, to advance the common good, and to achieve in some measure the *shalom* proclaimed by Scripture.

In several ways, the Reformation contributed to the development of civil law. For example, one outcome of the Protestant understanding of marriage as a created ordinance, as opposed to a Christian sacrament, was the development of civil marriage law with respect to consent, witness, and grounds of divorce. Education meanwhile came increasingly to fall within the civic realm, while the office of the magistrate, outside the immediate control of the church, was of growing significance.[4]

f *Nationalism*—Within the Reformed tradition, the different confessions played a role in forming national churches, as in the Belgic and Scots Confessions. Reformed churches were committed to the shaping of societies often modeled on the example of biblical Israel as a covenanted nation. By the seventeenth century, we see the emergence in Europe of powerful and autonomous states that are now related to each other by international law rather than imperial power, even though these states were inclined to engage in empire-building in other parts of the world. Religious forces played a part in this process.

Yet the relationship between theology and nationalism has often been an uneasy one. Some scholars have argued that the Romantic nationalism which emerged through the Enlightenment, with its stress on land, language, and ethnicity, was a replacement for more traditional forms of religion.[5] Others, echoing criticisms from the political left, see it as lurching toward an aggressive idolatry of kinship and place that divides peoples and threatens a more virtuous commitment to internationalism.[6] For the church, the loyalty commanded by the nation can threaten the allegiance of the baptized to the body of Christ, a polity that transcends language and tribe. And at other times a theory of national exceptionalism, again modeled on the Israel of the

---

4. See John Witte Jr, "Introduction," in *Christianity and Law: An Introduction*, ed. John Witte Jr and Frank S. Alexander (Cambridge: Cambridge University Press, 2008), 1–32.

5. See Adrian Hastings, *The Constructions of Nationhood: Ethnicity, Religion and Nationalism* (Cambridge: Cambridge University Press, 1997).

6. Eric Hobsbawm, *Nations and Nationalism since 1780: Programme, Myth and Reality* (Cambridge: Cambridge University Press, 1992).

Old Testament, has generated attitudes of hostility and superiority to those who belong elsewhere.[7]

Nevertheless, nationalism could also provide a way of promoting the common good of a people, as well as articulating legitimate protest against tyranny, colonialism and globalizing tendencies.[8] There are positive examples of its functioning as a force for liberation and of attracting a commitment to goals wider than those of individual and family. In relation to language, society, and territorial boundaries, it is difficult to see how a political philosophy can avoid some acknowledgement of nationhood in comprehending how a *polis* is to be delineated.

A sense of national identity is closely aligned with the Reformed concept of covenant when applied to human associations. This was a feature of political thought in the work of Johannes Althusius and others.[9] Drawing upon Scriptural and confessional accounts of covenant, the social order could be conceived according to a succession of covenants to which each of us is bound. In some respects, this parallels Catholic notions of the common good and subsidiarity. A society is structured by covenantal commitments which are a function of our creaturely status. This had at least two important advantages for Reformed political thought. First, it offered an account of society that did not depend upon a sacral concept of kingship that legitimized a top-down authority. Instead, political office is justified by its capacity to facilitate a covenant that binds each member of the state together. Its jurisdiction extends over a territorial region that will tend to be marked by a shared history, customs, languages, laws, and faith. Within this territory, the civil authorities, as part of their covenantal function, will enforce the rule of law and seek to protect the citizens of the realm, though this can include a respect for liberty of conscience on matters over which the state should not legislate. The law does not derive from the will of the ruler but has its ground in natural law and divine law which are not of our own making. Moreover, our natural condition is to enter into social bonds each of which has its own sphere of operation and rules of conduct. This generates a second advantage of the covenant concept, namely its capacity to perceive a society as comprising not one collective but a variety of interconnected covenantal communities each of which has its own traditions, practices, and norms. The capacity of covenantal politics to articulate different consocial spheres

---

7. See the discussion in Karl Barth, "Near and Distant Neighbours," in *Church Dogmatics* III/4 (Edinburgh: T&T Clark, 1961), 285–323.

8. Jonathan Hearn, *Rethinking Nationalism: An Introduction* (London: Palgrave Macmillan, 2004); Doug Gay, *Honey from the Lion: Christianity and the Ethics of Nationalism* (London: SCM, 2013).

9. See, for example, Thomas O. Hueglin, "Covenant and Federalism in the Politics of Althusius," in *The Covenant Connection: From Federal Theolog to Modern Federalism*, ed. Daniel J. Elazar and John Kincaid (Lanham: Lexington, 2000), 31–54.

was a feature of later Dutch Calvinism, particularly in the work of Abraham Kuyper.

g *Economics.* Much of the discussion in this field has been dominated by the Weber thesis regarding the causal link between Protestantism and the rise of capitalism. The thesis has been largely discredited on account of the ways in which capitalism similarly flourished in societies less committed to forms of Protestant Christianity.[10] But recent scholarship has also pointed to features of Calvin's writings which display a strong ethical concern for the poor and commitment to economic justice. First published in 1959, André Biéler's landmark study of Calvin's economic thought drew attention to his extensive deliberations on economic issues, especially in his commentaries and sermons.[11] Though neglected by later Reformed thinkers, this material focuses on biblical concerns for the underprivileged and destitute. Starvation and homelessness are an affront to God, as is the exploitation engendered by lending money at punitive rates of interest.

The Vestiges of Christendom?

What emerges from this historical sketch is a rich social theology that commits the church to promoting political and civic well-being. Much is attractive in this vision, and anticipates modern developments though under more secular conditions. But the problems of the founding Reformed vision need to be recognized. In particular, the emergence of ideals of tolerance and pluralism generated formidable challenges. The Reformed vision of a godly commonwealth in which the proper worship of God was upheld by the civil magistrate invoked Old Testament ideals of a society united by a common faith—the church or the nation could even be described as a new Israel. This extended to the suppression of other forms of worship and religious association that were adjudged blasphemous or idolatrous. In the face of early modern arguments for religious diversity and later claims for freedom of expression, such invocation of a single confessional identity proved impossible to maintain. A range of arguments was advanced that made appeal to the New Testament example of the free and non-coercive expression of faith, the value of peaceful negotiation over violent struggle, the presence of moral consensus amid doctrinal difference, the possibility of different faith groups learning from one another in ways that were mutually beneficial, and the need to protect freedom of conscience in matters of religious adherence. Through the eighteenth century, Reformed churches gradually came to deplore compulsory

---

10. See Johan J. Graafland, "Weber Revisited: Critical Perspectives from Calvinism on Capitalism in Economic Crisis," in *Calvinism and the Making of the European Mind*, ed. Gijsbert van den Brink and Harro M. Höpfl (Leiden: Brill, 2014), 177–98.

11. André Biéler, *Calvin's Economic and Social Thought* (Geneva: World Council of Churches, 2005).

measures in religion and to assign a more limited role to the civil authorities in the regulation of faith communities.

But just as the old model brought dangers of suppression, intolerance, and violation of human dignity, newer secular approaches also generate their own difficulties. These have been the focus of recent criticism of political liberalism. Where does the political order find its moral and spiritual basis if not by reference to the religious life of its people? Alternatives have been found to be too thin, incoherent, or incapable of commanding allegiance. The go-to option has been the language of human rights. But can this be sustained without earlier theological references to human beings as created in the image of God and the frequent injunctions in Scripture to attend to the needs of the marginalized, the alien, and the dispossessed? And if we are to adopt a substantive secularism in which religious discourse and commitment are confined to a semi-private or voluntary domain does this not prevent citizens and groups from expressing their deepest social commitments in the terms that make sense to them? This can readily develop into a secular intolerance of all public expressions of religion. In response, approaches that favor a procedural (as against programmatic) secularism have been advocated—this invites all exponents of deeply held religious views to express themselves in ways that are accessible to their fellow citizens.[12]

Under these pressures, European churches with long-established or national status have evolved in ways that reflect an accommodation of tolerance and diversity. At the same time, however, elements of their status have been retained and adapted to new circumstances. In an oft-quoted distinction, Wesley Carr, an Anglican writer, has distinguished high and earthed elements of establishment.[13] At ground level, parish churches have continued to view their immediate geographic community as the locus for service and mission. This takes place through the provision of ordinances for birth, marriage, and death, and also in hosting a variety of support groups including youth organizations, counseling services, recreational activities, and in generating support for charitable bodies. The involvement of the church in education has also been important in this context, and might be seen as part of a wider process in which a society can continue to be Christianized, though again the limits of this should be recognized. Meanwhile, the national identity of churches continues to be recognized in national and local ceremonial events, corresponding to Carr's higher level. These involve a fusion of religious and civic functions but suggest a spiritual dimension or setting for the wider community.[14] Here I am thinking of the presence of a religious input to

---

12. See, for example, Rowan Williams, *Faith in the Public Square* (London: Bloomsbury, 2012), 23–36.

13. Wesley Carr, "A Developing Establishment," *Theology* 102 (1999): 2–10.

14. This is explored by Linda Woodhead with reference to the Church of England and the Lutheran Church in Denmark. See "Can We Trust the Church?" in *Schools of Faith: Essays in Honour of Iain R. Torrance*, ed. David Fergusson and Bruce McCormack (London: T&T Clark, 2018), 193–202.

important state occasions such as the opening of a parliament, the coronation of a new monarch, the remembrance of the war dead, the marking of some public tragedy, or the celebration of an important national landmark. Admittedly, there are perennial dangers here of church captivity with the resultant loss of the prophetic responsibility to speak truth to power.[15] Striking a balance between the offer of support and the challenge of criticism is familiar to every pastor. But it is difficult to see how this can be avoided except through a sectarian withdrawal from society which has never been consistent with the foundational vision of the Reformed churches.

A more acute problem surrounds the disconnect between these two dimensions of Christian social engagement that has come about through the rapid process of secularization since the 1960s. The national dimension of religious engagement only makes sense where this is an expression of something that is already embedded at the local level in parish communities. Without this traction, the high-profile ceremonial and civic actions of the church can quickly become quaint, bizarre, or absurdly pompous. Unless it is the expression of the genuinely held faith of a substantial body of people across different sections of society, then these functions of the church become increasingly questionable. Consider some statistics from my own context in Scotland where the national church recognized by an Act of Parliament in 1921 is Reformed and Presbyterian. This state recognition belongs to an era in which Scotland could reasonably be considered a Protestant society in which the majority of its citizens adhered to the Church of Scotland. But since reaching a peak in 1955, the adult membership of the church has declined by about 80 percent to around 300,000 which today represents only about 6 percent of the population. This decline is continuing at a rate of 4 percent per annum. While the statistics reveal some implicit commitment to religion, more than one half of the population (58 percent) identified in 2017 as belonging to no religion.[16] Although this group is not hostile to the church, it undoubtedly displays a large measure of indifference. And given that the church is disproportionately represented by an older generation, these trends are likely to continue for the foreseeable future.

As already suggested, the notion of a "national church" is fraught with problems which are accompanied by numerous historical illustrations. We might note four difficulties. First, a national church risks becoming the organ of the state through an exchange of privilege for compliance. In providing a spiritual underpinning of state authority, it can too easily deliver a political quietism. This can masquerade as a strategy of "keeping religion out of politics" while in effect offering tacit support to the regnant powers. A related difficulty arises when the church purports to express the religious identity of a collective such as the Volk or the nation. This can result in a sense of exclusion among those who belong to other churches or

---

15. This is argued by Jonathan Chaplin in his recent advocacy of Anglican disestablishment. *Beyond Establishment: Resetting Church-State Relations in England* (London: SCM, 2022).

16. https://www.bbc.co.uk/news/uk-scotland-41294688.

faiths, or, more dangerously, for migrants whose identity cannot be articulated in similar religious terms. A third problem concerns the extent to which a claim to be exclusively a national church can impede ecumenical cooperation. In this context, it is too tempting for national churches to pretend that they alone have a concern for the society beyond its walls. Other churches have a distinguished, and sometimes better, record of service, charitable giving, and social engagement. It is not the sole prerogative of a national church to function in this way. A final problem concerns the incomprehension of churches in the majority world when faced with these older European models. Their different histories do not easily incline toward an adapting of these models. Social engagement and witness can function without any singular recognition on the part of the state. The Christendom model is not a marketable export.[17]

In the face of these challenges, so-called national churches might recognize the problems they have faced in the past and thus welcome, in at least one respect, the greater dissociation of church and society that secularization has brought. The loosening of ties with the state that arises through the sociological phenomenon of "a differentiation of functions" is to be welcomed. Belonging to a national church no longer confers privileges in terms of holding office, receiving a university education, entering the professions, casting votes, or entering parliament. Equality legislation firmly excludes this. The resultant distancing of the church from the political state enables a degree of autonomy that facilitates social criticism and independence of action. Instead of presenting itself as a spiritual expression of a single national identity, the church can enhance its breadth by offering an open door to all comers. A focus on its surrounding parish, when suitably inflected, might offer scope for ethnic, spiritual, and theological diversity. At this (more important, to my mind) "earthed" level with an openness to local communities in their particularity and diversity, a national church can adapt to different circumstances.[18] If this arises as an accident of history, so be it. At the same time, these churches, with their particular historical associations with the nation, may find themselves in a position where they can broker relations with other churches and faiths—the Protestant churches of Europe have a decent record in terms of ecumenical commitment and involvement. Admittedly, the risk of patronizing other groups remains ever-present, and in any case maybe this function is for a time only. Nevertheless, the capacity of long-established churches to function in a constructive ecumenical and multi-faith manner is evident in some quarters today. We should recognize that these are the genuine possibilities of what Adrian Hastings calls a "weak establishment" in which the subordination of the temporal

---

17. See, for example, Kwame Bediako, *Christianity in Africa: The Renewal of a Non-Western Religion* (Edinburgh: Edinburgh University Press, 1995), 249.

18. See Elaine Graham, "The Establishment, Multiculturalism and Social Cohesion," in *The Established Church: Past, Present, and Future*, ed. Mark Chapman, Judith Maltby, and William Whyte (London: Bloomsbury, 2011), 124–40. None of this, I should stress, precludes other churches from doing much the same and at least as well.

to divinely ordained standards can be acknowledged.[19] If these provisions prove transient, again so be it. We should not cling to the vestiges of establishment if it becomes apparent that it is long past its sell-by date. But the position in which we currently find ourselves is ineluctable.

Where then does this leave the notion of a national church that continues to have a presence, albeit reduced, in every parish across the land? Here I suspect some honesty and humility will be required in accepting a diminished social influence, a lower profile, and the need for a greater concentration of energies on tasks such as church planting and evangelism. Those of us who continue to support national churches should beware of inflated arguments that fail to register the applicability of these arrangements to historically particular contexts that are continually evolving.

The sociopolitical responsibility of a church does not repose upon its size or status. The Scriptural commitment to God's justice generates an imperative that is not contingent upon particular historical circumstances, a point recognized by Bonhoeffer in his prison cell reflections on a *this-worldly Christianity*."

> Unlike believers in the redemption myths, Christians do not have an ultimate escape route out of their earthly tasks and difficulties into eternity. Like Christ ("My God ... why have you forsaken me?"), they have to drink the cup of earthly life to the last drop, and only when they do this is the Crucified and Risen One with them, and they are crucified and resurrected with Christ. This-worldliness must not be abolished ahead of its time; on this, NT and OT are united.[20]

No church can avoid facing outward with a view to enriching the life of its host society. In fields of health and education, this has long been apparent in different contexts. And in relation to the state, the church cannot avoid taking a view on political representation, on war, on the care of children, on rule by law, on the fair distribution of resources and so forth. How and when it acts in an advocacy role is not always clear, but there is no prospect for sealing off the sociopolitical domain from Christian witness and action.

Transpositions of Reformed Social Theology

The aforementioned elements of Reformed social thought need to find expression in different circumstances. At a time of polarization, fragmentation, and prognostications of a crisis for democratic societies, the following suggestions are

---

19. Adrian Hastings, *Church and State: The English Experience* (Exeter: Exeter University Press, 1991).
20. Dietrich Bonhoeffer, *Works, Vol. 8, Letters and Papers from Prison*, ed. John W. de Gruchy (Minneapolis: Fortress, 2010), 447–8.

intended as a Reformed contribution to preserving and improving our politics today.

a *Politics as a vocation.* The tendency to treat elected officials with contempt represents a threat to democratic societies. If we construe our politicians as self-serving, cynical, venial, power-hungry or simply entertaining this will likely have two effects. The first is that decent and talented people will be disinclined to commit to public service. The second is a self-fulfilling prophecy in which people will tend to live down to our expectations, if they are not held accountable to higher standards or provided with better possibilities. We need to offer support and encouragement to political representatives, as to every holder of public office in our midst. They deserve our prayers, our understanding, and our interest in what they do. This critical support that is owed our political representatives can too easily degenerate into cynicism when a negative register becomes so relentless that it suppresses any degree of sympathy or solidarity with those set apart for political office.
In this regard, the churches can exercise political responsibility by the formation of their people for political service whether at local, regional, or national level. This can work through providing motivation and a vision of covenanted goods. Much has been written about the importance of social capital generated by faith communities. The capacity of citizens to network, interact, and apply their skills in other domains has been documented by Robert Putnam.[21] Moreover, models of living together can be imaginatively transposed from the ecclesial to the civic level, while the rich traditions of Christian political thought can be harnessed for new situations.[22]
b *Civil resistance*—this strand of our tradition should remind us that support is never uncritical or unqualified. The task of speaking truth to power is a perennial one, as the Hebrew prophets teach us. For this to take place, there needs to be fair scrutiny, accurate reporting, and informed judgment according to our interpretation of the Word of God. This requires education, access to information, and a free press that can function apart from political control or excessive pressure. Politicians did not get a free pass from the Reformers, nor should they today. The two most significant Protestant declarations of the twentieth century were the Barmen Declaration (1934)

---

21. For example, Robert D. Putnam, *Bowling Alone: The Collapse and Revival of American Community*, revised ed. (New York: Simon and Schuster, 2020). See also Jeffrey Stout, *Blessed Are the Organized: Grassroots Democracy in America* (Princeton: Princeton University Press, 2012).

22. Emmanuel Katongole argues that African churches need to offer an alternative social vision to avoid either political quietism or a more activist cooption by the civil state. See *The Sacrifice of Africa: A Political Theology of Africa* (Grand Rapids: Eerdmans, 2011), 50.

and the Belhar Confession (1982). While these acknowledged the God-given authority of political rulers, each offered a stark criticism of the circumstances in which they were set. Neither the ideology of the Deutsche Christen nor the policies of apartheid were to be tolerated by a community whose first loyalty was to the God of Jesus. Here theological arguments based on Scripture were deployed in the cause of resistance. These landmark protests are now part of our international Reformed identity and should be studied afresh by each generation.

c *Coordination of church and state.* The goal of social transformation through the coordination of church and state is an aspiration that is again commanded by the gospel. In the past, this was expressed by the ideal of a religiously monolithic society in which church and state were fully integrated. This has now been abandoned by recognition of modern principles of freedom of conscience, the protection of different religious groups under the law, and the accommodation of a diversity of traditions within the public square. Yet this relative distancing of the state from any single expression of faith does not invalidate the possibility of a constructive partnership or engagement in societal issues. In the late nineteenth century, the partnership was sometimes renegotiated through a distinction between the church and the kingdom. The church was concerned rightly with the preaching of the Word, the administration of the sacraments, and the pastoral care of its members. But its wider social commitments included working alongside secular agencies to advance the work of the kingdom of God. This could typically involve a concern with better housing, improved working conditions, fairer remuneration, and universal adult suffrage. In its corporate life, the church was called to be a sign of the coming reign already inaugurated by Christ. Yet other social actors that also contribute toward the divine commonwealth were recognized; these make a vital contribution to civil society, for example in domains such as art, science, education, law, industry, and business. This more recent facet of our tradition can also prevent social theology from adopting only a negative posture. If we say "no" to many things, we should be prepared to give an account of that to which we are willing to say "yes."[23]

d *Democracy.* Current political trends suggest that democracy is not the default position of every society through improved education and greater material affluence. This whiggish narrative is now in some doubt with the rise of strong populist leaders commanding significant levels of support among younger voters. If we remain persuaded of the value of democracy over against other systems of government, then this will need the tacit

---

23. Isaac Phiri proposes a constructive social role for African churches in increasingly pluralist states. Again, this resembles a model of critical support adapted to a different context. See *Proclaiming Political Pluralism: Churches and Political Transitions in Africa* (Westport: Praeger, 2001).

support of churches and other groups within civil society to maintain the necessary degree of social cohesion and commitment to institutions that buttress it—an independent judiciary, respect for the rule of law, forms of safeguarding that afford minorities protection of their human rights, a welcome recognition of the pluralist and patchwork nature of our societies, the defense of an unfettered press, and the cultivation of habits of civility that enable us to disagree honestly and to find ways of compromising. In this respect, a social theology may sometimes have a conservative caste in preserving and maintaining forms of life that produce cohesion amid diversity and difference. The institutions of civic life are there to shape us and to contribute to the overall function of a healthy society. But if they are merely occasions for performance or entertainment, they become denigrated.

Recent studies suggest that democracy may be more contextual and fragile than we have long assumed. It cannot be taken for granted as the default setting of our societies. As we face stagnating income levels, identity politics, the power of social media, and suspicion of educated elites, there is an evident risk to democratic institutions.[24] In these circumstances, a theological re-visiting of the case for democracy is needed. The commitment to popular consent, covenant partnership, the rule of law, and balanced reporting requires reinvigorating.[25]

e *Law*. While there has undoubtedly been a growing separation of church from state with respect to the development of positive law, some important connections persist and deserve closer theological attention. Three areas are worthy of consideration. The first concerns the metaphysical links between law and religion. A legal system should reveal both an "inner morality" and an "inner sanctity."[26] In the former, it reposes upon a deep sense in any society of what is fundamentally just and fair. Without this shared sentiment, it will tend to lack tacit support. Closely related to this is the capacity of the law to command respect and obedience on the part of citizens. Without something approaching reverence for the rule of law, its authority is weakened, even when enforced by sheer power. The ways in which legal systems appropriate the symbolism and rituals of religion—dress, processions, court room architecture, and appeal to authoritative texts and interpreters—also provide a powerful visual illustration of this connection.

---

24. See, for example, David Runciman, *How Democracy Ends* (London: Profile Books, 2018), Yascha Mounk, *People vs Democracy: Why our Freedom is in Danger and How to Save It* (Cambridge, MA: Harvard University Press, 2018).

25. The theological case for democracy is examined by Richard Harries, *Faith in Politics? Rediscovering the Christian Roots of our Political Values* (London: Darton, Longman and Todd, 2010), 51–70, and Jonathan Chaplin, *Faith in Democracy: Framing a Politics of Deep Diversity* (London: SCM, 2019).

26. See Witte, "Introduction," 28.

A second domain concerns the development of positive laws. Areas of recent tension are evident—marriage, divorce, sexuality, abortion, assisted dying, and capital punishment. But these should not prevent us from appreciating the ways in which strong alliances can be constructed, for example in applying principles of equity, ensuring that the criminal justice system can accommodate notions of forgiveness and rehabilitation, and in seeking to establish the truth in possible miscarriages of justice. Finally, in protecting the free expression of religion, theological and secular arguments for liberty of conscience can coalesce, at least in some ways—these need not be in opposition. This area commands widespread attention today, particularly where some forms of free expression generate tensions with other protected characteristics.

f *Nationalism*. Karl Barth insisted that the divine command meets us as people who are bound to one another by links of history, culture, and language.[27] We can take a justifiable pride in our local identities—our homeland is where we start from and we should remain loyal to it. Yet we are also called to move outward to meet those more distant and to recognize our solidarity with them. This is a Christian vocation, dramatically manifested on the day of Pentecost and in the eschatological vision of a community transcending tribal and linguistic divisions. While community, land, and culture are created goods to be preserved and celebrated, these should be subordinated to wider goals that include hospitality, international cooperation and a recognition of the dangers that have accompanied forms of ethnic nationalism.

Nationalism has often functioned best as a protest movement in the face of imperialist or totalitarian rule. Religion can be a powerful mobilizing force in relation to articulating a shared identity or providing a micro-culture in which dissent can be fostered. The case of Poland under Soviet rule offers one striking example.[28] At other times, however, the linkage of faith to national identity can become exclusive and threatening to those who belong to a different church or religion. Vituperative verbal attacks on Irish Catholic immigrants by Scottish Presbyterians in the 1920s and 1930s became one of the most shameful episodes in the recent history of my own church.[29] In this context, there is a particular obligation upon "national" churches to promote ecumenical and inter-faith relations precisely to avoid

---

27. Karl Barth, *Church Dogmatics* III/4 (Edinburgh: T&T Clark, 1961), 286–323. See also Nigel Biggar, *Between Kin and Cosmopolis: An Ethic of the Nation* (Eugene: Cascade, 2014).

28. For a survey of the diverse links between religion and nationalism see Christophe Jaffrelot, "Religion and Nationalism," in *The Oxford Handbook of the Sociology of Religion*, ed. Peter B. Clarke (Oxford: Oxford University Press, 2011), 406–18.

29. See Stewart J. Brown, "Reform, Reconstruction, Reaction: The Social Vision of Scottish Presbyterianism," *Scottish Journal of Theology* 44 (1991): 489–518.

any false equation of religious identity with citizenship. To this extent, at least, secularization may have done the Western churches a favor. With growing numbers now self-identifying as belonging to no religion, the case for a religiously inflected nationalism is greatly weakened. This should caution against exclusive association of a church with any single ethnic group or political faction.

g *Economics.* The commitment to more egalitarian forms of economic distribution has at least two motives. One is the priority given to poor relief in the tradition. This extends not merely to monetary income but to affordable access to education, housing and health care. There is a good deal in the Reformed social vision to support this. In addition, there is a growing realization that societies exhibiting the greatest disparities in wealth are also functioning less well. They lose their necessary cohesion, their sense of a common good and collective purpose with a resultant reaction against comfortable elites and those institutions that appear to support them. Here a properly regulated nationalism may have something to offer in generating a sense of a wider corporate identity without lurching into exclusionary sentiments. The social covenant is damaged by excessive levels of economic inequality together with acquiescence in growing poverty and disadvantage. These may have no simple remedy, but to ignore the problem or to attempt some form of ideological justification is to fly in the face of the Reformed tradition.

In a series of essays, Nicholas Wolterstorff has noted the resistance to poverty found in the writings of Calvin. This, he argues, proceeds not from a sense of sympathy so much as a recognition of the right of the poor to a fairer distribution of resources. It is grounded in the doctrine of the *imago Dei* and in the command to honor God. Failure to take advantage of readily available measures to alleviate poverty is an offence against God.[30] In similar vein, Bruce Gordon notes the extent of Calvin's preaching from Deuteronomy and the responsibility of Geneva toward refugees. "Landlords should not charge them higher rates, citizens should employ them, and magistrates should judge them as they did others."[31] The relevance of this teaching to predatory loan practices today hardly needs to be underscored.

---

30. Nicholas Wolterstorff, "The Wounds of God: Calvin's Theology of Social Injustice," in *Hearing the Call: Liturgy, Justice, Church, and World*, ed. Nicholas Wolterstorff (Grand Rapids: Eerdmans, 2011), 114–32.

31. Bruce Gordon, *Calvin* (New Haven: Yale University Press, 2009), 298.

Conclusion

Our churches will no doubt find different ways of interpreting and enacting these theological imperatives. A strategy of retrieval, criticism, and adaptation is necessary, whereas withdrawal, renunciation, or simple condemnation are all impossible options for social theology today. A positive engagement with our societies needs to be negotiated—this will be shaped in part by the history of our churches, our current social condition, and the possibilities that we can identify in each time and place. Even at a time of increased secularism, these persist in new and promising ways. The above elements of a Reformed social theology are not exhaustive, but these point to ways in which the tradition needs to be rearticulated amid increased fragmentation and the loss of a hopeful political vision. Constructive responses to many of our current ailments are latent within Scripture and our traditions. By considering these, the church can continue to demonstrate the political salience of its witness.

Chapter 16

THEOLOGY AND THERAPY

In the mid-twentieth century, there were concerted efforts to bring theology into closer interaction with theories of counseling and psychotherapy. This served several purposes. One was to enlist emerging therapeutic discourses and practices in the service of the church. A more informed and professionalized understanding of pastoral ministry was sought, with particular reference to meeting more adequately the needs of those inside and outside the churches. This coincided with a significant growth of counseling centers, the emergence of specialist ministries, and a plethora of writings and conferences dedicated to the interaction of theology with therapeutic practice. The theological syllabus in colleges and universities also underwent some important changes from around the 1960s with the growth of courses and programs of study in pastoral theology and counseling. Insights from psychology were increasingly valued, these being accommodated by theology and church practice, not least in the self-understanding of clergy whose lack of training and own shortcomings in this area were more openly acknowledged. This was a particular attraction of Frank Lake's clinical theology. Today it is now commonplace for many dioceses and presbyteries to provide counseling and support to clergy who themselves experience psychological stress and burnout. Comparative work with other professions has proved useful, not least in tackling the hitherto neglected problem of bullying within congregations.[1]

Reading some of the literature from that period, one is impressed by its thoughtful, wide-ranging, and informed reflections on the ways in which theology and psychotherapy can benefit from closer interaction. By contrast, the contemporary theological scene has become more fragmented with too much specialism and insufficient interaction between the different components of the syllabus and other disciplines with overlapping interests. Significant attention continues to be devoted to the relationship between theology and psychotherapy, especially in the United States, but this has become an increasingly specialist

---

1. See for example the 2001 report submitted by the Society of Mary and Martha. http://www.balmnet.co.uk/clergystress.htm.

branch of pastoral theology by contrast with which more "mainstream" activity has become remote. This is a source of recurrent complaint from theological educators today.[2] The professional formation of clergy suffers from the manner in which the standard components of the theological curriculum fail properly to connect with each other. There is also impatience in many quarters with the division between systematic and practical theology, particularly among practitioners in those parts of the world where academic theology is more closely related to the interests of the church. Some repair work is now needed that can bring the different subjects of theological reflection into closer contact, without sacrificing the rigor and scholarly depth that often characterize specialist inquiry in a more clearly delineated field. Similar remarks might be made about the professionalization of counseling as a parallel process which has similarly encouraged specialization and differentiation, with some resultant disconnection from other forms of inquiry.

One danger in attempting interdisciplinary research is to over-simplify the other field as if one can quickly identify consensus findings that can be readily appropriated and integrated with one's primary expertise. Psychotherapy itself may be at least as variegated as theology and church life. Populated by different and sometimes competing approaches, it is a field that itself has experienced much fragmentation and internal conflict.[3] For the theologian, however, one place to begin is with those broader philosophical accounts which seek to situate therapy for the client in a wider context of meaning and fulfillment, including notions of the spiritual, the sacred, the religious, and the transcendent.[4] In understanding ourselves and our life stories, we carry within ourselves these broader categories of meaning, even if they remain implicit, half-formed, and fluid. The openness of such approaches to wider questions of meaning and context generates the possibility of drawing upon resources from other areas of inquiry, including theology.

In relating the discrete disciplines of theology and psychotherapy, many exponents were decisively influenced by the development of personalist thought in the first half of the twentieth century. This afforded several advantages, in particular the possibility of a holistic and relational account of the human person that could accommodate the insights of different discourses without prioritizing any one of these. It is not surprising, therefore, that personalist themes were appropriated by theologians, psychologists, and psychotherapists on both sides of the Atlantic. For theologians, in particular, there were further links with Trinitarian doctrine

---

2. See Dietrich Werner, "Ecumenical Learning in Theological Education: The World Council of Churches Perspective," *Expository Times* 123 (2011): 1–11.

3. A recent study has likened the disruption of schools of psychotherapy to the schismatic nature of Presbyterian churches. See Trevor Dobbs, *Faith, Theology and Psychoanalysis: The Life and Thought of Harry S. Guntrip* (Eugene: Pickwick, 2007).

4. Here I am alluding not to those "humanistic-existential" approaches which can function as one type of psychoanalytic theory (over against others) so much as a philosophy that seeks to offer some underpinning and contextualization within which different theories can be situated.

and anthropology that were already recognized before the more popular appeal of writers such as Moltmann, Zizioulas, Boff, and Pope John Paul II.[5]

Many of the personalist approaches that flourished in education and psychology from the mid-twentieth century borrowed extensively from the philosophy of John Macmurray (1891–1976).[6] Macmurray was a philosopher who sought to bring his subject into close contact with wider trends in social and intellectual life. A leading figure in the Christian left during the 1930s, he interacted with churches and a range of professional bodies. Frustrated by the narrower interests of many philosophical colleagues, he proved more influential outside than inside his own professional guild. His output was marked not so much by articles in specialist journals as by popular writings, BBC radio broadcasts, and numerous talks and lectures.[7]

Macmurray's work from the 1920s onward represents an attempt to develop a personalist vision of philosophy which can be employed in different fields of study and professional practice. Although expressed more analytically, it resonates in many ways with the work of Martin Buber on the European continent. The self is not the disembodied and detached mind of the Western tradition, as for example in the *Meditations* of Descartes. Instead, the self is an agent that is positioned in a physical and social world. Its identity cannot be exhausted by material or organic patterns of explanation. These are important to understanding the human being, but an adequate description requires also the language of the personal which is not reducible to material or organic causal laws. A relational self, the person interacts with other persons in ways marked by freedom, love, and friendship. Self-fulfillment is therefore found only in community, and it is in its promotion of community life that the real significance of religion is to be found.

---

5. E.g. C. J. Webb, *God and Personality* (London: Allen and Unwin, 1918) and Leonard Hodgson, *Doctrine of the Trinity* (London: Nisbet, 1944). Again, I am referring to personalism more as a philosophical framework for understanding approaches to counseling and therapy than as a distinctive type of therapy as in Carl Rogers's "person-centred" or "client-centred" therapy. See Richard Nelson-Jones, *Theory and Practice of Counselling and Therapy*, 5th ed. (London: Sage, 2011), 85–115.

6. In what follows, I have borrowed from a more detailed study of the influence of Scottish philosophical traditions upon person-centered approaches to counseling and psychotherapy. See David Fergusson, "Persons in Relation: The Interaction of Philosophy, Theology and Psychotherapy in 20th century Scotland," *Journal of Practical Theology* 5, no. 3 (2013): 287–306. For a fuller exploration of the period see Gavin Miller, *Miracles of Healing: Psychotherapy and Religion in Twentieth-Century Scotland* (Edinburgh: Edinburgh University Press, 2021).

7. For further information see John Costello S.J., *John Macmurray: A Biography* (Edinburgh: Floris Books, 2002) and Esther McIntosh, *John Macmurray's Religious Philosophy: What it Means to be a Person* (Aldershot: Ashgate, 2011).

All this may be summed up by saying that the unit of personal existence is not the individual, but two persons in personal relation; and that we are persons not by individual right, but in virtue of our relation to one another. The personal is constituted by personal relatedness. The unit of the personal is not the "I" but the "You and I".[8]

This holistic approach requires that the patient or client be viewed as a person and not merely an organic entity. This personal context determines the relationship that exists between professional and client, and hence it must also condition the former's understanding of the situation, needs, and direction of the client. The person aims at friendship, freedom, and love; this cannot be entirely bracketed out of professional relationships. In addressing professional groups, Macmurray would remind his audience that in working with their clients, patients, or pupils they were dealing with persons and not mere objects of study.[9] If we do only the latter—seek to present our subject—then we will fail to attend to the important personal dimension of the teacher–pupil relationship. This applies also to the relationships between doctor and patient, and therapist and client.

A proper understanding of the setting of human life is one that aspires not toward independence or detachment but toward the realization of codependency and interrelatedness. The paradigm for this is the mother–child relationship. From the beginning, it is a highly structured complex of interactions and patterns of behavior which not only enskill the child and enable it to take its place in a community of relations, but also provide a source of mutual delight for mother and child. In growing up, the child does not cease to be interrelated and dependent but rather transposes these into the terms of mature adult existence, in particular with reference to free, conscious activity.

When dealing with issues in medicine, Macmurray insists upon the importance of the whole psycho-physical field in understanding the condition of the patient.[10] While conceding that he speaks as a layperson in this respect, he points out that each of us knows what it is to be a patient in a doctor's surgery. In almost all cases, the patient is asking the doctor to help him or her, and in doing so is generally anxious about a condition, an ailment, or a problem. The reaction of the doctor can increase or diminish this anxiety.[11] Often the underlying condition is explained by a physiological cause that can be remedied by the appropriate prescription of drugs. However, we cannot assume that this is always the case. There are forms of anxiety that do not have a primary organic explanation and it is these with which the psychotherapist, counselor, and pastor are typically faced. Although genuinely

---

8. *Persons in Relation* (London: Faber and Faber, 1961), 61.
9. "A Philosopher Looks at Psychotherapy," *Individual Psychology Pamphlets* 20 (1938): 10.
10. See ibid., 9–22.
11. Macmurray does not consider whether doctors may also experience some levels of anxiety in relation to fulfilling their role.

felt, much of this anxiety is imaginary and groundless; its cure lies in achieving the dominance of more positive motivations. These comprise faith, trust, and love of others. To establish these, there must be mutual confidence between doctor and patient, therapist and client. Their relationship itself is an instance of the personal, a token of trust and friendship.

One of the few sources that are cited in his Gifford Lectures is Ian Suttie's 1936 study *The Origins of Love and Hate*. Macmurray had encountered this work shortly after its publication. Its thesis is that love as the need for companionship was a deeper need than Freud had understood and is the primary element in a child's relationship with its mother. Macmurray found in Suttie's work the empirical confirmation for lines of argument that he had been developing philosophically, and in his subsequent output Suttie is used extensively. Prior to his premature death in 1935, Suttie had moved to the Tavistock Clinic in London, an organization that undertook pioneering work in psychotherapy. Its first director, Hugh Crichton-Miller, also wrote on the subject of religion and psychology in ways that further resonate with this person-centered relational philosophy.[12] Macmurray's work was later appropriated by an array of groups, practitioners, and theorists across the world. These include Harry Guntrip in Leeds, R. D. Laing in Glasgow, Francis McNab in Melbourne, and Ray Anderson in Pasadena.

This approach resonates with much of the work of the churches from the 1960s onward with its stronger accent on pastoral care, on counseling centers, and on the importance of house groups where people could meet, converse and interact in ways that were less constrained by the more formal activities and physical environment of the churches. Further inspiration came from the Iona Community and the vision of its founder, George McLeod. The focus on community, incarnation, and a reaching-out to the physically and emotionally deprived were apparent. House groups became not an alternative to patterns of worship and church organization, but a complementary activity that created a non-threatening space for different types of interaction among members and adherents. More specialist chaplaincy ministries became increasingly common, these no longer being limited to the armed forces, but established in hospitals, universities, prisons, and industrial workplaces. Programs in practical theology emerged, these often combining psychological and theological approaches.

Perhaps not surprisingly, the relationship between psychotherapy and theology was jeopardized by attempts to achieve a premature integration or synthesis of different disciplines and forms of activity. In many ways, this was understandable. The religious roots and motivation of several key practitioners led to an enthusiasm to reach a single discourse of therapeutic theology or equally theological psychotherapy. This could lead to two contrasting problems. On the one side, there was a tendency to pour religion into the molds that had been created by

---

12. For a recent discussion of Suttie's important for the independent tradition in British psychoanalysis see Gabriele Cassullo, "Back to the Roots: The Influence of Ian. D. Suttie on British Psychoanalysis," *American Imago* 67 (2010): 5–22.

psychotherapeutic theories. As a result, much that was distinctive in theology was at risk of being reduced to an epiphenomenon or a spiritual dimension of psychotherapeutic goals. In some cases, the translation of theological categories into psychological ones seemed to evacuate the language of God of any real significance and reduce Jesus to the status of teacher or moral exemplar. Of course, there are legitimate theological arguments and disagreement around these issues, but these are primarily theological, not psychotherapeutic. To reach too quickly for a synthesis of discourses runs the risk of distortion and loss of understanding; this may have been a particular temptation for those who were fleeing traditional patterns of Christian belief and affiliation in the mid-twentieth century. But there was also a danger from the other side. The appropriation of psychotherapy could be similarly eclectic and amateurish, undoubtedly a problem given the diversity and contested discourses of experts in the field. The difficulty in acquiring expertise and in making critical judgments about competing approaches could too easily elude the non-specialist. Even more problematic is the notion that there might be a distinctively Christian type of psychotherapy which could quickly be pressed into the service of some highly specific and determinate confessional assumptions. A looser fit might work better. The notion of a distinctively Christian counseling or psychotherapy, contrasted with other therapies, is one that probably needs to be resisted, as opposed to a more professional counseling or psychotherapy carried out by individual Christians, or institutionally facilitated by the churches, or set within the context of a Christian worldview.[13] At the same time, a narrow and over-medicalized approach to psychotherapy may tend to bracket the wider spiritual questions that are present on both sides of the client-therapist relationship. In this context, Liz Bondi has written that "the therapeutic process . . . cannot survive the instrumentalization implicit in 'efficiency'. Rather, the psychotherapeutic process eschews such calculation and needs to enable 'nothing to happen' or 'time to be wasted' and similar 'inefficiencies.'"[14]

The need for a premature integration of disciplines and methods should be resisted. There are good precedents here from other discourses and fields of inquiry, for example, history, medicine, and the natural sciences. We tend to think in terms of complementary patterns or layers of understanding and explanation, discourses that might repose upon each other in important ways but which remain distinct and irreducible. Stephen Jay Gould's famous notion of NOMA (non-

---

13. The Association of Christian Counselling, while stressing the importance of a Christian worldview, also acknowledges a legitimate diversity of approaches practiced by its counselors. Christian counseling is described as "that activity which seeks to help people towards constructive change and growth in any or every aspect of their lives through a caring relationship and within agreed relational boundaries, carried out by a counsellor who has a Christian worldview, values and assumptions." See http://www.acc-uk.org/1410/.

14. "Research and Therapy: Generating Meaning and Feeling Gaps," *Quantitative Inquiry* 19, no. 1 (2013): 9–19 (10). There are some striking parallels here with those traditions in spiritual theology which emphasize prayer as "time wasted" with God.

overlapping *magisteria*) might serve quite well in this domain also, especially as there is a growing need to relate psychotherapy to a plurality of faiths and not simply Judaism and Christianity. These disciplines represent different domains with their own descriptive terms and methods of evaluation. There are points of contact and tension which can shift and alter across time, but we are dealing here with different and complementary forms of understanding each of which has its own integrity and scope. The relationship is one in which partial analogies and links can be made, but with an awareness of the different conceptualities that are employed. These are neither reducible one to another, nor capable of full systematic integration.[15] The philosophical description of personhood in Macmurray and others may work well in this context precisely because it is neither theologically nor psychotherapeutically freighted in any strong way. While providing a set of concepts which enable fruitful connections to be drawn between the two disciplines, it also affords space for different forms of understanding to flourish. For example, a description of sin, forgiveness, and reconciliation is central to a Christian theological account of the self in relation to God and others. Yet this discourse should neither suppress nor itself be supplanted by psychotherapeutic descriptions which can offer an awareness of the dynamics of the self in relation to others. The successful use of one set of concepts, with its own grammar and vocabulary, does not preclude coexistence with another. The real enemy here is a totalizing approach which assumes that one type of description is exhaustive and therefore exclusive. The task of juxtaposition and connecting may present some problems, but it may be better to leave this open and unresolved than too readily to dismiss key insights for the sake of an enforced, comfortable, or lazy coherence.

In surveying the work that was undertaken in the twentieth century, one cannot avoid the sense that much of the impetus was lost after about the 1960s and 1970s, particularly after the passing of some of the inspirational and pioneer figures. Concerted attempts at integration of theology and psychotherapy have been less conspicuous, at least in the UK, although there remain some important examples. Why is this so? One factor is that psychotherapy and counseling have moved, perhaps inevitably, toward a greater degree of professionalization and specialism in terms of training, accreditation, and association. This has generated an understandable shift toward independence and professional autonomy. As far as the churches are concerned, these have been in rapid decline in most Western societies since this period, a decline that currently shows no signs of arresting. The causes of this process have been explored by Hugh McLeod in his study of the religious crisis of the 1960s.[16] One effect of this was that energy and resources

---

15. A similar methodological relationship is defended by Deborah van Deusen Hunsinger in *Theology and Pastoral Counseling: A New Interdisciplinary Approach* (Grand Rapids: Eerdmans, 1995). This is illustrated by the ways in which forgiveness and healing can coincide while remaining conceptually distinct and asymmetrical.

16. Hugh McLeod, *The Religious Crisis of the 1960s* (Oxford: Oxford University Press, 2007).

were increasingly required to shore up declining institutions—this left less time and opportunity for more outward-facing, exploratory ministries. Reviewing the work of Ronald Gregor Smith and others on secular Christianity, a contemporary scholar is likely to be struck by the confidence they displayed in the position of the church in society and its capacity to exercise widespread influence. There has also been a theological reaction against the perceived liberalism of the mid-twentieth century, both in Protestant and Roman Catholic circles. This has resulted in concerns about the dilution of distinctive Christian tenets. As a result, we have witnessed a consequent reassertion of theologies that are less inclined to enter into conversation and accommodation with other disciplines and activities. This may now be becoming superseded by fresh trends which reflect the drive toward greater interdisciplinarity in the academy and in government research councils.

At the same time, it can be argued that the disappearance of wider philosophical and theological appropriations of psychotherapy has resulted in a narrowing of focus that is unhelpful for the latter. Noting the "therapeutic turn" in contemporary culture, Charles Taylor points out that the restriction of strategies to biochemical and medical approaches can lead to a bracketing-out of wider notions of meaning. The therapeutic avoidance of these existential notions may lead to their suppression or displacement in ways that can be restrictive or even damaging. Macmurray's philosophy points to the personal goals of love, freedom, and relational integrity; yet if psychotherapy restricts itself to the language of "cure," then its goals will tend to be confined to treating pathological symptoms rather than articulating and realizing some wider holistic ends, which admittedly may be much harder to realize and to quantify. Such an approach will reduce the personal to the level of the organic.

> [T]o have tried to get rid of an unease that one really needed to understand is crippling; the more so in that within the culture of the therapeutic, the various languages, ethical and spiritual, in which this understanding can be couched become less and less familiar, less and less available to each new generation. . . . The issue is whether one can speak of a pathology alone, or whether there is also a spiritual or ethical hermeneutic to be made.[17]

Twentieth-century debates have taught us much about the ways in which the languages of psychotherapy and religion can fruitfully interact. These are positive and enduring gains which include a better understanding of the self with its unconscious and half-conscious anxieties and hurts. It is such selves that are the focus of pastoral care and so a fuller understanding of their dynamics is needed. Similarly, the holistic understanding of the person as embodied, social, and relational resonates with much of the biblical tradition and provides a corrective to theologies that privilege the spiritual over against the physical as if we could detach the true self from all the material, organic and psychological conditions that contribute to its formation.

---

17. Charles Taylor, *The Secular Age* (Boston: Harvard University Press, 2007), 622.

Attention given to the relationship of therapist to client has much pastoral and theological significance also, particularly in its underscoring of the need for respect, love, attentiveness, and acceptance within the parameters of that relationship. The moral and spiritual significance of love itself requires to be explored. At this juncture, further questions tend to arise. Why does this matter so much to us, and what does it tell us about who we are and how we ought to live? The activity of the psychotherapist raises issues about the moral and spiritual framework within which we understand our personhood and its goals. Don Browning points to "the question as to whether the agent of change is the finite relationship or what it implies about some over-belief that testifies that neither a person's mother nor father, sister nor brother, shaman nor psychotherapist, is the exhaustive source of the client's worth but rather that some larger structure of meaning and being is this source."[18]

Clients hold a range of presuppositions and spiritual assumptions that are deeply related to the sense that they make of themselves, others, and the world. To bracket these out or suppress them in counseling can lead to frustration or at least a narrowing of goals. While many assumptions will require to be challenged, refined, or even abandoned, this process itself will involve attention to wider philosophical and theological concerns. Here a fruitful dialogue is needed that brings together a broad array of disciplinary interests, not for the sake of achieving a totalizing discourse but for the promotion of more holistic strategies toward psychological well-being and personal fulfillment.[19]

The therapeutic context is one of several in which theological claims need to be engaged and constantly reevaluated. It is at this interface between practical and systematic theology that the most creative work is sometimes conducted.[20] The increasingly technical and professionalized approach to theology in the modern academy may conceal some of the resources of the church's doctrinal and ethical traditions that have long had a therapeutic quality. Rooted in biblical stories and injunctions, these constitute a powerful resource that is surprisingly salient in a therapeutic setting.[21] The following examples offer some illustration of this feature

---

18. Don Browning, *Reviving Christian Humanism: The New Conversation on Spirituality, Theology and Psychology* (Philadelphia: Fortress, 2010), 102. For a measured attempt at showing how theological notions can both complement and adjust more secular approaches see Alastair V. Campbell, *Rediscovering Pastoral Care* (London: Darton, Longman and Todd, 1981).

19. See for example William West (ed.), *Exploring Therapy, Spirituality and Healing* (Basingstoke: Palgrave Macmillan, 2011).

20. In this respect, David Lyall draws attention to the importance of "cross-grained experience" in pastoral theology. See *The Integrity of Pastoral Case* (London: SPCK, 2001), 87. For an example of an approach to theodicy oriented toward pastoral contexts see Marilyn McCord Adams, *Christ and Horrors: The Coherence of Christology* (Cambridge: Cambridge University Press, 2006).

21. Similarly, a narrow and more medically inflected approach to psychotherapy might ignore some of the wider humanistic concerns of early pioneer figures.

of our traditions. These might be characterized as theological fragments, drawn from wider systems of theology and ethics, but capable of shedding sudden light in a secular context.[22]

Self-love. At least since Augustine, the importance of loving oneself, as well as God and neighbor, has been stressed. This is a responsibility that is laid upon each person, yet it can readily be neglected for at least two reasons. Self-love can be presented as selfish and even narcissistic, and hence inimical to the love of one's neighbor in the outward orientation of the self. This can hardly be denied. Yet, when properly constituted, the love of one's self is correlative to the capacity to dispose oneself properly to the other, including God. If the aforementioned philosophical description of the person is along the right lines, then the realization of the self can only occur in the encounter with other persons. In the right ordering of relationships, the self is properly constituted. This is one way of reading Jesus' instruction about losing one's life in order to find it. A second reason for neglecting the love of self emerges from the tendency to over-stress guilt, particularly in a liturgical context. This may be a particular feature of Western Christianity with its deep-seated fear of Pelagianism. Yet the language of repeated confession, if not tempered by other themes such as thanksgiving for what has been accomplished by divine grace—sadly reserved too often for funeral orations—can contribute to a self-loathing and an inability to overcome past burdens that prevent the practice of self-love. This applies to both body and soul. The abuse of one's health through substance addiction and unhealthy diet can proceed from an incapacity to love the self. Similarly, self-love is necessary for the life of the spirit in orienting itself toward God and love of one's neighbor.[23] To divide physical and spiritual health among different sets of experts is to ignore the ways in which the whole person functions.

The traditional stress on sanctification in Reformed theology might be viewed as proceeding from the recognition that we carry a responsibility to make the most of ourselves through the resources afforded by divine grace, even while acknowledging that this is never a smooth, unproblematic, or perfected process. An account of proper self-love can thus function in a way that is correlated with love of God and love of one's neighbor, allowing all three to be inter-linked in ways that are vital for each.[24] Love of self, when properly ordered, can be viewed as a necessary correlate of the love of one's neighbor in terms of maintaining commitment to one's insights, responsibilities, and integrity. In loving the other,

---

22. I have borrowed this notion from Duncan Forrester, *Theological Fragments: Essays in Unsystematic Theology* (London: T&T Clark, 2005).

23. In this context, Thomas Aquinas could affirm the importance of loving oneself and one's own body; see *Summa Theologiae* 2a2ae, Q25.4–5. Werner Jeanrond notes how this is strangely lacking from the 2006 Papal encyclical *Deus caritas est*; see his *Theology of Love* (London: Continuum, 2010), 165.

24. This argument for "right self-love" is developed by Darlene Fozard Weaver, *Self-Love and Christian Ethics* (Cambridge: Cambridge University Press, 2002).

the self requires a unity of purpose, organization of time, adherence to core commitments and reciprocity of respect and freedom.[25]

In an important study, Stephen Pattison notes the ways in which the discourse of sin and forgiveness can reinforce patterns of chronic shame instead of providing the intended release. A sense of worthlessness and defilement, often the result of abusive relationships, may be deepened by faulty notions of God as inquisitorial, these being further reinforced by liturgical practice. Unless complemented by other themes, monotonous confession that "there is no health in us" can merely confirm the absence of self-esteem. A clearer discrimination between genuine guilt and chronic shame is here required. "While guilty people need forgiveness, shamed people need a sense of valued self."[26] This is required both by those who care for others, and those who are the recipients of such care.

Providence. The need to find a pattern to one's life runs deep in most of us, hence the importance of meaning-making in psychotherapy. This is unlikely to be a predetermined route or carefully charted course to which we constantly adhere. Very few life stories have that narrative shape. But there persists a striving for an existence that admits of meaning. This might take the form of making some sense of what happens to us, of resolving hurt and recognizing failure, of discerning a value in one's typical activities, and of reaching a place of increased wisdom. These elements can be grouped together under the theological rubric of providence.

The theology of providence is historically beset with mistakes—a near-fatalism that ascribes too much to the rule of predetermined forces, a predestinarianism that substitutes God for fate, and an introspective preoccupation that tends to read too much significance into the myriad details of one's own individual biography.[27] Nevertheless, the providence attested in the Bible often describes the limitless capacity of divine grace for securing meaning and positive outcomes from the most unpromising of circumstances. Adam and Eve are promised a victory of sorts, even as they are banished from Eden. Joseph is reconciled with his brothers down in Egypt. The return from exile in Babylon is through the liberating army of Cyrus. The foolishness of the cross is the wisdom of God to those who are perishing. This divine providence does not govern only nations and empires, but is found in hidden and insignificant places. A pattern of crucifixion and resurrection belongs to all baptized lives. The parables of the kingdom suggest small beginnings and a secret working of divine grace. These are found in the everyday and mundane

---

25. See the discussion in Gene Outka, *Agape: An Ethical Analysis* (New Haven: Yale University Press, 1972), 55–74. For a measured assessment of arguments for the necessity of self-love in Christian ethics, see Oliver O'Donovan, *The Problem of Self-Love in St Augustine* (New Haven: Yale University Press, 1980).

26. Stephen Pattison, *Shame: Theory, Therapy, Theology* (Cambridge: Cambridge University Press, 2000), 245.

27. I have sought to develop these ideas in "Theology of Providence," *Theology Today* 67 (2010): 261–78.

contexts of ordinary human lives. The providential work of God is not reserved for the powerful, the successful, or the fortunate; by contrast, it is more apparent in lives that would otherwise be regarded as weak, failing, or unlucky.[28]

A particular stress on the improvising power of divine providence can rescue us from the sense that our lives have parted company from God's purpose or have become so hopelessly broken that they cannot be mended or given any meaningful shape. The pattern that emerges from such accounts resonates with recent work on narrative therapy. Divine providence always gives us another chance; the future is never devoid of some potential. J. R. Lucas stresses the reactive, improvising, and resourceful dimension of this providence. In his teaching, he often cited the analogy of the Persian carpet-maker whose skills could incorporate the successive mistakes of his apprentice son.[29]

Vocation. If notions of providence can sometimes carry the risk of appearing too passive—much work in this area presents human beings as the objects rather than the agents of God's providence[30]—the concept of vocation points to ways in which persons can understand their activity as a unique exercise and accomplishment of what God intends for them. Vocation was an idea that was universalized at the time of the Reformation with Luther's argument for its secularization. We can encounter God's call in the home and the workplace as much as in the monastery or church. While these notions of the estates in which vocation is discovered were rather static and overly concentrated on occupation, Luther's argument is still valid and widely accepted in modern ecumenical accounts of the ministry of the whole people of God, especially in Vatican II's *Lumen Gentium*. According to the New Testament, vocational gifts are distributed to the whole membership of the body of Christ. Karl Barth makes the point that throughout Scripture conversion is closely linked with the call of God—faith is always accompanied by a commission to service. In discovering this, the prophets and the apostles find themselves and their identity in relation to God. Similarly, a life today can be reoriented and have a meaning conferred through the discernment of some vocation. This does not require bright lights or loud voices, but only the discovery of a significance bestowed by God upon opportunities that are placed before us. This may require a process of discernment, but it can be a means of liberation when it replaces a sense of ennui or aimlessness.

Healing: The twentieth-century attention to psychotherapy and counseling has also contributed to a re-appropriation of the language of healing in theology.

---

28. For a fictional exploration of this see Francis Spufford, *Light Perpetual* (London: Faber, 2021).

29. This account of providence is developed in J. R. Lucas, *Freedom and Grace* (London: SPCK, 1976).

30. An exception is Ellen Charry, *God and the Art of Happiness* (Grand Rapids: Eerdmans, 2010) which stresses the ways in which human beings can sometimes be the agents of God's providential rule.

The Synoptic Gospels are of course replete with stories of people being healed, cured and made whole by Jesus but too often this has been occluded in Western approaches to the work of Christ, the Christian life and the sacraments with an overly exclusive focus on guilt and remission of sins. In recent theology and exegesis, particularly Pauline studies, greater weight has been given to the more participationist themes employed to express the work of Christ. Here the language of the *admirabile commercium* has been recovered and revitalized in both theology and liturgy; our lives and Christ's are brought together in a wondrous exchange. Thus the "physical" notion of redemption which has been privileged in the Eastern tradition of the church has now been set alongside the juridical themes that have hitherto dominated in the Latin west. These insights are now all commonplace and are found in many contemporary approaches to pastoral care.[31] A study of recent liturgy and hymnody reflects many of these gains from last century. In striking more pastoral and therapeutic notes, this has proved practically fruitful in its enrichment of worship.

> I will weep when you are weeping;
> when you laugh I'll laugh with you;
> I will share your joy and sorrow
> till we've seen this journey through.[32]

What has been offered here is one theologian's attempt to recover important links with the practice of psychotherapy. In this encounter, theology does not remain unchanged—it functions as more than a catalyst—since its practice needs to be informed and partly shaped by descriptions of human personhood that offer insights from related discourses. Through this interaction, we can identify some therapeutic qualities of theology and its resonance in surprising ways. This is offered neither in the interests of compromising the distinctive subject matter of theology nor of pressing for a swift fusion of discourses. But theology can succeed here through displaying its salience for persons who are shaped by their striving for freedom and love. The interaction with psychotherapy is needed on both sides of the disciplinary divide, and there are sufficient resources out there to provide encouragement for the undertaking of that work today.[33]

---

31. See the use of the image of the "wounded healer" in Alastair V. Campbell, *Discovering Pastoral Care* (London: Darton, Longman and Todd, 1986), 37–46.

32. *Church of Scotland Hymnary*, 4th ed. (Norwich: Canterbury Press, 2005), 694. For a discussion of the relationship between liturgy and pastoral care, see William H. Willimon, *Worship as Pastoral Care* (Abingdon: Nashville, 1982).

33. This chapter is based on a lecture delivered in October 2012 at the Uniting Church Centre for Theology and Ministry in Melbourne. It derives from an AHRC/ESRC-funded project at the University of Edinburgh to investigate the relationship between Christianity, Psychotherapy, and Spirituality in Scotland in the latter half of the twentieth century. I am particularly grateful to my colleague Professor Liz Bondi for many helpful comments on an earlier draft.

Chapter 17

THE PLACE OF CHRISTIAN THEOLOGY IN THE UNIVERSITY

Introduction

The wide variety of settings in which Christian theology is pursued today entails that there is no simple answer to questions about its rationale and relevance. Responses will vary according to the context in which the question arises. Theology has been taught in the ancient universities of Europe since their foundation, this reflecting the age of Christendom, whether before or after the Reformation. The first chairs to be established were often in theology.[1] But, even here, there have been some notable differences between, for example, Germany, Scandinavia, and the UK. What seems relevant in one place may appear egregious in another. Even within the UK, there are significant differences. The so-called "Cathedrals group" is likely to offer somewhat different arguments for the study of Christian theology than elite Russell Group institutions.[2]

Whilst Christian theology has often been pursued in the universities of Europe, this has never been its only setting. Seminaries, monasteries, religious houses, vicarages, and manses have all been the locus for important contributions to the discipline. We should guard against the assumption that theology cannot flourish without a university home.[3] This diversity may actually be increasing in

---

1. In Cambridge, the Lady Margaret Chair of Divinity was created in 1502 and in Edinburgh, the Chair of Divinity was founded in 1620.

2. The Cathedrals Group is an umbrella organization of fifteen English universities which were formerly church-established teaching training colleges. Their distinctiveness is expressed by a commitment to educating the "whole person." See "Find out about us | Cathedrals Group" (CCUC). The Russell Group, by contrast, represents twenty-four institutions. These tend to be larger, older, and more research-intensive. The Group includes Oxford and Cambridge and is sometimes assumed to comprise the elite of the UK system. St Andrews, inter alia, might reasonably contest the assumption. "Russell Group | Our universities."

3. John McLeod Campbell's seminal work *The Nature of the Atonement* (1856) has sometimes been hailed as the greatest single theological work to appear in Scotland. Yet it was written by the minister of an independent congregation who had been earlier been banished from the established church.

our own day with the advent of online and distance-learning programs. These locations of theological study have varied, but so too have the media. Theology, moreover, has not been pursued always through texts—we can find it embedded in works of art, in liturgy, in architecture and other artifacts. These may even have been the principal forms of theological transmission in societies where literacy rates were low.[4]

In the 1980s, David Kelsey in Yale produced an important study arguing that contemporary models of theological education need to negotiate between ancient ideals of *paideia* and the modern paradigm of professional training.[5] When we consider the contemporary university both models are problematic for related reasons. The academy has ceased to be a place that cultivates a religious identity. Students are expected to display their academic competence in a range of subjects, rather than demonstrate their spiritual development. There are no confessional tests or requirements in religious formation; indeed, many begin and end their studies without espousing any religious faith. Degree courses in theology recruit large numbers of students who have no intention of seeking ordination. Some may and will be better formed for the tasks of ministry, but this cannot be assumed of all or most of the student body. Reassuring parallels with professional schools of law and medicine start to break down when only a small minority of divinity graduates enter the ranks of the ordained ministry.

In a societal context of religious decline, we often hear questions about the "relevance" of theological study, often from exponents of other disciplines. Yet the concept of "relevance" has raised some hackles in recent discussion. Few people are attracted to an institution that is anxious about its own future; similarly, few are likely to be persuaded to study a subject that constantly frets about its relevance and is unsure of its place. Nicholas Wolterstorff has complained about strategies of *adaptation*. He writes: "The theologian looks around for developments in the contemporary academy that seem to be generally esteemed, and tries to sail a bit of theology under those colors."[6] Sometimes this has resulted in theologians

---

4. See, for example, Thomas O'Loughlin, "Theology in Scotland before Scholasticism," in *History of Scottish Theology, Vol. 1: From Celtic Origins to Reformed Orthodoxy*, ed. David Fergusson and Mark W. Elliott (Oxford: Oxford University Pres, 2019), 12–24.

5. David Kelsey, *Between Athens and Berlin: The Theological Education Debate* (Grand Rapids: Eerdmans, 1003), 99–220.

6. Nicholas Wolterstorff, "To Theologians: From One Who Cares about Theology but Is Not One of You," *Theological Education* 40, no. 2 (2005): 79–92 (83). For further discussion see Wolterstorff's, *Religion in the University* (New Haven: Yale University Press, 2019), 117–54. Wolterstorff's comments echo the oft-quoted remark of John Milbank, "The pathos of modern theology is its false humility. For theology, this must be a fatal disease. . . . If theology no longer seeks to position, qualify, or criticize other discourses, then it is inevitable that these discourses will position theology." John Milbank, *Theology and Social Theory: Beyond Secular Reason*, 2nd ed. (Oxford: Wiley Blackwell, 2006), 1.

following intellectual fashions in philosophy in the hope of gaining a measure of academic respectability. Speaking as a philosopher, Wolterstorff deplores this as a failure of nerve and a dereliction of one's responsibility to the faith community in which Christian theology finds its primary location. On the other hand, he argues against *protectionist* strategies which tend to isolate theology, leaving it incapable of interacting with the cultural mainstream. I fear that this may be the unintended consequence of attempting to reposition theology as the "queen of the sciences."

In one of his last essays, John Webster argues for a robust Christian theology that holds all things together in the university, disclosing to other disciplines their essence and relationship to a transcendent source in a world that is both fallen and redeemed.[7] There is something impressive in his contempt for all defensive measures. Yet these arguments have an abstract feel. They are unlikely to have much traction in the wider academy, and even within theology they tend to conceal the contested nature of our subject matter and the need to reckon with the realities of pluralism. In her recent salvo, Linn Marie Tonstad fiercely attacks such approaches. Complaining that they assume a moral and intellectual high ground, she accuses them of a false humility and lack of self-awareness.[8] While I consider this criticism of Webster et al. to be overstated for reasons that I will come to, nevertheless Tonstad has a point. The reassertion of such an Olympian position may play well in some theological circles, and it may even function as a necessary jolt to a few lazy assumptions. But it will struggle with the particular questions that continue to be pressed by critics and which haunt theologians themselves. The answers we offer need to have some traction in our contemporary secular and ecclesial contexts.

Despite local variations, I shall assume that the arguments presented today against the ongoing pursuit of Christian theology in the academy are broadly similar in a European context. These arguments come from two sides—one is largely secular and skeptical, the other, more surprisingly perhaps, is ecclesial and confessional. In what follows, I shall respond to each of these, while offering in a middle section a less defensive approach to what theology offers the university.

Secular Skepticism

A position that has sometimes been argued—I used to hear it most starkly rehearsed at examiners' meetings by the late John Hinnells, a distinguished

---

7. John Webster, "God, Theology, Universities," in *God Without Measure: Working Papers in Christian Theology, Vol. 2 Virtue and Intellect* (London: Bloomsbury T&T Clark, 2016), 157–72.

8. Tonstad, "(Un)wise Theologians: Systematic Theology in the University," *International Journal of Systematic Theology* 22, no. 4 (2020): 494–511.

exponent of religious studies—is that we live in a pluralist society in which all faiths are treated as equal under the law. The British taxpayer, Hinnells insisted, does not fund higher education in order to promote the cause of any religion. Therefore, to embark upon a confessional theology in the academy is in effect a breach of contract with the funding agencies. Is this valid? While there are some obvious dangers in drawing a straight line from the wishes of the average taxpayer to the provisions of the university syllabus, other considerations can be advanced to support this case. These include the increased secularization of European societies where churchgoing is now as low as 2 percent in some quarters. Given the age profile of adherents, these numbers are set to go in only one direction for the foreseeable future. This creates some unease, particularly in older universities in which Christian theology has always been taught. Theology suddenly seems a less familiar and natural part of the landscape. Within a predominantly Christian society, its presence in a university may once have seemed unremarkable. But now it has ceased to be the default option, and its case requires some careful consideration. Have we become strangers in our own house, former owners who now find themselves cast as embarrassing tenants?

Why continue with teaching and research in Christian theology? One answer to this question is simple, if somewhat utilitarian. Christian theology will flourish in the university for as long as there are people who wish to study it. One of the paradoxical features of theology in the UK today is that there are more people studying the subject at graduate level and teaching it than there were in the heyday of Christendom, even as churches empty and close all around us.[9] There might be two explanations for this. The first is that although Christian affiliation is in rapid decline in Europe, especially among younger generations, it blossoms in other parts of the world, thus ensuring an international constituency, particularly within our graduate programs. In an increasingly secular society, we may find it easy to forget that *c.* 85 percent of the world's population adheres to one of the world religions. Secularization does not appear to be taking over on a global scale—it looks more like a regional phenomenon in the heartlands of Christendom.

A second explanation for student demand, particularly within our undergraduate and Master's programs, may be an intellectual curiosity no longer encumbered by expectations of conformity to ecclesiastical standards of orthodoxy. Although not entirely absent from university life, intellectual contempt and indifference are being replaced by puzzlement, surprise and even appreciation of religion. The questions it asks, the answers that it has given, its canonical texts, its societal influences—these all remain of interest to students today. Moreover, if questions about spiritual meaning and religious truth emerge in other disciplines, then

---

9. Admittedly, recent evidence suggests a worrying decline over the last decade in numbers at A-level and undergraduate courses in theology and religious studies. Whether this can be halted or reversed is currently an open question, though the resurgence of classics over the last twenty years may offer some hope. "Theology and Religious Studies provision in UK Higher Education | The British Academy."

students will find their ways to the study of theology. My own recent experience of taught postgraduate recruitment in Edinburgh and Cambridge suggests a steady flow of students "converting" to theology from other fields.

This takes us into a more substantive kind of response. If theology is concerned with some of the most fundamental questions that face us, then it would be surprising if it were excluded from academic life. Why is there something and not nothing? Why are we here? What is a human being? What wisdom can be gathered from long-standing spiritual traditions and their classical texts? What makes a life worth living? The latter is a question that we have pondered amid lockdown restrictions. Why are the sciences so successful? Or Bonhoeffer's oft-quoted question: Who is Jesus Christ for us today?

To suppress these normative questions or to refuse even to entertain them in an academic context would result in a narrowing of focus, even an ideological curtailment of free inquiry, though it would not be long before they resurfaced in other disciplines. Simone Weil described herself as occupying a boundary between the church and the world. She wrote of the ways in which questions about ourselves, the world, God, suffering, and love are all deeply intertwined. While these may not admit of ready answers, in pursuing them we are drawn inevitably into theological territory. To suppress or bracket our deepest existential questions in an academic context would result only in a lazy avoidance.

Theology alone cannot answer these questions. It must travel in conversation with other approaches, methods of inquiry, and their findings. This is why the juxtaposition of theology with biblical criticism, church history, and religious studies can work well, despite inevitable tensions. Most of our predecessors would have assumed that was the case; indeed, they would have had difficulty recognizing the division of labor in today's academy with its guilds and carefully regulated boundaries. At its best, theology works alongside other disciplines neither in subservient adherence to intellectual fashions nor in dictatorial mode. If the latter tendency blighted the past, then the former may be the greater danger today.

These trends will continue and are unlikely to be reversed in any foreseeable future. Plurality and diversity are celebrated as intellectually enriching, socially inclusive, and reflective of our society and world. I welcome these for the stimulus and intellectual freedom that they have offered me in my own time. We might also note that a degree in Christian theology within a multidisciplinary context can nurture all the skills that accompany the best liberal arts programs—linguistic, historical, philosophical, literary, and social scientific. As transferable skills, these are developed across a theology and religious studies degree program.[10]

Should theology be a confessional enterprise? Yes, but not in a partisan or sectarian spirit. The judgment of theologians will reflect their own confessional commitments, though these must be open to challenge, correction and adjustment. The centuries-long history of our Chairs of Divinity suggests that theology is mobile. It is not mere repetition, clarification, or retrieval of what was

---

10. See the webpage "Why Study TRS at University?" *Theology and Religious Studies UK*.

accomplished in the thirteenth, seventeenth, or twentieth centuries. Interrogation of earlier expressions of the tradition is necessary. Without its historical focus and attempt to articulate a living, breathing tradition, theology quickly lapses into a more abstract philosophy of religion. There is a constant return to the canonical texts of the discipline in the conviction that these can illuminate the present. Yet this conversation with the past is always critical and constructive. Few of us believe what was once taught about predestination, hell, other religions, the suppression of heresy, and the inerrancy of Scripture. Meanwhile, the diversity within Christian theology has probably never been greater than it is today, given that the majority of Christians live outside the West.

The study of theology commits us ineluctably to normativity. There is no Archimedean point of neutrality. Every position, including atheism, skepticism, and naturalism, is freighted with normative judgments about God, spirituality, religion, the world and human existence. Theology offers evaluative comments, and ventures truth claims, even when practiced in its most deconstructive mode.[11] If it could not do so, it would soon lose its significance and its appeal to contemporary audiences. A critic may argue that we should confine ourselves to the *history* of Christian thought, but that again would represent some scarcely concealed normative judgments and bracket out some of the biggest questions. It would be odd to include the study of Augustine, Aquinas, and Schleiermacher in the syllabus, while arguing in effect that, if they applied for a job in one of our universities, we would not consider them appointable on account of the confessional claims that they make. In following Jesus, the Christian is committed to seeking the truth wherever it is to be found, to the *logos* that is everywhere in the world. Simone Weil writes:

> One can never wrestle enough with God, if one does so out of pure regard for the truth. Christ likes us to prefer truth to him, because being Christ, he is truth. If one turns aside from him, to go toward the truth, one will not go far before falling into his arms.[12]

Here there is an obvious objection that will already have occurred to the reader. Why privilege the study of *Christian* theology in our university? The only answer that can be given to that question is along the lines already offered. The study of theology has been around for as long as the university and of course this has historically reflected the Christian culture of our society. If there is a continuing demand, then under the appropriate conditions, the case for the supply persists. Yet we should recognize that the religious character of our host society has

---

11. For a striking analysis from North America of the problem of normativity among theologians in the contemporary academy, see Miroslav Volf and Matthew Croasmun, *For the Life of the World: Theology That Makes a Difference* (Grand Rapids: Brazos Press, 2019), 35–59.

12. Simone Weil, *Waiting on God* (London: Routledge and Kegan Paul, 1951), 36.

changed significantly. Different theologies and world views deserve expression in our universities—Jewish, Muslim, Hindu, Buddhist, and others. The voice of Christian theology will have increasingly to be heard in conversation with other normativities—this is both a necessary and an exciting venture. In the future, the self-understanding of the church will require to be positioned in a multi-faith context, not in mono-faith isolation.[13]

A further reason, and here I risk raising some hackles, is that the study of theology is a necessarily cohesive element in any faculty or school of divinity. What is it that prevents our different disciplines from sheering off in disparate directions whether toward classics, history, philosophy, literature or the social sciences? Each of us could find a location there, and indeed we already have valued conversation partners in these fields of study. What then holds us together? Might it be a shared commitment to offering some insight into the religious self-understanding of human beings and of the world in which we are situated? This is at root a theological enterprise in the broadest sense. It does not require a consensus in favor of any creed, confession, community, or worldview—indeed, it may be more invigorating and stimulating if these are contested—but it does entail a commitment to pursuing some questions of perennial importance in the time and place in which we find ourselves.

What Can Theology Offer the University?

What might theology offer the wider university? Instead of mounting a rearguard action, can theology position itself at the center of university life without embarrassment? Theology may be more embedded in the academy than some appearances may suggest. Having recently written a REF environment statement for my unit,[14] I have been impressed with how many of my colleagues are engaging with other scholars in the university—in the sciences, health care, Islamic studies, literature, Asian studies, and of course with classics, history and philosophy. We bring something to these conversations, though their potential may not always be fully realized. The future prosperity of the subject will require a capacity to work not only with the theologies of other faith traditions but also with our partner disciplines in the university. Graduate students today need to be encouraged not

---

13. From his Reformed Dutch context, Gijsbert van den Brink argues along similar lines for the positive multicultural contribution that a faculty of theology can make to the ideological diversity of the university. "The Future of Theology at Public Universities," *In die Skriflig* 54, no. 2 (2021): 1–9.

14. The Research Excellence Framework (REF) is a government initiative to assess the quality, impact, and infrastructure of research in UK universities. Since the 1980s, these exercises have been undertaken approximately every seven years. There are financial and reputational advantages in securing a high score for one's subject area, though the investment of institutional time in preparing for the REF is often perceived as excessive.

to become too narrow in their intellectual interests or to neglect opportunities to find out what is happening beyond their own field. We should not sit at home or in the library because someone is reading a paper at a research seminar which does not appear relevant to our own field of study.

Theology also has a distinctive role to play in the wider strategic aims of our universities as reflected in their mission statements. I offer two examples which sit close to what the University of Cambridge professes regarding freedom of inquiry and sustainability.

The first concerns democracy—here I echo some remarks of David Ford in *The Future of Christian Theology*.[15] There has long been a tacit assumption that Christian theology exists in a positive relationship to the ideals of a democratic society. Of course, that has not always been the case and it may be under some strain in our own day. But, for most in the academy and the churches, democracy is worth defending at a time of emboldened totalitarianism and rising tides of populism with erosion of those institutions that provide the necessary checks and balances for the functioning of a well-regulated democracy. David Runciman has recently written about "executive aggrandisement."[16] In this context, the contribution of faith communities to the health of our fragile democracies continues to be important. This has been explored in Jeffrey Stout's *Blessed are the Organized* which points to ways in which local organizations equip people with the necessary skills, motivation, and leadership to maintain the traditions of democracy.[17] Without such input, democratic culture becomes thinner and more fragile, suffering from a lack of involvement and mobilization. Here churches and other faith bodies have a key role to play in their local forms of service and organization. These generate democratic capital and attract people with the energy and skill to make a positive difference. Their contribution to "political liberalism" is not to be underestimated, and this is generally aligned with the aims of the university. The capacity of theology to establish links between the academy and civil society is strikingly evident in this context, not least with the more theoretical support that can be provided for notions of consent, equality, and solidarity.[18]

Academics have a responsibility toward the professional groups that they serve and from which they draw support—that applies to medicine, law, education, and also to theology. The recent attention to public engagement is only a reaffirmation of what has long been the case. For theology to demonstrate its relevance, we should expand rather than contract the scope of these relationships, for example

---

15. David Ford, *The Future of Christian Theology* (Oxford: Wiley Blackwell, 2011), 21–129.

16. David Runciman, *How Democracy Ends* (London: Profile Books, 2018), 30.

17. Jeffrey Stout, *Blessed Are the Organized: Grassroots Democracy in America* (Princeton: Princeton University Press, 2010).

18. Jonathan Chaplin argues the theological case for democracy on the basis of principles of consent, participation, and defense against tyranny, *Faith in Democracy: Framing a Politics of Deep Diversity* (London: SCM, 2021), 3–30.

with a wider range of churches, other faith bodies, and schoolteachers. These exemplify the capacity of theology to contribute to the fulfillment of those aims that typically appear in the mission statements of our contemporary universities.

Democracy is one example. Another is the multifaceted challenge of global sustainability. The recently published *Living Planet Report* of the World Wildlife Fund states: "A deep cultural and systemic shift is urgently needed, one that so far our civilization has failed to embrace: a transition to a society and economic system that values nature."[19] As COP 26 has vividly illustrated, this is easier said than done if "rhetorical leadership gets mistaken for the real thing."[20] If we are to make such a "deep cultural shift," then the world religions will have to play an important role by working among themselves and with other agencies to articulate a strong sense among their adherents of our connectedness to the natural world, to other creatures, and to future generations. The capacity of religion to give normative expression to the importance of our descendants and our temporary stewardship of the planet is well attested. If sustainability is a strategic aim of the university, then it will need to engage with religion along the way. Theologies of creation have an important role to play in shifting perceptions within our faith communities and these are most effectively developed in close conversation with other academic disciplines. The Christian doctrine of creation has historically suffered from two related problems. Either it merely stands as a prelude or scene-setting to the doctrine of redemption, or else it has become too anthropocentrically focused with its concentration on the *imago Dei*. Attention to our embeddedness in the natural world, the sharing of our habitat, and the significance of other creatures is steadily shifting or being shifted by grassroots theological opinion in advancing a more expansionist account of creation. Again, a theology situated in the university provides valuable links between the academy and an important section of civil society. And, in doing so, it promotes in its distinctive way one of the typical aims of the contemporary university.

Ecclesial Criticism

These reflections are offered in response to a possible secular critic. Since studying philosophy in the 1970s, I have always assumed that secularism would present the most familiar and formidable challenges to theologians. Yet now I detect a threat from elsewhere, namely the church. Anxiety about traditional models of theological education is acutely felt as ordinands train for different forms of ministry in a society that has largely seceded from its earlier Christian affiliation. Instead of maintaining an already Christianized society, the church faces a tougher challenge

---

19. *Living Planet Report 2020* | Official Site | WWF (panda.org) (accessed December 15, 2021).

20. COP26: The issues that stand in the way of progress—BBC News (accessed November 1, 2021).

of missional engagement, service, and outreach within a rapidly changing context marked by indifference, loss of institutional attachments, and unfamiliarity with the rituals, practices and beliefs of Christian faith. Might an apprentice model of ministry work better in which candidates are rooted in parishes, working alongside other ministers, and gaining their theological education through day-release or distance-learning modes? Can this generate greater resilience and a spiritual formation that is difficult to provide in a university setting? I do not doubt the greater need for resilience and spiritual formation in this setting, nor the need for changes in ordination training. *Gaps* and poorly fitting elements in any form of ministerial formation are not difficult to detect. Yet there remains an advantage in being exposed to current teaching and research in the theological disciplines and in mixing with students from a wide variety of backgrounds. The university can itself be seen as a microcosm of our wider society, the context in which ministry is to be exercised. The church can, and should, be enriched by exposure to scholarly excellence in the study of religion.

Here I recall an exchange that took place during a review at the Church of Ireland College in Dublin some years ago. Arriving at Trinity College, the Archbishop of Dublin was asked for his views on the quality of an educational program that involved church candidates spending time studying for a university degree. He said to the review body something along the following lines. Here I paraphrase. "I don't much like having to write a large cheque each year for our ordinands to be taught here, but I'm unwilling to tolerate a situation in which our clergy are preaching to congregations who are better educated than they are." In any case, while much Christian theology will be pursued in other settings, for example in church colleges, most of the teaching will continue to be undertaken by people who have obtained their doctorates in a residential university setting. This point has been made forcibly in reports on theological education in the United States. Even if the churches cease to outsource much of their theological education to the universities, they will continue to require educators who are university-trained.

A wide-scale ecclesiastical retreat from the university system would remove theological education from an important part of our cultural mainstream and the advantages of studying in a context enriched by multiplicity of approaches to the study of religion. Jonathan Sacks once wrote about the importance of people of faith being saved from believing too much in the wrong things.[21] The critical study of theology in the academy can be an important part of that process.

In summary, the pursuit of Christian theology offers an entry into the deepest and unavoidable questions that confront us as human beings. Such questions are embedded in all the major world religions. This pursuit will ensure an abiding interest on the part of students, while also generating a set of skills that are as adaptable as any in a liberal arts education. Enriched by location within a broad-spectrum university, research and teaching in theology can provide multiple

---

21. I discuss this in *Faith and Its Critics: A Conversation* (Oxford: Oxford University Press, 2009), 145.

points of constructive contact with civic society. These are readily aligned with the mission of the modern university. I have always regarded it as a mistake to adopt too defensive a posture on the place of theology in the university; even writing an essay on relevance has caused some unease. Does this arise from fear of extinction? One valuable lesson I learned from my teachers, especially John McIntyre, Tom Torrance, and James Mackey in Edinburgh and Basil Mitchell in Oxford, is that you should not apologize to anyone for studying theology. Instead, you should immerse yourself in the life of both your discipline and your institution, believing that you have the capacity to make as constructive and scholarly a contribution as anyone else.

EPILOGUE

Chapter 18

THEOLOGY AND LAUGHTER

One merry countenance may diffuse cheerfulness to many. . . . Laughter is none of the smallest bonds of common friendship. (Francis Hutcheson, "Thoughts on Laughter.")

Do you engage . . . faithfully, diligently, and cheerfully to discharge the duties of your ministry? (Church of Scotland, "Order for the Ordination of a Minister.")

Of all the theologians I can recollect, none has caused such hilarity in classrooms and conference halls (at least not intentionally) as George Newlands. So often self-effacing, his humor is infectious. A mark of that generosity he has long advocated, it has elicited the appreciation of students and colleagues, even among those who regularly find themselves in disagreement with him. The following is offered gratefully to him as a modest reflection on a neglected, but not unimportant, subject.

One should probably begin by noting that the subject of humor seems unpromising for a theological essay. Both the apparent lack of Scriptural allusions to this topic and also the relative paucity of resources in the history of the tradition present obstacles. And yet humor is so pervasive in our teaching, writing and collegial relations that it demands to be placed in some relation to theological descriptions of the virtues and skills required for living well together. Perhaps it is surprising too that with the (occasionally bombastic) stress upon community, fellowship and relationality in much contemporary theology, so little attention is devoted to the role of humor in maintaining and fostering friendship.[1]

Hutcheson versus Hobbes

One notable contribution to the sparse philosophical literature on the subject was made by Francis Hutcheson in the eighteenth century. Born into a Presbyterian

---

1. Recent exceptions include Kevin Hector, *Christianity as a Way of Life: A Systematic Theology* (New Haven: Yale University Press, 2023), 184–7, and Jan Martijn Abrahamse, "Appropriate Divine Laughter," *Journal of Reformed Theology* 15 (2021): 185–207.

manse in Ulster, Hutcheson entered the University of Glasgow in 1710 where he trained in classics and philosophy before beginning his Divinity course under John Simson. Returning to Ulster in 1718, he was licensed by the Presbytery of Armagh although he never held a ministerial charge; instead, he went to Dublin to take up a position in an academy for Presbyterian and other nonconformists. In 1729, following the death of Gershom Carmichael, Hutcheson was appointed to the Chair of Moral Philosophy in Glasgow. Although his views aroused some suspicion in the courts of the Church of Scotland, Hutcheson was a highly popular lecturer. (Is there a causal connection here?) From the 1730s, he abandoned the older practice of using Latin as the medium of instruction, preferring instead to teach in English.[2]

Typical of the Scottish Enlightenment to which he contributed so much, Hutcheson's philosophy is rooted in a providential theism that describes our natural constitution to equip us under the right conditions for intellectual, moral, and religious fulfillment. Yet in important respects this theism is quite distant from the Reformed orthodox traditions of Hutcheson's family background. His reflections on laughter are found in a set of three letters written for *The Dublin Journal* in 1725.[3] In an attack on Hobbes's egoistic thesis, Hutcheson offers a series of empirical observations about the different contexts of laughter and the functions that it serves. Hobbes had argued that the prime purpose of humor is to enable us to enjoy a pleasing comparison with the failings of others or even our own former selves. According to the account offered in the *Leviathan*, laughter is a "sudden glory" arising in persons that is "caused either by some sudden act of their own, that pleaseth them; or by the apprehension of some deformed thing in another, by comparison where they suddenly applaud themselves."[4]

This self-regarding account of laughter—it is often labeled as a superiority theory of humor—is seen as reductive and implausible by Hutcheson. Much of what makes us laugh bears little or no comparative relation to ourselves. We do not have to assume an attitude of superiority to the object or occasion of wit in order to laugh. In any case, much of what is far beneath us excites only our indifference, disgust or pity, but seldom our amusement. While admitting that on occasion we

---

2. For biographical information on Hutcheson see W. R. Scott, *Francis Hutcheson: His Life, Teaching and Position in the History of Philosophy* (Cambridge: Cambridge University Press, 1900).

3. The letters were republished as *Thoughts on Laughter and Observations on "The Fable of the Bees"* (Glasgow, 1758). They are reproduced with introductory comments in Gordon Graham (ed.), *Scottish Philosophy: Selected Writings 1690–1960* (Exeter: Imprint Academic Press, 2004), 25–37.

4. Thomas Hobbes, *Leviathan*, ed. C. B. Macpherson (Hardmondsworth: Penguin, 1972), I.6. For excerpts and comment on the leading philosophical literature on laughter see John Morreall (ed.), *Philosophy of Laughter and Humour* (Albany: State University of New York Press, 1987).

do enjoy ridiculing others in a self-satisfied manner, Hutcheson cannot find here an exhaustive account of laughter. Other explanations must be sought.

One source of non-egoistical laughter is described by Hutcheson as "parody and burlesque allusion." We are often moved by an incongruity of image or event, without ever imagining ourselves superior or more fortunate than another. He offers the following example.

> Many an orthodox Scotch Presbyterian (which few sects accuse of disregard for the holy scriptures) has been put to it to preserve his gravity, upon hearing the application of scripture made by his countryman, Dr Pitcairn, as he observed a crowd in the streets about a mason, who had fallen along with his scaffold, and was overwhelmed with the ruins of the chimney which he had been building, and which fell immediately after the fall of the poor mason: "blessed are the dead which die in the Lord, for they rest from their labours, and their works follow them."[5]

Discussing this example, Hutcheson notes that the humor arises not from any sense of superiority to the doctor, the apostle or the stonemason whose demise prior to the doctor's remark would have excited no pleasure or feeling of pre-eminence. The burlesque instead is generated by a sudden juxtaposition of images with contrary ideas and associations, or the drawing of resemblances from quite unlikely sources. In this case, it is the solemn pronunciation of a familiar sacred text in a situation in which it applies incongruously. Even an unintended pun in the course of an otherwise grave discourse can arouse our laughter without in the least diminishing our good opinion of the speaker. Hutcheson tends to focus on the notion of incongruity of image or circumstance as the key explanatory concept. Whether this is sufficiently comprehensive is not altogether clear. At the very least, a broad account of incongruity will be required to capture everything that causes laughter. Much humor arises from impropriety of behavior, although this might be represented as an incongruous set of actions or dispositions that deviate startlingly from norms of appropriateness.[6]

Yet Hutcheson seems broadly correct to point to the communal goods served by laughter as opposed to the narrower account of Hobbes. In this respect, his incongruity theory is more adequate than Hobbes's superiority theory. The function of humor is a social one, as opposed to the narrowly individualist explanation offered by Hobbes. Its contribution to cheerful and friendly society is not to be disaggregated into its value for the ends of each individual. Laughter, Hutcheson observes, is contagious, and promotes widespread merriment which is to everyone's benefit.

---

5. *Thoughts on Laughter*, 7–8.

6. This is discussed in the excellent analysis of Elizabeth Telfer, "Hutcheson's Reflections Upon Laugher," *Journal of Aesthetics and Art Criticism* 53 (1995): 359–69.

However, like other natural tendencies, the laughter of the ridiculous needs to be ordered by virtuous judgment. According to Hutcheson, some forms of ridicule are inappropriate, even contemptible. They can demean and dishonor. Some might consider the incident of the deceased stonemason to be lacking in propriety. On the other hand, the "engine of ridicule" when judiciously driven can chasten or amuse in the right context. It can cure us of our small faults, more effectively perhaps than a weighty sermon. Ridicule can deflate pomposity or exaggerated claims, as the example from another culture of Elijah and the prophets of Baal indicates. In this respect, laughter has a therapeutic value when properly exercised and regulated within friendship. Hutcheson assumes that a virtuous, sensible person will not be amused by demeaning forms of ridicule. Yet this may be contested. It is possible to perceive the ridiculing of individuals as both funny and hurtful. Jonathan Watson, the BBC Scotland sports impresario, once noted that some of the most amusing material sent to him has to be excluded on the grounds that it would be too offensive to its subjects.[7] Not all tabloid newspapers respect this boundary, and much of what is widely read involves a ridiculing that is intrusive, salacious, and demeaning. Here a more Hobbesian reading of public manners suddenly seems appropriate. The lampooning of politicians, celebrities and others does not always serve a legitimate communal purpose.

Hutcheson has little to say about laughter in relation to God and the religious life, yet he seems to regard the functions of laughter, like our innate sense of goodness and beauty, as a mark of providential design. "The implanting then a sense of the ridiculous, in our nature, was giving us an avenue to pleasure, and an easy remedy for discontent and sorrow."[8] The presence of laughter in human societies serves a wise and happy purpose; this is part of the way human nature has been constituted by its Maker. It promotes happiness and is not the least of the bonds of friendship. Quite how this occurs is not pursued by Hutcheson. It appears that the incongruous simply gives rise to that particular feeling of pleasure that is expressed in laughter. This is how we are made. Other accounts might of course be offered either as alternatives or as complements to the providential theistic explanation. There may indeed be some survival advantage through having a developed sense of humor. We rub along better with other persons through the uses of laughter. Laughter may even be conducive to our physiological condition as in the case of Mark Twain's observation of the old man who "laughed loud and joyously, shook up the details of his anatomy from head to foot, and ended by saying that such a laugh was money in a man's pocket, because it cut down the doctor's bills like everything."[9]

---

7. *Sunday Times—Scotland*, December 31, 2006.

8. *Thoughts on Laughter*, 36f.

9. Mark Twain, *The Adventures of Tom Sawyer* (New York: Modern Library Edition, 1940), 208. I owe this reference to Doris Donnelly, "Divine Folly: Being Religious and the Exercise of Humour," *Theology Today* 48 (1992): 396.

Hutcheson delineates many of the positive functions of humor; these include the hilarity of the burlesque, the conviviality of laughter, its contribution to friendship, and also some of the morally sobering effects of ridicule. At the same time, he acknowledges ways in which inappropriate laughter can diminish and corrupt us. Yet the roles of humor and laughter may be more various and wide-ranging even than conceived here, different types serving different purposes. There is little about its hopeful role amid suffering, its capacity to serve as a mark of redemption, or its enabling us to recognize our fragility and fallibility at critical moments in life, though this latter is suggested in his remarks about self-directed humor.

Laughter in Scripture

As a final-year philosophy student in Glasgow, I had a tutor who used to inform us that if had he to select between Socrates and Jesus, he would always choose the former because there was not a single joke in any of the gospels. Whether we were to take this remark seriously was not altogether clear, but it raises some interesting issues about the seeming absence of humor in Scripture. There are some sporadic references to laughter in Scripture. Yet these are infrequent, never indulgent, and often bracing. An early incidence in the canon occurs in Genesis 18:12 when the elderly Sarah laughs to herself on overhearing the divine promise that she and her husband will conceive a son. In part, this is a form of ridicule. The sheer improbability of their conceiving provokes a spontaneous reaction of mirth. We can also detect an element of the burlesque in this incident with its solemn promise of pregnancy to an elderly, incapacitated couple. When confronted by God, Sarah denies her laughter—it betokens a lack of faith—yet at the birth of Isaac in Genesis 21:6 laughter now finds its proper expression: "God has brought laughter for me: everyone who hears will laugh with me." The humor of ridicule and mockery now gives way to a shared celebration of the unexpected. Having earlier been the object of laughter, God is now its subject. The previous derision which divided Sarah from God is now overcome by a carnival atmosphere in which people are gathered to celebrate an event that is good for the whole community.

This disjunction of two forms of humor—mockery and celebratory—is also reflected in the Psalms. The laughter of derision or scoffing is both a mark of sinners (Psalm 1:1) but also of God whose own laughter will soon overcome and trump that of Israel's enemies (Psalm 2:4). Here there is a division of victor and defeated that is the occasion of a haughty scorn. The tables are turned on the scoffers of unrighteousness by God. *Wer zuletzt lacht, lacht am besten.* Jeering is the prerogative of the victor, an incidence of humor that offers some support to the Hobbesian. Hints of the satisfaction and derision that result from the defeat of one's enemies are present in other parts of Scripture, particularly in the apocalyptic literature. This may have a role in exhorting the faithful to persevere while on the underside of history, yet it cannot be the most befitting form of laughter for those who see their salvation as the outcome of divine mercy and love. Elsewhere in the Psalms, there is gifted by God a laughter of consolation and reward that gathers people together. It occasions a celebration, in which joy is enhanced by the element of surprise. "When the Lord restored the fortunes of Zion, we were like those who dream. Then our mouth was filled with laughter, and our tongue with shouts of joy" (Psalm 126:2).[10]

Compare this with Abraham's earlier laughter at Genesis 17:17 when he prostrates himself before God and laughs at the promise of a son. This humbling of self before God is not equivalent to the more impertinent laughter of Sarah in Genesis 18:12. There is an intermingling of disbelief with trust that the text seems to affirm. In this context, Abraham's laughter tilts in the direction of faith rather than despair or cynicism. Doubt is embraced by a practical obedience, a commitment that prevails over his natural skepticism. It is a laughter that is given its proper place; tolerated by God, there is no attempt to suppress it or any suggestion that it is misplaced. In his study of laughter, Karl-Josef Kuschel questions whether this image has been given its proper place in Christian theology.[11] It is certainly not invoked by Paul in his interpretation of Abraham in Romans 4, although Judaism's religious use of humor may have something to teach us here in the ways it resonates with the pattern of Abraham's response to God. Witness the ways in which Jewish humor can display a faithfulness that does not suppress questions, a gentle self-mockery that can also expose the flaws in others, together with a commitment to perseverance in the faith even in difficult times. A Jewish father once complained that his son had converted to Christianity. "What did you do?" his friend inquired of him. "I spoke to God about it," he replied. "And what did God say?" "God told me that his son had done the same. So I then asked him what he did about it. God replied, 'I wrote a new testament.'"[12]

The New Testament says little explicitly about laughter that is of a positive nature. Attempts by some exegetes to depict the gospel story as replete with comic incident can easily become contrived, if not indeed laughable in themselves. To give but one example—the incident over the legitimacy of paying taxes to Caesar is held by one commentator to end hilariously since we must assume, it is argued, that Jesus simply pocketed the coin that was handed to him.[13] Yet this is never stated by the gospel writers nor does the reaction of Jesus' audience suggest it. It is an ingenious and creative reading of the text, but it reveals the danger attending arguments from silence. Nowhere do we read that Jesus laughed; instead, we find others mocking him at his trial and crucifixion. It is his detractors alone who scoff.

---

10. This is echoed by Dante's arrival in Paradise when he hears the choir of angels singing praises to the Trinity. He writes, "*mi sembiava un riso/ de l'universo*"—"it seemed like the laughter of the universe" (*Paradiso*, Canto 27). I owe this allusion to Harvey Cox, *The Feast of Fools* (Cambridge, MA: Harvard University Press, 1969), 155–6.

11. Karl-Josef Kuschel, *Laughter: A Theological Reflection* (London: SCM, 1994). In much of what follows, I am indebted to his analysis.

12. See ibid., 106.

13. Attributed to Robert Funk, this is discussed by Donnelly, "Divine Folly," 390.

Nevertheless, there are aspects of the gospel story that resonate with the laughter of Abraham, Sarah and the redeemed of Psalm 126. The joy that is occasioned by the wonderful birth of Jesus, the gospel message of the divine commonwealth, and the breaking news of the Resurrection is of this type. It occasions surprise and joy as God's people are united in praise. Mourning gives way to celebration, darkness finally yields to light. Although it is not said that those who laugh are blessed—indeed those who laugh now are warned in Luke 6:25—nevertheless the Beatitudes provide an occasion for celebration among the downcast faithful. Their joy results primarily from their being uplifted by God, not in their scoffing at those who are excluded. The tension between Hutchesonian and Hobbesian approaches to laughter appears to be resolved by God's grace in favor of the former, even though one cannot deny that this tension is present in Scripture and parts of church tradition.[14]

A stronger argument from silence than the one noted above will plausibly claim that the prevalence of feasting, healing, conviviality and the celebration of divine grace in the ministry of Jesus provides scope for an appropriate theology of laughter.[15] "The wedding guests cannot fast while the bridegroom is with them, can they?" (Mark 2:19). In light of this, how could humor be missing from Jesus' table fellowship? Such laughter will have performed several functions—a reinforcement of physical healing and personal transformation together with a defiance of alien cosmic forces, but not a self-satisfied mockery. Schillebeeckx once wrote of "the impossibility of being sad in the presence of Jesus."[16]

Redemptive Humor

Three types of humor theory are prevalent in much philosophical and psychological discussion. Already we have alluded to two of these: theories of superiority and incongruity. A third type, often associated with Freud, is the theory of relief.[17] Jokes, laughter, and humor provide release from inhibition or restraint. Like dreams, a joke may be a way in which we outwit or overcome suppressed fear or anxiety. In doing so, the joke brings release from some internal or external censor. According to Freud, though not all humor functions in one way, this is one type that can be

---

14. It would be worth considering in this context whether the historical attraction of the doctrine of double predestination partly resides in the manner in which the beauty and pleasures of heaven are positively enhanced by the righteous damnation of the reprobate in hell. In this respect, dualism is a feature of some theological aesthetics. A final eschatological separation can here be depicted as a transcendental theatre of cruelty. "It is not enough to succeed. Others must fail."

15. See Kuschel, *Laughter*, 74.

16. Edward Schillbeeckx, *Jesus: An Experiment in Christology* (London: Collins, 1979).

17. For a survey of these theories, see D. H. Monro, "Humour," in *Encyclopedia of Philosophy*, Vol. 4, ed. P. Edwards (New York: Macmillan, 1967), 90–3.

identified.[18] Without committing to a Freudian explanation of what is going on here, one can acknowledge the contribution of humor to release from anxiety and the overcoming of fear. The laughter that is occasioned by sudden and unexpected liberation, as in the aforementioned Psalm 126, belongs in this neighborhood. The sudden deliverance from captivity and restoration of the people's well-being is naturally occasioned by the outbreak of laughter and joy.

Even amid near hopeless circumstances, humor has a role to play in affirming faith and in the positive reassertion of the self when threatened by despair. This emerges in Brian Keenan's haunting description of his long imprisonment in Beirut after he and others had been taken hostage. Together with his cell companion John McCarthy, he maintained his faith by a dogged recourse to laughter. So, he concludes, God is to be found decisively in humor.

> We would imitate different characters as we played, or more frequently we would create characters out of our imagination. With these characters we entertained ourselves for many hours. Through them we brought other people into the cell to be with us, to talk to us or to make us laugh. In that laughter we discovered something of what life really is. We were convinced by the condition we were kept in and the lives that we managed to lead that if there was a God that God was above all else, a comedian. In humour, sometimes hysterical, sometimes calculated, often childish, life was returned to us.[19]

Of the three types of humor noted earlier—superiority, incongruity and relief—all can be detected in portions of Scripture. My claim is that the second and third are more appropriate to a gospel of grace, although the force and temptation of the first should not be underestimated, particularly among those who seem so often on the losing side of life. Given the centrality of humor to the ways we live, it would be surprising if faith did not find ways of appropriating laughter and recognition as a divine gift.

The tradition, however, has sometimes been nervous around the phenomenon of laughter. Whilst acknowledging that it can have a proper place, John Chrysostom cautions his hearers against a complacent, lighthearted, and frivolous attitude to life. The spectator sports and entertainments of his day are condemned. Now living in an age when Christian persecution has diminished, his congregation must attend to the seriousness of faith. Preaching on the journey of the Magi in Matthew 2, Chrysostom urges his hearers against complacency and an easy lifestyle. God is known through tears of weeping, not by laughter. To enter the kingdom of heaven, we must avoid the "senseless mirth" of those who scorned Noah's efforts to construct an ark of salvation.

---

18. Sigmund Freud, *The Joke and Its Relation to the Unconscious* (London: Penguin, 2002). Freud's study itself contains not a few good jokes, particularly those drawn from his Jewish heritage.

19. Brian Keenan, *An Evil Cradling* (London: Vintage, 1993), 172.

The things then being so great, for which thou art to give account, dost thou sit laughing and talking wittily, and giving thyself up to luxury. . . . Therefore it is that Christ discourses to us much of mourning, and blesses them that mourn, and pronounces them that laugh wretched. For this is not the theatre of laughter, neither did we come together for this intent, that we may give way to immoderate mirth, but that we may groan, and by this groaning inherit a kingdom.[20]

Much in Chrysostom's strictures against laughter is present in later medieval and Protestant theology. The fear of trivializing human life, of diminishing our responsibility and of dishonoring God prevented a proper appropriation of humor. This has led to frequent complaints of repressiveness, particularly among Scottish literati. With their tight-lipped brilliance, Crichton Smith complained, the black-hatted and white-collared gentlemen of the church have suppressed the magic of the theatre.[21] On the other hand, the capacity of humor to be misappropriated and overextended remains a legitimate worry. We see this today in some examples of Protestant worship that have become little more than forms of light entertainment. A preacher can use humor creatively, but when he or she starts to play for the laughs then the act of worship is demeaned.

To some extent, the views of Chrysostom may reflect the influence of an earlier Greek tradition.[22] While recognizing the legitimacy of some forms of humor, both Plato and Aristotle express anxiety about its capacity to take over and so to distort human relations and understanding. For Plato, in particular, laughter is viewed with deep suspicion. At times, it can represent a mocking of others that is unworthy and demeaning. On other occasions, it produces a loss of affective control that is particularly unhelpful for educating and disciplining the young. Comedy is always an inferior form of literature for this reason. As one might expect, Aristotle qualifies the Platonic account. Laughter has some useful functions, while an ordered humor forms part of the make-up of the most attractive personalities. In describing a moderated humor, Aristotle offers one of the best examples of his doctrine of the virtuous mean. The gentle, ironic humor of his ideal citizen avoids both the grim disposition of the humorless and the folly of those who lacks genuine seriousness. There is here a balanced recognition of the proper place, yet capacity for distortion that laughter affords. At least formally, this moderated approval of humor might usefully be appropriated by the theologian.

---

20. "Homily VI on Matthew 2:1-2," in *Nicene and Post-Nicene Fathers*, First Series, Vol. 10, 41.

21. Iain Crichton Smith, *Murdo: The Life and Works* (Edinburgh: Birlinn, 2001), 227. While this may have some limited application, it does not function well as a blanket condemnation of Scottish Presbyterianism.

22. Set in the middle ages, Umberto Eco's celebrated novel *The Name of the Rose* explores the clash between an Aristotelian humanism and Augustinian Christianity. In this context, the question of whether Christ laughed is raised.

Those who carry humour to excess are thought to be vulgar buffoons, striving after humour at all costs, and aiming rather at raising a laugh than at saying what is becoming and at avoiding pain to the object of their fun; while those who can neither make a joke themselves nor put up with those who do are thought to be boorish and unpolished. But those who joke in a tasteful way are called ready-witted, which implies a sort of readiness to turn this way and that; for such sallies are thought to be movements of the character, and as bodies are discriminated by their movements, so too are characters. [23]

Aristotle's Athenian gentleman, however, may himself be quite limited ethically. Regulated by a particular social status, he is unaware of the biblical humility that arises from an awareness of one's dependence on God's mercy. Humility is not one of his virtues. This different context affords opportunities for laughter at oneself, divine grace, and the incongruity of the "treasure in earthen vessels." These too can afford a moderated humor, albeit one that differs in outlook from the aristocratic model. It may be worth comparing this with some remarks of Karl Barth about the importance of humor in the theologian.[24] As self-directed, humor should remind us of our status as sinners *simul iustus et peccator*. This enables us in turn to laugh at others, though never spitefully or with *Schadenfreude*.[25] In Barth's case, one manifestation of this self-deprecation was a commendable lack of interest in producing pupils who would slavishly adopt his patterns of thought.[26] Laughter may also be defiant; it is an affirmation of God's "Yes" amid suffering and the potential for despair, not unlike Keenan's recourse to comedy as a means of maintaining dignity and hope in the most harrowing of circumstances.[27] Finally, humor is a mark of the freedom of the Christian; it is a sign of the gospel that elicits beauty and joy. In the context of his theological aesthetics, Barth claims that any expression of the faith that lacks beauty or humor is deficient; it can offer only an attenuated account of the good news of God.[28]

---

23. Aristotle, *Nicomachean Ethics*, trans. Sir David Ross (London: Oxford University Press, 1972), 1128a1.

24. E.g., *Ethics* (Edinburgh: T&T Clark, 1981), 506–12. Barth notes that one problem we have to face in reading Calvin is his inability to laugh.

25. Hans Frei, however, worried that Barth's self-deprecating humor only reinforced some of his failings. "His protective device against his own, as well as others', pretensions was frequent ironization, self-ironization and self-needling, sometimes in mock-solemn, mock-elevated language. It is an interesting but double-edged instrument, and it says much about Barth.. . . Ritual exorcism by humor all too often reaffirms the tenant rights of the very demons seemingly expelled, especially in the case of forceful personalities." *Types of Christian Theology* (New Haven: Yale University Press, 1992), 151.

26. This is noted by Daniel L. Migliore in his account of the role of humor in Barth's theology. "Editorial," *Theology Today* 43 (1986): 309–15.

27. Harvey Cox speaks about laughter as hope's last weapon. See *The Feast of Fools*, 157.

28. See also *Church Dogmatics* III/4 (Edinburgh: T&T Clark, 1961), 665ff.

Set in this light, laughter is occasioned, perhaps even demanded, by a theology of the forgiveness of sins, the ethical demands under which this places us, and the final hope that it occasions. When pressured to describe the essence of the faith in ten words, Will Campbell finally produced eight. "We're all bastards, but God loves us anyway."[29] Amid the many forms of gratitude that this theme occasions, there is surely a place for endless laughter.

---

29. His companion "didn't comment on what he thought about the summary except to say, after he had counted the words on his fingers, 'I gave you a ten word limit. If you want to try again you have two words left.' I didn't try again but he often reminded me of what I had said that day." Will Campbell, *Brother to a Dragonfly* (London: Continuum, 2000), 220.

BIBLIOGRAPHY

Abraham, William J. *Divine Agency and Divine Action: Systematic Theology*, Vol. III. Oxford: Oxford University Press, 2018.
Abrahamse, Jan Martijn. "Appropriate Divine Laughter." *Journal of Reformed Theology* 15 (2021): 185–207.
Adams, Marilyn McCord. *Christ and Horrors: The Coherence of Christology*. Cambridge: Cambridge University Press, 2006.
Ahnert, Thomas. *The Moral Culture of the Scottish Enlightenment 1690–1805*. New Haven: Yale University Press, 2015.
Aisthorpe, Steve. *The Invisible Church*. Edinburgh: St Andrew Press, 2016.
Althaus, Paul. *Theology of Martin Luther*. Philadelphia: Fortress, 1966.
Altmann, Alexander. "*Homo Imago Dei* in Jewish and Christian Theology." *Journal of Religion* 48, no. 3 (1968): 235–59.
Alvey, James. *Adam Smith: Optimist or Pessimist?* Aldershot: Ashgate, 2004.
Anselm. "Proslogion." In *Anselm of Canterbury: The Major Works*, edited by Brian Davies and G. R. Evans, 82–104. Oxford: Oxford University Press, 2008.
Ariarajah, Wesley. *The Bible and People of Other Faiths*. Geneva: World Council of Churches, 1989.
Aristotle. *Nicomachean Ethics*, translated by David Ross. London: Oxford University Press, 1972.
Atkins, Peter. *On Being: A Scientist's Exploration of the Great Questions of Existence*. Oxford: Oxford University Press, 2011.
Atwell, Robert, Christopher Irvine, and Sue Moore. *A Time for Creation: Liturgical Resources for Creation and the Environment*. London: Church House Publishing, 2020.
Augustine. *City of God*, edited by David Knowles, translated by Henry Bettenson. Harmondsworth: Penguin, 1972.
Augustine. *Confessions*, translated by Henry Chadwick. Oxford: Oxford University Press, 1992.
Auld, Graeme. "*Imago Dei* in Genesis: Speaking in the Image of God." *Expository Times* 116 (2005): 259–62.
Auld, Graeme. "Pluralism Where Least Expected: Joshua 22 in Biblical Context." *Expository Times* 122, no. 8 (2011): 374–9.
Baggini, Julian, ed. *Hume on Religion*. London: Routledge, 2010.
Baillie, Donald M. *God Was In Christ: An Essay on Incarnation and Atonement*. London: Faber and Faber, 1948.
Baillie, John. *Our Knowledge of God*. Oxford: Oxford University Press, 1939.
Barr, James. *Biblical Faith and Natural Theology*. Oxford: Clarendon, 1993.
Barrett, Justin L. *Cognitive Science, Religion, and Theology: From Human Minds to Divine Minds*. West Conshohocken: Templeton, 2011.
Barth, Karl. *Church Dogmatics* II/1, edited by Thomas F. Torrance and Geoffrey W. Bromiley. Edinburgh: T&T Clark, 1957.
Barth, Karl. *Church Dogmatics* IV/3, 2 vols, edited by Thomas F. Torrance and Geoffrey W. Bromiley. Edinburgh: T&T Clark, 1962.
Barth, Karl. *Dogmatics in Outline*. London: SCM, 1949.

Barth, Karl. *Ethics*. Edinburgh: T&T Clark, 1981.
Barth, Karl. *The Knowledge of God and the Service of God*. London: Hodder & Stoughton, 1938.
Barton, John. *The Nature of Biblical Criticism*. Philadelphia: Westminster John Knox, 2007.
Bauckham, Richard. *Jesus and the Eyewitnesses*. Grand Rapids: Eerdmans, 2006.
Bauckham, Richard. "Reading Scripture as a Coherent Story." In *The Art of Reading Scripture*, edited by Ellen F. Davis and Richard B. Hays, 42–3. Grand Rapids: Eerdmans, 2003.
Bavinck, Herman. *Reformed Dogmatics: God and Creation*, Vol. 2. Grand Rapids: Baker, 2004.
BBC News. *COP26: The Issues that Stand in the Way of Progress* [webpage]. 2021. https://www.bbc.co.uk/news/science-environment-59114255 (accessed October 10, 2023).
Beattie, James. *Essay on the Nature and Immutability of Truth*. Dublin: Thomas Ewing, 1773.
Bediako, Kwame. *Christianity in Africa: The Renewal of a Non-Western Religion*. Edinburgh: Edinburgh University Press, 1995.
Bentley Hart, David. *The Doors of the Sea: Where Was God in the Tsunami?* Grand Rapids: Baker, 2005.
Bergjan, Silke-Petra. *Der Fürsorgende Gott*. Berlin: De Gruyter, 2002.
Berkhof, Hendrikus. *Christian Faith: An Introduction to the Study of the Faith*, revised ed. Grand Rapids: Eerdmans, 1986.
Berkouwer, C. G. *Holy Scripture*. Grand Rapids: Eerdmans, 1975.
Berners-Lee, Mike. *There Is No Planet B: A Handbook for the Make or Break Years*. Cambridge: Cambridge University Press, 2021.
Berry, Wendell. *The Unsettling of America: Culture & Agriculture*. San Francisco: Sierra Books, 1977.
Biéler, André. *Calvin's Economic and Social Thought*. Geneva: World Council of Churches, 2005.
Biggar, Nigel. *Between Kin and Cosmopolis: An Ethic of the Nation*. Eugene: Cascade, 2014.
Blackburn, Simon. "Playing Hume's Hand." In *Religion and Hume's Legacy*, edited by D. Z. Phillips and Timothy Tessin, 3–16. Basingstoke: Macmillan 1999.
Bond, Helen K. *The Historical Jesus: A Guide for the Perplexed*. London: T&T Clark, 2012.
Bondi, Liz. "Research and Therapy: Generating Meaning and Feeling Gaps." *Quantitative Inquiry* 19, no.1 (2013): 9–19.
Bonhoeffer, Dietrich. "Letters and Papers from Prison." In *Collected Works*, Vol. 8, edited by John W. de Gruchy, translated by Christian Gremmels et al. Minneapolis: Fortress Press, 2010.
Bosch, David J. *Transforming Mission: Paradigm Shifts in Theology of Mission*. Maryknoll: Orbis, 1991.
Broadie, Alexander. *History of Scottish Philosophy*. Edinburgh: Edinburgh University Press, 2009.
Broadie, Alexander. "Sympathy and the Impersonal Spectator." In *The Cambridge Companion to Adam Smith*, edited by Knud Haakonssen, 158–88. Cambridge: Cambridge University Press, 2006.
Brooke, John Hedley. "Natural Law in the Natural Sciences: The Origins of Modern Atheism?." *Science and Christian Belief* 4, no. 2 (1992): 83–103.
Brooke, John Hedley and Geoffrey Cantor. *Reconstructing Nature: The Engagement of Science and Religion*. Edinburgh: T&T Clark, 2000.

Brown, David. *Divine Generosity and Human Creativity: Theology through Symbol, Painting and Architecture*, edited by Christopher R. Brewer and Robert McSwain. London: Routledge, 2017.
Brown, David. *Divine Humanity: Kenosis Explored and Defended*. London: SCM, 2011.
Brown, Stewart J. "Moderate Theology and Preaching c. 1750–1800." In *The History of Scottish Theology: The Early Enlightenment to the Late Victorian Era*, Vol. II, edited by David Fergusson and Mark W. Elliott, 69–83. Oxford: Oxford University Press, 2019.
Brown, Stewart J. *Providence and Empire 1815–1914*. Harlow: Longman, 2008.
Brown, Stewart J. "Reform, Reconstruction, Reaction: The Social Vision of Scottish Presbyterianism." *Scottish Journal of Theology* 44 (1991): 489–518.
Brown, William P. *The Ethos of the Cosmos: The Genesis of Moral Imagination in the Bible*. Grand Rapids: Eerdmans, 1999.
Browning, Don. *Reviving Christian Humanism: The New Conversation on Spirituality, Theology and Psychology*. Philadelphia: Fortress, 2010.
Bruce, A. B. *The Providential Order of the World*. New York: Scribner's, 1905.
Brueggemann, Walter. *Theology of the Old Testament: Testimony, Dispute, Advocacy*. Minneapolis: Augsburg Press, 1997.
Brunner, Emil. *Die Mystik und Das Wort: Der Gegensatz zwischen moderner Religionsaufassung und christlichem Glauben dargestellt an der Theologie Schleiermachers*. Tübingen: J. C. B. Mohr, 1928
Buber, Martin. *Eclipse of God: Studies in the Relation between Religion and Philosophy*. Princeton: Princeton University Press, 2016.
Buckley, Michael J. *At the Origins of Modern Atheism*. New Haven: Yale University Press, 1987.
Busch, Eberhard. *Karl Barth: His Life from Letters and Autobiographical Texts*. London: SCM, 1975.
Caird, Edward. *The Evolution of Religion*. Glasgow: Maclehose, 1893.
Calderwood, Henry. *David Hume*. Edinburgh: Oliphant, Anderson & Ferrier, 1989.
Calvin, John. *Institutes of the Christian Religion*, 2 vols, edited by John T. McNeill, translated by Ford Lewis Battles. Philadelphia: Westminster Press, 1960.
Campbell, Alastair V. *Rediscovering Pastoral Care*. London: Darton, Longman and Todd, 1986.
Campbell, Gordon. *The Bible: The Story of the King James Version*. Oxford: Oxford University Press, 2010.
Campbell, John McLeod. *The Nature of the Atonement*. London: Macmillan, 1856.
Campbell, Will. *Brother to a Dragonfly*. London: Continuum, 2000.
Carey, Daniel. "Francis Hutcheson's Philosophy and the Scottish Enlightenment: Reception, Reputation and Legacy." In *Scottish Philosophy in the Eighteenth Century: Morals, Politics, Art, Religion*, Vol. 1, edited by Aaron Garrett and James A. Harris, 36–85. Oxford: Oxford University Press, 2015.
Carr, Wesley. "A Developing Establishment." *Theology* 102 (1999): 2–10.
Cassullo, Gabriele. "Back to the Roots: The Influence of Ian. D. Suttie on British Psychoanalysis." *American Imago* 67 (2010): 5–22.
Chalmers, Thomas. *On the Power, Wisdom, and Goodness of God as Manifested in the Adaptation of External Nature to the Moral and Intellectual Constitution of Man*, 2 vols. London: W. Pickering, 1833.
Chaplin, Jonathan. *Beyond Establishment: Resetting Church-State Relations in England*. London: SCM, 2022.

Chaplin, Jonathan. *Faith in Democracy: Framing a Politics of Deep Diversity*. London: SCM, 2021.
Charry, Ellen. *God and the Art of Happiness*. Grand Rapids: Eerdmans, 2010.
Cheyne, A. C. *The Transforming of the Kirk: Religious Scotland's Victorian Revolution*. Edinburgh: St Andrew Press, 1983.
Church of England Archbishops' Council. *Common Worship: Services and Prayers for the Church of England*. London: Church House, 2000.
Church of Scotland Panel on Worship. *Church of Scotland Book of Common Order*. Edinburgh: St Andrew Press, 1994.
Clough, David L. *On Animals: Systematic Theology*, Vol. 1. London: T&T Clark, 2011.
Coakley, Sarah. *Powers and Submissions: Spirituality, Philosophy and Gender*. Oxford: Blackwell, 2002.
Cochrane, Arthur C. *Reformed Confessions of the 16th Century*. London: SCM, 1966.
Coffey, John. *Persecution and Toleration in Protestant England 1558–1689*. Harlow: Longman, 2000.
Collins, Francis. *The Language of God: A Scientist Presents Evidence for Belief*. New York: Free Press, 2006.
Collins, John J. *The Bible After Babel: Historical Criticism in a Postmodern Age*. Grand Rapids: Eerdmans, 2005.
Cone, James H. *The Cross and the Lynching Tree*. New York: Orbis, 2011.
Costello, John. *John Macmurray: A Biography*. Edinburgh: Floris Books, 2002.
Cottingham, John. *Philosophy of Religion: Towards a More Humane Approach*. Cambridge: Cambridge University Press, 2014.
Cox, Harvey. *The Feast of Fools*. Cambridge, MA: Harvard University Press, 1969.
Craig, Cairns. *Intending Scotland*. Edinburgh: Edinburgh University Press, 2009.
Craig, William Lane. *The Only Wise God: The Compatibility of Divine Foreknowledge and Human Freedom*. Eugene: Wipf & Stock, 1999.
Cross, Richard. *Duns Scotus*. Oxford: Oxford University Press, 1999.
Currie, Thomas Christian. *The Only Sacrament Left To Us: The Threefold Word of God in Karl Barth's Theology and Ecclesiology*. Eugene: Pickwick, 2015.
Daley, Brian. *God Visible: Patristic Christology Reconsidered*. Oxford: Oxford University Press, 2018.
Davie, Grace. *Religion in Britain: A Persistent Paradox*. Oxford: Wiley Blackwell, 2015.
Davies, Brian. *The Thought of Thomas Aquinas*. Oxford: Clarendon, 1992.
Davis, Ellen F. "Teaching the Bible Confessionally in the Church." In *The Art of Reading Scripture*, edited by Ellen F. Davis and Richard B. Hays, 9–26. Grand Rapids: Eerdmans, 2003.
Davison, Andrew. *Astrobiology and Christian Doctrine*. Cambridge: Cambridge University Press, 2023.
Dawkins, Richard. *The God Delusion*. London: Bantam, 2006.
de Gruchy, John. *Being Human: Confessions of a Christian Humanist*. London: SCM, 2006.
Deane-Drummond, Celia. "God's Image and Likeness in Humans and Other Animals: Performative Soul-Making and Graced Nature." *Zygon* 47, no. 4 (2012): 934–48.
DeHart, Paul R. "Leviathan Leashed: The Incoherence of Absolute Sovereign Power." *Critical Review* 25, no. 1 (2013): 1–37.
Dell, Katharine J. *The Lord by Wisdom Founded the Earth: Creation and Covenant in Old Testament Theology*. Baylor: Baylor University Press, 2023.
Dennett, Daniel C. *Breaking the Spell: Religion as a Natural Phenomenon*. London: Penguin, 2007.

Dennett, Daniel C. *Darwin's Dangerous Idea: Evolution and the Meanings of Life*. London: Penguin, 1995.
Dixon, John W. *The Christ of Michelangelo: An Essay on Carnal Spirituality*. University of South Florida: Scholars Press, 1994.
Dobbs, Trevor. *Faith, Theology and Psychoanalysis: The Life and Thought of Harry S. Guntrip*. Eugene: Pickwick, 2007.
Donnelly, Doris. "Divine Folly: Being Religious and the Exercise of Humour." *Theology Today* 48 (1992): 381–507.
Donnelly, Michael. *Scotland's Stained Glass: Making the Colours Sing*. Edinburgh: Historic Scotland, 1997.
Dowey, Edward A. "Law in Luther and Calvin." *Theology Today* 41 (1984): 146–53.
Dowey, Edward A. *The Knowledge of God in Calvin's Theology*. New York: Columbia University Press, 1952.
Dowey, Edward A. "The Word of God as Scripture and Preaching." In *Later Calvinism: International Perspectives*, edited by W. Fred Graham, 5–18. Kirksville: Northeast Missouri State University, 1994.
Dulles, Avery. *Models of the Church*. New York: Image Books, 2014.
Dyrness, William A. *Reformed Theology and Visual Culture: The Protestant Imagination from Calvin to Edwards*. Grand Rapids: Eerdmans, 2004.
Eco, Umberto. *The Name of the Rose*. San Diego: Harcourt, 1994.
Elliott, Mark W. *Providence Perceived: Divine Action from a Human Point of View*. Berlin: De Gruyter, 2015.
Emerson, Ralph Waldo. *Political Writings*, edited by Kenneth S. Sacks. Cambridge: Cambridge University Press, 2008.
Eze, E. C., ed. *Race and the Enlightenment: A Reader*. Oxford: Blackwell, 1997.
Falkenstein, Lorne. "Hume on 'Genuine', 'True', and 'Rational' Religion." *Eighteenth-Century Thought* 4 (2009): 171–201.
Fergusson, David. "Adam Smith on Ethics and Religion." *Humanities and Culture* 52 (2020): 53–72.
Fergusson, David. "Aesthetics of the Reformed Tradition." In *Worship and Liturgy in Context: Studies of Theology and Practice*, edited by Duncan B. Forrester and Douglas C. Gay, 23–35. London: SCM, 2009.
Fergusson, David. *Faith and Its Critics: A Conversation*. Oxford: Oxford University Press, 2009.
Fergusson, David. "Hume Amongst the Theologians." In *History of Scottish Theology: The Early Enlightenment to the Late Victorian Era*, Vol. II, edited by David Fergusson and Mark W. Elliott, 301–13. Oxford: Oxford University Press, 2019.
Fergusson, David. "Jesus and the Faith-History Problem Today." In *Jesus Christ Today: Studies of Christology in Various Contexts*, edited by Stuart G. Hall, 265–82. Berlin: Gruyter, 2009.
Fergusson, David. "Kenosis and Divine Humility." In *Kenosis: The Self-Emptying of Christ in Scripture and Theology*, edited by Paul T. Nimmo and Keith L. Johnson, 194–211. Grand Rapids: Eerdmans, 2022.
Fergusson, David. "Mapping the Church: Current Challenges of History and Mission." In *Engaging Ecclesiology*, edited by Andrew McGowan, 1–17. Eugene: Wipf & Stock, 2023.
Fergusson, David. "Natural Theology after Darwin." In *Darwinism and Natural Theology: Evolving Perspectives*, edited by Andrew Robinson, 78–95. Newcastle: Cambridge Scholars Publishing, 2012.

Fergusson, David. "Persons in Relation: The Interaction of Philosophy, Theology and Psychotherapy in 20th Century Scotland." *Journal of Practical Theology* 5, no. 3 (2013): 287–306.
Fergusson, David. "Politics, Society and Law." In *The Oxford Handbook of Reformed Theology*, edited by Michael Allen and Scott Swain, 592–608. Oxford: Oxford University Press, 2020.
Fergusson, David. "Providence after Darwin." In *Theology After Darwin*, edited by Michael Northcott and R. J. Berry, 73–88. Milton Keynes: Paternoster, 2009.
Fergusson, David. "Providence and Analytic Theology." In *The T&T Clark Companion to Analytic Theology*, edited by James Arcadi and James Turner, 155–64. London: T&T Clark, 2021.
Fergusson, David. "Reformed Social Theology." In *The Calling of the Church in Times of Polarization, Studies in Reformed Theology*, edited by Heleen Zorgdrager, Pieter Vos, and Eddy van der Borght, 179–97. Leiden, Brill, 2022.
Fergusson, David. "The Absence of God and its Contextual Significance in Hume." *Journal of Scottish Philosophy* 11, no. 1 (2013): 69–85.
Fergusson, David. "The Bible and Modernity." In *The Bible: Culture, Community and Society*, edited by Neil Messer and Angus Paddison, 9–30. London: Bloomsbury T&T Clark, 2013.
Fergusson, David. "The Last Judgement." In *Theological Theology: Essays in Honour of John Webster*, edited by R. David Nelson, Darren Sarisky, and Justin Stratis, 75–88. London: T&T Clark, 2015.
Fergusson, David. "The Place of Christian Theology in the Academy Today." *International Journal for the Study of the Christian Church* 21, no. 3/4 (2021): 212–21.
Fergusson, David. *The Providence of God: A Polyphonic Approach*. Cambridge: Cambridge University Press, 2018.
Fergusson, David. "Theology and Laughter." In *The God of Love and Human Dignity: Essays in Honour of George M Newlands*, edited by Paul Middleton, 107–16. London: T&T Clark, 2007.
Fergusson, David. "Theology and Therapy: Maintaining the Connection." *Pacifica* 26 (2013): 3–16.
Fergusson, David. "Theology of Providence." *Theology Today* 67 (2010): 261–78.
Fergusson, David. "Types of Natural Theology." In *The Evolution of Rationality: Interdisciplinary Essays in Honor of J. Wentzel van Huyssteen*, edited by F. Le Ron Shults, 380–93. Grand Rapids: Eerdmans, 2006.
Fergusson, David. "Visual Images and Reformed Anxieties: Some Scottish Reflections." *Princeton Theological Review* 21, no. 1 (2017): 25–34.
Fergusson, J. D. *Modern Scottish Painting*. Glasgow: Luath Press, 2015.
Finlay, Graeme, Stephen Lloyd, Stephen Pattemore, and David Swift. *Debating Darwin, Two Debates: Is Darwinism True and Does It Matter?* Milton Keynes: Paternoster, 2009.
Finney, John. *Finding Faith*. Swindon: British and Foreign Bible Society, 1992.
Fishbane, Michael. *The Garments of Torah*. Bloomington: Indiana University Press, 1989.
Flett, John. *The Witness of God: The Trinity, Missio Dei, Karl Barth and the Nature of Christian Community*. Grand Rapids: Eerdmans, 2010.
Flint, Robert. *Theism*. Edinburgh: Blackwood, 1877.
Flint, Thomas. *Divine Providence: The Molinist Account*. Ithaca: Cornell University Press, 1998.

Flint, Thomas. "The Possibilities of Incarnation: Some Radical Molinist Suggestions." *Religious Studies* 37 (2001): 125–39.
Ford, David. *The Future of Christian Theology*. Oxford: Wiley Blackwell, 2011.
Forde, Gerhard. *The Preached God: Proclamation in Word and Sacrament*. Grand Rapids: Eerdmans, 2007.
Forrester, Duncan. *Theological Fragments: Essays in Unsystematic Theology*. London: T&T Clark, 2005.
Forsyth, Alexander C. *Mission by the People: Re-discovering the Dynamic Missiology of Tom Allan and His Scottish Contemporaries*. Eugene: Wipf & Stock, 2017.
Frei, Hans. *Types of Christian Theology*. New Haven: Yale University Press, 1992.
Fretheim, Terence. *God and World in the Old Testament: A Relational Theology of Creation*. Nashville: Abingdon, 2005.
Freud, Sigmund. *The Joke and Its Relation to the Unconscious*. London: Penguin, 2002.
Fulkerson, Mary McClintock. "Contesting the Gendered Subject: A Feminist Account of the Imago Dei." In *Horizons in Feminist Theology: Identity, Tradition and Norms*, edited by Rebecca S. Chopp and Sheila Greeve Davaney, 99–115. Minneapolis: Fortress, 1997.
Garrett, Don. "What's True About Hume's 'True Religion.'" *Journal of Scottish Philosophy* 10, no. 2 (2012): 199–220.
Garside, Charles. *Zwingli and the Arts*. New Haven: Yale University Press, 1966.
Gaskin, J. C. A. *Hume's Philosophy of Religion*. Basingstoke: Macmillan, 1978.
Gaventa, Beverly Roberts. "Power and Kenosis in Paul's Letter to the Romans." In *Kenosis: The Self-Emptying of Christ in Scripture and Theology*, edited by Paul T. Nimmo and Keith L. Johnson, 24–40. Grand Rapids: Eerdmans, 2021.
Gay, Doug. *Honey from the Lion: Christianity and the Ethics of Nationalism*. London: SCM, 2013.
Geach, Peter. *Providence and Evil*. Cambridge: Cambridge University Press, 1977.
Gerrish, Brian. "Tradition in the Modern World: The Reformed Habit of Mind." In *Toward the Future of Reformed Theology: Tasks, Topics, Traditions*, edited by David Willis and Michael Welker, 3–20. Grand Rapids: Eerdmans, 1999.
Gerrish, Brian. *The Old Protestantism and the New*. Edinburgh: T&T Clark, 1982.
Goldenberg, Robert. *The Nations that Know Thee Not: Ancient Jewish Attitudes Towards Other Religions*. Sheffield: Sheffield Academic Press, 1997.
Gordon, Bruce. *Calvin*. New Haven: Yale University Press, 2009.
Goris, Harm. "No Creation Stories in the Holy Scripture: Von Rad's View on the Relation Between Covenant and Creation Revisited." In *Strangers and Pilgrims on Earth: Essays in Honour of Abraham van de Beek*, edited by Eduardus van der Borght and Paul van Geest, 669–82. Leiden: Brill, 2012.
Goudriaan, Aza. *Reformed Orthodoxy and Philosophy, 1625–1750*. Leiden: Brill, 2006.
Graafland, Johan J. "Weber Revisited: Critical Perspectives from Calvinism on Capitalism in Economic Crisis." In *Calvinism and the Making of the European Mind*, edited by Gijsbert van den Brink and Harro M. Höpfl, 177–98. Leiden: Brill, 2014.
Graham, Elaine. "The Establishment, Multiculturalism and Social Cohesion." In *The Established Church: Past, Present, and Future*, edited by Mark Chapman, Judith Maltby, and William Whyte, 124–40. London: Bloomsbury, 2011.
Graham, Gordon. "Adam Smith and Religion." In *Adam Smith: His Life, Thought and Legacy*, edited by Ryan Patrick Hanley, 305–20. Princeton: Princeton University Press, 2016.
Graham, Gordon. *Philosophy, Art and Religion: Understanding Faith and Creativity*. Cambridge: Cambridge University Press, 2017.

Graham, Henry Grey. *The Social Life of Scotland in the 18th Century*. London: A&C Black, 1899.

Graham, Ralph E. *Ecclesiastical Discipline in the Church of Scotland, 1690–1730*. PhD diss., University of Glasgow, 1964.

Graham, Roderick, *The Great Infidel: A Life of David Hume*. Edinburgh: Birlinn, 2006.

Gregersen, Niels Henrik, ed. *Incarnation: On the Scope and Depth of Christology*. Minneapolis: Fortress, 2015.

Greggs, Tom. *Dogmatic Ecclesiology: The Priestly Catholicity of the Church*, Vol. 1. Grand Rapids: Baker, 2019.

Grenz, Stanley. *The Social God and the Relational Self: A Trinitarian Theology of the Imago Dei*. Louisville: Westminster John Knox, 2001.

Guder, Darrell L. "Reformed Theology, Mission and Ecumenism." In *The Cambridge Companion to Reformed Theology*, edited by Paul T. Nimmo and David Fergusson, 319–34. Cambridge: Cambridge University Press, 2016.

Gunton, Colin E. *Act and Being: Towards a Doctrine of the Divine Attributes*. London: SCM, 2002.

Hall, Christopher A. and John Sanders. *Does God Have a Future? A Debate on Divine Providence*. Grand Rapids: Baker, 2003.

Hampson, Daphne. *Theology and Feminism*. Oxford: Blackwell, 1990.

Harries, Richard. *Faith in Politics? Rediscovering the Christian Roots of our Political Values*. London: Darton, Longman and Todd, 2010.

Harris, James. "Hume's Use of the Rhetoric of Calvinism." In *Impressions of Hume*, edited by M. Frasca-Spada and P. J. Kail, 141–59. Oxford: Clarendon, 2005.

Harris, James. "The Place of the Ancients in the Moral Philosophy of the Scottish Enlightenment." *Journal of Scottish Philosophy* 8, no. 1 (2010): 1–11.

Harrison, Peter. "Adam Smith and the History of the Invisible Hand." *Journal of the History of Ideas* 72, no. 1 (2011): 29–49.

Hart, David Bentley. *Atheist Delusions: The Christian Revolution and its Fashionable Enemies*. New Haven: Yale University Press, 2010.

Hart, David Bentley. *That All Shall Be Saved: Heaven, Hell and Universal Salvation*. New Haven: Yale University Press, 2019.

Hart, David Bentley. *Tradition and Apocalypse: An Essay on the Future of Christian Belief*. Grand Rapids: Eerdmans, 2022.

Harvard-Smithsonian Center for Astrophysics. *How Can Astronomy Improve Life on Earth?* [webpage]. 2021. https://pweb.cfa.harvard.edu/big-questions/how-can-astronomy-improve-life-earth (Accessed October 10, 2023).

Hasker, William. *Providence, Evil and the Openness of God*. London: Routledge, 2004.

Hastings, Adrian. *Church and State: The English Experience*. Exeter: Exeter University Press, 1991.

Hastings, Adrian. *The Constructions of Nationhood: Ethnicity, Religion and Nationalism*. Cambridge: Cambridge University Press, 1997.

Hauerwas, Stanley and William H. Willimon. *Resident Aliens*. Nashville: Abingdon, 1993.

Hayes, Zachary. *Visions of a Future: A Study of Christian Eschatology*. Wilmington: Glazier, 1989.

Hazlett, W. I. P. "Ebbs and Flows of Theology in Glasgow 1451–1843." In *Traditions of Theology in Glasgow 1450–1990*, edited by W. I. P. Hazlett, 1–26. Edinburgh: Scottish Academic Press, 1993.

Hearn, Jonathan. *Rethinking Nationalism: An Introduction*. London: Palgrave Macmillan, 2004.

Hebblethwaite, Brian. *The Christian Hope*. Basingstoke: Marshall, Morgan and Scott, 1984.
Hector, Kevin. *Christianity as a Way of Life: A Systematic Theology*. New Haven: Yale University Press, 2023.
Heidegger, Martin. *Being and Time*, translated by John Macquarrie and Edward Robinson. Oxford: Blackwell, 1962.
Heinz, Johann. "The 'Summer That Will Never End': Luther's Longing for the 'Dear Last Day' in His Sermon on Luke 21 (1531)." *Andrews University Studies* 23, no. 2 (1985): 181–6.
Helm, Paul. *The Providence of God*. Downer's Grove: InterVarsity Press, 1993.
Helmer, Christine. *Theology and the End of Doctrine*. Louisville: Westminster John Knox Press, 2014.
Hengel, Martin. *The Son of God: The Origin of Christology and the History of Jewish-Hellenistic Religion*. Minneapolis: Fortress, 1976.
Hesselink, I. John. *On Being Reformed: Distinctive Characteristics and Common Misunderstandings*. Ann Arbor: Servant Books, 1983.
Heydt, Colin. "The Problem of Natural Religion in Smith's Moral Thought." *Journal of the History of Ideas* 78, no. 1 (2017): 73–94.
Hick, John. "Jesus and the World Religions." In *The Myth of God Incarnate*, edited by John Hick, 167–85. London: SCM, 1977.
Hill, Lisa. "The Hidden Theology of Adam Smith." *European Journal of the History of Economic Thought* 8, no. 1 (2001): 1–29.
Hilton, Boyd. "Chalmers as Political Economist." In *The Practical and the Pious: Essays on Thomas Chalmers (1780–1847)*, edited by A. C. Cheyne, 141–56. Edinburgh: St Andrew Press, 1985.
Hitchens, Christopher. *God Is Not Great: The Case Against Religion*. London: Atlantic Books, 2007.
Hobbes, Thomas. *Leviathan*, edited by Christopher Brooke. London: Penguin, 2017.
Hobsbawm, Eric. *Nations and Nationalism since 1780: Programme, Myth and Reality*. Cambridge: Cambridge University Press, 1992.
Hodge, Charles. *What is Darwinism?* London: Nelson, 1874.
Hodgson, Leonard. *Doctrine of the Trinity*. London: Nisbet, 1944.
Hogg, James. *The Private Memoirs and Confessions of a Justified Sinner*, edited by Peter Garside. Edinburgh: Edinburgh University Press, 2002.
Holden, Thomas. *Spectres of a False Divinity*. Oxford: Oxford University Press, 2010.
Holland, Tom. *Dominion: The Making of the Western Mind*. London: Little, Brown, 2019.
Hopkins, Gerard Manley. "God's Grandeur." In *The Major Works*, edited by Catherine Phillips, 128. Oxford: Oxford University Press, 1986.
Hueglin, Thomas O. "Covenant and Federalism in the Politics of Althusius." In *The Covenant Connection: From Federal Theolog to Modern Federalism*, edited by Daniel J. Elazar and John Kincaid, 31–54. Lanham: Lexington, 2000.
Hume, David. *Dialogues Concerning Natural Religion*. London: Penguin, 1999.
Hume, David. *Dialogues Concerning Natural Religion*, edited by Norman Kemp Smith. Oxford: Clarendon, 1935.
Hume, David. *Enquiry Concerning Human Understanding*, edited by L. A. Selby-Bigge, 3rd ed. Oxford: Oxford University Press, 1975.
Hume, David. *Selected Essays*. Oxford: Oxford University Press, 1996.
Hume, David. *The History of England from the Invasion of Julius Caesar to the Revolution in 1688*, 6 vols. Indianapolis: Liberty Fund 1983.
Hume, David. *The Natural History of Religion*. London: A. and H. Bradlaugh Bonner, 1757.
Hunsinger, Deborah van Deusen. *Theology and Pastoral Counseling: A New Interdisciplinary Approach*. Grand Rapids: Eerdmans, 1995.

Hurtado, Larry. *At the Origins of Christian Worship*. Carlisle: Paternoster, 1999.
Hurtado, Larry. *Honoring the Son: Jesus in Earliest Christian Devotional Practice*. Bellingham: Lexham Press, 2018.
Hutcheson, Francis. "Thoughts on Laughter and Observations on 'The Fable of the Bees.'" In *Scottish Philosophy: Selected Writings 1690–1960*, edited by Gordon Graham, 25–37. Exeter: Imprint Academic Press, 2004.
Hutcheson, Francis. *A System of Moral Philosophy: In Three Books*. London, 1755.
Huxley, T. H. *Hume*. London: Macmillan, 1879.
Immerwahr, John. "Hume's Aesthetic Theism." *Hume Studies* 22, no. 2 (1997): 325–37.
Iverach, James. *Evolution and Christianity*. London: Hodder & Stoughton, 1894.
Jaffrelot, Christophe. "Religion and Nationalism." In *The Oxford Handbook of the Sociology of Religion*, edited by Peter B. Clarke, 406–18. Oxford: Oxford University Press, 2011.
Jaki, Stanely. *Lord Gifford and his Lectures*. Edinburgh: Scottish Academic Press, 1995.
Jeanrond, Werner. *Theology of Love*. London: Continuum, 2010.
Jeeves, Malcolm. "Mind Reading and Soul Searching in the Twenty-first Century." In *What About the Soul? Neuroscience and Christian Anthropology*, edited by Joel Green, 13–30. Nashville: Abingdon, 2004.
Jensen, Alexander S. *Divine Providence and Human Agency: Trinity, Creation and Freedom*. Aldershot: Ashgate, 2014.
Jenson, Robert W. *Systematic Theology: The Triune God*, Vol. 1. New York: Oxford University Press, 1997.
Jenson, Robert W. *Systematic Theology: The Works of God*, Vol. 2. New York: Oxford University Press, 1999.
Jenson, Robert W. "The Great Transformation." In *The Last Things: Biblical and Theological Perspectives on Eschatology*, edited by Carl E. Braaten and Robert W. Jenson, 33–42. Grand Rapids: Eerdmans, 2002.
John, Chrysostom. "Homily VI on Matthew 2:1-2." In *Nicene and Post-Nicene Fathers, First Series*, Vol. 10, edited by Philip Schaff, 34–41. Edinburgh: T&T Clark, 1888.
Johnstone, William. *Exodus 20–40*. Macon: Smyth & Helwys, 2014.
Jordan, Will R. "Religion in the Public Square: A Reconsideration of David Hume and Religious Establishment." *Review of Politics* 64, no. 4 (2002): 687–713.
Jowett, Benjamin. "On the Interpretation of Scripture." In *Essays and Reviews*, 3rd ed., 330–433. London, 1860.
Juhasz, Gergely. "Resurrection or Immortality of the Soul?: A Dilemma of Reformation Exegesis." *Reformation* 14 (2009): 1–47.
Jüngel, Eberhard. "The Last Judgement as the Act of Grace." *Louvain Studies* 15 (1990): 389–405.
Katongole, Emmanuel. *The Sacrifice of Africa: A Political Theology of Africa*. Grand Rapids: Eerdmans, 2011.
Kay, James. *Preaching and Theology*. St Louis: Chalice Press, 2007.
Kay, James. "The Place of Prayer in Theological Method: A Conversation with Sarah Coakley." In *Schools of Faith: Essays on Theology, Ethics and Education in Honour of Iain R. Torrance*, edited by David Fergusson and Bruce L. McCormack, 117–28. London: T&T Clark, 2019.
Keenan, Brian. *An Evil Cradling*. London: Vintage, 1993.
Keller, Catherine. *On the Mystery: Discerning Divinity in Process*. Minneapolis: Fortress, 2008.
Keller, Catherine. *The Face of the Deep: A Theology of Becoming*. New York: Routledge, 2007.

Kelly, J. N. D. *Early Christian Creeds*, 3rd ed. London: Longman, 1972.
Kelsey, David. *Between Athens and Berlin: The Theological Education Debate*. Grand Rapids: Eerdmans, 2003.
Kelsey, David. *Eccentric Existence: A Theological Anthropology*, Vol. 1. Louisville: Westminster John Knox Press, 2009.
Kelsey, David. *Eccentric Existence: A Theological Anthropology*, Vol. 2. Louisville: Westminster John Knox Press, 2010.
Kennedy, Gavin. "Adam Smith on Religion." In *The Oxford Handbook of Adam Smith*, edited by Christopher J. Berry, Maria Pia Paganelli, and Craig Smith, 464–86. Oxford: Oxford University Press, 2013.
Kerr, Fergus. *After Aquinas: Versions of Thomism*. Oxford: Blackwell, 2002.
Kerr, Fergus. *Theology After Wittgenstein*, 2nd ed. Oxford: Blackwell, 1997.
Kerr, Fergus. *Twentieth-Century Catholic Theologians: From Neoscholasticism to Nuptial Mysticism*. Oxford: Blackwell, 2007.
Kessler, Edward. "Judaism." In *The Blackwell Companion to the Bible and Culture*, edited by John Sawyer, 119–34. Oxford: Wiley Blackwell, 2006.
Kilby, Karen. *God, Evil and the Limits of Theodicy*. London: T&T Clark, 2020.
Kilby, Karen. "The Seductions of Kenosis." In *Suffering and the Christian Life*, edited by Rachel Davies and Karen Kilby. London: T&T Clark, 2020.
Kingdon, Robert M. "Calvinism and Resistance Theory 1550–1580." In *The Cambridge History of Political Thought 1450–1700*, edited by J. H. Burns, 193–218. Cambridge: Cambridge University Press, 2008.
Kirkpatrick, Frank. *Together Bound: God, History and the Religious Community*. New York: Oxford University Press, 2004.
Koffeman, Leo J. "'Ecclesia reformata semper reformanda': Church Renewal from a Reformed Perspective." *HTS Teologiese Studies/Theological Studies* 71, no. 3 (2015): 1–5.
Kuschel, Karl-Josef. *Laughter: A Theological Reflection*. London: SCM, 1994.
Laffin, Michael Richard. *The Promise of Martin Luther's Political Theology: Freeing Luther from Modern Political Narrative*. London: Bloomsbury, 2016.
Lash, Nicholas. "Up and Down in Christology." In *New Studies in Theology*, edited by Stephen Sykes and Derek Holmes, 31–46. London: Duckworth, 1980.
Law, David R. "Kenotic Christology." In *The Blackwell Companion to Nineteenth Century Theology*, edited by David Fergusson, 251–79. Oxford: Wiley Blackwell, 2010.
Lewis, Alan E. *Between Cross & Resurrection: A Theology of Holy Saturday*. Grand Rapids: Eerdmans, 2001.
Lewis, Alan E. "Ecclesia ex Auditu: A Reformed View of the Church as the Community of the Word of God." *Scottish Journal of Theology* 35 (1982): 13–31.
Lindbeck, George A. "The Church." In *Keeping the Faith: Essays to Mark the Centenary of Lux Mundi*, edited by Geoffrey Wainwright, 179–208. Philadelphia: Fortress Press, 1988.
Lindbeck, George A. *The Church in a Postliberal Age*. London: SCM, 2002.
Lindbeck, George A. *The Nature of Doctrine*. London: SPCK, 1984.
Livingston, James C. *Religious Thought in the Victorian Age*. London: T&T Clark International, 2006.
Livingstone, David. *Darwin's Forgotten Defenders: The Encounter between Evangelical Theology and Evolutionary Thought*. Grand Rapids: Eerdmans, 1987.
Livingstone, David. *Dealing with Darwin: Place, Politics and Rhetoric in Religious Engagements with Evolution*. Baltimore: Johns Hopkins University Press, 2014.

Lohse, Bernhard. *Martin Luther's Theology: Its Historical and Systematic Development.* Edinburgh: T&T Clark, 1999.
Louth, Andrew. "Pagans and Christians on Providence." In *Texts and Culture in Late Antiquity: Inheritance, Authority, and Change*, edited by J. H. D. Scourfield. Swansea: Classical Press of Wales, 2007.
Lucas, John R. "Foreknowledge and the Vulnerability of God." In *Royal Institute of Philosophy Lecture Series: 25, in The Philosophy in Christianity*, edited by Godfrey Vesey, 119–28. Cambridge: Cambridge University Press, 1989.
Lucas, John R. *Freedom and Grace.* London: SPCK, 1976.
Lukes, Stephen. *Power: A Radical View.* London: Macmillan, 1974.
Luther, Martin. *Werke: 36.* Weimar: H. Böhlhaus, 1883.
Luther, Martin. *Werke: Briefe, 9.* Weimar: H. Böhlhaus, 1883.
Lyall, David. *The Integrity of Pastoral Case.* London: SPCK, 2001.
MacCulloch, Diarmaid. *A History of Christianity.* Hardmondsworth: Penguin, 2009.
Mackie, J. L. *The Miracle of Theism.* Oxford: Oxford University Press, 1982.
MacKinnon, Donald M. *Themes in Theology: The Threefold Cord.* Edinburgh: T&T Clark, 1987.
Macmurray, John. *Persons in Relation.* London: Faber and Faber, 1961.
Macmurray, John, "A Philosopher Looks at Psychotherapy." In *Individual Psychology Pamphlets 20.* London: C. W. Daniel, 1938.
Macquarrie, John. *In Search of Humanity.* London: SCM, 1985.
Macquarrie, John. *Jesus Christ in Modern Thought.* London: SCM, 1990.
Marshall, Christopher. *Beyond Retribution: A New Testament Vision for Justice, Crime and Punishment.* Grand Rapids: Eerdmans, 2001.
Marshall, Bruce D., ed. *Theology in Dialogue: Essays in Conversation with George Lindbeck.* Notre Dame: University of Notre Dame Press, 1990.
Mason, Roger, ed. *Knox: On Rebellion.* Cambridge: Cambridge University Press, 1994.
May, Gerhard. *Creatio Ex Nihilo: The Doctrine of "Creation out of Nothing" in Early Christian Thought*, translated by A. S. Worrall. London: T&T Clark, 2004.
McCormack, Bruce L. "The Being of Holy Scripture is in Becoming: Karl Barth in Conversation with American Evangelical Criticism." In *Evangelicals and Scripture: Tradition, Authority and Hermeneutics*, edited by V. Bacote, Lauran C. Miguelez and Dennis L. Okholm, 55–75. Downer's Grove: IVP, 2004.
McCormack, Bruce L. *The Humility of the Eternal Son: Reformed Kenoticism and the Repair of Chalcedon.* Cambridge: Cambridge University Press, 2021.
McDermott, Gerald R. "Review Essay." *Pro Ecclesia* 14 (2005): 487–93.
McFadyen, Alister. "Imaging God: A Theological Answer to the Anthropological Question?" *Zygon* 47, no. 4 (2012): 918–33.
McFarland, Ian A. *The Word Made Flesh: A Theology of the Incarnation.* Louisville: Westminster John Knox, 2019.
McGrath, Alister. *Emil Brunner: A Reappraisal.* Oxford: Wiley Blackwell, 2015.
McIntosh, Esther. *John Macmurray's Religious Philosophy: What it Means to Be a Person.* Aldershot: Ashgate, 2011.
McLeod, Hugh. *The Religious Crisis of the 1960s.* Oxford: Oxford University Press, 2007.
Mercadante, Linda A. *Belief Without Borders: Inside the Minds of the Spiritual But Not Religious.* Oxford: Oxford University Press, 2014.
Michalski, Sergiusz. *The Reformation and the Visual Arts: The Protestant Image Question in Western and Eastern Europe.* London: Routledge 1993.
Migliore, Daniel L. "Editorial." *Theology Today* 43 (1986): 309–15.

Milbank, John. *Theology and Social Theory: Beyond Secular Reason*, 2nd ed. Oxford: Wiley Blackwell, 2006.
Miller, Gavin. *Miracles of Healing: Psychotherapy and Religion in Twentieth-Century Scotland*. Edinburgh: Edinburgh University Press, 2021.
Minnear, Paul. *Images of the Church in the New Testament*. Louisville: Westminster John Knox Press, 2004.
Mizuta, Hiroshi. *Adam Smith's Library: A Catalogue*. Oxford: Clarendon Press, 2000.
Moberly, R. W. L. "'Interpret the Bible Like Any Other Book?' Requiem for an Axiom." *Journal of Theological Interpretation* 4 (2010): 91–110.
Moltmann, Jürgen. *God in Creation: An Ecological Doctrine of Creation*. London: SCM, 1985.
Moltmann, Jürgen. *The Coming of God*. London: SCM, 1996.
Monro, D. H. "Humour." In *Encyclopedia of Philosophy*, Vol. 4, edited by P. Edwards, 90–3. New York: Macmillan, 1967.
Moore, Aubrey. "The Christian Doctrine of God." In *Lux Mundi*, edited by Charles Gore, 57–112. London: John Murray, 1889.
Moore, James. "Deconstructing Darwinism: The Politics of Evolution in the 1860s." *Journal of the History of Biology* 24 (1991): 353–408.
Morreall, John, ed. *Philosophy of Laughter and Humour*. Albany: State University of New York Press, 1987.
Morse, Christopher. *Not Every Spirit: A Dogmatics of Disbelief*. Valley Forge: Trinity Press International, 1994.
Mossner, E. C. *Life of David Hume*. London: Nelson, 1954.
Mounk, Yascha. *People vs Democracy: Why our Freedom is in Danger and How to Save It*. Cambridge, MA: Harvard University Press, 2018.
Murray, Paul, ed. *Receptive Ecumenism and the Call to Catholic Learning: Exploring a Way for Contemporary Ecumenism*. Oxford: Oxford University Press, 2008.
Nelson-Jones, Richard. *Theory and Practice of Counselling and Therapy*, 5th ed. London: Sage, 2011.
Newbigin, Lesslie. *A Word in Season: Perspectives on Christian World Mission*. Grand Rapids: Eerdmans, 1994.
Newman, John Henry. *The Dream of Gerontius*. Edinburgh: Constable, 1910.
Newman, John Henry. *University Sermons*. London: SPCK, 1970.
Nietzsche, Friedrich. *Thus Spoke Zarathustra*, edited by Adrian Del Caro and Robert Pippin. Cambridge: Cambridge University Press, 2005.
Nimmo, Paul T. and David Fergusson, eds. *Cambridge Companion to Reformed Theology*. Cambridge: Cambridge University Press, 2016.
Nimmo, Paul T. and Keith L. Johnson, eds. *Kenosis: The Self-Emptying of Christ in Scripture and Theology*. Grand Rapids: Eerdmans, 2021.
Noll, Mark. *The Civil War as a Theological Crisis*. Durham: University of North Carolina Press, 2006.
Numbers, Ronald L. *Galileo Goes to Jail and Other Myths about Science and Religion*. Cambridge, MA: Harvard University Press, 2010.
O'Collins, Gerald. *Christology: A Biblical, Historical and Systematic Study of Jesus*, 2nd ed. Oxford: Oxford University Press, 2009.
O'Collins, Gerald. *God's Other Peoples: Salvation for All*. Oxford: Oxford University Press, 2008.
O'Donovan, Oliver. *The Desire of the Nations*. Cambridge: Cambridge University Press, 1996.
O'Donovan, Oliver. *The Problem of Self-Love in St. Augustine*. New Haven: Yale University Press, 1980.

O'Loughlin, Thomas. "Theology in Scotland before Scholasticism." In *The History of Scottish Theology: From Celtic Origins to Reformed Orthodoxy*, Vol. 1, edited by David Fergusson and Mark W. Elliott, 12–24. Oxford: Oxford University Press, 2019.

Oakley, Francis. "The Absolute and Ordained Power of God in Sixteenth and Seventeenth-Century Theology." *Journal of the History of Ideas*, 59, no. 3 (1998): 437–61.

Oord, Thomas J. *The Death of Omnipotence and the Birth of Amipotence*. Grasmere: SacraSage Press, 2023.

Oord, Thomas J. *The Uncontrolling Love of God: An Open and Relational Account of Providence*. Downer's Grove: InterVarsity Press, 2016.

Orr, James. *David Hume and His Influence on Philosophy and Theology*. Edinburgh: T&T Clark, 1903.

Oslington, Paul. "Divine Action, Providence and Adam Smith's Invisible Hand." In *Adam Smith as Theologian*, edited by Paul Oslington, 61–76. London: Routledge, 2011.

Oslington, Paul. "God and the Market: Adam Smith's Invisible Hand." *Journal of Business Ethics* 108, no. 4 (2012): 429–38.

Oslington, Paul. "The 'New View' of Adam Smith in Context." *History of Economics Review* 71, no. 1 (2018): 118–31.

Otto, Rudolf. *The Idea of the Holy*, translated by John W. Harvey. Oxford: Oxford University Press, 1958.

Outka, Gene. *Agape: An Ethical Analysis*. New Haven: Yale University Press, 1972.

Pannenberg, Wolfhart. *Systematic Theology*, Vol. 1. Grand Rapids: Eerdmans, 1991.

Pannenberg, Wolfhart. *Systematic Theology*, Vol. 2. Edinburgh: T&T Clark, 2004.

Pannenberg, Wolfhart. *Systematic Theology*, Vol. 3. Edinburgh: T&T Clark, 1998.

Parker, T. H. L. *Calvin's Preaching*. Edinburgh: T&T Clark, 1992.

Partee, Charles. *The Theology of John Calvin*. Louisville: Westminster John Knox Press, 2008.

Pattison, Stephen. *Shame: Theory, Therapy, Theology*. Cambridge: Cambridge University Press, 2000.

Paul, Diane B. "Darwinism, Social Darwinism and Eugenics." In *The Cambridge Companion to Darwin*, edited by Jonathan Hodge and Gregory Radick, 214–39. Cambridge: Cambridge University Press, 2003.

Pauw, Amy Plantinga. *Church in Ordinary Time: A Wisdom Ecclesiology*. Grand Rapids: Eerdmans, 2017.

Pelikan, Jaroslav. *The Emergence of the Catholic Tradition (100–600)*. Chicago: University of Chicago Press, 1971.

Penelhum, Terence. "Hume's Views on Religion: Intellectual and Cultural Influences." In *The Blackwell Companion to Hume*, edited by Elizabeth Radcliffe, 323–37. Chichester: Wiley Blackwell, 2008.

Pew Research Center. *The Digital Pulpit: A Nationwide Analysis of Online Sermons* [webpage]. 2019. https://www.pewresearch.org/religion/2019/12/16/the-digital-pulpit-a-nationwide-analysis-of-online-sermons/ (accessed October 10, 2023).

Phillips, D. Z. *Wittgenstein and Religion*. Basingstoke: Macmillan, 1993.

Phillipson, Nicholas. *Adam Smith: An Enlightened Life*. London: Allen Lane, 2010.

Phiri, Isaac. *Proclaiming Political Pluralism: Churches and Political Transitions in Africa*. Westport: Praeger, 2001.

Placher, William. *Mark*. Louisville: John Knox Press, 2010.

Plantinga Pauw, Amy. *Church in Ordinary Time: A Wisdom Ecclesiology*. Grand Rapids: Eerdmans, 2017.

Pope Francis. *Laudato Si': On Care for our Common Home*. Vatican City: Libreria Editrice Vaticana, 2015.

Pusey, Edward. *The Day of Judgement*. Oxford: John Henry Parker, 1839.
Putnam, Robert D. *Bowling Alone: The Collapse and Revival of American Community*, revised ed. New York: Simon and Schuster, 2020.
Putnam, Robert D. and David E. Campbell. *American Grace: How Religion Unites and Divides Us*. New York: Simon and Schuster, 2010.
Rahner, Karl. "Current Problems in Christology." In *Theological Investigations*, Vol. 1, 149–200. London: Darton, Longman and Todd, 1962.
Rahner, Karl. *Foundations of Christian Faith*. London: Darton, Longman and Todd, 1978.
Rainy, Robert. *Evolution and Theology*. Edinburgh: Maclaren & Macniven, 1874.
Ratzinger, Joseph. *Eschatology: Death and Eternal Life*, 2nd ed. Washington, DC: Catholic University of America Press, 1988.
Raven, Charles. *In Praise of Birds*. London: Allen and Unwin, 1950.
Raven, Charles. *Natural Religion and Christian Theology: The Gifford Lectures First Series, Science and Religion*. Cambridge: Cambridge University Press, 1953.
Richardson, Alan. *An Introduction to the Theology of the New Testament*. London: SCM, 1958.
Ruether, Rosemary Radford. "Anti-Semitism in Christian Theology." *Theology* 30, no. 4 (1974): 365–81.
Runciman, David. *How Democracy Ends*. London: Profile Books, 2018.
Ryrie, Alec. *Protestants: The Radicals Who Made the Modern World*. London: Collins, 2017.
Sanders, John. *The God Who Risks: A Theology of Providence*. Downer's Grove: InterVarsity Press, 1998.
Schillbeeckx, Edward. *Jesus: An Experiment in Christology*. London: Collins, 1979.
Schleiermacher, Friedrich. *On Religion: Speeches to its Cultured Despisers*, edited and translated by Richard Crouter. Cambridge: Cambridge University Press, 1988.
Schleiermacher, Friedrich. *The Christian Faith*, 2 vols, edited by Catherine L. Kelsey and Terence N. Tice. Louisville: Westminster John Knox Press, 2016.
Schleiermacher, Friedrich. *The Christian Faith*, edited by H. R. Mackintosh and J. S. Stewart. Edinburgh: T&T Clark, 1928.
Schweiker, William. *Dust that Breathes: Christian Faith and the New Humanisms*. Oxford: Wiley Blackwell, 2010.
Schwöbel, Christoph. "Last Things First? The Century of Eschatology in Retrospect." In *The Future as God's Gift: Explorations in Christian Eschatology*, edited by David Fergusson and Marcel Sarot, 217–41. Edinburgh: T&T Clark, 2000.
Scott, W. R. *Francis Hutcheson: His Life, Teaching and Position in the History of Philosophy*. Cambridge: Cambridge University Press, 1900.
"Second Helvetic Confession." In *Reformed Confessions of the Sixteenth Century*, edited by Arthur C. Cochrane, 220–301. London: SCM Press, 1966; *The Creeds of Christendom*, 3 vols, 4th ed., edited by Philip Schaff, 220–301. Grand Rapids: Baker, 1977.
Sen, Amartya. "The Contemporary Relevance of Adam Smith." In *The Oxford Handbook of Adam Smith*, edited by Christopher J. Berry, Maria Pia Paganelli, and Craig Smith, 581–92. Oxford: Oxford University Press, 2013.
Smith, Adam. *An Inquiry into the Nature and Causes of the Wealth of Nations*, edited by R. H. Campbell, A. S. Skinner, and W. B. Todd. Indianapolis: Liberty Fund, 1981.
Smith, Adam. *The Theory of Moral Sentiments*, edited by D. D. Raphael and A. L. Macfie. Indianapolis: Liberty Fund, 1982.
Smith, Iain Crichton. *Murdo: The Life and Works*. Edinburgh: Birlinn, 2001.
Smith, Norman Kemp. *The Philosophy of David Hume: A Study of Its Origins and Central Doctrines*. London: Macmillan, 1941.
Sonderegger, Katherine. *Systematic Theology: The Doctrine of God*, Vol. 1. Minneapolis: Fortress, 2015.

Soskice, Janet. *Naming God: Addressing the Divine in Philosophy, Theology and Scripture*. Cambridge: Cambridge University Press, 2023.

Spufford, Francis. *Light Perpetual*. London: Faber, 2021.

Spurlock, Scott. "Boundaries of Scottish Reformed Orthodoxy 1560–1700." In *History of Scottish Theology, Vol. 1: Celtic Origins to Reformed Orthodoxy*, edited by David Fergusson and Mark W. Elliott, 359–76. Oxford: Oxford University Press, 2019.

Srikosz, Meric and Rebecca Watson. *Blue Planet, Blue God: The Bible and the Sea*. London: SCM, 2017.

Stevens, Wallace. "Sunday Morning." In *Selected Poems*, 33. London: Faber and Faber, 1953.

Stewart, M. A. "Two Species of Philosophy: The Historical Significance of the First Enquiry." In *Reading Hume on Human Understanding*, edited by Peter Millican, 67–95. Oxford: Clarendon, 2002.

Stockitt, Robin and S. John Dawson. *Leaving Church: What Can We Learn from Those Who Are Done with Church?* Cambridge: Grove Books, 2020.

Stout, Jeffrey. *Blessed Are the Organised: Grassroots Democracy in America*. Princeton: Princeton University Press, 2010.

Stump, Eleanore. *Wandering in the Darkness: Narrative and the Problem of Suffering*. Oxford: Oxford University Press, 2010.

Sugirtharajah, R. G. *The Bible and the Third World*. Cambridge: Cambridge University Press, 2001.

Swinburne, Richard. *Providence and the Problem of Evil*. Oxford: Clarendon, 1998.

Swinburne, Richard. *The Coherence of Theism*, 2nd ed. Oxford: Oxford University Press, 2016.

Swinburne, Richard. *The Existence of God*, 2nd ed. Oxford: Clarendon, 2014.

Sykes, Stephen. *Power and Christian Theology*. London: Continuum, 2006.

Talia, Maina Vakafua. *Am I Not Your TŪ/AKOI? A Tuvaluan Plea for Survival in a Time of Climate Emergency*. PhD diss., Charles Sturt University, 2022.

Tanner, Kathryn. *God and Creation in Christian Theology: Tyranny or Empowerment?* Oxford: Blackwell, 1988.

Tanner, Kathryn. *Theories of Culture: A New Agenda for Theology*. Minneapolis: Augsburg Fortress, 1997.

Taylor, Barbara Brown. *Leaving Church*. Norwich: Canterbury Press, 2011.

Taylor, Charles. *A Secular Age*. Cambridge, MA: Harvard University Press, 2007.

Taylor, Richard C. "Primary and Secondary Causality." In *The Routledge Companion to Islamic Philosophy*, edited by Richard C. Taylor and Luis Xavier López-Farjeat, 225–35. London: Routledge, 2016.

Telfer, Elizabeth. "Hutcheson's Reflections Upon Laugher." *Journal of Aesthetics and Art Criticism* 53 (1995): 359–69.

Temple, Frederick. *Religion and Science*. London: Macmillan, 1884.

The British Academy. *Theology and Religious Studies Provision in UK Higher Education* [web publication]. 2019. https://www.thebritishacademy.ac.uk/publications/theology-religious-studies-provision-uk-higher-education/ (accessed October 11, 2023).

The Confession of Faith. Edinburgh: Blackwood, 1957.

The Iona Community. *A Communion Liturgy of the Iona Community* [webpage]. 2020. https://media.acny.uk/media/Communion_Liturgy_Iona_2020.pdf (accessed October 10, 2023).

The Society of Mary and Martha. *Submission on Clergy Stress* [webpage]. 2001. https://www.balmnet.co.uk/clergystress.htm (accessed October 10, 2023).

Thiselton, Anthony C. *First Epistle to the Corinthians*. Grand Rapids: Eerdmans, 2000.
Thiselton, Anthony C. *Life After Death: A New Approach to the Last Things*. Grand Rapids: Eerdmans, 2012.
Thomas, Aquinas. *Summa Contra Gentiles*, Vol IV, 2nd ed., translated by Charles J. O'Neil. Notre Dame: University of Notre Dame Press, 1975.
Thomas, Aquinas. *Summa Theologica*, 10 vols, 2nd revised ed., translated by Fathers of the English Dominican Province. London: Burns, Oates and Washbourne, 1920–2.
Thomas, Keith. *Man and the Natural World: Changing Attitudes in England 1500–1800*. London: Penguin, 1983.
Thomson, J. Arthur and Patrick Geddes. *Evolution*. London: Williams & Norgate, 1912.
Ticciati, Susannah. "Anachronism or Illumination? Genesis 1 and Creation *ex nihilo*." *Anglican Theological Review* 99, no. 4 (2017): 691–712.
Tiessen, Terrance. *Providence & Prayer: How Does God Work in the World?* Downer's Grove: InterVarsity Press, 2000.
Tindal, Matthew. *Christianity as Old as the Creation or the Gospel a Republication of the Religion of Nature*. London, 1731.
Tonstad, Linn Marie. "(Un)wise Theologians: Systematic Theology in the University." *International Journal of Systematic Theology* 22, no. 4 (2020): 494–511.
Torrance, James B. *Worship, Community and the Triune God of Grace*. Carlisle: Paternoster, 1996.
Torrance, T. F. *Karl Barth: Biblical and Evangelical Theologian*. Edinburgh: T&T Clark, 1990.
Tracy, David. "Lindbeck's New Program for Theology: A Reflection." *The Thomist* 49 (1985): 460–72.
Tribe, Keith. *The Economy of the Word: Language, History and Economics*. Oxford: Oxford University Press, 2015.
TRS-UK. *Why Study TRS at University?* [webpage]. 2020. https://trs.ac.uk/studying-trs/why-study-trs-at-university/ (accessed October 10, 2023).
Twain, Mark. *The Adventures of Tom Sawyer*. New York: Modern Library Edition, 1940.
van Asselt, Willem. *The Federal Theology of Johannes Cocceius (1603–1669)*. Leiden: Brill, 2001.
van den Brink, Gijsbert. *Almighty God: A Study of Divine Omnipotence*. Kampen: Kok Pharos, 1993.
van den Brink, Gijsbert. "The Future of Theology at Public Universities." *In die Skriflig* 54, no. 2 (2021): 1–9.
van Huyssteen, Wentzel. *Alone in the World? Human Uniqueness in Science and Theology*. Grand Rapids: Eerdmans, 2006.
van Til, Howard. "The Creation: Intelligently Designed or Optimally Equipped?." *Theology Today* 55 (1998/9): 344–64.
Veldhuis, Henri. "Absolute and Ordained Power in Scotus' Ordinatio I:44." *Vivarium* 38, no. 2 (2000): 222–30.
Victorin-Vangerud, Nancy M. "Thinking Like an Archipelago: Beyond Tehomophobic Theology." *Pacifica* 16 (2003): 153–72.
Viner, Jacob. *The Role of Providence in the Social Order*. Princeton: Princeton University Press, 1972.
Vogel, Winfried. "The Eschatological Theology of Martin Luther, Part I: Luther's Basic Concepts." *Andrews University Seminary Studies* 24, no. 3 (1986): 249–63.

Volf, Miroslav. *Captive to the Word of God: Engaging the Scriptures for Contemporary Theological Reflections*. Grand Rapids: Eerdmans, 2010.

Volf, Miroslav. "The Final Reconciliation: Reflections on a Social Dimension of the Eschatological Transition." In *Theology and Eschatology at the Turn of the Millennium*, edited by James Buckley and L. Gregory Jones, 89–111. Oxford: Blackwell, 2001.

Volf, Miroslav. "Theology for a Way of Life." In *Practicing Theology*, edited by Miroslav Volf and Dorothy C. Bass, 245–63. Grand Rapids: Eerdmans, 2002.

Volf, Miroslav and Matthew Croasmun. *For the Life of the World: Theology That Makes a Difference*. Grand Rapids: Brazos Press, 2019.

Volf, Miroslav and G. Talal, eds. *A Common Word: Muslims and Christians on Loving and Neighbour*. Grand Rapids: Eerdmans, 2010.

von Rad, Gerhard. *Old Testament Theology*, Vol. 1. Edinburgh: Oliver and Boyd, 1962.

von Skarżyński, W. *Adam Smith als Moralphilosoph und Schoepfer der Nationaloekonomie: Ein Beitrag zur Geschichte der Nationaloekonomie*. Berlin: Verlag von Theobold Grieben, 1878.

Wainwright, Geoffrey. *Doxology: A Systematic Theology*. London: Epworth, 1980.

Wallace, R. S. *Calvin's Doctrine of the Word and Sacrament*. Edinburgh: Oliver & Boyd, 1953.

Walls, Andrew. *The Cross-Cultural Process in Christian History*. Edinburgh: T&T Clark, 2002.

Walsham, Alexandra. *Providentialism in Early Modern England*. Oxford: Oxford University Press, 1998.

Wandel, Lee Palmer. *The Reformation: Towards a New History*. Cambridge: Cambridge University Press, 2011.

Watson, Francis. "Are There Still Four Gospels?" In *Reading Scripture with the Church: Towards a Hermeneutic for Theological Interpretation*, edited by A. K. M. Adam, Fowl Stephen E., Kevin J. Vanhoozer, and Francis Watson, 95–116. Grand Rapids: Baker, 2006.

Weaver, Darlene Fozard. *Self-Love and Christian Ethics*. Cambridge: Cambridge University Press, 2002.

Webb, C. J. *God and Personality*. London: Allen and Unwin, 1918.

Webster, John. "Eschatology, Anthropology and Postmodernity." *International Journal of Systematic Theology* 2, no. 1 (2000): 13–28.

Webster, John. *God Without Measure: Working Papers in Christian Theology: God and the Works of God*, Vol. 1. London: Bloomsbury T&T Clark, 2016.

Webster, John. "God, Theology, Universities." In *God Without Measure: Working Papers in Christian Theology: Virtue and Intellect*, Vol. 2, 157–72. London: Bloomsbury T&T Clark, 2016.

Webster, John. *Holy Scripture: A Dogmatic Sketch*. Cambridge: Cambridge University Press, 2003.

Weil, Simone. *Waiting on God*. London: Routledge and Kegan Paul, 1951.

Welker, Michael. "Creation and the Image of God: Their Understanding in Christian Tradition and the Biblical Grounds." *Journal of Ecumenical Studies* 34, no. 3 (1997): 436–48.

Welker, Michael. *Creation and Reality*. Minneapolis: Fortress, 1999.

Wells, Sam. "How Common Worship Forms Local Character." *Studies in Christian Ethics* 15 (2002): 66–74.

Welz, Claudia. "A Theological Phenomenology of Listening: God's 'Voice' and 'Silence' after Auschwitz." *Religions* 10, no. 3 (2019): 139.

Werner, Dietrich. "Ecumenical Learning in Theological Education: The World Council of Churches Perspective." *Expository Times* 123 (2011): 1–11.
West, William, ed. *Exploring Therapy, Spirituality and Healing*. Basingstoke: Palgrave Macmillan, 2011.
Westermann, Claus. *Genesis 1–11*. London: SPCK, 1984.
Westermann, Claus. *The Living Psalms*. Edinburgh: T&T Clark, 1989.
Whale, J. S. *Christian Doctrine*. Cambridge: Cambridge University Press, 1941.
White, Thomas Joseph. *The Incarnate Lord: A Thomistic Study in Christology*. Washington: Catholic University of America Press, 2015.
White, Vernon. *Purpose and Providence: Taking Soundings in Western Thought, Literature and Theology*. London: T&T Clark, 2015.
Wilckens, Robert. *The Spirit of Early Christian Thought*. New Haven: Yale University Press, 2003.
Williams, Delores S. *Sisters in the Wilderness: The Challenge of Womanist God-Talk*. New York: Orbis, 2013.
Williams, Richard. *Sex and Buildings: Modern Architecture and the Sexual Revolution*. London: Reaktion, 2013.
Williams, Rowan. *Christ the Heart of Creation*. London: Continuum, 2018.
Williams, Rowan. *Faith in the Public Square*. London: Bloomsbury, 2012.
Williams, Rowan. *On Christian Theology*. Oxford: Blackwell, 2000.
Williams, Rowan. *Why Study the Past? The Quest for the Historical Church*. London: Darton, Longman and Todd, 2005.
Willimon, William H. *Worship as Pastoral Care*. Nashville: Abingdon, 1982.
Wirzba, Norman. *From Nature to Creation: A Christian Vision for Understanding and Loving Our World*. Grand Rapids: Baker, 2015.
Witte, John, Jr. "Introduction." In *Christianity and Law: An Introduction*, edited by John Witte Jr. and Frank S. Alexander, 1–32. Cambridge: Cambridge University Press, 2008.
Wittgenstein, Ludwig. *Lectures and Conversations on Aesthetics, Psychology and Religious Belief*. Oxford: Blackwell, 1966.
Wittgenstein, Ludwig. *Philosophical Investigations*. Oxford: Blackwell, 1953.
Wollheim, Richard. *Hume on Religion*. London: Collins, 1963.
Wolterstorff, Nicholas. *Divine Discourse*. Cambridge: Cambridge University Press, 1995.
Wolterstorff, Nicholas. "God and Darkness in Reid." In *Thomas Reid: Context, Influence, Significance*, edited by Joseph Houston, 77–102. Edinburgh: Dunedin Academic Press, 2004.
Wolterstorff, Nicholas. *Hearing the Call: Liturgy, Justice, Church, and World*. Grand Rapids: Eerdmans, 2011.
Wolterstorff, Nicholas. *Religion in the University*. New Haven: Yale University Press, 2019.
Wolterstorff, Nicholas. "The Christian Humanism of John Calvin." In *Re-Envisioning Christian Humanism: Education and the Restoration of Humanity*, edited by Jens Zimmermann, 77–94. Oxford: Oxford University Press, 2016.
Wolterstorff, Nicholas. "The Migration of the Theistic Arguments: From Natural Theology to Evidentialist Apologetics." In *Rationality, Religious Belief and Moral Commitment*, edited by Robert Audi and William J. Wainwright, 38–81. Ithaca: Cornell University Press, 1986.
Wolterstorff, Nicholas. "To Theologians: From One Who Cares about Theology but Is Not One of You." *Theological Education* 40, no. 2 (2005): 79–92.
Wolterstorff, Nicholas. *Until Justice and Peace Embrace*. Grand Rapids: Eerdmans, 1987.

Wood, Charles. *The Question of Providence*. Louisville: Westminster John Knox Press, 2008.
Woodhead, Linda. "Can We Trust the Church?" In *Schools of Faith: Essays in Honour of Iain R. Torrance*, edited by David Fergusson and Bruce McCormack, 193–202. London: T&T Clark, 2018.
Wright, David F. "'The Common Buke of the Kirk': The Bible in the Scottish Reformation." In *The Bible in Scotland's Life and Literature*, edited by David F. Wright, 155–78. Edinburgh: St Andrew Press, 1988.
WWF. *Living Planet Report 2020* [webpage]. 2020. https://web.archive.org/web/20200910083915/https://livingplanet.panda.org/en-GB/, archived from the original at https://livingplanet.panda.org/en-GB/ (accessed October 10, 2023).
Yong, Amos. *Theology and Down Syndrome: Re-imagining Disability in Late Modernity*. Waco, TX: Baylor University Press, 2007.
Zachman, Randall. *Image and Word in the Theology of John Calvin*. Notre Dame: University of Notre Dame Press, 2007.
Zachmann, Randall. *Reconsidering John Calvin*. Cambridge: Cambridge University Press, 2012.
Zahl, Simeon. "Non-Competitive Agency and Luther's Experiential Argument Against Virtue." *Modern Theology* 35, no. 2 (2019): 199–222.
Zimmermann, Jens. *Humanism and Religion: A Call for the Renewal of Western Culture*. Oxford: Oxford University Press, 2012.
Zink, Jesse. "Five Marks of Mission: History, Theology, Critique." *Journal of Anglican Studies* 15, no. 2 (2017): 144–66.

INDEX

Abrahamse, Jan Martijn   255 n.1
academia   25, 140, 206–7, 228–9, 235–6, 241–51
Adams, Marilyn McCord   65, 236 n.21
agnosticism   114, 117, 123, 134, 198
analytic philosophy   8–12, 17, 62, 70–80, 153
Anglicanism   41, 44, 62, 171, 190–5, 218 n.15, 219 n.16
   Hume on   120, 124
Anselm   23, 28, 65, 160
apokatastasis   2, 103–4, 108
Apostles' Creed   24, 42–3, 53
Aquinas, Thomas   8–14, 22, 53, 82, 98–102, 142–4, 246
   Thomism   71, 75, 161
Aristotle   82, 129, 161, 183, 263–4
art   19, 37, 52, 96, 171–9, 223, 242
   music   103, 124, 168, 173, 178, 193
   novels   37, 173, 263 n.22
   painting   99–100, 177
   poetry   20, 37, 47, 52, 97–9, 103, 173, 260 n.10
atheism   112–18, 123–6, 148–9, 187–8, 198, 246
atonement   12, 35, 65, 134, 159–60
Augsburg Confession   182
Augustine   18, 43, 186, 237
   in curricula   184, 246
   on ecclesiology   181–2
   on eschatology   30, 97–102
   on *imago Dei*   81–4
   on sacraments   160, 167

Baillie, Donald   67
Baillie, John   20–1, 175 n.13
von Balthasar, Hans Urs   15, 35, 104
Barmen Declaration   16, 222
Barth, Karl   22, 56, 239, 264
   on Christology   35, 58, 209–10
   on ecclesiology   165, 182 n.8

   on eschatology   104–7
   on nationalism   216 n.8, 225
   on natural theology   12–16, 26, 46, 153–5
Barton, John   200, 207
Bauckham, Richard   58, 199, 205
Bavinck, Herman   11, 12 n.13
Beattie, James   111, 123 n.35
Bentley, Richard   30, 54
Berkhof, Hendrikus   14–15, 168 n.22
biblical criticism   46, 57–9, 102, 199–201, 205, 207, 245
biblical interpretation   102–4, 108, 167–70, 196–211
Bonhoeffer, Dietrich   92, 180, 210, 221, 245
Brown, David   2, 19 n.32, 35 n.29
Brown, Stewart J.   129 n.3, 225 n.29
Brunner, Emil   19, 153
Bullinger, Heinrich   71, 136, 166–7, 176–8
Burns, Robert   124, 127, 173

Calvin, John   3–4, 52, 82, 136, 167 n.19, 170, 264 n.24
   Calvinism   3, 53, 71, 75, 114, 130, 172–3, 217
   on ecclesiology   181, 196
   on eschatology   101–2
   on images   171–6
   methodology   18, 29, 144
   on politics   213–17, 226
   on providence   71–6
Christology   12, 46, 53
   and anthropology   75, 82–3, 89–90, 201
   Chalcedon   33–4, 59–69
   and divine power   26, 34–7
   and hermeneutics   104, 205, 209–10
   kenosis   34–7, 61–2, 77–9, 150
church of Scotland
   history of   112–14, 124, 128–9, 189

liturgy of 44, 240, 255
and mission 193, 219
and Scottish culture 173
Cicero 18, 129
Coakley, Sarah 37, 160 n.4
creation 31, 38–54, 85–94, 140–55
  ex nihilo 9, 25, 33, 38, 42–3, 49–50, 78
crucifixion 27, 36, 69, 104–5, 171, 221, 238, 260

Darwin, Charles/Darwinism 83, 117–18, 125, 140–55, 187
Davison, Andrew 63 n.22
Dawkins, Richard 125, 145
deism 38, 47, 77, 154
  Hume and 114–20
  and natural theology 9, 141–50, 197–8
  providential deism 71, 129, 134–5
democracy 186, 214–15, 223–4, 248–9
Descartes, René 81, 230
divine attributes 7–23, 30–9
divine hiddenness 8, 17, 26, 123, 143 n.6
dualism 39, 42, 47–9, 84
Dulles, Avery 183–4, 191
Duns Scotus 10, 29

Eastern orthodoxy 33, 70, 74, 179, 195
ecclesiology 45, 56–7
  and the Bible 195–6, 209–11
  and Christology 63–7
  establishment 25, 120–1, 135, 189, 218–24
  and mission 180–94
  and politics 213–17, 220–3, 249–51
  and worship 159–70
ecological theology 19, 30–2, 40–54, 84, 86, 92, 152, 191, 249
ecumenism
  and doctrine 56–7, 65, 182–4, 239
  and establishment 220, 225
  and mission 191 n.29
  and sacraments 162, 170, 181
election 30, 32, 128, 183

the Fall 75, 82–3, 89, 91, 93, 130, 243
Ford, David 248
Forrester, Duncan 237 n.22
Frei, Hans 19 n.30, 55–6, 144 n.8, 264 n.25
Freud, Sigmund 144, 232, 261–2

Gerrish, Brian 3, 23 n.46, 208
Gnosticism 17, 49
Gore, Charles 35, 48
Graham, Gordon 133 n.15, 171, 177, 256 n.3
Gunton, Colin 7–14

Hart, David Bentley 2 n.4, 48 n.21, 104 n.20, 187 n.19
Hauerwas, Stanley 55, 161
Hector, Kevin 255 n.1
Hegel, Georg W. F. 12, 124
Heidegger, Martin 9, 84
hell 95–104, 246, 261 n.14
Hobbes, Thomas 25, 197, 255–61
holy spirit 27, 37–9, 43–4, 164–8
  and Scripture 144, 196, 202, 206–10
Hume, David 9, 111–27, 130–6, 144–6, 173, 198 n.5, 203
Hurtado, Larry 58, 159 n.2
Hutcheson, Francis 113, 124–36, 173, 255–61
Huxley, T. H. 114, 118, 145–6

idolatry 8 n.3, 18, 49, 215, 217
  and the Bible 13, 163
  and images 174–7
  and natural theology 10–11, 46, 143, 153
  and power 26, 37
imago Dei 30, 44, 51, 81–94, 176, 201, 218, 226, 249
interfaith relations 12 n.14, 19, 63, 203–4, 219–20, 244
Irenaeus 49, 205
Islam 42, 47, 69, 73, 201–4, 247

Jeanrond, Werner 237 n.23
Jenson, Robert 12–17, 95–6, 107
John Chrysostom 262–3
Judaism 247, 260
  imago Dei in 90–1
  Jesus and 61, 68–9, 200
  relationship with Christianity 17, 43, 46, 57, 64 n.24
  scripture in 169, 203–5

Kant, Immanuel 12, 20, 102, 117, 123–4, 129, 152–3

Katongole, Emmanuel 222 n.22
Keller, Catherine 38, 50 n.24
Kelly, J. N. D. 42, 43 n.6
Kelsey, David 43, 62–3, 89–92, 242
Kerr, Fergus 11, 20 n.35, 84, 143 n.6
Kilby, Karen 37 n.35, 86 n.13
Knox, John 172, 213

Lash, Nicholas 68
Lindbeck, George 13 n.15, 55–69, 161, 182 n.9
liturgy
  and creation 31, 41–6
  and doctrine 17, 38, 58, 66–7, 97–8, 159–69
  and mission 19, 189, 193
  in Protestantism 121, 184
  and Scripture 25, 195, 210
  and self-image 237–42
Locke, John 9, 141–4, 198
Lucas, J. R. 72 n.10, 76–7, 239
Luther, Martin
  eschatology 100–1, 108
  and images 171, 174
  Lutheranism 3, 166–7, 171, 179, 210, 212–13, 218 n.15
  methodology 12–13
  on monarchy 214
  on Scripture 166, 208
  on vocation 189 n.24, 239

McCormack, Bruce 60
McIntyre, John 251
Mackey, James 251
Macmurray, John 230–2
Macquarrie, John 34, 61 n.16, 67, 84 n.10
metaphysics
  in analytic theology 153
  and Christology 59–60, 66–9
  and the doctrine of God 7, 9, 24, 26, 131
  and evolution 148
  God-world relationship 50, 73
  and law 224
  methodology 12, 22
  and natural science 125
Milbank, John 242 n.6
Mitchell, Basil 251

Moltmann, Jürgen 36, 51 n.27, 89–90, 98 n.5, 104, 230

natural sciences 40, 43, 73, 83, 233–4
  astronomy 52, 63, 175–6
  evolution 117–18, 140–55
natural theology 16, 46, 80, 113–23, 140–55
negative theology 11–12, 16, 108, 142–4
New Atheism 112, 116–17, 125, 145, 184–5
Newlands, George 255
Newman, John Henry 103, 154
Nicene Creed/Nicaea 24, 42, 43 n.5, 59 n.10, 66, 181–2
Nietzsche, Friedrich 123, 126, 184
non-competition 33, 68, 73

O'Collins, Gerald 61 n.16, 104 n.21
O'Donovan, Oliver 28, 238 n.26
Oord, Thomas Jay 38, 78–9

Pannenberg, Wolfhart 21–2, 68, 181
pantheism 20, 47
Pascal, Blaise 12, 113
patristic theology 8, 17–18, 146, 159–60
Pauw, Amy Plantinga 45–51, 63
Phiri, Isaac 223
Plantinga, Alvin 10, 143, 153
Platonism 8, 12, 18, 70, 73, 263
political theology 25–7, 32, 65, 67, 121, 130, 187–9, 212–27, 248
prayer
  and agency 33, 74, 77, 80
  and art 20, 177
  and Christology 37, 61, 164
  and doctrine 10–12, 55, 103, 159–60, 162
  Hume on 118
preaching 161–70, 174–8, 195–7
  biblical scholarship and 200, 206
  creeds in 66
  and ecclesiology 182, 209–10
  on the Hebrew Bible 47, 226
  humor in 263
  in the New Testament 204
  in the Scottish church 129
Presbyterianism
  Burns and 124
  and the Enlightenment 111, 128

Hume and 126
   and humor 257
   and images 178
   and Irish Catholics 225
   liturgy 44
   schisms in 229 n.4
   and Scottish culture 172–3, 219, 263 n.21
   Smith and 135
process thought 28, 38, 78–9
providence 31–4, 70–80, 91–2, 114–18, 129–39, 141–52, 238–9

Rahner, Karl 20, 60, 67–8, 84, 104
Reformed theology
   anthropology of 139
   and church reform 186
   disputes within 113
   and the Enlightenment 124
   and images 171–9
   predestination in 29
   providence in 135
   sacraments in 165–70
   sanctification in 237
   social thought of 189, 212–27
Reid, Thomas 4, 111, 122–6, 128, 173
resurrection 35, 39, 66, 69, 89, 92, 95–105, 221, 238, 261
Roman Catholicism 30, 47, 103–4, 134, 161, 167, 184, 193, 235

sacraments 87–9, 164–70, 174–83, 191–2, 240
   baptism 106, 159–60, 162, 176, 181–2, 196, 213, 215, 238
   Christology and 58, 67
   Eucharist 31, 43–5, 159–63, 175, 195–6
   in the Scottish church 124
Schleiermacher, Freidrich 7, 19–22, 28, 46, 59–60, 153, 199, 246
Schwöbel, Christoph 95
Scots Confession 183, 215
Second Helvetic Confession 71, 166–7
secularism 184–92, 211–13, 218–20, 225–7, 243–4
semper reformanda 3, 179, 186, 196
sensus divinitatis 18, 22, 144

sin
   and anthropology 83, 144
   in the Christian narrative 43, 62–3, 104, 106, 108, 159, 234, 240, 265
   God and 71, 73, 75, 90, 97
   and growth 78, 238
   and illness 32
   and law 214
   in liturgy 41
Smith, Adam 111–24, 128–39
Smith, Iain Crichton 172, 263
Sonderegger, Katherine 11–14, 17, 63 n.19
Soskice, Janet 11 n.11
Spinoza, Baruch 124, 197
Spufford, Francis 37, 239 n.29
Stoicism 70, 113, 129, 132–7
Stump, Eleanore 79–80, 153
Swinburne, Richard 8–10, 77, 153

Tanner, Kathryn 33 n.24, 56
Taylor, Barbara Brown 20
Taylor, Charles 71, 122–3, 129, 235
theodicy 36, 38, 48, 72–4, 78, 83, 115, 125, 150–1, 236
Thiselton, Anthony 27, 106–7
Ticciati, Susannah 50
Torrance, James B. 164
Torrance, Thomas F. 154, 251
Trinity 7, 9, 14, 18, 21, 43, 56, 59 n.10, 66, 196
   and humans 81–2, 229–30
   inner relations 62, 85–6, 165, 190

van den Brink, Gijsbert 28 n.10, 34 n.26, 247 n.14
Vatican II 57, 98, 167 n.17, 182–3, 239
Volf, Miroslav 107–8, 161–2, 204, 207–8, 246 n.12

Weber, Max 25, 217
Webster, John 7, 17, 95, 206 n.21, 243
Weil, Simone 245–6
Welker, Michael 3 n.7, 51 n.28, 86
Westminster Confession 101, 113, 182 n.7
Westminster Directory of Publick Worship 32
Westminster Larger Catechism 168

Westminster Shorter Catechism   163
Williams, Rowan   33 n.23, 33 n.25, 187, 218 n.13
Wittgenstein, Ludwig   55–6, 84, 102, 117, 124, 160
Wolterstorff, Nicholas   4, 123 n.34, 141, 170, 209 n.27, 226, 242–3
Woodhead, Linda   218

worship   23, 74, 124, 191–3, 195, 217, 232, 240, 263
   and doctrine   4, 13, 159–70
   and ecotheology   43–5
   images in   171–9

Zahl, Simeon   33 n.23
Zwingli, Huldrych   3, 174–5, 182 n.7

www.ingramcontent.com/pod-product-compliance
Lightning Source LLC
Chambersburg PA
CBHW071237230426
43668CB00011B/1479